D1570069

James and Esther Cooper Jackson

James and Esther Cooper Jackson

Love and Courage in the Black Freedom Movement

SARA RZESZUTEK HAVILAND

UNIVERSITY PRESS OF KENTUCKY

Copyright © 2015 by The University Press of Kentucky

Scholarly publisher for the Commonwealth,
serving Bellarmine University, Berea College, Centre College of Kentucky,
Eastern Kentucky University, The Filson Historical Society, Georgetown
College, Kentucky Historical Society, Kentucky State University,
Morehead State University, Murray State University, Northern Kentucky
University, Transylvania University, University of Kentucky, University of
Louisville, and Western Kentucky University.
All rights reserved.

Editorial and Sales Offices: The University Press of Kentucky
663 South Limestone Street, Lexington, Kentucky 40508-4008
www.kentuckypress.com

Cataloging-in-Publication data is available from the Library of Congress.

ISBN 978-0-8131-6625-4 (hardcover : alk. paper)
ISBN 978-0-8131-6626-1 (epub)
ISBN 978-0-8131-6627-8 (pdf)

This book is printed on acid-free paper meeting
the requirements of the American National Standard
for Permanence in Paper for Printed Library Materials.

Manufactured in the United States of America.

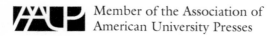 Member of the Association of
American University Presses

Dedicated to the memory
of my grandparents,
Wojciech and Maria Rzeszutek
and Roland and Phyllis Bibeault

Contents

Photographs follow page 186

Introduction

Love and Activism

When Esther Cooper met James Jackson, or Jack, as his family and friends called him, she was already committed to her principles. By 1939 she was, like Jack, a member of the Communist Party USA (CPUSA) and eager to do her part to unravel the system of Jim Crow segregation that consumed the South. Over the next sixty-eight years, she and Jack fought together to promote radical change in the United States. The long black freedom movement, spanning the Popular Front, the McCarthy period, the civil rights years, and the post–civil rights era, offered the couple many avenues to navigate in their pursuit of racial and economic justice. They fought for black freedom through the Great Depression, World War II, the Cold War, and beyond. Their focus on activism was a prominent part of their marriage and family life. Esther and Jack described themselves as "dedicated revolutionaries" who recognized that the fight for racial and economic justice "was going to be a long struggle."[1] Their lives offer a story of freedom and repression, persistence and change, and love and activism in the long black freedom movement.

Esther and Jack's love and activism illustrate that, in the face of major political transformations, activists responded to new political contexts and drew on personal experiences to frame and reframe conversations about black freedom in the United States. Their relationship offers a way of understanding how individuals developed, adapted, and understood their own politics and participated in the black freedom movement as major events shaped the nation. The Jacksons steered themselves as a couple through difficult circumstances and continued to fight for black freedom in the twentieth-century United States, but their approaches changed as politics shifted, as their family grew, and as their relationship evolved. Their work also influenced their political viewpoints, and Esther and Jack, as individuals and as a couple, changed as a result of their activism. As a collective biography of two people who weathered the twentieth century with one another, *James and Esther Cooper Jackson* serves as a unique format for connecting political ideology, the black freedom movement, and individuals' lives by using personal history as a reflection of and catalyst for political change.

The Great Depression, World War II, and the Cold War shaped activist strategies to achieve black freedom across the twentieth century because national priorities in each period differed. While a liberal civil rights mobilization saw successes in the mid-1950s and the 1960s, a number of scholars have argued that the civil rights movement had its roots in a radical southern activist tradition dating back to the New Deal era through such groups as the Southern Negro Youth Congress (SNYC), the National Negro Congress, and the CIO.[2] In the years known as the Popular Front period, the CPUSA took an active hand in influencing a wide-ranging progressive and leftist coalition of groups by opening up and reaching out. Activists in these years drew on communism to emphasize radical economic reform, interracial working-class unity, and equal access to opportunities and resources as a way to dismantle Jim Crow. Though these activists no doubt contributed to a long black freedom movement that fought for equality, political enfranchisement, and economic rights, whether they constituted one of the earliest stages of the civil rights movement itself is up for debate.

The context of the Cold War reformulated this early wave of protest in part because the activists in the 1930s and 1940s emphasized radical economic restructuring, a goal out of step with the mounting emphasis on capitalism's benefits after World War II. While these organizations and activists were important in the 1930s and 1940s black freedom movement, many of their strategies and goals, along with the political context in which they operated, distinguished them from the civil rights movement that emerged a decade later. If the Cold War marginalized black radicals, it also provided liberal organizations like the National Association for the Advancement of Colored People and the Southern Christian Leadership Conference with the opportunity for new triumphs.[3] Yet, pushed to the sidelines by the Cold War, these Popular Front radicals did not disappear or disengage. They reconfigured their participation in the black freedom movement as they weathered these changes, aged, and responded to new questions and demands. Their voices remained part of the struggle.

Tracing one couple's political evolution across these distinct eras, organizations, and political climates offers the opportunity to study waves of social movements through the distinct lens of two individuals who worked with and loved one another. While studies of organizations or political moments offer insight into how activists mobilized in a given period, following a couple like the Jacksons across a lifetime provides an understanding of how they responded to new developments and adapted their participation in movements as they grew older and as their own needs and goals changed. Not only did dominant contexts, questions, and organizational styles shift as the couple remained active, but their own priorities, as individuals and as a couple, varied on the basis of circumstances in their personal lives. My intent is neither to lionize them nor to condemn their choices but to understand how Esther and Jack saw the various scenarios before them, interpreted their options, considered the range of consequences, and moved forward with that knowledge. This method provides insight into the texture of moments and movements as they unfolded. The Jacksons were historical actors who did great things and made mistakes, and they were also two people who, like everyone else, determined a course of action in response to their interpretation of the information available to them.

Esther and Jack's lifelong activism both supports historiographic analyses that categorize the black freedom movement in separate eras and belies the notion that there were clear breaks within that struggle. Other biographers have offered similar arguments about the work of activists who participated across movement eras. Of the activist Ivory Perry, George Lipsitz has written that his persistent presence in activist circles "suggested an extraordinary continuity beneath the appearance of rupture" that "reflects moral and intellectual resources honed through a lifetime of personal and collective experiences."[4] Erik Gellman and Jarod Roll have argued that the activism of the southern preachers Claude Williams and Owen Whitfield provides insight into the utility of biography by offering "a clear picture of the messy history experienced by racially, culturally, and regionally diverse groups" that "blurs neat conventional historical categories" and "[challenges] us to rethink the dominant narratives of American history."[5] Esther and Jack's collective biography connects their public life to their marriage, illustrating how love and activism intertwined in building a relationship, a set of careers, and two lifetimes of dedication to black freedom. The links between their personal and their activist lives provide insight into the shifting political, social, and cultural backdrops they navigated.

A collective biography of the Jacksons is especially useful for understanding the Cold War's influence on leftists in black social movements and the individuals who were instrumental in advocating for radical change. The Jacksons had their political coming of age as part of the Popular Front, but they remained active throughout their lives, and they participated in the black freedom movement continuously. They were each active in different areas of work: Jack spent the majority of his career as a committed CPUSA functionary and one of its key experts on race, and Esther focused on work that hovered on the perimeter of the Party's reach, more directly entrenched in the broader black freedom movement. Their experiences and influence illustrate that the Popular Front generation shaped the civil rights movement in the 1950s and 1960s as they made their organizational styles, methods, and ideas into a useful resource for young activists. The generation's influence also came from people like the Jacksons who were still participating and contributing to the struggle.

Esther and Jack's life together contributes to a growing analysis of the relationship between the CPUSA and the black freedom movement. A number of Cold War–era histories argue that the deceitful Communist International manipulated African American Communists into joining the Party.[6] Black ex-Communists who described this perspective reacted to an array of circumstances ranging from genuine feelings of manipulation to frustration over the Party's changing positions and priorities.[7] Some of the scholars who have utilized the experiences of black ex-Communists have done so in an effort to discredit the Party's periodic successes. They suggest that African American radicals were hoodwinked by the Party, which took away their ability to determine which political course most suited their needs.

The Party indeed erred egregiously in numerous instances in crafting its policies on foreign issues, labor, race, women, and homosexuals and its relationship to the political mainstream, especially as the Cold War took shape. Efforts to adhere to ideological positions that were untenable in the face of on-the-ground political realities occurred alongside the mounting persecution of Communists and fellow travelers. The Party lost influence, grew paranoid, engaged in purges, and isolated itself in the American political landscape. Leaders who had lived through the heyday of the Popular Front years mismanaged the postwar political climate and, believing the advent of US fascism was imminent, turned inward to purify the organization. The Party supported Stalin's regime even as evidence of his atrocities was coming to light. Some continued to talk around the issue, seek to justify the facts, or compare the crimes to similar brutality in other parts of the world after the rumors were verified.[8] While it is useful to understand the psychological minefield Communists faced in these trying moments, the Party's actions contributed to its rapid decline. The Communists who stayed, like Jack, worked feverishly to revive the Party, and they actively and deliberately chose to attempt to give the organization life support because they continued to believe that it could provide correct solutions to pressing problems.

In spite of these problems, more recently historians have argued that many African Americans who chose communism did so because they had reflected on political and economic circumstances, witnessed the Party's efforts in the fight for black freedom, and found that the Party helped give meaning to the lives of poor, segregated blacks.[9] These individuals, like Hosea Hudson and Ben Davis, for instance, weathered the Party's crises because they preferred CPUSA positions and activism in support of African Americans to those of other organizations. And they were less influenced by the tumultuous shifts in international communism than were their white counterparts. Of Hosea Hudson's experience, Nell Painter argues that, unlike white Communists who defected after the Party took what they saw as unfavorable policy positions on European crises, "blacks felt more strongly about what happened in this country. . . . [B]lack communists cared more about domestic questions that related directly to black interests."[10] Ben Davis made a similar distinction between the perceptions of external influences on and the actual priorities of black Communists. After being asked in the late 1930s whether his position at the *Daily Worker* was "to carry out the anti-American policy of Moscow," he replied: "My job is to work in the interests of democracy and peace, and to oppose jim-crow and lynch law against Negroes."[11] For blacks who saw the black freedom movement in the United States as the most pressing and immediate concern, the Party was, in various moments, an attractive option.

In this respect, it is important to recognize that Jack and Esther, along with the multitude of people they influenced over the course of their long activist careers, were not dupes or pawns of the Soviet Union. They analyzed their options, observed the world around them, and concluded that communism offered the best opportunity to attain their goals for racial justice in the United States. They did not always choose popular or easy paths, and the CPUSA and the Communist International have surely opened the door to substantive critique. But exploring Esther and Jack's individual commitments to communism alongside their relationship to the black freedom movement illustrates that the fight for black freedom was not monolithic or uniform: activists approached it with a wide array of methods and philosophies and made distinct contributions along the way.

Esther and Jack were rational, compassionate, intelligent people. They loved their family and each other and believed in the fundamentals of American democracy. Jack served in the army in World War II, and each partner expressed outward patriotism even during times of political strife. This book explores how two such individuals came to embrace a political philosophy that was vilified by the US government and feared by the American people for over half a century. In the process, it humanizes people who believed that communism would solve the social, political, and economic ills of the United States by explaining the rationales behind their choices and the circumstances that informed their beliefs. It also offers context for understanding the way the Party and the black freedom movement functioned and overlapped in the lives of members and participants.

As a biography of two individuals, this work is not an in-depth study of Communist Party policy or doctrine. Each partner's role in and relationship to the Party was complex, and exploring those relationships provides an understanding of how and why the couple embraced certain goals and abided by or deviated from the Party line in a variety of situations. Esther withdrew from formal Party functions in 1956, and Jack remained a committed Party leader until the end of the Cold War. The couple embraced their connections to the Party, the black freedom movement, their family, the nation, race, gender, and region, and all those commitments informed their activism. Jack and Esther not only used the Communist Party and civil rights organizations to create change; they also mobilized social, political, and diplomatic contexts to shape the Party and civil rights organizations. Their relationship with the Party and the black freedom movement sheds light on the links between individuals, organizations, and states and helps explain shifts in social movements and political discourse.

Esther and Jack grew up understanding that opportunities came differently for black and white, male and female, rich and poor. In the South, Jim Crow further stratified opportunity, and even the black middle and upper classes found themselves in a lower social category than whites of a similar class background. When the Depression hit in 1929, struggling people across the nation began to question capitalism's validity, and Communist Party membership grew. But, in many instances, Communist ideology did not come from an intellectual or philosophical tradition. In her biography of the Alabama Communist Hosea Hudson, Nell Painter writes: "Jim crow and hard times had created a radical black constituency in Alabama of men . . . who did not find political sufficiency in church or lodge."[12] As the historian Robin D. G. Kelley has argued, poor and working people in Alabama embodied a radicalism that grew out of their economic and racial exploitation, and their ideals matched Communist ideology.[13] In other areas, the CPUSA found itself adapting to a local context, meeting the needs and desires of people who demanded particular types of change.[14]

The Jacksons fused their political sensitivity to inequality with their intellectual backgrounds. They were part of a growing trend among Depression-era students who got involved in leftist organizations and joined the Communist Party as a result of connections they made in college.[15] But, for a couple who identified not only with their classmates but also with poor, disenfranchised, and segregated African Americans, the CPUSA had meaning that was deeper than simply an ideological and philosophical political affiliation. The Jacksons' exposure to poverty and racial segregation sparked their political awareness, and, in many ways, their intellectual adoption of communism was organic. The conclusion that communism was a good solution for the nation's racial and class problems was rooted in a long tradition of fighting oppression and did not require a distinct moment of philosophical epiphany. As Lipsitz has argued about organic intellectuals, individual commitment to activism needs "no traumatic break with the past . . . no cathartic transformation from accommodation to resistance."[16] A unique fusion of experiences—growing up in segregated southern communities, witnessing racialized poverty, being raised by parents who were involved in activist organizations, and having the opportunity to attend college during a time of vast economic despair—made communism a natural choice for the Jacksons.

But joining the Communist Party did not mean that the CPUSA was always their top priority. Becoming members near the rise of the Popular Front era allowed the couple to explore the relationship between Party politics and grassroots social movements that were independent of political organizations. Both partners led the SNYC and committed themselves to promoting the cause of black freedom first. Though Communist Party politics influenced the SNYC, the organization's leaders focused on the needs of local communities, organizations, and individuals. The SNYC worked hard to approach black southerners with an array of ideas about social movements, and, in addition to offering support for unionization efforts and promoting leftist ideas, the organization also opened its doors to more conservative southern activists. In this regard, Esther and Jack's early communism fused political ideology with the pragmatic needs and goals of black southerners. The couple's priorities shifted as their organizational commitments changed, with communism and Party work becoming central or peripheral depending on the setting. In the 1950s, when Jack was indicted under the Smith Act, the Party was important to the couple's approach to black freedom. In later years, Jack drew closer to the Party in his activism, and Esther pulled away from it.

Linking Esther and Jack's love and activism provides a useful framework for considering gender, family dynamics, and personal life as important components of social movements. The Jacksons crafted a radical, gender egalitarian marriage in which both partners were equally active and committed to their careers. Jack and Esther put their gender ideology into practice and mobilized it to participate in the black freedom movement and keep their household happy. Their gender egalitarianism added complexity to their political positions as it made the space for each part-ner to carve individual niches in social movements. It also formed a foun-dation that helped Jack and Esther respect one another's political choices when they disagreed on particular issues. The nature of their marriage suggests that the Jacksons both embraced aspects of what would become second-wave feminism, as many of the questions they grappled with while building their marriage and the answers they found would be rehashed during the women's movement of the 1960s and 1970s.

Esther and Jack's marriage was unique in many regards. Historians have offered substantial analysis of marriage in the twentieth century, examining issues like patriarchy, divorce, race, class, and love. Much of the work on married life examines the gaps between the perception of domestic bliss and the reality of the work that goes into maintaining a household. In the dominant model, either women are victims of patriar-chy, or their marriage fails, despite their efforts at asserting autonomy.[17] For many married couples, black and white, equal relations in marriage meant sacrificing power and not performing normative gender roles, and performing traditional gender roles meant inequality between partners. For the poet Paul Laurence Dunbar and his wife, Alice, for instance, despite equal artistic talent and drive, marriage meant that the pair of elite African Americans would need to be an example of Victorian respectabil-ity. The Dunbars married partly to rectify Paul's rape of Alice during their courtship. Because they courted during a time when a rape meant that Alice's "honor was gone," marriage was the only avenue for preserving her good, respectable name.[18] The couple ultimately split after Paul vio-lently attacked Alice and nearly killed her. The Dunbar marriage offers an example of power and patriarchy taken to the extreme.

The historian Martin Summers notes a particular deviation from patriarchal domination for black couples during the Harlem Renaissance. Focusing on Wallace Thurman and Louise Thompson, Zora Neale Hur-ston and Herbert Sheen, and Paul and Eslanda Goode Robeson, he sug-gests a changing outlook on marriage during the 1920s. According to Summers, these three black couples experimented with the idea of "mod-ern marriage" in the 1920s. During this period, he argues: "Marriage was no longer solely defined as a union between a man and a woman for the purpose of starting a family that would, in turn, fit into a larger social network. Rather, marriage was becoming more of a means through which to experience individual self-fulfillment."[19] In all three of these unions, however, the couples became discontented and either divorced or led entirely separate private and public lives. For these sets of partners, aspiring toward a new kind of married life did not mean that the men were able to overcome fully their internalized ideas about gender roles within a marriage.

For black couples, a breaking from the traditional model of marriage was different than it was for white couples. Because many blacks had fought hard since Reconstruction to marry legally and embrace a normative middle-class model of marriage—husbands working and supporting, wives enjoying the domesticity that they were denied during slavery—black couples whose gender expression deviated from tradition were engaged with a different marital discourse than white couples who did the same. In addition, the hypersexualization of black men and women in mainstream culture meant that black couples had significantly more at stake in maintaining respectable, patriarchal marriages than did white couples. For black couples, there was an added pressure to defy stereotypes and prove themselves successful at normative models of marriage. This aspiration is predominantly associated with black couples who either had or sought to attain middle-class status.[20] Black and white couples who experimented with gender roles in their marriage may have been aspiring to the same egalitarian ideal, but, for black couples, this move resonated with a long history of invalidated relationships and the exploitation of male and female labor.

Still, Esther and Jack's marriage was not a total historical anomaly. Others in Esther and Jack's SNYC cohort had similar modern marriages. Ed and Augusta Strong and Louis and Dorothy Burnham also practiced the same sort of gender egalitarianism.[21] For Communists like Esther and Jack, fundamentally restructuring the economic system in the United States took priority over attaining a bourgeois ideal. They did not seek to create a black middle class as a parallel to the white middle class through their roles within their marriage; instead, they believed that racial equality needed to be attained through more sweeping change. The couple believed that inherent in the emergence of a new economic system would be the transformation of gender relations in public and private life. Their gender and class politics, and accordingly, their marriage, were vital to their activism against racism. For Esther and Jack, then, a modern marriage worked well because both were deeply committed to being in love and to leading activist lives and both believed strongly in women's equality.

The historian Stephanie Coontz notes that the concept of love as an essential feature in a successful marriage is a relatively recent phenomenon. Toward the end of the eighteenth century, love became increasingly important to matching potential mates. By the time the Jacksons were married, sentimental love and interpersonal attraction accompanied other forms of compatibility in building marriages. In the normative construction, Coontz writes: "[Compatible couples] must love each other deeply and choose each other unswayed by outside pressure. From then on, each must make the partner the top priority in life, putting that relationship above any and all competing ties. A husband and wife, we believe, owe their highest obligations and deepest loyalties to each other and the children they raise."[22] Esther and Jack built their love for one another alongside their activism and agreed that their commitment to one another was tied to their political ideologies and, in particular, informed by their communism. Their politics and the accompanying obligations fueled their romance.

Esther and Jack could have a functional modern marriage partly because they each grew up with strong female role models in their mothers and in other women in their lives. Esther was raised in a household where women were independent, strong thinkers and active in politics. Jack's ideas about female activism emerged from his mother's influence, the women in his neighborhood, and his specific interpretation of Marxism. For Jack, being a good Marxist required shared responsibility for all sorts of work and the acceptance and encouragement of women's leadership abilities. As Esther's role in the SNYC expanded, Jack took on additional household responsibilities.[23] Esther and Jack learned over the course of their early marriage to work through their differences while maintaining an egalitarian relationship. Esther reflected on the couple's perspective on marriage: "We used to joke that if anybody comes and tells you their marriage is perfect, one person is dominating the other and the other's just saying, 'Yes dear, yes dear,' if they don't have any differences."[24] There were certainly particular moments within Esther and Jack's marriage when their lived experiences did not meet their ideals, but they strove to hold themselves to an egalitarian standard.

Their life together also offers a counterpoint to the normative nuclear family model that became a diplomatic tool in the Cold War, because the couple emphasized race and activism as key factors in understanding family life. Their work was intertwined for much of their life together, and many of the obstacles Jack confronted as a Communist Party leader led his wife to act in his defense and to protect their daughters. But her activism on behalf of her husband and family was part of a broader left-ist political struggle, not simply adherence to traditional maternal norms. Positioning herself as a normative maternal figure was especially potent in the 1950s, but doing so as a black Communist activist also defied the conventional logic about the intersections of family and politics. Esther's activism as a wife and mother offers a counterpoint to the idealized image of Cold War domestic life. Her work points to racism and anticommunism as forces aimed at the destruction of family and as factors in the changing black freedom movement.[25]

Jack fully supported his wife's independent activism and aspirations. He respected her ambition, intellect, and activist goals and believed that "to be a good Communist you struggled on the woman question."[26] In this regard, he used his Communist principles as guiding factors in his life. He embraced Communist ideals to understand gender, race, class, region, and nation, and he mobilized those ideals to help the CPUSA make tangible change in the United States. Believing that communism had relevance for everyday life, he tried to help the CPUSA reach wide audiences and disseminate its approaches to social problems. Most of Esther's career took place outside formal Party functions. She had not joined with the intent of becoming a full-time functionary. Rather, she supported the Party's ideas and included it in her long résumé of political connections.

Jack and Esther remained adamant about their democratic right to hold political ideas that they believed would best serve the causes about which they were passionate. That their political affiliation was neither popular nor mainstream makes understanding their choices all the more historically valuable. The Jacksons' love and activism illustrate that personal and political factors shaped individual lives and the black freedom movement. Even within the Jackson household, where one couple endured unique hardships as a result of their communism, the Cold War and the black freedom movement produced distinct individual experiences and political opinions. As individuals, the Jacksons valued their political differences not only as an expression of their commitment to debate as a source of political inspiration but also as a representation of their love and respect for each other. While the world changed, Esther and Jack drew on their closest personal connection—each other—to persevere in the fight to make the world they desired.

When I first met Esther and Jack in late 2002, I was one scholar in a long line of historians, literature scholars, art historians, documentarians, and archivists to come through their door. That I, as an undergraduate, was there at all reflects a triumph in their work. From the late 1970s through the early years of the twenty-first century, many people with an array of projects about all aspects of their lives and experiences contacted them, including Nell Painter, Robin D. G. Kelley, Patricia Sullivan, Jonathan Holloway, Erik McDuffie, Erik Gellman, David Levering Lewis, Mary Helen Washington, and Yolanda Parks, among others. The Jacksons embraced the opportunity to tell their story, granting many interviews over the decades and offering critical support to scholars working on the history of the black Left. By the turn of the twenty-first century, historians were well into the process of reevaluating and complicating civil rights history. In addition to all the couple offered to immediate freedom struggles during their life together, a significant part of their legacy has been their influence on the preservation of a black radical past. This book, which I hope makes a contribution to preserving that black radical tradition, is as much a product of their work as activists and as the keepers of their own history as it is my words on the page. To know the Jacksons is to admire them, and, to do them justice as a historian, I have endeavored to highlight their humanity, reveal their attributes and flaws, and show their complexity as individuals and as activists. It is as a result of their own efforts that the things they did, the changes they shaped, and the people they worked with will not be forgotten.

1

Jack and Esther's Paths to Activism and Each Other

When James Edward Jackson Jr. was a small boy in Richmond, Virginia, in the early twentieth century, he would stand outside his father's pharmacy on the corner of Brook Road and Dubois Avenue every evening and wait. The strong stench of sweat and tobacco wafted his way before he saw anything coming, and then a throng of people appeared in the distance. The procession was composed of tobacco workers heading home from the city's tobacco factories. These workers were black, mostly female, and desperately poor. Many were clad in burlap tobacco sacks that they had taken from the factory because they could not afford clothes. As Jack observed: "The struggle for survival in poverty was written in the ragged clothes and shoelaces and the conditions of the houses they lived in."[1] The women were exhausted, often ill, and trapped in dire poverty. Even though their circumstances were difficult, they would sing and shout with joy as they headed north toward their homes. Jack said good evening to each woman as she walked by the pharmacy, and he would stand outside until the last worker passed. His lifelong activism for black freedom, his membership in the Communist Party USA (CPUSA), and the development of his political outlook were rooted in this memory.[2]

Jack's political coming of age was a product of growing up middle-class with politically minded, progressive parents in a segregated southern city that included deep poverty. His parents had embraced the politics of middle-class respectability and racial uplift and worked to raise their children with opportunities and awareness of the world around them. His future wife, Esther Cooper, was raised in a similar household. Her mother was a model of black female respectability and social engagement, and she instilled in her daughters the value of education, the fight for racial equality, and female independence. In both families, black progressivism offered a framework for embracing social justice, upward mobility, and uplift. Progressivism informed their upbringings, and Jack and Esther fused that exposure to the political context of the Great Depression, during which they became politically active.

For African Americans, the Progressive era offered a combination of setbacks and advancements. Progressivism emerged as a social and political movement in the late nineteenth century and led Americans to reconsider the relationship of the individual and the state, gender roles, industrialization, wealth, status, and social difference.[3] Progressivism in its broadest sense altered American life dramatically, particularly for the middle class and for whites. More concerned with social welfare, charity, purity, and improved labor conditions, Progressives employed a new sense of morality as a way of measuring the individual. Settlement houses offered hope to impoverished immigrants, schools revamped curricula and received renewed support, and factories were overhauled to ensure the safety of workers and products alike. But, in the wake of extensive efforts to improve the moral, economic, and political quality of life for white Americans, white southerners continued to scramble to adapt to African American freedom after slavery. Massive violence against African Americans in the South had been a widely accepted approach to stamping out black assertions of equality, but it was neither practical nor sustainable. To maintain an ordered, moral society, white southerners determined that segregation was the most appropriate way to simultaneously prop up white supremacy and adhere to a strict Progressive moral code.[4]

The cloak of civility emerged as a disguise for the persistent oppression of African American southerners. Civility dictated social behavior, mobilizing one's manners and gentility as a marker of status and ability to contribute to a polite society. As the historian William Chafe argues, whites used civility to promote consensus and avoid social conflict, and African Americans were forced to accommodate it: "As victims of civility, blacks had long been forced to operate within an etiquette of race relationships that offered almost no room for collective self-assertion and independence. White people dictated the ground rules, and the benefits went only to those who played the game."[5] Segregation offered the appearance of a polite alternative to direct racial violence, but, for African Americans in the Progressive era, the threat of white violence nonetheless loomed large. Any perceived step out of segregation's boundaries riled white reaction and often resulted in lynching. Segregation was designed "to send an unmistakable message of racial inequality that would intimidate blacks and reassure whites [and] deprive blacks of so much economic and political opportunity that they would never threaten white power."[6] Nationwide, white progressives rationalized segregation as a positive alternative to race war, but the inequality that Jim Crow engendered also produced a heightened drive for resistance among African Americans.

Not all white progressives embraced racial segregation as an essential component of an ordered world. In 1910, white and black Progressives joined together to form the National Association for the Advancement of Colored People (NAACP). At its outset, the NAACP modeled itself on abolitionist groups. Among its leaders, W. E. B. Du Bois believed that, as the historian David Howard-Pitney writes, "the South in 1919, as in the 1850s, was a reactionary society that stifled all dissent": "Then as now, the South stood alone against rising national and international trends toward democracy and freedom."[7] The NAACP fought segregation's legal roots and worked to improve education for African Americans, focusing on opportunity and change. For the black middle class in the South, education, self-help, entrepreneurship, and professionalism promised a path toward a better future in spite of racial obstacles. These assets contributed to constructing what Du Bois referred to as *the talented tenth*. Well-educated and established blacks, a small elite in the United States, could use their skills and standing to "oversee a community in crisis." Du Bois argued: "The Negro race, like all races, is going to be saved by its exceptional men."[8]

Jack's family, like that of his future wife, fit the model of the talented tenth. Both sets of parents provided their children with a comfortable life, educational opportunities both in school and at home, and a moral upbringing. Jack and Esther each grew up with the foundations to build comfortable, middle-class lives for themselves as adults. But both were exposed to extreme poverty, and both became full-time activists. Jack and Esther each carried forward the principles of their socially conscious, talented-tenth childhoods, particularly concern for the politically, socially, and economically disenfranchised, and fused them with communism. As they were becoming adults, the Great Depression, the Popular Front, the rise of the American Communist movement, the changing relationship between the United States and the Soviet Union, and the ongoing black freedom movement all made clear the relevance of socialism as a means to racial equality. Familial progressivism and individual convictions, combined with the looming social, political, and economic context, made Jack and Esther's embrace of communism in the midst of the Depression a reasonable choice.

Jack's father exerted a powerful influence on his social consciousness and participation in the black freedom movement. A respected pharmacist and graduate of Howard University, James E. Jackson Sr. had earned the admiration of the black community. He was the second black pharmacist in Richmond's history.[9] The Jackson family's standing was a product of James's education, profession, and status as a business owner along with his wife's educational achievements. His wife, Clara Kersey Jackson, also graduated from Howard. She was a member of one of the first classes to accept female students and studied in the Conservatory of Music.[10] The couple married on December 14, 1905.

While the Jackson family held an elevated social position in the community, they were not the economic equivalent of an average middle-class white family. As the historian Martin Summers has written: "The black middle class is defined more by its self-conscious positioning against the black working class—through its adherence to a specific set of social values and the public performance of those values—than by real economic and occupational differences."[11] James "envisioned the emergence of a large monied [sic] Negro business class as both a possibility in the American free enterprise market of the turn of the century, and as a necessity to ensure a minimum of economic independence and self-sufficiency to the Negro masses."[12] However, his position did not divide him geographically or socially from the poor black community in Richmond. Middle-class status was no shield from the insults of white racism in the South, and the indignities of segregation shaped the family's approach to politics. James stood as a symbol of hope, compassion, and upward mobility for the community.[13]

In early twentieth-century Richmond, a strong sense of community guided the city's African Americans through changing times. New segregation laws and white political backlash against blacks led to a reconfiguration of the city's spatial, social, and political structure, and African Americans adapted accordingly. The Jackson family lived in a neighborhood known as "Jackson Ward," a section that had "political, social, and economic importance even after white city councilmen gerrymandered the district out of existence in 1903."[14] Jackson Ward lived on in memory, imagination, and mythology and represented African American claims to the social terrain of Richmond. The historians Elsa Barkley Brown and Gregg D. Kimball write that it was "a function of history, collective memory, mythology, and power . . . a function of legislation, politics, and inequality . . . an act undertaken by black people, a distinction that turned it into a place of congregation as well as segregation."[15]

African Americans in Richmond made claims to community and geographic space even as white city authorities attempted to segregate and disenfranchise them. Within their community, class and gender divisions created internal conflict and drew the ire of whites. For instance, black middle- and upper-class women in Richmond strove for an image of respectability, and their dress epitomized their status within the community. They were set apart from poor and working-class women, who could not afford stylish clothing. To whites, black women who were not well dressed became the objects of spectacle and speculation, as their class status and race suggested that they might be prostitutes, criminals, or simply lazy. But stylish black women did not escape the racist scorn of whites. Whites thought that professional African American women who were well dressed threatened the status of white women, whose "money was being used to finance an extravagant, wasteful, and most important, non-subservient lifestyle of black women who more appropriately belonged in domestic work."[16] Professionalism and middle-class status distinguished the Jackson family socially from poor blacks within the African American community and gave them some status with whites, but they were no less a part of Jim Crow's rigid social hierarchy.

In general, James had a positive rapport with powerful whites in Richmond. The head of the Cliff Weil Cigar Company described him in a reference letter as "honorable and in every way high class in his dealings . . . as clean a cut merchant and darkey as [I have] ever met."[17] While Jim Crow sharply divided Richmond and racism colored the cigar merchant's portrayal of him, James was the type of man who defied white Virginians' stereotypes about African Americans. But his good relationship with local whites did not mean that he accommodated racism. He insisted on respect from all the merchants with whom he did business and expected them to "address him as 'Mr.' or 'Dr.,' and refer to his wife as 'Mrs.'"[18] White merchants usually complied, if begrudgingly so. Yet, in one frightening instance, bullets flew through a window a few feet from Jack's infant sister Clara's crib in the family's apartment above the store. The threat of white violence loomed large for any black businessperson who demanded equal treatment.[19]

Beyond demanding cordiality from white merchants, James fought segregation and racism head on. He and his friends once successfully impeded the segregated trolley car transit system in Richmond for several hours, a battle in which James was "beaten bloodily and jailed, but not before he had defended himself."[20] He believed that the problem of racism extended beyond the segregated South and spoke against World War I, declaring that it was "an imperialist war of thieving nations whose hands would be forever stained with the innocent blood of the outraged African and Asian peoples."[21] In the 1920s, he served as treasurer of the Richmond Committee of Civic Improvement League. The organization played a leading role in protesting racially restrictive housing covenants in Richmond and won a victory in a legal battle that went to the Supreme Court.[22]

James's drugstore served as a base for his political activities as local men converged to discuss "the whole galaxy of human knowledge and experience."[23] His circle embraced the liberationist attitude of W. E. B. Du Bois, which was expressed in the 1906 *Credo* of the all-black Niagara movement. Du Bois declared: "We [i.e., black Americans] will not be satisfied to take one jot or tittle less than our full manhood rights . . . and until we get these rights we will never cease to protest."[24] Du Bois's militancy inspired James's social circle to political struggle. Like Du Bois, most of these men opposed Booker T. Washington's "policy of conciliation."[25]

Washington was the first principal of the Tuskegee Institute in Alabama, where young African Americans learned trade skills, teaching, and domestic work and were urged to appreciate manual labor as a path to advancement. He famously advocated the public accommodation of segregation. He earned recognition by urging southern blacks, "Cast down your bucket where you are," in the process drawing on their skills and immediate surroundings to create lives for themselves and aspiring to comfort within the confines of the South's inflexible racial order. "In all things that are purely social," Washington declared, "we can be as separate as the fingers, yet one as the hand in all things essential to mutual progress."[26] Moderate whites responded well to Washington, and he was invited to dine at the White House in 1901 with President Theodore Roosevelt.

But many blacks, like Du Bois and James's circle, disagreed with Washington and argued that social, economic, educational, and political parity with whites was the only way forward for African Americans. They favored the "education of the whole man to enable him to exercise all the functions as a citizen of democracy." Nonetheless, Washington's tactics inspired debate. One man in James's group insisted that Washington's tactics were indeed subversive. He "would expound on the hidden meaning, the 'tricking-the-white-folk' wisdoms" of Washington's methods.[27] This man perceptively saw resistance lurking behind Washington's public persona. While Du Bois's public posture was far more militant than Washington's, the Tuskegee principal did indeed work behind the scenes to fight legalized segregation.[28]

James Jackson Jr. was born on November 29, 1914. He had an older sister, Alice. His younger sister, Clara, was born a few years later. His parents also had two other children, both of whom died in toddlerhood before Alice was born. As a boy, Jack observed his father, uncles, and neighbors as they debated politics and planned protests in the back room of the pharmacy. James offered his children Du Bois's teachings, feeding them a "steady diet of readings from 'As the Crow Flies,'" the youth section of the NAACP periodical *The Crisis*.[29] Jack absorbed his father's militancy and developed a political astuteness that drove his intellect and activities.

For a young black boy growing up in segregated Richmond, it was not difficult to develop an understanding of how race and class provided or denied opportunities. Early on in school, Jack excelled. His classmates and neighbors were the desperately poor children of tobacco workers. He noticed that many of the poor students who had some academic successes faced difficulties as they grew older. As they became increasingly able, these children "were a part of the bread-winning combination of their families": "After school and on weekends, they worked long hours selling papers, shining shoes, gathering junk, hauling groceries."[30] The economic demands of struggling families in a struggling community forced intellectually capable students to leave school for unskilled positions that would sustain their family but would not help them advance. Jack saw clearly the privileges that his family's more comfortable economic status afforded him, and the difficulties his classmates faced never left his mind.

As Jack became aware of Richmond's stark social and economic divisions, he immersed himself in scholarly, artistic, and athletic endeavors. As a senior he designed the cover of the Armstrong High School yearbook. The image depicted two figures, each climbing upward. As Jack described: "The figure holding the torch represents the graduating student, bearing the torch of knowledge, obtained at Armstrong; by means of its light he is able to aid his weaker brother as he climbs the ragged mountain of life, to attain the success which lies on the summit of the heights."[31] Jack's upbringing and education distinctly shaped his worldview. The opportunities he had and the support his family offered, he believed, would not limit his ability to succeed. He had a responsibility to use his success to help others who had been denied the chances he had.

When he was about twelve years old, Jack organized the first black troop to be admitted into the Boy Scouts of America in Virginia. Geared toward middle-class youths, the Boy Scouts of America formed in 1910 alongside a number of other youth organizations that sought to provide structure and regulation to children's recreation. Scouting reinforced "boys' work" as an essential component of developing the masculinity that drove politics and patriotism during this period.[32] Jack saw in the Scouts an opportunity for "a life of evangelical work in strictest conformity to the credo and laws of the worthy order."[33] The Scouts "emphasized the drive for individual achievement but also the necessity of team play" as part of the organization's mission.[34]

A Boy Scout uniform usually would draw the respect of fellow citizens, as it meant that the young man wearing it had resisted "the overwhelming temptation of illicit and soul-destroying pleasures" in favor of social responsibility and respectable manhood.[35] This did not apply to Jack. Shortly after acquiring his uniform, Jack once wrote Esther: "I inadvertently sat beside an aged, dignified, aristocratic looking white couple on the rearmost seat of the Chamberlyn Avenue bus—apologizing as I did so." Though Jack was well versed in the Jim Crow way of life, his youth, his uniform, and his faith in humanity had not prepared him for what happened next:

> Like some knight accosted by a dragoon, [the white man] leaped up, seized my Scout ax and holding it menacingly over my head with tremulous hand and in hysterical phrases ordered me ("filthy, black little nigger") to stand up where I belonged. I searched the eyes of his woman companion with eyes wide with pain and soul searing shock. I questioned her eyes to find a reprimand there for his act of barbarian manners but I saw only cold, steel grey pools of religious, racial arrogance there. Something in me dies, never to be born again. And something new was born . . . : a ferocious hatred for the haters of my people—later to be enlarged to embrace all the oppressed of the world. . . . From 12 to 16 I lived in a world of hate.[36]

As an adolescent, Jack saw not only the ferocity of the man's racism and its potential to turn "dignified, aristocratic" whites into monsters but also the cold indifference of the female companion, who disregarded Jack's age and visible status when he mistakenly crossed a segregation barrier. The humiliation and fear that accompanied this experience led Jack to guard himself against the pain of racism by using hatred as a shield.

Jack graduated from high school at the age of sixteen. That same year, his politics and interest in activism grew better defined as he had several transformational experiences. He continued in the Boy Scouts until he was sixteen, when he earned the rank of Eagle Scout. The ceremony where new Eagle Scouts received their honors from the governor of Virginia reinforced for Jack that his accomplishments did not supersede his race in the eyes of the most powerful man in Virginia.

At the John Marshall Hall, known as the "'society' sanctuary of white supremacy," where the ceremony was held, Jack recalled, "the only entrance for blacks was the freight elevator." Jack was allowed to invite only his father along, though several family members accompanied most other scouts. The only other black guest at the ceremony was a man named William Jordan. In spite of the high honor that came with the rank of Eagle Scout, the black honoree and attendees navigated their way around the building and through an alleyway to find the freight elevator entrance.[37] Once inside, James and Jordan sat off to the side of the rest of the audience in wooden folding chairs. Jack sat on one side of the platform, and the eleven white scouts sat on the other.

When the time came for Virginia governor John Garland Pollard to pin the badges on the new Eagle Scouts, he honored each white scout with his badge and a handshake or congratulatory pat on the head. When he saw Jack, "he stepped back and just grunted . . . for me, he tossed [the award] and I caught it." Though this was cause for humiliation, Jack used the moment as an opportunity to exhibit the character traits of a proud Eagle Scout. Recovering quickly from the shock of the affront, he pinned the badge on his own shirt and put his hand to his forehead in salute. He recalled: "The audience applauded that. And they separated themselves from the rudeness of the governor."[38]

Following the event, Jack took a stand. At sixteen, he was keenly aware of the injustice he had just encountered, but he remained hopeful about his ability to catalyze a change within the Boy Scouts. He wrote a letter to James E. West, the chief scout of the Boy Scouts of America, hoping that a respectable, well-written, and well-reasoned argument against segregation would highlight the absurdity of racial division within the organization. He described his encounter with the Virginia governor at the Eagle Scout ceremony and his frustration with separate white and black Scouting. He pointed out that racial segregation within the Boy Scouts was an obvious injustice and insisted that the Scouts be integrated. But West sent a defensive reply, and Jack resigned in protest.[39]

Jack enrolled at Virginia Union University in February 1931 at the age of sixteen. Virginia Union had grown out of the Richmond Theological Seminary and was founded as a historically black college on February 17, 1900. Although the university earned most of its financial support from the American Baptist Home Missionary Association, it was officially nonsectarian. It absorbed neighboring Hartshorne Memorial College, a similar institution for black women, in 1932. It boasted respected faculty members and was one of just five higher education institutions for blacks in the state.[40] Virginia Union and Hartshorne stood in view of the Carrington and Michaux Tobacco Stemming Company. This juxtaposition of menial labor and higher education illustrated the contrast in economic prospects for black Richmond youths.

Because he had developed a sense of class consciousness and witnessed deep poverty in Richmond, despite his family's status Jack came of age believing that college students felt superior to the surrounding community. He knew the cost of higher education made it a prohibitive luxury, and many of his high school classmates, no matter how gifted, could barely entertain the notion of college, let alone make it reality. Initially, despite enrolling in Virginia Union, he tried to stay true to his roots and "rather ridiculously strained to keep himself 'pure' of any real identification with the manners of the collegian." When he became immersed in college culture, however, he learned that his earlier viewpoint was misguided. He discovered that most college students "weren't the 'arrogant conceited asses'" of his stereotype but regular young men and women, "toiling at odd jobs after school hours and throughout the summer months; denying themselves the small pleasures, and along with their parents pinching and saving that they might buy the tools of a higher learning and 'make something really worthwhile' out of their lives."[41] This realization was crucial in the development of his politics. Growing up surrounded by poverty and racism gave him empathy and insight into the daily struggles of the working class, and his education became the foundation for his efforts on their behalf.

Jack was particularly fortunate to attend college during the Great Depression. The economic crash of 1929 resulted in a 25 percent unemployment rate nationwide. For many African Americans in the South, poverty was not new, but the breadth of poverty during the Depression years put economic and educational opportunities for African Americans even further out of reach. As the political scientist Ira Katznelson writes: "The world economy's collapse after 1929, especially as it affected agriculture, deepened the poverty experienced by the vast majority of the South's black workforce. . . . [T]he small, fragile black middle classes on both sides of the Mason-Dixon line came under intense pressure, having gained only a very tenuous attachment to stable jobs with regular wage incomes, cultural respectability, and chances for mobility before the depression hit."[42] Even as government efforts to assuage the worst of the Depression brought some relief, blacks were almost wholly excluded from the benefits of the New Deal. James's career as an entrepreneur and pharmacist made him vital to his community and afforded his children opportunities even in the face of widespread economic despair.

Though earning only average academic marks, Jack's reputation as a charismatic campus leader started early in his college career when he became president of the freshman class. He encouraged his peers to use their education to improve the conditions of the working class worldwide.[43] He delivered a speech on Freshman Day entitled "The Student and the World beyond the Campus." It was reprinted in *The Intercollegian* and the *Richmond Times-Dispatch*.[44] As his perspective on the social position of college students had evolved, he saw in his classmates' passion, ambition, and sense of sacrifice the potential for global change. He began his speech by asking his fellow students to imagine walking beyond the pristine campus to another section of Richmond. He described the despair poverty had wrought for blacks in other parts of the city and then connected that to the problem of poverty worldwide. He closed: "Ten million Chinese are destitute—no food—no homes—no hope. . . . A coolie misses his evening 'rice'—we echo the pangs of his hunger. . . . There is a world beyond the campus."[45] He described how the adversity caused by Richmond's racial and economic divisions was not unique to the city, the state, or the South. He related local struggles to an international economic context.

The connections Jack drew between local situations in the US South and the global struggle against race and class oppression echoed one of his primary influences, W. E. B. Du Bois. Du Bois had long emphasized "worldwide networks that encompass Europe, Africa, the industrial United States, and the 'colonies that belt the globe.'"[46] In an essay on the start of World War I titled "The African Roots of the War," he presented a line of thinking that Jack drew from when connecting his college classmates to Chinese peasants. He wrote that World War I was "the result of jealousies engendered by the recent rise of armed national associations of labor and capital whose aim is the exploitation of the wealth of the world mainly outside the European circle of nations."[47] The war, Du Bois argued, consisted of the conflicts between white Europeans who stood to profit from the natural and human resources in other parts of the world.

While the United States avoided the conflict until it was nearly over, its own racial and class tensions were enmeshed with Europe's. Du Bois argued that discontented white workers in the United States were mollified by threats that black workers would replace them should they decide to strike. The result would be that "we gain industrial peace at home at the mightier cost of war abroad." In other words, anxieties about labor were quelled by reassuring whites that their supremacy was intact, but uniting whites on this basis only contributed to the larger tensions that were brewing across the globe. To Du Bois, the larger problem was the global color line, and people of color worldwide grew increasingly restless as Europeans fought for democracy on their own small continent. He argued that Europe needed to grant the "democratic ideal to the yellow, brown, and black peoples" in order to avoid even deeper calamity.[48]

Following Du Bois, Jack argued that people of color across the globe bore the brunt of white competition over capital, that the hunger pangs of his Chinese peasant resulted from the same racist ideology that separated black Americans from white Americans. When Du Bois visited China several years after Jack's speech, he remarked: "A little white boy of perhaps four years order[ed] three Chinese out of his imperial way on the sidewalk. . . . It looked quite like Mississippi."[49] As Jack reconciled his privileged upbringing against the backdrop of acute poverty, he began to acknowledge that his education was more than a means for economic upward mobility. He, like his classmates, had an opportunity as an African American earning a college degree during the Great Depression to work against the barriers that capitalism, racism, and class divisions created worldwide. His Freshman Day speech urged Virginia Union students to "dedicate their lives to the people as the sole motive and justification for their more favored circumstances."[50]

Impressed by the speech, Jack's classmates nominated him to attend an interracial seminar in North Carolina the following summer. At the YMCA conference at Kings Mountain, he met the first white people who did not treat him as though he was inferior. Until 1926, Kings Mountain had been a segregated YMCA training school for blacks, and whites from the Southeast met at nearby Blue Ridge. The YMCA had long been the most widely represented youth organization for African Americans, but its segregation policies came under fire as blacks and whites increasingly agitated for "Christian brotherhood" across racial lines. Neither Blue

Ridge nor Kings Mountain integrated easily, particularly because many southern white YMCA members remained attached to segregation. But a few whites were more open to meeting at Kings Mountain, and the seminar Jack attended was integrated.[51] The seminar deepened Jack's belief that productive change in the conditions in the South should include all members of society, that people of all races working together to improve the social, economic, and political climate could make an impact.

After conversations with a young white Communist at this seminar, Jack devoted the summer of 1931 to the study of Marxism and joined the Communist Party.[52] He recalled that this moment of transformation initiated "wonderful years heralding the revolution and toppling of the gods of bourgeois respectability in every direction."[53] This flowery recollection of his early experiences with the CPUSA points to a young man who had been searching for a way to reconcile his privilege as a member of the middle class with the ways he had experienced racism and oppression and translate his experiences into useful actions. The Communist Party offered Jack a path away from the hatred he had harbored for whites, as he saw the organization as a vehicle for productive change for impoverished and struggling people around the globe.

The CPUSA gained increasing popularity across the United States as economic despair ravaged the country. In the face of capitalism's apparent failure, more Americans were amenable to the notion that the US economic structure could change. For African Americans, the CPUSA offered a unique opportunity for political advancement and economic parity that was unavailable with other American political organizations. The Party worked actively to court African Americans during the Depression as well and sought to provide solutions to racial problems in the South. In 1928, it offered a formal statement on the "Negro Question" and articulated the "Black Belt thesis." The latter argued that black Americans living in the Deep South constituted a nation within a nation and that this status afforded them the right to self-determination. The Party encouraged blacks to move to areas within the Black Belt to secure black self-determination. Modeled on the Soviet Union's republics, the Black Belt thesis became the Party's doctrine on African Americans. By considering black Americans a separate nation within the United States, the Party acknowledged the prevalence of race in the United States and encouraged black support by offering a clear focus on the domestic problems blacks faced.[54] The Black Belt thesis offered African Americans a claim to the South, where they constituted the majority of the labor force but reaped few of the benefits.

In 1931, the Party solidified its standing with African Americans when it became involved in the legal defense of nine black boys charged with raping two white women. On March 25, 1931, the nine, aged twelve to nineteen, were riding a freight train in Chattanooga, Tennessee. Their names were Haywood Patterson, Roy Wright, Willie Roberson, Eugene Williams, Olen Montgomery, Ozie Powell, Andy Wright, Clarence Norris, and Charles Weems. Two white women, Ruby Bates and Victoria Price, also hopped onto the train. After a conflagration between the black boys and a group of white men, Price and Bates asserted that "twelve black men" had gang-raped them. Despite Bates's later recantation, the Scottsboro boys' legal trouble lasted into the 1950s. Haywood Patterson, the last of the boys to leave Alabama, did so in a dramatic escape from prison in 1948. The CPUSA and its legal arm, the International Labor Defense (ILD), notoriously defended the boys, and the NAACP competed for the case. The boys and their parents remained loyal to the ILD in part because of the NAACP's bureaucratic approach to the boys.[55] African Americans responded favorably to the CPUSA's work with the Scottsboro boys in part because so many similar cases in the past had led directly to lynching without any intervention from the justice system.

Angelo Herndon's struggle against the Georgia justice system was another case that united African Americans and Communists. Herndon, a nineteen-year-old black Communist originally from Ohio, moved to Fulton County, Georgia, in 1932. He had traveled to the South to help organize unemployed workers, both black and white. Southern police feared him and arrested him after he led a group of destitute southerners in a demonstration at the Fulton County courthouse. Having had no legitimate reason to arrest Herndon, police excavated an arcane anti-insurrection law dating back to 1861 that was originally written to apply to slave rebellions. Herndon was convicted and sentenced to eighteen to twenty years in prison but was released in 1934 after an appeals process. His case had rallied the support of African Americans and international observers and again solidified the CPUSA and ILD's standing with African Americans during the Depression.[56]

The Angelo Herndon case also signified the start of a new pattern in radical Communist-influenced protest during the Depression years. By leading both white and black workers at the Fulton County courthouse, Herndon, and his so-called insurrection, exemplified interracial working-class unity, which was growing more popular as the Depression wore on. For many white workers, it became disadvantageous to distance themselves from blacks, and unity seemed to be an appropriate approach for combating capitalism's failure. The proletariat, it appeared, was no longer divided along racial lines, and this class solidarity among poor blacks and whites terrified southern authorities. It surely contributed to Herndon's prosecution, but it also reflected the CPUSA's growing influence on social movements. Jack learned through the CPUSA's writings "that the Negro people have a powerful ally in the white workers and that it is to the self-interest of both to unite in common struggle . . . [and] that the task of correct leadership was to fight for this unity of the Southern people—Negro and white workers—to weld it, and to win allies for them in the nation and throughout the world."[57]

Jack's middle-class upbringing afforded him a set of privileges that set him apart from most of his community, and his understanding of communism was grounded in a complex intellectual and theoretical tradition. But his arrival at the conclusion that communism was the best path to justice for poor and working-class African Americans was rooted in his everyday exposure to the depths of economic oppression and racism. As his experience at his Eagle Scout ceremony illustrates, Jack's achievements were always tempered in the eyes of whites by his race. Despite his family's economic standing, the insults of segregation meant that his intellectual approach to communism was fused with lived experience.

Jack's membership in the CPUSA was the result of both his intellectual background and his exposure to racism and poverty, and his story differed from the stories of many other college students who joined the Party in the Depression. For the white college student Junius Scales, embracing communism was the result of an intellectual journey during his first year of college. A student at the University of North Carolina at Chapel Hill from an affluent background, Scales was an astute observer

of social and political injustice. He opposed segregation and labor exploitation and sought a political ideology to reflect this. He read widely and
had a number of conversations with fellow students about the benefits of
communism. While he ultimately disliked some of communism's most
outspoken ideologues, he decided the Party offered an opportunity to
realize his "old dream of building the brotherhood of man." He was also
drawn to Communists' "camaraderie and . . . privileged sense of belong-
ing." He was soon dissatisfied with his decision and planned to drop out
of the Party after a few months but then met a Communist who gave the
Party renewed meaning. The Communist recognized Scales's disillusion-
ment and explained: "It's working people and Negroes that make the
Party tick. They don't join in a burst of idealism like a lot of students do.
They join because they need it."[58]

While Jack's path to the Communist Party was a product of his education, his conclusion that Communist ideology was a correct approach
to racial and class activism was as much an organic result of his social and
geographic context as it would have been for a poor tobacco worker.
As the historian Robin D. G. Kelley writes, working-class radical men
and women "came from the farms, factories, mines, kitchens, and city
streets, not as intellectual blank sheets but loaded down with cultural
and ideological baggage molded by their race, class, gender, work, community, region, history, upbringing, and collective memory."[59] The Alabama Communist Hosea Hudson recalled that, during a meeting led by a
Communist who detailed the disadvantages blacks faced in the South, he
thought to himself: "My grandmother, my mother, my brother and I and
so many more of us hoped to go to school—and we never stopped hoping—we never did get a chance. Right here and now we Blacks are the last
to be hired and the first to be fired."[60] In this reflection, Hudson realized
that his personal situation was aligned with the Communist leader's ideas,
regardless of his illiteracy and lack of education.

The discovery of communism allowed Jack to strike a balance between
his loyalties to poor and working-class black Richmond and his elite educational background. Though he grew up with professional, educated
parents, in the midst of the Great Depression his community illustrated to
him the worst that abject poverty had to offer. Tobacco workers stream-
ing past his father's pharmacy and schoolmates whose chances to advance

in education were stunted by economics reminded him of his good fortune. Communism transformed Jack from a boy whose faith in humanity was dashed by a racist white couple, whose world was full of hate and suspicion, into a young man who had a renewed faith in the power of unity and the potential for change. The Party would provide his activism, intellect, and accomplishments with meaning. Communism also forced him to consider the importance of national and international economic and racial systems, emphasizing unity among workers.

Jack's growing commitment to Communist theory and practice initially caused some strife with his parents. His newfound politics led him to push at racial barriers, and in one instance he participated in a "'mass' violation of Jim Crow seating at [an] Inter-racial Commission meeting creating consternation and humiliating [his] mother before all of her 'fine' friends." At one point, his protest activity nearly got him expelled from Virginia Union. At his father's pharmacy, he attempted to assuage some of the pain of the Depression for Richmond's poor blacks, leading to "violent anti-filial arguments over giving away [his] father's drugs to [the] unemployed."[61]

These conflicts were political as much as they were normal generational disagreements between parents and children. James was of a generation that viewed the "self-made man as the epitome of success."[62] His education, entrepreneurship, and profession paved a path out of the mire of racial poverty and gave him standing in both the admiring black community and the reluctant white community. Though James openly protested racist practices, his status as a middle-class professional cemented the notion of racial uplift as his political ideology. As the historian Kevin K. Gaines writes, men like James "believed that they were replacing the racist notion of fixed biological differences with an evolutionary view of cultural assimilation, measured primarily by the status of the family and civilization." By creating a household culture of individual responsibility and family unity to exemplify racial respectability, they "dissemble[d] in order to survive in a racialized world not of their own making."[63] When Jack adopted communism, he not only rebelled against his father's authority as a parent; he also dismissed the politics that structured the whole of his father's racial being.

Nevertheless, Jack did not rebel completely against his father. From

Virginia Union University, he followed in James's footsteps and received his pharmacy degree from Howard University. He became a well-known student activist and was best remembered at Virginia Union for organizing the Marxist Club, the Proletarian Students Party, and the Cooperative Independents Club. He remained active as a graduate student at Howard between 1934 and 1937. As a member of the Young Communist League, the Marxist Study Circle, and the Liberal Club, he participated in strikes for the passage of antilynching legislation, against war, and against the high cost of living.[64] As a student activist, he protested school segregation at the Virginia capitol building with the University of Virginia student leader Palmer Weber. He fought unfair hiring and expressed support for the Scottsboro boys.[65]

While he was at Howard, Jack gave a speech on behalf of the National Executive Committee of the National Student League (NSL) to the Labor Committee of the House of Representative to express his support for the Lundeen Bill. The Lundeen Bill, or the Workers' Unemployment and Social Insurance Bill, offered federal protection for the unemployed, maternity leave, and aid to families with dependent children and guaranteed protections for as long as workers sought jobs. It was a more progressive version of the Social Security act that the Roosevelt administration later passed.[66] Jack argued that the bill appealed to the NSL "both in our capacity as students, that is as sons and daughters of workers, and in our capacity as potential workers . . . who . . . will be out there competing against our jobless elders." He highlighted the privilege college students had in the Depression but emphasized that even college students struggled. He pointed out that economic hardship made it difficult for students to stay in school, noting: "It was not until the fifth year of the depression that Federal funds became available to the destitute college students who had somehow found their way into colleges. This aid is so small that it can hardly be said to constitute relief."[67] As a student activist, Jack increasingly integrated his educational opportunities with efforts to support students and workers in the midst of the economic crisis. His communism informed his perspective, fusing his lived experience, his exposure to poverty, and his growing academic background.

As Jack completed his education, he faced a dilemma. Since the time he was a small boy, his family and community had expected that he would eventually take over his father's business. As a toddler, he played with chemistry sets. His educational path pointed to pharmacy as a career. But, as he prepared to fulfill the promise of his upbringing, he found himself more concerned with the social and economic inequality blacks faced across the Jim Crow South. His student activism at both Virginia Union and Howard captivated his imagination more than his science and pharmacology courses. He managed to be both a pharmacist and an activist for a few years after graduating from Howard, but it was clear that his passion was not his father's career.

Jack found a new outlet for activism not long after graduating from Howard, attending the February 14–16, 1936, organizing conference of the National Negro Congress (NNC) in Chicago. The NNC, an organization that had ties to the CPUSA, the Brotherhood of Sleeping Car Porters, the Urban League, and the CIO, offered black Americans a left-wing alternative to the liberal NAACP. As the historian Marc Solomon writes: "For the hundreds of blacks and whites who gathered in Chicago—and for the millions whom they represented—the quest for racial justice had become an integral part of the struggle for economic, political, and social progress. Not since the founding of the NAACP had the Negro Question become such an essential element of a broad progressive agenda."[68] The NNC was designed to "activate and politicize the grass roots of the black community" by "endorsing the organization of black labor, attacking lynchings, and supporting black businesses."[69] As a Popular Front organization, as Erik Gellman notes, it "combined several strands of protest movements from African American history, the labor movement, and radical political parties into a black-led, interracial, mass movement that catalyzed both labor unions and black advancement organizations to see these tactics as necessary and employ them across urban America."[70] For Jack, the NNC offered a bold, ideal outlet that was firm in its uncompromising approach to destroying Jim Crow.

The NNC offered a link between CPUSA influence and black freedom organizations. Before the Depression and the New Deal, the relationship between the CPUSA and organizations designed to help African Americans was a tense one. At the outset, the CPUSA approached racial struggles from a class perspective. Focusing on the large number of poor and working-class African Americans, it appeared dismissive and at times hostile to middle-class blacks and "moderate protest and betterment organizations the 'black bourgeoisie' supported."[71] According to Solomon, the Party exhibited particular enmity toward the Urban League for "fawning before the capitalists" and the NAACP for its "solid middle-class credentials, its anticommunism, its faith in the legal system, and its status as a pillar of the community." The NAACP and the Party had a consistently strained relationship, and, while other groups with distinct ideologies might coexist, Communists and racial liberals could not. The Party believed that the NAACP inhibited mass action by catering to the bourgeois legal system, that it did "the job of social fascists—diverting blacks and whites from forming 'fighting alliances' in the streets."[72] The NAACP adopted a similarly antagonistic stance toward the Party. Du Bois, who would later join the CPUSA, represented NAACP opinion on the Party in 1931 when he called Communist activity in the South "too despicable for words." He later wrote in an editorial for *The Crisis* that the CPUSA lacked the "honesty, earnestness and intelligence of the NAACP during twenty years of desperate struggle."[73] When the Party went head-to-head with the NAACP over the Scottsboro case, this animosity intensified.

Only when the Popular Front began did the anxieties between the CPUSA and the NAACP dissipate. The Popular Front, which grew out of the global economic Depression, unified activists in the 1930s behind progressive causes. Initiated in 1935 by the Communist International and the Soviet Union, it introduced some flexibility into the CPUSA and altered the notion that all Party policy came directly from Moscow. It also represented the earliest opposition to the rise of fascism across Europe. In the United States, the goal of the Popular Front movement was to unite leftist organizations and quietly influence activism across the nation and the world with Communist ideas. Communists got involved in a wide network of labor unions, civil rights organizations, and any other groups that explicitly opposed fascism. Instead of forcing these organizations to adopt strict Communist principles, Party members subtly influenced them with their ideas, suggestions, and methods. Between 1936 and 1938, the Communist Party doubled its membership, from about forty thousand to about eighty-two thousand, and the Popular Front's antifascist, reform-minded platform was at the heart of that growth. Earl Browder, a

CPUSA leader, declared: "Communism is twentieth-century American-ism." Many Popular Front organizations in the United States were inter-racial and working-class, devoted to labor reform and civil rights.[74] The NNC was part of the Popular Front movement in the United States.

It is no coincidence that the Popular Front emerged when it did. Global economic depression brought about the rise of both liberalism and a leftist critique of liberalism in the United States. On the basis of the notion that capitalism and democracy were inextricably linked, liber-als fought economic depression from within the system. Liberalism was rooted in the notion that the government was the solution to the nation's ills and that reform could be implemented by using existing social, legal, political, and economic structures. As liberalism emerged as the next major political movement, liberal politicians actively distanced themselves from socialism by promoting, preserving, and rescuing capitalism. While Franklin D. Roosevelt was not as overtly anti-Communist as the liberal presidents who followed, some of his efforts to assuage the difficulties of the Depression worked to bolster capitalism.

But, for those on the political Left, the Depression solidified the idea that capitalism needed to be discarded, not revived. When the Popu-lar Front movement unleashed communism from its hierarchical struc-ture, Left-leaning and Communist activists had little difficulty winning the support of the down-and-out. Communism, in its milder Popular Front form, not only appeared to offer new long-term solutions to the economic woes of the nation's workers; it also helped exploited workers, African Americans, and disenchanted activists feel that they were making active contributions to immediate change. Just as Jack's upbringing in a politically progressive, middle-class household where he was also exposed to desperate poverty led him to embrace communism, the Popular Front fused an intellectual and theoretical movement to the needs of individuals experiencing real-life economic despair. In this unique political moment, the Communist Party was able to generate a response unlike anything it would see in later eras.

Jack was excited by the prospects of an organization like the NNC. But, along with his friends Edward Strong and James Ashford, he believed that young black southerners would benefit from an organization that emphasized southern concerns, rather than a northern-dominated national organization. The young activist Augusta Strong wrote: "Numbers of militant youth came to the [NNC] meeting. They felt at once that the acute problems of their people in the North were indissoluble [*sic*] from those of the South. . . . All were agreed that a successful Southern Negro youth movement would be a powerful force in winning equality and opportunity for all young Negroes and for raising their standards of life in general."[75] In the past, it happened that most progressive southern organizations had been branches of northern organizations, making the concept of a southern-based and -administered black youth organization unique. Jack, Strong, and Ashford felt that southerners needed an organization that represented their unique circumstances and understood the particularities of contemporary southern racial culture.

Ashford proposed the organization of the Southern Negro Youth Congress (SNYC) to Edward Strong, the NNC youth chairman. Strong, a Texarkana, Texas, native, was the son of a Baptist minister. His family moved north to Flint, Michigan, when he was twelve, by which point he knew "what it meant to pick a hundred pounds of cotton a day, and to have absorbed the feeling for the folkways of the Negro people—their music, their leaders, and the fervent oratory of the church." While his family worked in Flint's industries, Strong "absorbed the talk of organizing unions."[76]

Before entering college, Strong had founded a Junior NAACP branch and had won a college scholarship.[77] He graduated from Central YMCA College in Chicago, a college-level program that grew out of YMCA business classes and eventually became Roosevelt University. He then became a youth leader at the Mount Olivet Baptist Church. In 1933, he attended the First International Youth Conference in Chicago and joined the Communist Party shortly thereafter. After abandoning his path toward leadership in the Baptist Church, he received a graduate degree in political science at Howard University. Though Ashford was the earliest proponent of the SNYC, Strong did most of the initial organizational work. He had planned to hold the first Southern Negro Youth Conference in November 1936 but postponed it to attend the World Youth Conference in Geneva, Switzerland, that year. He passed the organizational responsibilities on to Jack, who spent the summer of 1936 piecing together plans for the first conference of the SNYC.[78]

The first All-Southern Negro Youth Conference was held on February 13–14, 1937—in honor of Frederick Douglass's birthday—in Richmond, Virginia. In all, 534 young men and women attended the conference. Delegates came from twenty-three states, the Belgian Congo, and China and represented two hundred thousand members of a large variety of religious, civic, fraternal, and political organizations.[79]

The organization established itself as "primarily concerned with the problems of black youth." Yet it was "convinced that the problems of adults and youth in the South were substantially similar and the solutions for black and white youth were virtually the same."[80] The organization encouraged its new members and leaders to commit to making the South represent American ideals, rather than abandoning the difficult struggle there. As Florence Castile recalled, the delegates at the first SNYC conference were "determined not to go to the crowded urban cities to try to compete for jobs in the North," and "they were persistent in their belief that the South, which was their home, must yield them a living, an education, full citizenship rights including the right to vote and the right to be free of terror."[81] At the first conference, Edward Strong gave a talk in which he emphasized the contrast between the "land of potential with plenty of science, natural resources and every possible equipment to place at the disposal of man" and the lack of legislation against lynching and poll taxes.[82] The newly formed SNYC validated black southerners' hope that democracy could be fought for and won, even amid the woes of the Great Depression.[83]

At the first SNYC conference, young black southerners issued the "Proclamation of Southern Negro Youth," challenging their country to deliver on the promise of equality and democracy that defined American political culture. The organization represented a wide range of black southerners from an array of economic backgrounds, but all agreed that the combination of segregation and economic oppression resembled an insidious virus that they needed to combat. Young black southerners also believed that the challenge of democracy was crucial to America's standing in the world community. Equality and justice were not only imperative in the lives of young black southerners; they were vital to the stature of the nation in the eyes of the rest of the globe.[84]

These young black southerners declared: "We shall sweep away all obstacles, real and imaginary, and make for ourselves, and for America, a wonderful greatness, an expression of civilized humanity, at peace with itself, at peace with the world, a proof that humankind can achieve a new order." In contrast to Marcus Garvey's popular belief a decade and a half earlier that black Americans should abandon hope in the United States and resettle in Africa, the SNYC's founders believed that America, and the South in particular, did provide the framework for the equality and justice that US democracy had not yet realized. According to the "Proclamation of Southern Negro Youth," young black southerners held the same potential as the most noteworthy black figures in history to make essential strides toward a new United States that fulfilled its promise. They optimistically planned to create a truly unified country that embraced the goal of democracy as a global ideal.[85]

From its inception, the SNYC sponsored, as the historian Robin D. G. Kelley states, "a politics of inclusion *and* self-determination—a vision of interracial democracy combined with black militancy."[86] It emphasized unity and racial pride as key components of social justice. The "Proclamation of Southern Negro Youth" addressed the tensions between young white and black southerners. It read: "These conditions are caused not by the many—but by the few, those who profit by pitting white labor against black labor to the harm of both." The SNYC offered its "hand in warmest brotherhood" to young white southerners, stating that whites and blacks could better their conditions only by working together.[87] But the organization also emphasized that race further compounded the problems of black southerners and set out to infuse political activism with racial pride and a sense that racial equality would benefit the entire nation.

As a part of the Popular Front, the SNYC included Communist leaders like Jack who believed in a radical overhaul of the social and economic structures of the United States as a path to social justice and equality for black Americans. But the organization also defined itself as nonpartisan. It included black southerners who held a range of political viewpoints, from Communists to followers of Booker T. Washington.[88] For Jack, though he had been a member of the CPUSA since 1931, the SNYC's political inclusiveness fostered his political maturation. His involvement with Richmond's black community, including his father's progressive social circle, his mother's dignified friends, his schoolmates, and impoverished tobacco workers, helped him adopt a broad interpretation of communism's ideals. Though his CPUSA membership and leadership would outlast the SNYC's existence by a half century, leading the SNYC was the defining role of Jack's political life.

The SNYC structure included the Adult Advisory Board, the Executive Board, officers and staff, SNYC clubs, affiliated clubs, and members at large. The organization earned nationwide credibility through its Adult Advisory Board. This group consisted of around thirty preeminent black academics, activists, and professionals, ranging from the presidents of southern black colleges to NAACP leaders and lawyers. During the SNYC's history, members of the Adult Advisory Board included the influential figures W. E. B. Du Bois, Charlotte Hawkins Brown, Mary McLeod Bethune, Mordecai Johnson, F. D. Patterson, Arthur Shores, and Charles Johnson.[89] These advisers participated in the SNYC's Executive Board meetings and provided budget approval, guidance, and encouragement, along with strong and respectable connections with the organizations that they represented.[90]

The Executive Board, officers, and staff were responsible for issuing club charters and organizing all major functions of the SNYC. SNYC clubs existed within trade unions, YMCAs, YWCAs, colleges, high schools, and neighborhoods.[91] Affiliated clubs were groups that already existed and wished to associate with the SNYC. Social clubs, athletic groups, and school, church, and fraternal organizations were represented among the affiliated clubs. Members at large were individuals who wished to affiliate with the SNYC but were not members of a club or an affiliate group. These branches of the organization combined to form the SNYC Community Council. SNYC leaders expected that delegates from each branch of the organization would gather at least once every two years at the All-Southern Negro Youth Conference, the organization's "highest governing body."[92]

One of the SNYC's first activities was aiding the unionization of over five thousand black female tobacco stemmers in Richmond, Virginia, the very group Jack had greeted nightly as a child. Of the tobacco campaign, Augusta Strong wrote: "As a movement may reflect the image of the personalities who lead it, the passion and drive of the Negro youth movement of this period were mirrored in James Edward Jackson, the Richmond,

Virginia youth, who inspired, and helped to achieve, the organization of the perennially exploited tobacco workers in his native city."[93] Jack advocated that the group work with the CIO to organize the tobacco workers into a union.

The deplorable conditions of Virginia's tobacco workers were rooted in a long history of racial and economic oppression. By the early twentieth century, black women in Virginia monopolized the stemming of tobacco. Tobacco rehandlers were 98 percent black, and these workers were unable to advance to skilled labor positions because the tobacco industry "developed a dualistic structure in which black and white workers sought employment in separate, non-competing job classifications at differing rates of pay."[94] To stem tobacco, a worker would fold the leaf in half and remove the stem. Efficient technology for tobacco stemming had not yet been developed. Black female workers in this occupation were paid on the basis of the weight of the stems they had removed from the leaves. On average, tobacco stemmers earned a meager five dollars per week, not nearly enough to make ends meet.[95]

Management cared about tobacco profits more than the welfare of the workers. Factories seldom contained adequate dressing rooms or toilets. Factory windows were kept closed to retain moisture in the leaves, making the rooms extremely warm for the workers, who had no choice but to wear clothes made from discarded burlap tobacco sacks.[96] Without ventilation, the air was not breathable, and workers had to cover their faces with handkerchiefs to avoid inhaling dust. The humidity was unbearable, and the cruelty of the bosses only made the working conditions worse.[97]

Bosses were particularly harsh on black female workers, who occupied the majority of the lowest-paying, most grueling positions. As the historian Robert Korstad writes of tobacco strikes several years later in Winston-Salem, North Carolina, black women were subjected to poor treatment on the basis of both race and gender. Foremen had "virtually no constraints when it came to black women."[98] They failed to allow regular breaks, even for women who were pregnant or menstruating, and regularly implemented speedups to increase production. As one Export Leaf Tobacco Company worker known as Mama Harris put it: "It took me just one day to find out that preachers don't know nothing about hell. They ain't worked in no tobacco factory."[99] Although women constituted the vast majority of Virginia's tobacco stemmers, the tobacco factories also employed elderly people and children as stemmers and men as skilled laborers.

Many of the children who left school at an early age to provide their families with additional income by working in the tobacco industry were the offspring of adult tobacco workers. Jack observed that the number of children who remained in Richmond's black schools was "reduced by the man's deep pocket." For these children, returning to school after they found a means for earning income in the tobacco industry was neither a priority nor an option. In 1912, the Tobacco Workers International Union (TWIU) of the AFL had offered membership that would lead to improved wages and conditions, and, by 1920, thirty-five hundred workers had enrolled. However, membership meant little to the workers, and conditions had not improved. By 1925, the TWIU retained only one hundred members in Richmond.[100]

On April 16, 1937, a spontaneous walkout of unorganized workers at the Carrington and Michaux plant began in response to a work speedup without a corresponding pay raise. The strikers petitioned the Richmond community for assistance in organizing and collective bargaining. For twenty-four hours, their plea went unanswered. The SNYC, which was in the beginning stages of working with the CIO, responded and hurriedly joined with a semiorganized citizen's committee to help the strikers. Demands included wage increases, forty-hour workweeks, and recognition of the union. Without the assistance of the TWIU, the workers and the SNYC decided to form a new union, the Tobacco Stemmers and Laborers Industrial Union. Within forty-eight hours, dialogue began between the union leaders and the tobacco bosses, and the contract was renegotiated just four days after the strike began. The state sent a representative from the Department of Labor to ensure that negotiations went smoothly; even the representative was appalled at the existing labor and work conditions. The quick settlement of the spur-of-the-moment strike at Carrington and Michaux reflected management's desire to get the factory running as expeditiously as possible. Unaccustomed to worker defiance, factory managers were not willing to risk the cost of a long strike, and, as the historian Richard Love argues, the strikers' "courage and determination had cost C&M little in terms of dollars . . . but represented a major challenge to the established sensibilities of Richmond's white employers."[101]

The Carrington and Michaux strike initiated a series of strikes in Richmond's tobacco industry that extended into 1938, and the SNYC remained involved in worker organization. By the end of April 1937, twenty-two-year-old Jack, along with the twenty-one-year-old Virginian Francis Grandison and Chris Alston, a twenty-three-year-old SNYC member who had been an autoworker and union organizer in Detroit, enrolled over five thousand stemmers in the Tobacco Stemmers and Laborers Industrial Union, newly an affiliate of the CIO. Jack became the education director for the unionization effort, while Grandison worked as the business agent for the union, and Alston was the union's main organizer.[102] Whereas the segregated AFL, from which the CIO had separated, had failed to make union membership meaningful for black workers, Jack and the SNYC promptly promised that conditions would change for the stemmers affiliated with the CIO.[103]

Strikes followed at I. N. Vaughn and Company, Larus Brothers, the Tobacco By-Product and Chemical Corporation, and the Export Leaf Tobacco Company. The strikes typically resulted in higher wages, paid overtime, and better conditions.[104] The Carrington and Michaux victory had inspired workers. In the three months following the spontaneous walkout, strikes at three factories resulted in settlements, and workers lost less than four total weeks of work. Love writes: "Whether this spoke to the union's power, or simply to the fact that wages for stemmers and laborers had been so low and business so good that it cost the companies relatively little to settle the strikes, was open to question." In spite of this, the strikes grew progressively more complicated and drawn out. As the union effort expanded in Richmond, the divisions between unskilled black laborers and skilled white laborers increased. The TWIU (AFL affiliated) and the Tobacco Stemmers and Laborers Industrial Union (CIO affiliated) competed for the right to control the union at Larus Brothers, and segregation intensified the struggle. In addition, as the strikes progressed, stemming was becoming a less stable segment of the tobacco industry. The industry expanded, but, as technology improved, fewer stemmers were needed, and this shift meant that the proportion of black women working in Richmond's tobacco industry was shrinking.[105]

National politics made the situation in Richmond's tobacco industry even more complex. In the midst of the series of tobacco strikes in June 1938, Congress passed the Wages and Hours Bill, a part of the Fair Labor Standards Act that provided for a forty-cent-per-hour minimum wage. The Fair Labor Standards Act also outlawed child labor.[106] Out of fear that this would significantly increase, or even double, the price of tobacco, Tobacco Manufacturers' Association president E. J. O'Brien called for a campaign to educate the public about the "humane paternalism" of the tobacco industry. He argued that increasing tobacco wages to ten dollars per week would prevent the industry from "providing 'a place for'" elderly, sickly, and disabled people to work. On close examination into the industry by the union, however, the workers discovered that the vast majority of tobacco workers were adults in their prime who received less than 2 percent of the tobacco profits.[107]

The strike at the Export Leaf Tobacco Factory started on August 1, 1938, and lasted for eighteen days. The company's stemmers were the lowest paid in Richmond. One striker pointed out the wage disparity in a sign that read, "EXPORT LEAF'S VICE PRES WAS PAID $34,047 A YR. WE STRIKE FOR $10 A WEEK."[108] At the outset of the strike, the powerful factory threatened to close its doors and reopen elsewhere. But, with the public's support, the strikers won pay raises, union recognition, and improved conditions. The movement in 1937–1938 was the first major series of strikes in Virginia since 1905 and the first major victory for organized black labor in Virginia. Richmond Urban League director Wiley Hall considered the CIO campaign "the most significant thing that has happened to Richmond Negroes since Emancipation."[109]

The tobacco workers' successes through their new union led other working-class laborers to express solidarity. In the Export Leaf strike, two hundred members of the predominantly white female Amalgamated Clothing Workers joined the black tobacco workers on the picket line and pledged fifty dollars to help the strikers.[110] In addition, the Newspaper Guild, the American Federation of Teachers, and the International Ladies Garment Workers Union offered their assistance.[111] Jack explained: "The black workers were the pace setters in the struggle. They had nothing to lose, everything to gain and very little to defend. . . . [T]his was the base of their militancy." He recognized that the distinct racial separation and the gendered division of labor were deliberate. He noted: "It was not accidental on the part of the [bosses] to utilize the racial factor to ensure against the unification of the working class." The addition of the Amalgamated Clothing Workers to the Export Leaf Tobacco Factory picket line illustrated to Jack the extent of labor exploitation and solidified his belief that unity among workers of all races and across gender lines could lead to dramatic change.[112]

Jack's understanding of the implications of gender in racial and economic exploitation reflected both his politics and his upbringing in Richmond along with the cultural backdrop of the New Deal. When the strikes began, he observed that the workers he watched pass his father's pharmacy throughout his boyhood had begun "appreciating . . . that the power was in the muscle and mind of the workers."[113] Jack saw the strength of these workers as both mental determination and physical fortitude. The image of a muscular, "manly worker," propagandized during the New Deal, represented an ideal of work as both gendered and physical. The historian Barbara Melosh describes the image of a muscular worker as a cultural response to political strife, "a reformation of masculinity that both revised and conserved older representations of class, race, and gender." In New Deal–era public art, sculptures and paintings offered muscle-bound men as reassurance that, in spite of massive economic strife, gendered norms would prevail and preserve the nation. As Melosh notes: "In the face of widespread unemployment and changes in work that threatened traditional skills, public art presented work as a domain of male control and camaraderie."[114]

Yet the Richmond strikes proved this gendered representation to be inaccurate. Jack described one of the workers, Mama Harris, as an articulate "spokesman of the rank and file . . . in a class by herself." Her husband was of powerful, muscular stature with "big arms," a quintessential manly worker. But he often sat quietly aside while his wife's loud voice boomed over the crowd.[115] For Jack, Mama Harris debunked the popular image of the manly worker. The Harrises provided Jack with an example of the power of muscle and mind in defeating exploitation and reversed popular representations of gender and power.

By the time the tobacco strikes ended, they had helped the SNYC establish itself as an influential force in the South. The success of the strikes was a victory for the Popular Front movement, and Communist activists like Jack earned the respect of those they represented. In the 1940s, Raleigh-Durham's tobacco industry followed Richmond's with a series of strikes that merged labor concerns with civil rights.[116] The SNYC's earlier campaign had led the way. Nonetheless, the expression of defiance bubbling up from Richmond's impoverished workers did not win the favor of everyone in the city. Divisions between the city's middle- and working-class blacks, one commentator suggested, might be exacerbated by the workers' disregard for standards of respectability and polite behavior as they fought for improvements. While no one would have suggested that the tobacco workers'/SNYC's victory was pyrrhic, it was not uncomplicated.[117] But, for Jack, the events in Richmond were the culmination of his upbringing, education, and young adulthood in Richmond.

In the midst of the Richmond strikes, the SNYC forged ahead with its Popular Front mission. The second All-Southern Negro Youth Conference took place in Chattanooga, Tennessee, April 1–3, 1938. Depression-era economics dominated the conference program, with special attention to interracial working-class unity as a key means for advancing a civil rights agenda. As the conference invitation emphasized: "Many of our problems, those of health, family life, religion, education and economic security are problems common to ALL youth. The economic and cultural level of the South as a whole can be raised to a position of equality with the rest of the nation only by joint co-operation between Negro and white people."[118] For the SNYC, the unification of black and white working-class youths was a means to economic security. The organization's victories in the Richmond tobacco strikes demonstrated that its methods produced results and that its goals could be reached. The SNYC entered its second year with a record of success and looked to broaden its agenda.

In 1938, the SNYC also began to give more explicit attention to international politics. As a Communist-influenced organization, it went against the isolationist grain of late 1930s American life. Most Americans opposed intervention in foreign affairs during this era for several reasons. Homegrown anti-Semitism helped them turn a blind eye to Adolf

Hitler's growing Nazi aggression, the economic crisis turned the nation inward, and the memories of the horrors of World War I loomed large.[119] For many African Americans, the specter of World War I was particularly resonant. Blacks had believed that they would win the respect of the nation in the Great War, that, "by showing themselves good citizens, they would win the sympathy of the whites and gain all the things which they had been deprived."[120] Instead, on returning from war, black veterans confronted some of the most virulent and violent racism in history.

Most SNYC leaders did not envision American involvement in a total war but believed that the United States needed to stay attuned to international affairs and take a clear position on injustices perpetrated by fascist regimes. War was brewing within Europe and China, and conflicts were extending into other regions as well. In 1935, the Italian army invaded Ethiopia to avenge a four-decades-old defeat that kept a sole African nation from the ravages of colonialism. In response to mounting overseas conflict, the Roosevelt administration passed Neutrality Acts in 1935, 1937, and 1939. The Neutrality Acts forbade the US government from providing aid to any belligerent nations and implemented trade embargoes. Roosevelt invoked the first act immediately to bar aid to Ethiopia and Italy. But African Americans saw hope for global black independence in Ethiopia's efforts to hold off colonization and wanted to help. They rallied across the nation, set up the Provisional Committee for the Defense of Ethiopia, and even tried to volunteer to fight on behalf of Ethiopia. Because the Neutrality Act forbade enlistment in foreign war, they rallied to send money instead.[121]

The next year, civil war broke out in Spain after Republicans defeated the conservative government in a popular election and Generalissimo Francisco Franco, a right-wing nationalist, led a coup. Roosevelt did not invoke the Neutrality Act in this instance but generally discouraged Americans from participating. Nonetheless, sympathetic leftists and African Americans who had protested the Italian invasion of Ethiopia and felt a need to participate organized "Abraham Lincoln Brigades" and traveled to Spain to fight. Because the war in Spain was civil and not a competition between two nations, the Neutrality Act had no jurisdiction. These events influenced the SNYC in the late 1930s and helped the organization craft its position on international conflict as total war approached.[122]

In addition, Popular Front policy reflected the Soviet Union's opposition to and anxiety about fascism. Tensions between the Soviet Union and Western Europe increased as Nazism began to consume Eastern Europe. Britain had attempted to quell the danger Hitler posed and tried to calm the growing Nazi regime through its policy of appeasement. In 1938, British prime minister Neville Chamberlain agreed to recognize Italy's authority in Ethiopia to preserve peace in the Mediterranean and allowed Germany to conquer the Sudetenland in order to avoid further conflict in Eastern Europe. The United States maintained its isolationist stance and applauded Britain's peacekeeping measures, but isolation and neutrality abetted fascism's expansion. The Soviet Union anticipated the consequences of spreading Nazism and expressed frustration at the appeasement policy coming from the West. Josef Stalin rebuffed Britain's and France's efforts to form an alliance in part because Germany's uncontested expansion into the Sudetenland threatened Russia's security and stability. Instead of putting confidence in Britain and France, Stalin began to pave his own path in dealing with Hitler's aggression.[123]

For Communists and leftists in the United States, the events of the late 1930s spelled impending disaster. Popular Front leaders across the country took political cues from the Soviet Union and applied them to an American context, articulating an antiwar position that did not isolate or neutralize the United States in international affairs. At the second SNYC conference, leaders juxtaposed a desire for peace with anxiety that the world was heading in the opposite direction. They wrote:

> Our bodies and our souls are destined for higher things than cannon fodder in banker-made wars. We see the world today careening on a precipice and about to lurch over in a gulf of destruction and chaos. . . . We must take our stand against the fascist bandits who hold Ethiopia in bondage, and who now seek to march steadily through Spain, China, and Austria. With the world asking, "Where will they strike next?" we join our voices with all those who would preserve peace and democracy in saying: "They have gone far enough. They must be stopped by the aroused sentiment of the people of the world, and by the concerted actions of all nations and peoples who still hold democracy dear."[124]

The SNYC leaders echoed Du Bois's World War I article, "The African Roots of War," by deeming that the approaching conflict was the will of capitalists. Those engaged in competition over access to resources and capital used international conflict as a path to profit without concern for the nations that would be trampled as collateral damage. The SNYC asserted that local struggles and international strife were interconnected. The organization's leaders believed that exploited workers and oppressed African Americans would pay the cost of war while capitalists reaped the benefits.

Shortly after the second conference, Jack took a leave of absence from the SNYC to pursue an opportunity as a researcher for Gunnar Myrdal's study *An American Dilemma: The Negro Problem and Modern Democracy*. He left home and toured the South, interviewing blacks across the region. He worked under Ralph Bunche, an ardent anti-Communist. But Bunche was open to Jack's interpretations, and Jack's Communist insight "provided information on labor and radical activities that escaped the notice of most political scientists."[125] The experience was invaluable for Jack, but the most significant part of his time as a researcher did not become a part of Myrdal's work. On assignment in Tennessee, he visited Fisk University, where he met a graduate student in sociology named Esther Cooper. She lived and worked in a Methodist settlement house in the city, and she showed Jack around when he arrived. Esther and Jack had a lot in common. By the time they met, they had each independently committed to fighting racism and capitalism.

Esther Cooper, an Arlington, Virginia, native, and Jack were cut from nearly identical cloth. Esther's mother, Esther Irving Cooper, instilled in her three daughters, Kathryn, Esther, and Paulina, an awareness of the world around them. The elder Esther Cooper and her husband, the army officer George Posea Cooper, lived in relative comfort and afforded their daughters opportunities that many black children growing up in the Jim Crow South were denied. The family spent summers in Sea Isle City, New Jersey, and regularly visited family in Ohio, where the children experienced integration and equality unavailable at home.

Esther Irving grew up in Cleveland, Ohio. As a young adult, she entered a business college and later won a position as a secretary to Ohio's first black state representative, Harry C. Smith. Smith was a black journalist who founded the *Cleveland Gazette* and won election to the Ohio state legislature in 1893. After leaving Cleveland, Irving made her way to Kentucky, where she worked as a secretary to Nannie Helen Burroughs at the Auxiliary to the National Baptist Convention in Louisville. The connection with Burroughs proved fruitful, and the two became lifelong friends and allies. Irving later taught at Burroughs's National Training School for Women and Girls in Washington, DC, where she subsequently pursued a career as a secretary in the Department of Agriculture. There, she met Lieutenant George Posea Cooper. The two married on September 10, 1913, and had three daughters.[126]

Esther Irving Cooper was a respectable, progressive black woman who was politically active and engaged, and she strove to raise daughters who were savvy, independent, and smart. As a Parent Teacher Association leader in Arlington, Irving Cooper ensured that her girls received a solid educational foundation in spite of the poor state of Virginia's segregated schools. Though she was dedicated to improving southern schools, she prioritized the quality of her daughters' education over her politics. All three Cooper children spent some time living with an uncle in Washington, DC, to attend the prestigious Dunbar High School. As the nation's first public high school for African Americans, Dunbar boasted an impressive roster of both faculty and alumni and provided the rare opportunity for black southerners to acquire an elite education. Irving Cooper was active in St. John's Baptist Church and participated in many of its outreach programs, including the Lott Carey Foreign Mission Society. She also helped found and lead the Jenny Dean Community Center Association, which bought land on which to develop YMCAs. The Jenny Dean group formed in 1931 in response to "a need for organized recreation for the youth of the community and for the extended services of a community center." Most significantly, in 1940 Irving Cooper founded and served as the president of the Arlington, Virginia, NAACP. Prior to the chapter's founding, she had long supported the Washington, DC, branch. Irving Cooper taught her daughters by example that it was possible and necessary for them, as young black women, to pursue racial justice and political rights.[127] Her middle daughter and namesake fused her mother's influence with her own experiences in her life of activism.

Born on August 21, 1917, Esther Victoria Cooper took her mother's instructions to heart and excelled in school. After graduating from Dunbar High School, she enrolled in Oberlin College in Ohio in 1934, where she was one of three black students on campus. Following her mother's lead, she was a pacifist at Oberlin, but her ideals were beginning to shift. She was acquainted with several students at Oberlin who had volunteered and died in the fight against Franco during the Spanish Civil War. To Esther, Franco represented an evil that needed to be defeated at any cost, and she began to rethink her commitment to pacifism during this time.[128] She also became interested in Dolores "La Pasionaria" Ibarruri, a Spanish Communist, because she was "not just a follower or leader of women": "She was the revolution."[129] Ibarruri gained recognition for her efforts to inspire Republican troops in the Spanish Civil War. She also encouraged Spanish women to get involved in the fight against Franco.[130]

As a master's student in the Sociology Department at Fisk University from 1938 to 1940, Esther gained her first exposure to the depths of poverty in the South. While she had a clear understanding of segregation from her childhood in Arlington, her parents had shielded her from the most abject poverty. But as she recalled: "I lived [in graduate school] in a Methodist settlement house in Nashville, and worked with the families who lived in the settlement house. And that was the worst poverty I'd ever seen, and I knew there was poverty in Arlington, but I didn't know it that well. It was just something that really hit me." At this point, Esther's communism began to take shape. Some of her strongest political influences "were radical professors, most of whom had come to Fisk from the North because they wanted to make a contribution, really, to the education of black youth."[131] Her professors provided her with Marxist and Communist literature and newspapers, including the CPUSA's main organ, *The Daily Worker.*

When a professor she respected asked her to sign up for Communist Party membership in the presence of her adviser, she decided to join. She recalled that she did not feel pressured to do so.[132] She nonetheless kept her new political affiliation private and did not think that adding the CPUSA to her political résumé was especially significant. As a woman in her early twenties, she prized her intellectual independence and did not want anything to compromise it. She was thoughtful about her new affiliation, its relationship to her college pacifism, and her developing sense of herself as a political person.

Much the way Jack's involvement in the Richmond tobacco strikes fused his upbringing, education, and politics, Esther's master's thesis forged her developing politics and her intellectualism into a cohesive ideology. Though she had not seen much poverty as a child, Esther observed that nearly all the poor black women she encountered worked as domestic servants in the homes of whites. "The Negro Woman Domestic Worker in Relation to Trade Unionism," her thesis, argued: "The problems faced by Negro women domestic workers are responsive to amelioration through trade unions." She acknowledged that unionizing these women was a difficult task because of racism and the failure of the AFL to make an effort to organize domestic and agricultural workers.[133] Her work, which drew on labor statistics, correspondence with domestics, interviews, union materials, and a comparison with labor conditions in Scandinavia, interrogated the significance of race, class, and gender in shaping domestic service. She suggested that unionization would not only improve the conditions of toil for domestic workers but also assuage some of the unique difficulties of working in a private home, including sexual harassment and violence.[134]

By looking specifically at black domestic servants, Esther contested a key component of New Deal labor politics. In 1935, President Franklin Roosevelt signed the Social Security Act into law. The act functioned as an economic safety net for workers across the nation by providing old age assistance, unemployment insurance, and benefits for dependent children. But, as Ira Katznelson notes, southerners had a hand in writing provisions into the act that prevented the federal government from "[interfering] with the way white southerners dealt with 'the Negro question.'" Southern lawmakers insisted that farmworkers and maids, two occupations that were heavily black, be excluded from receiving the benefits of the act. These lawmakers codified their regional way of life into national law, retaining a firm grip on their white supremacy for generations to come by ensuring that poor and working-class blacks could not collect old age pensions under the new Social Security benefits.[135] Minimum wage and maximum hour laws used some of the same exclusions.

The law, in essence, defined farm and domestic work as a status, not an occupation worthy of recognition. Esther's thesis suggested that organizing domestic workers into labor unions would help redefine black women as employees who were embedded in the national economy, both through their own income and by allowing the white women who employed them the leisure time to consume. Her thesis was grounded in both the development of New Deal liberalism and her Marxist perspective. Esther merged her mother's progressivism and her generation's Popular Front ideals with New Deal liberal politics.

Esther and Jack were drawn to one another. They went to see a movie, and Jack slept through the whole film, but it did not matter to Esther. Even though they were each seeing other people at the time, their attraction was undeniable. Swept up in romance, Jack wrote: "I remember her with a persistency that's altogether pleasant . . . sweet, unaffected, clean, open-faced innocence, like a bit of sunshine imbedded in one's heart, as it were."[136] He also admired her seriousness, her commitment to her ideals, and her intellect. Jack left Nashville to continue his research, but Esther remained in his thoughts. When a letter from him would arrive in her mailbox, she would take out a pencil and correct his spelling and grammatical errors. She liked him, and she liked his imperfections. Through this correspondence, their romance blossomed.

In 1939, Esther attended the Birmingham conference of the SNYC and was impressed by the organization's focus and by the members' courage.[137] In 1940, Ed Strong and Jack, who had finished his roughly one-year stint as a researcher for Myrdal, invited her to join the staff in Birmingham. They asked her to come register voters for the summer and to loan the organization money so that they could get out of dire financial straits.[138] Esther, who had also been invited to pursue a Ph.D. at the University of Chicago under the famed sociologist Robert Park, faced a dilemma similar to Jack's decision about whether to pursue pharmacy or activism. When she considered whether to follow her path to academe or accept the SNYC invitation, Esther turned to her mother for advice. Her mother agreed that the opportunity to change the South was important. She chose the SNYC and stayed well beyond the one summer Jack and Strong originally suggested. Her decision was mostly political, but her romantic involvement with Jack was also a factor.[139] She became one of a handful of paid staff members and an elected officer after a summer spent registering voters.[140] Esther never regretted her choice to abandon her promising path toward an academic career. She wrote of her time in Birmingham: "The fact that salaries were small and irregular never once dampened our spirits or blunted the ardor in our enthusiasm."[141] She also became the embodiment of the organization's position on women's leadership.

Though the organization was not immune from some sexism, most of the men in the SNYC consistently pressed for the full participation of women in leadership roles and speaking positions. Many of the men who had families also participated in housework and child care.[142] While she was a member of the organization, Esther observed: "Women were promoted on an equal basis. In fact, some of us that didn't particularly want to speak were . . . [told by] people like Edward Strong, who always called me 'Cooper,' [that] we weren't to be there just to run the mimeograph machine and hand out things but get up and speak and organize."[143] The SNYC's position on women's leadership derived from an interpretation of Marxism that required the full inclusion of women as a component of the struggle for social justice.[144] The SNYC men "read Engels' *The Origin of Family* and took a Marxist position on women's involvement" and "were extraordinarily different and advanced in their thinking."[145] Jack challenged himself to embrace an egalitarian view of women, and, while he was not immune to occasional chauvinism, he worked hard to view Esther as his equal.

The couple's political and intellectual foundations brought them together and set the stage for their love and their activism. On May 8, 1941, Esther and Jack married in Bessemer, Alabama. Unlike many radical couples who forsook marriage in favor of a noninstitutionalized romantic commitment, they felt it was important to have a codified union.[146] Still, Esther, who is recorded as "Ester Copper" on her marriage certificate, elected to keep her maiden name as an expression of her independence. She and Jack determined together that, in their marriage, they would focus on their activism and that they would both play equal roles in the household and in their work life. In the 1930s and 1940s, the idea that women needed to sacrifice external fulfillment or employment in order to be happily married was the dominant narrative. Partly a result of the economic circumstances of the Depression, which made employment scarce, women who worked outside the home alongside their husbands drew scorn, and employers discouraged hiring married women, even in professional positions. In addition, women who did work outside the home in the Depression years typically did so to shore up their families, not to have extra spending money or external stimulation. This changed the broader cultural meaning of work for women: it was not about personal fulfillment or material gain but out of necessity.[147] Esther's career as an activist in a social justice organization that prioritized women's equality made her work and married life different from the norm. She and Jack defied common expectations about love and domesticity, as their shared activism was part of their marriage. Almost immediately after their wedding, Jack left for a two-week trip to New Orleans for SNYC duties, and Esther set straight to work as the organization's new administrative secretary.[148] As she later teased her husband: "Some honeymoon!"[149]

As Esther and Jack began to build the foundations of their marriage, the shaky remains of global stability crumbled. The pair of activists remained devoted to the SNYC as they helped shepherd it through a tense, changing international context, adapting its mission and using the CPUSA as one guide while war took center stage. As the organization matured into a seasoned front for social justice, Esther and Jack gained experiences and insight that contributed to their developing political ideologies. They prepared to face a world at war with confidence in their convictions, their plans, and each other. Their activities during the war also helped them determine their philosophy about their marriage, which would become a significant piece of their activist life together.

2

Radical Marriage on the Front Lines of the Double Victory Campaign

June 16, 1945, was a dull, hot, and sticky day along the Ledo Road in Burma. Jack, now a corporal in the army, sat down in his barrack to write a letter to Esther, who was still in Birmingham. Several pages passed as he commented on the debate within the Communist Party USA (CPUSA) over whether to expel Earl Browder for suggesting that communism and capitalism could peacefully coexist. Then, in a moment of self-reflection, he realized that his letter did not quite offer his wife the affection she might need to sustain interest in her husband while he was overseas. Jack did typically write political letters, and it was not uncommon for him to receive similar political letters from his wife. Still, he found humor in the nature of his marriage. Did his wife ever just wish he would send her a flowery note, free from the world's drama? he wondered. "Politics, politics, politics!!!" Jack joked. "'What a lover,' you must say, 'he quotes Marx on the class struggle and other girls get Keats and Shelly and Browning on 'June Moon's' and stuff. . . . Whatta dope!' (Smiles!)"[1]

When Esther received the letter, she was probably too busy to have spent much time on poetry. She was serving as the executive secretary of the Southern Negro Youth Congress (SNYC) during the World War II years. Her busy position entailed endless committee meetings, travel, investigations, budgeting, publishing organizational materials, and keeping up with the many SNYC councils and affiliate groups throughout the South, all for very little money. In the midst of political discussion, planning an application for a Rosenwald Fellowship, reporting on a new Alabama law to force prospective voters to interpret the Constitution, and an update on their daughter, Harriet Dolores, Esther found a moment to reply to her husband's kidding. Esther wrote: "Yes, I do like Shelly, Browning, and Keats like other girls but please don't slow up on the politics. I'd rather discuss everything with you than anyone in the world."[2]

In World War II, the combination of politics and romance was integral to sustaining Esther and Jack's relationship over time and distance.

The interplay of love and activism in Esther and Jack's marriage during World War II sheds light on how the couple built their partnership around both personal concerns and their participation in the black freedom movement. SNYC work, army service, communism, and activism were infused in their family life. The way Esther and Jack interpreted, cultivated, and maneuvered through the intersections of personal and political life during World War II shows how larger political changes influenced individuals and families and ultimately helps explain the ways in which the black freedom movement adapted to a changing world. As the US relationship with the Soviet Union shifted between alliance and animosity, the national discourse on permissible social justice activism changed as well and reshaped the fundamental structure of the struggle for black civil rights. World War II also elicited questions about the benefits of patriotism for black Americans fighting to preserve a segregated democracy. As Esther and Jack gained exposure to a wider world in conflict and as their family grew, their personal and political priorities changed. Their activism reflected their wartime experiences. During the war, they planned for a postwar life together where they could continue to be active in mainstream civil rights work while retaining their Popular Front and Communist ideals. In spite of the devastating and difficult times they would face in the early Cold War years, the way they imagined their future during World War II helped them carve out individual niches in the black freedom movement without compromising their ideological integrity. These visions for their future together offer a glimpse into how black radicals interpreted events as they unfolded and how they integrated their activism and their needs as a family encountering a changing world.

Because Esther and Jack were married for only about two busy years before Jack was drafted into the army, the couple crafted their radical political marriage largely through correspondence during the three-year period of separation. During these years, Esther was able to cultivate her independence within her marriage and assert herself against the common expectation that a woman would have to choose between her career and her love. The historian Nancy Cott argues that media reinforced the dominant marriage paradigm. She states that "an entanglement of econ-

omy, society, and state" propped up "the economic framework of marriage [that] prescribed that husbands would be the primary earners in
families and wives their economic dependents." She notes that women
were "free to choose *either* marriage and family *or* vocational ambition—
and she was predicted to choose the first, if she was 'normal.'" Even
in wartime, commentators expressed concern about the implications for
family life and social stability as increasing numbers of women worked
outside the home.[3]

That Esther sacrificed neither familial nor career satisfaction makes
her unique, and it also makes Jack, who expected her to mobilize her
talents outside the home, unusual. Of course, Esther and Jack's communism and activist commitments meant that they prioritized different
outcomes from their marriage than those suggested by mainstream culture. But their mutual desire to create an egalitarian marriage did not
completely negate the impact of normative cultural ideas on their world-
views. While he was overseas, Jack had the opportunity to reconcile any
internalized expectations he held for a traditional marriage with both his
deep belief in female equality and the pride he took in his wife's career
and ambition. All these dimensions of the couple's politics and relationship must be understood as products of and factors in their love for each
other. They used the context of war to define their marriage alongside
their increased exposure to internationalism and SNYC activism on the
home front.

The SNYC remained the couple's main outlet for political activism.
As a Popular Front organization, the SNYC followed the Communist
Party when planning its political trajectory in the early stages of war.[4]
In response to the Soviet Union's entry into the Nazi-Soviet Pact on
August 28, 1939, it argued that US assistance to Britain would jeopardize
the autonomy of the world's only socialist nation. By the end of 1940,
efforts to maintain peace through appeasement were falling apart, and
the United States began to plan to provide military equipment to Britain.
The Roosevelt administration designed the Lend-Lease program to be an
"arsenal of democracy" that would serve to buttress the barrier that Britain and its colonies built between fascist regimes and the Americas.[5] In an
S.N.Y.C. News bulletin printed in January 1941, SNYC leaders referred to
the Lend-Lease program as a "war-mongering" effort to be "a co-partner

of Britain in an imperialist adventure for the redivision of the world which would leave the U.S. monopolists in the dominant position."[6] In this period, the Communist Party lost popularity as it appeared aligned with Hitler. The SNYC, like the National Negro Congress (NNC), did struggle because it attempted to fuse complex global politics with the immediacy of local needs. But the organization worked to retain the loyalty of its constituency by attempting to make its anti-imperialism message relevant and real without directly linking it to Soviet influence.

Leaders explained how their position coalesced with the interests of the South's black youths and working-class citizens. After addressing the inconsistency of Roosevelt's defense of democracy abroad through support of Britain—a country whose vast empire oppressed and exploited Africans and Indians—the article continued:

> Roosevelt can speak of defending democracy abroad when 10,000,000 adults in our own Southland are voteless, when the spectra of the lynch rope yet waves over the heads of the Negro people and working men of the South; when political bosses . . . rest like ulcers on our body politic . . . when 9,000,000 able bodied Americans walk the streets of the nation in a vain search for jobs; when our so-called Citizen's Army relegates Negro youth to the most menial tasks; when the Navy and Air Corps refuse to admit Negroes, when the great armament aircraft industries refuse to hire Negroes and one third of a nation is still "ill-housed, ill-clad, and ill-fed."[7]

The SNYC's interpretation of Roosevelt's contradictory policies linked political tensions at home and abroad. Though its view of the conflict was influenced by the CPUSA and Popular Front ideology, its antiwar sentiment remained aligned with the isolationism of the majority in the United States. Its economic arguments were still palatable for a population of black and white citizens fighting the Great Depression, even though the Communist Party lost much of its appeal in building an alliance with Nazi Germany.

When Germany invaded the Soviet Union on June 22, 1941, the SNYC shifted its focus from ways in which a war would perpetuate the oppression of black citizens to how the struggle against global fascism would aid oppressed people of color across the globe. The connections among the different forms of racial exploitation remained a prevalent theme for the SNYC in the World War II period. Jack expressed SNYC opinion when he wrote that young men should be enrolled in the military for the greater benefit of oppressed people worldwide. He argued: "This is a World Wide struggle, a Total War between the new forces of Barbarism and World Slavery—represented by the Hitler-Hirohito-Mussolini Axis and the freedom loving peoples of the World as represented by the United Nations. This is a struggle between freedom and slavery; between civilization and savagery. . . . ALL MANKIND includes those nations and peoples who already enjoy considerable democratic rights as well as the 'subject' peoples who have yet to win full suffrage rights, such as the Negro people in the South, the people of India, Africa, the conquered countries."[8]

Jack highlighted the connections between the South and other parts of the world through oppressed people's common lack of a right to a voice in government. He and the SNYC proposed that winning this voice and defeating oppression entailed military participation in worldwide political struggles.

Gender equality was also an essential component of the SNYC's agenda during the war. The SNYC urged women to become "militant and able leaders in the youth movement," to fight poll taxes and segregation, and to unite with "white women who believe in democracy and who support the rights of Negroes in the United States." SNYC leaders maintained: "On through the history of our country, Negro women have been ever faithful and brilliant leaders. . . . Negro women want peace and security."[9] Throughout the war, women constituted approximately half the SNYC's leadership.

The SNYC's goals during World War II aligned with black Americans' across the nation in expressing loyalty, patriotism, and enthusiasm for the cause of global democracy. In a 1942 report, SNYC leaders affirmed that the organization's constituencies were loyal to wartime causes, that they had "traditionally been partisans of democracy" because democratic ideals offered a solution to their own racial struggles. The report continued: "Our people have always been ardent anti-fascists because they saw in the obnoxious race theories and brazen acts of the [uncivilized] which characterized the Axis powers a threat to themselves and all minority and disadvantaged people." But the report noted that these same African Americans hesitated to express this sentiment because of "the thousands of adverse circumstances that prevail in the every day life of Negro youth simply because of the color of their skin."[10]

To the SNYC, patriotism in wartime was important in its campaigns to support the war effort and build racial equality. In 1943, Organizational Secretary Louis Burnham delivered an address on *Wings over Jordan*, a CBS-sponsored black radio program. Burnham was a Barbados native who was raised in New York City and had graduated from Hunter College. Like Esther and Jack, he was inspired to become an activist after college and moved to Birmingham with his wife, Dorothy, to join the SNYC. The two couples forged a lifelong friendship. In his address, Burnham discussed the pervasive image of war in the South. He stated: "[Any student is] likely to witness in front of his school building an Army jeep populated with soldiers from a nearby camp. . . . He may talk to the soldiers. . . . In all of this he finds himself drawn closer to the war effort, he finds added stimulation for the purchase of war stamps and bonds." According to Burnham, purchasing war stamps and bonds represented "unusual sacrifices and small acts of self-denial" through which black youths who were not enlisted or drafted into army service could participate.[11]

SNYC leaders organized a number of ways for black southerners to understand and engage with the war effort. For instance, they urged members to see the Frank Capra–produced *The Negro Soldier*.[12] Released in 1944 by the War Department, the propaganda film glorified African American military participation in American wars in an effort to recruit new soldiers. In the film, military segregation is a clear fact, though it is presented without commentary.[13] While the SNYC promoted black participation in the war effort, it rallied to change national and regional racist customs and asserted that full African American participation needed to be rewarded with political equality.

The organization emphasized ways to promote equality in the United States by both participating in and critiquing the war. Employment discrimination provided fertile ground for the SNYC to accomplish this.

SNYC leaders, like many other black activists during the war, believed that equal employment opportunities would not only increase the number of employed black youths and finally begin to unravel the Depression's effect on African Americans but would also represent the furthering of US democratic ideals.

The SNYC's attention to employment opportunities was part of a national movement among African Americans during the war. NNC president and founder of the Brotherhood of Sleeping Car Porters A. Philip Randolph led the March on Washington movement, which made substantial steps forward in the push for equal employment. Randolph generated a mass movement that boasted significant female leadership and widespread grassroots support for employment equality. He promised the presence of one hundred thousand black Americans on the White House lawn on July 1, 1941, to protest employment discrimination.[14] Roosevelt was skeptical and believed that Randolph had issued "an extraordinary bluff." Nonetheless, he responded to Randolph's plan—which, in his interpretation, would present an image of national disunity—by establishing via Executive Order 8802 the President's Fair Employment Practices Committee (FEPC). By creating the FEPC, Roosevelt ensured that, in a time of increased production such as war, it was illegal for the war industries to discriminate in hiring practices.[15] For SNYC members, as for other African Americans, the establishment of the FEPC meant the same relief from the Depression that many whites were receiving through employment in the war industry. It also indicated that the federal government was obligated to correct some of the problems that Jim Crow produced.

Yet the FEPC was not always entirely effective, despite efforts at enforcing Executive Order 8802. Budgetary problems and the lack of power to follow through with complaints made it more symbolic than useful. After the reorganization of war agencies in 1942, the FEPC fell under the auspices of the War Manpower Commission (WMC), which impeded the FEPC's productivity. The WMC insisted on filling the manpower needs of the war industry as expeditiously as possible, disregarding the FEPC's authority to guarantee fair hiring practices. The WMC held no FEPC hearings.[16]

The historian John Morton Blum asserts that most complaints against employers were filed "in the Northeast, where blacks were more conscious of their rights than they were anywhere else in the country," and that "the opportunity to file complaints . . . improved morale."[17] But southerners, including SNYC members, saw potential for equal employment opportunities in the FEPC too. They repeatedly petitioned for federal support in their employment campaigns in Birmingham. The SNYC established the Citizen's Committee on Jobs and Training in Birmingham to ensure that job-training classes at the Bechtel-McCone-Parsons Airplane Modification Plant remained open to black citizens. In 1943, the committee secured FEPC intervention, "with the result that classes in chipping, caulking, riveting, and welding have been maintained for a small number of Negroes."[18] The Citizen's Committee and the FEPC succeeded in guaranteeing the hiring of seventeen thousand black workers, five hundred of whom would learn specific skills, at various companies in Birmingham.

Yet SNYC successes with the FEPC were limited in various ways. The Bechtel-McCone-Parsons plant refused "to train a single Negro woman for skilled or semi-skilled work, although 60% of the working force at the plant is composed of women." The striking disparity between male and female skilled laborers highlighted some of the important shortcomings of the FEPC. In addition to the discrimination against women, the Citizen's Committee on Jobs and Training noted that many of the black men who did have specific skill training still worked primarily in low-level jobs as truck drivers or porters. The SNYC worked to arouse public sympathy to "break this bottleneck in essential war production caused by discriminatory practices."[19]

Voting rights were another important component of the SNYC's wartime agenda. Alabama, Arkansas, Georgia, Mississippi, South Carolina, Texas, and Virginia required that voters pay a poll tax, which disenfranchised those states' poor citizens, both black and white. Blacks in Alabama were also required to pass an examination measuring civic knowledge and literacy in order to register to vote. Voter registrars were often barely literate themselves but held the authority to provide or deny citizens access to the franchise. The test consisted of obscure questions about the Constitution and the legal system, including things like: "What is meant by *non compos mentis* when it is applied to a citizen in legal jeopardy?"[20] Such questions discouraged eligible voters from registering.

Esther, who held an M.A. from Fisk University, was well equipped to pass the test. Nevertheless, she noted: "Even when I went to register to vote in Birmingham I had to take the test three times before they said that I understood the Constitution enough, and I finally passed."[21]

In 1940, the SNYC implemented a Right to Vote campaign under Jack's direction. The SNYC held frequent community forums to educate citizens on how to answer likely questions, how to register, and the times and places of registrations.[22] In the May 1942 issue of *Cavalcade*, the SNYC's artistic and political newsletter, the organization invoked a speech by Roosevelt to urge black citizens to fight for their rights. One article read: "If we are to attain the full citizenship rights with freedom from fear and freedom to vote and freedom from all discriminations which operate to limit our service to our nation in its hour of peril . . . it's up to you to help speed the day of Victory by building and strengthening the organization which works for the mobilization of the youth for Victory."[23] The Right to Vote campaign represented a key struggle to win democracy at home. Jack wove the wartime language of democratic rights into the larger narrative of the black freedom movement in order to rally support and promote the SNYC's cause.

In addition to holding community classes, SNYC leaders frequented local mines and unions to distribute literature and instruct workers on how to register to vote. In the summer of 1942, the twenty-three-year-old white folksinger Pete Seeger, an SNYC supporter, performed for the steel workers and coal miners in Birmingham while Jack spoke against poll taxes and provided instructions on registering. In addition to advocating voting as a necessary function of citizenship, Jack and Seeger took the opportunity to topple racial stereotypes. Black and white workers, in accordance with segregation laws, sat separately. Seeger and Jack entered the room as though they were going to perform the opposite functions— Jack with Seeger's banjo in hand. When Jack passed the instrument to Seeger, their audiences were surprised to see that Jack was the speaker and Seeger the musician.[24] Seeger's performance debunked racist stereotypes and generated a point to which black and white miners could relate.[25]

The SNYC regularly used cultural events, including concerts, to unite black and white youths of varying educational levels and social backgrounds. Organization leaders and members admired the singer and political figure Paul Robeson. Robeson, who graduated as valedictorian of his class at Rutgers University in 1919, used his fame as a stage performer and singer to promote progressive and leftist ideals along with civil rights and black internationalism. He visited Spain in 1938 to support the Republican forces. As he stated: "I love the cause of democracy in Spain . . . as a Black. I belong to an oppressed race, discriminated against, one that could not live if fascism triumphed in the world." Like other Communist-influenced activists, Robeson fully supported the US war effort after the German invasion of the Soviet Union in 1941. But, where the CPUSA threw its full support behind the Soviet Union and began to neglect domestic problems in the United States, including the Negro Question, Robeson promoted the black freedom movement as an essential component of democracy's triumph.[26]

Robeson normally refused to perform in the South because of the restrictions that segregation placed on audiences. Though most cultural and entertainment events in the Deep South were segregated, the SNYC worked to ensure integrated audiences for its major functions. It organized an integrated Robeson performance at its fifth conference in Tuskegee in 1942. The program proclaimed that Robeson was a hero for African Americans "at a time when democracy, sorely pressed, needs heroes." The invitation to the conference stated: "Perhaps no other single artist so completely represents the strivings of the common people in all parts of the world for democratic cultural growth and for social progress. Certainly no other artist has more effectively made of the unique songs of the Negro—*and of America*—a durable bond which unites our people with all men and women who today hold high the banner of freedom in face of Hitler's onslaught."[27] The writer Ramona Lowe, the artist Arthur Price, and the poets Langston Hughes and Waring Cuney also performed at SNYC events. Through its integrated cultural events, the SNYC created a forum in which blacks and whites could jointly experience entertainment, culture, and political education.

In its effort to advance cultural knowledge and understanding, the SNYC also integrated visual art, poetry, and politics in *Cavalcade: The March of the Southern Negro Youth,* its main organ from 1941 to 1942. The magazine highlighted the work of black artists and promoted the history and tradition of black cultural expression. As a predecessor of the black arts movement of the 1960s and 1970s and of *Freedomways, Cavalcade* published the work of high-profile poets alongside the work of its local members. For example, Eugene B. Williams, a member of the SNYC New Orleans Council, published work in the magazine. *Cavalcade* also carried the writings of Waring Cuney, a Harlem Renaissance poet who authored a number of songs on folk singer Josh White's famous 1941 album *Southern Exposure*. In "Uncle Sam Says," which was published in *Cavalcade* and also appeared as a song on White's album, Cuney explored segregation in wartime:

Uncle Sam says
Two camps for black and white
But when trouble starts
We'll all be in the same big fight.[28]

Cavalcade was one example of the SNYC's belief in cultural production as an important educational and expressive component of activism. The organization also used puppet shows, through its Caravan Puppeteer program, to provide information to black southerners on how to register to vote. Cuney and Seeger, among others, supported and performed with the Puppeteers.[29] As an organization that existed within strict Jim Crow confines and worked with populations in the South experiencing deep plight, the SNYC also drew together an impressive coalition of artists, activists, and performers who both came to the South to engage with local communities and used their national platforms to support its cause.

In the SNYC, Esther and Jack found a vehicle for change and a place to anchor their political goals. The organization's political and gender ideologies also helped them foster and sustain their egalitarian relationship. As they contributed to developing the organization, the couple honed their political philosophies and priorities. But wartime also complicated life and raised challenges for young newlyweds. For Esther and Jack, it introduced a three-year separation into their marriage.

Drafted into the army in 1943, Jack left his wife and infant daughter, Harriet Dolores, in Birmingham. He went overseas excited about the opportunity to defend democracy against fascism. The couple reunited in February 1946. In the three years they were apart, Esther and Jack wrote each other every day. Roughly twelve hundred pages of World War II letters between them constitute the basis for understanding how they developed their views about national and international politics, their strategies for the black freedom struggle in the South, their ideas about marriage, and how all this was linked.[30]

Days at a time would pass without any mail for either Esther or Jack. Then letters would arrive in bundles. Two, six, nine days' worth of correspondence at a time would reflect a series of anxieties: "Do you have to wait so long as I for letters? Oh, I hope not!" "I pray nothing is wrong with you. . . . I get so anxious about you when mail is tardy." "I had often feared that as the months rolled on your memory would grow dim, and I would feel alone as if you had gone forever."[31] Esther and Jack did not dwell on these anxieties for long, however, and, after a paragraph or two, they would each go on to recount the day's events, analyze reading material and current affairs, and offer each other thoughts on the war, the South, and their future together.

Esther and Jack maintained a strong and communicative relationship during their time apart. After discussing marriage with her sister, Kat, whose husband was also serving overseas, Esther was stunned to hear how much her sister and brother-in-law kept from each other. They feared sharing their secrets and worries because they believed it would hurt the other's morale. Esther expressed relief that she and her husband had such an open line of communication and wrote Jack: "I'm so happy we don't believe in that prevalent idea about sheltering each other from our problems. . . . I'm not only your wife, but your best friend and companion. And darling—if you disagree with anything I've said or done—tell me always. Our marriage must serve as an 'example' to all our friends, relatives, and the youth of the South."[32] Esther and Jack had built a relationship that was connected to their politics and believed that activists should embody their politics in their personal lives. They agreed that the example of marriage and gender relations they offered was connected to the more straightforward political advances the SNYC fought to achieve.

Esther and Jack's wartime correspondence highlights how love raised morale in the fight against fascism. The couple placed great importance on family unity and a faithful marriage as key factors in maintaining their wartime morale. Almost all the letters contain a few paragraphs of deeply personal romance. Although Jack devoted a lot of space to political analysis, many of his letters included long quotes from poems, and Jack and Esther each spent a lot of time reflecting on the nature of their marriage. Their discussions of politics, romance, and war morale in their letters link seemingly separate facets of life and show how the context of war brought the private sphere into the public, and vice versa.

The comfort of Esther and Jack's relationship was crucial to easing the psychological trauma of war. On May 4, 1945, Jack described a particularly gruesome scene that resulted in the death of a soldier who "couldn't understand why and for what [he was dying] and . . . needed more time to learn such things: how to die like a hero for a cause." Clearly shaken, he wrote Esther: "Such a day leaves one weary and sick of all the blood and broken flesh and pallid faces . . . and then your letters come like a mountain breeze quaffing the dead leaves away and leaving the bright green blades swaying in the sunlight. . . . [T]ogether we shall triumph over every hardship and forlorn mood and no matter what tomorrow brings—it will be good because you love me."[33] This experience illustrated for Jack just how important his marriage was in maintaining his stability through the war. It also led him to reflect on the problem of infidelity while husbands were overseas. He argued that women who were unfaithful were "performing a service to the enemy": "One such case can undermine the spirit of a whole battalion for the one reward every soldier expects is for 'his girl' to remain 'true' to him."[34] Love, Jack argued, was an act of support for the Allied cause.

Esther and Jack's correspondence also linked love and morale to political strategies. World War II allowed for a tremendous fluidity of political ideologies for black activists. The black freedom struggle in the war years was rooted in both the desire to defeat fascism and a desperate need to address the contradictions of fighting fascism with a segregated army, workforce, and homeland. Historians have addressed the multifaceted layers of black activism and leadership during World War II and have shown that, either through organizations or on an individual basis, protest activities ranged from using the framework of the federal government to employ workers to "everyday resistance" to rioting.[35] Esther and Jack would often vent their disgust with racism in the United States and in the army and then use their letters as a place to convert their outrage into productive energy.

Beyond writing letters to editors and his wife, there was little Jack could contribute to the struggles in the South from the Ledo Road, an area that was isolated from much of the world and even from the rest of the war. The China-Burma-India (CBI) Theater of the war was not as immediate a priority as the European Theater or the Pacific Theater. It started as a Lend-Lease project to assist in building roads to transport equipment across remote areas. Over 60 percent of the engineers sent to the CBI Theater were black. By late 1944, when Jack arrived, the purpose of the theater was to keep Japanese attention divided. Jack worked as a pharmacist with the 823rd Engineering Battalion, and his unit rarely saw much of the action that any of the combat units in the theater might have seen. In fact, by March 1945, only a couple of months after Jack arrived, a military victory in Lashio meant that in the Burma-India section of the theater the Allies had accomplished the most important of their combat goals. That section subsequently focused its resources on offering "logistical support" to the China and Southeast Asian sections.[36] Many of the injuries Jack witnessed, then, were caused by equipment malfunctions or were the result of incidents that the 823rd encountered but did not participate in. Nonetheless, the area was still very dangerous.

Though the CBI Theater was not a part of as many landmark World War II battles as were the Pacific and European Theaters, there was still substantial violence. In 1942, Japanese forces raided Assam, India, and the Japanese presence meant the constant threat of combat.[37] Other dangers loomed as well. Trucks regularly fell off cliffs, the monsoon season meant frequent landslides, the climate was malarial, and many soldiers had encounters with tigers, snakes, and other dangerous animals and insects in the Burmese jungle. Whether by intent or coincidence on the part of the War Department, many political dissidents and military undesirables were stationed in the CBI Theater.[38] The theater was rife with personnel problems, and most of the soldiers stationed there "wanted nothing better than the speediest possible return to what they half jokingly, half fondly called 'Uncle Sugar.'"[39] Jack's unit included soldiers who were politically active like him and soldiers who were alcoholics or had other issues. In fact, the doctor in the 823rd was often so drunk that Jack, who had only pharmaceutical training, often performed medical procedures and made diagnoses.[40]

As much as Jack was excited to participate in a war to save democracy, he felt stifled in this context. He wanted to produce real progress toward democracy, and, since he had been drafted, World War II seemed to him like an ideal way to make a broad contribution to his internationalist vision of justice. Instead, the dizzying heat, torrential rain, and "picayune" commanders on the Ledo Road made him want to "consign the army and all of its components to a choice spot in hell."[41] In Burma, he wrote letters to the editors of many of the newspapers his wife supplied him with, corresponded with activists in the CPUSA and the black freedom movement in the South, and met with local activists to talk about colonialism, imperialism, and socialism. He also was lucky to cross paths with his close friend Ed Strong, a fellow SNYC leader who was also stationed in the CBI Theater.

Jack's heart was on the front lines of the black freedom struggle in the American South. Even though he looked forward to telling "Junior," the son he and Esther hoped for on his return, about "how [he] won the war," Jack could not produce real democracy in his immediate surroundings, let alone the whole world.[42] As demonstrated by his decision to leave the pharmacy business to run the SNYC and unionize the Richmond tobacco stemmers, he was not the kind of man who worked well behind the scenes.[43] On the Ledo Road, he needed Esther not only to build his morale by making him feel loved but also to help him feel like he was making real contributions to real struggles at home.

Esther tried to place herself in his shoes. She could not imagine how difficult it must have been to be so accustomed to fighting on the front lines only to be relegated to the Ledo Road, which was important but in the background of the larger Pacific Theater. Reflecting on this, she wrote: "I began to . . . feel the humiliation—the failure to recognize talent and ability, seeing stupid and prejudiced men placed above me from whom I must take orders—I tried to feel all of this which has been your life for so many months—and I realize for the first time how much more I could have done to share your hardships."[44] She began to understand the difficulty of fighting in an army that provided inferior resources to Jack because of the color of his skin, that would not accept the highly educated intellectual into Officer Training School, and that put racists who placed segregation before democracy in charge. She knew that Jack's suggestions for the SNYC were not only beneficial to the organization but also crucial to his morale. His marriage allowed him to stay engaged in the fight at home.

The connection between Esther and Jack's marriage and politics offers unique insight into how the pair developed political ideologies with one another before presenting their ideas to public audiences. During World War II, the SNYC used the government's democratic rhetoric to push for improvements for blacks in the South. With Jack on leave from his position as education director and Esther running the organization as executive secretary, the SNYC became a vehicle for the couple's political expression and a site where they could bond over a common experience.

Jack often vented his personal frustrations with segregation in the South and in the military with his wife in ways that he certainly would not have in formal settings. Military life was frustrating for black soldiers, and the insults of segregation took their toll. The contradiction of fighting a war for democracy within a segregated army reinforced the urgency of SNYC work for the couple. Jack wrote on June 10, 1945: "I am so damn sick of this life I could cry about it. If anybody tells me about the 'remarkable' breakdown of prejudice in this damn jim crow Army I'll spit in their eye. From where I sit, nothing is improving, it's getting worse and worse. (Now the rest camps in this theater have been separated—one for black, one for white)." He continued, noting that the Red Cross in Calcutta had built a six-story building for a white soldiers' rest camp and gave black soldiers only a small rest area.[45]

In another instance, Jack told his wife about an aquatic training session at a white camp near the Tuskegee Air Force Base, where part of his training took place. Jack's unit ate dinner at the camp, where "it was jim crow from 'soup to nuts.'" After describing the rigid segregation patterns at the camp, Jack continued: "Damned little cracker imbeciles were stationed everywhere to see that we sat apart from the white soldiers. . . . Southern bigots, everyone. Enforcing their jim crow pattern like they were commissioned by God to do so. . . . I have never really known the full measure of my hatred for the South and its native fascist way of life until I came here."[46]

Jack, who grew up in Richmond, Virginia, and had also lived in Birmingham, Alabama, was no stranger to segregation. Indeed, one of his earliest recollections of segregation's meaning was, as we have seen, the near assault on the Richmond bus while he wore his Boy Scout uniform. However, the enthusiasm with which white southerners maintained racial separation while waging a war against fascism fueled his disgust. Had he published an anecdote about this incident in an SNYC newsletter, for instance, he surely would have told the story differently. While he would not have masked the insult of segregation, he certainly would have excised much of the more emotional language. The way in which he described this incident to his wife, however, demonstrates that even black activists who regularly presented polished, flowery prose to promote their causes still had thoroughly human responses to the pure offensiveness of racial segregation. Jack needed an audience like his wife when he voiced his raw frustration before he could generate the refined language he would share with the public.

Both partners used their correspondence to air their uncensored disgust with the South in the confines of their relationship and then move forward, generating broad strategies for change through discussion of SNYC activities and plans. With Esther as his correspondent, Jack could release his revulsion with segregation to a woman who both was a confidante and had the ability to address some of his concerns with action. After assuaging his disgust with his angry letter, he sought to use his frustration productively by suggesting strategies for the SNYC to address the problems of segregation in the army and in the South. He discussed plans for veterans' issues in the postwar period. On April 15, 1944, he suggested that the National Council of the SNYC establish a veterans' commission. The commission, Jack offered, "would have as its objective the formulation of plans and activities for the promotion of soldier welfare during the war [and] for the integration of Negroes in all post war soldier welfare programs."[47] A veterans' commission was established, and Colonel Campbell C. Johnson, the executive assistant to the director of the Selective Service, spoke at the SNYC's 1944 Atlanta conference on the reintegration of black veterans into American society.[48] In this respect, Jackson's letters illustrate how his raw emotional outrage elicited strategic suggestions that influenced the SNYC and the South.

Esther's letters contain a similar combination of disdain for the South and energy directed toward changing it. The insults she confronted were subtler in nature, and the way she described her frustration was somewhat more reserved. In one instance, she wrote about a visit to a white doctor's office. Normally, she visited black doctors, but Harriet needed to see a specialist, so Esther's regular doctor recommended a white doctor he believed was progressive on race issues. Esther recalled that the doctor was so insulting that she was sick to her stomach.[49] Overall, however, Harriet's checkup went well "until the nurse called me Esther . . . and we had it!" Addressing her by her first name suggested a familiarity that Esther did not reciprocate and that was rooted in the condescension with which whites approached adult African Americans in the Jim Crow South. In addition, Harriet kept trying to run into the white waiting room to play with the other children. Esther wrote: "Ah! It's so senseless—sometimes I want to pack up and go to shield Harriet from the humiliations of being a Negro in the South. But perhaps she will be a wiser and more understanding person being here—we must live for a year in a country free from race prejudice for her sake."[50]

The following day, however, Esther attended a meeting for the Recy Taylor Committee, a class, and an Executive Board meeting for the SNYC.[51] She channeled her frustration with the insults of segregation into real efforts to end racial injustice, empower young black southerners, and organize black leadership.

Jack beamed with pride, impressed by his daughter's activities and his wife's continual efforts to improve the South. He wrote: "Indeed! Harriet is already making her contribution toward the removal of the color line. I am sure she charmed Dr. Neely for a lasting impression. . . . My! I don't know how you do it. FEPC, Recy Taylor committee, Round Table, etc. plus a full day at the office and H.D. [Harriet Dolores]! You should sleep well each night with the comforting satisfaction of knowing that you are doing fully more than your share."[52] This series of events that Esther described in her letters, along with Jack's reply, indicates that segregation's offensiveness could function in two ways: it could drive blacks to leave the South, or, in Esther and Jack's case, it could instigate activism and motivate leaders to work for racial justice.

Esther's activism in response to southern racism, along with her husband's pride in her ambition and accomplishments, points to a connection between her and Jack's marriage and her activism in the SNYC. The SNYC had a very progressive position on female leadership, and Esther embodied that position when she took the role as the organization's executive secretary. She believed that she could prove through her example that "it is possible to be completely happily married and still be 'a progressive'!"[53] Given this perspective, it was impossible for her to take a backseat to her husband's activities, and, likewise, it was impossible for her to stand on the sidelines in the organization.

Jack, in fact, looked forward to working together with his wife when he returned. Though he planned and hoped to work equally with his wife, he did express some dismay at her pace while he was absent. He wrote: "Your letters read like 'My Day' by Super Woman. . . . [O]n reading your letter, I said to myself, 'It isn't necessary for anyone to be that busy, not even Stalin.' . . . Does this letter read like I'm sore? Well, I am. . . . I figured we'd have a busy time together 'changing the world' when I got back. But at the pace you're going all I'll have to do is live in it." Jack's frustration grew primarily out of concern about the negative consequences of his wife's pace on her health, even though he was jealous of the contribution Esther made while he felt unproductive in the CBI Theater. He wrote: "Take it easy, Honey. There is just no sense in tearing yourself to pieces so early in the game. If you don't, I'll be spending my post war vacation nursing you, and all those rosy dreams we cherish will be still-born."[54]

Jack was also concerned about Esther's safety. Part of her busy schedule entailed visiting small towns in Alabama to investigate riots, rapes, and lynching for the SNYC. For instance, Esther visited Abbeville and Eufaula, Alabama, to investigate two rape charges. She wrote: "The lynch spirit surrounds Eufaulia [sic]. All Negroes are ordered off the streets by 9 o'clock (We left at 8:30). The highway police & M.P.'s were called in by Gov. Sparks."[55] Jack replied: "I don't like the idea of you taking trips into these little lynch towns on riot investigations. . . . [O]ne out of the family in enemy country at a time is enough, my sweet!"[56] Jack's worries and frustrations, though, were ultimately tempered by the pride he took in his wife's success. The couple, in this instance, became an ideal representative of the Double Victory campaign that black Americans and the *Pittsburgh*

Courier initiated during the war. Double Victory promoted the idea that the war provided an opportunity for global freedom that encompassed an end not just to fascism on a global scale but to segregation and racism at home as well. Of this one couple, Jack was fighting for democracy abroad, and Esther was fighting for it on the home front.

The fervor with which Jack wrote on SNYC issues derived not only from his passion for social justice work but also from a deep sense of the individuals who would be most affected by change. He wrote: "Be full of courage and confidence in the great work you and Louis [Burnham] and others are doing—it is the difference between life and death for our children, the difference between hope and despair for ourselves."[57] For Jack, activism meant devotion not only to an idealistic better world but also to the future of his family and friends. His personal life, his love, and his concerns for the individuals around him were intimately connected to broader political ideals. Love was integral to his and Esther's activism.

Jack wanted to change the world with his wife as an equal partner when he returned from war. On July 6, 1945, he replied to a June 23 *Baltimore Afro-American* article by Irene West entitled "Females Halfway to Hell." West disparaged women's new position during the war. From Burma, Jack wrote: "That woman is inherently the inferior of man . . . would be considered simple-minded even by the male supremacists out here in the Far East." He continued by comparing West's position on women's wartime activities to that of fascists, who "have always advocated such a program of shackling women to the penury of the kitchen as part of their design for the super-exploitation, oppression, and ultimate enslavement of *all* mankind."[58] This gendered analysis of the struggle against fascism was inherently linked to his interpretation of the black freedom struggle in the South.

In the same letter, Jack argued that West's concerns about women could easily be employed by southern "mobs" aiming to drive black women from their war industry jobs "back to the 'white folks' kitchen and $3.00 a week." He continued, voicing his perspective on women's liberation in the United States: "The measure of our civilization's progress is to be seen in the extent to which women have achieved their liberation from the tyranny of male domination and the degree of equality attained in all fields of endeavor." Finally, he offered some examples of strong black female leaders: "May [Irene West] some day encounter Mary McLeod Bethune, Thelma Dale, Jeanetta Welch Brown, or my own wife, Esther Cooper."[59] For Jack, understanding the wartime world and planning for the postwar peace meant recognizing that struggles around gender were integral to the fight for democracy. Highlighting female activists, including his wife, would contradict any claims to the contrary. His marriage to Esther was inextricably linked to his outlook on national and international politics.

As his letter to the *Baltimore Afro-American* suggests, on the Ledo Road Jack had a lot of time to read, write, and think about the future he planned with his wife. Though the psychological trauma of war was profound and there was still considerable violence in the CBI Theater, very few of Jack's letters describe wartime action. According to the historian Gwendolyn Midlo Hall, this trend was common among soldiers. Aside from censorship regulations, soldiers also sought to shield their loved ones from the horror and grisliness of battle scenes. Jack's letters were uncommon in their intimacy, as many soldiers censored themselves to avoid embarrassment in front of the officials who intercepted mail.[60]

Jack also frequently discussed immediate steps toward improving the racial climate in the Jim Crow South. Blending his experiences in the segregated military and his prior work with the SNYC, he offered advice on how to urge young black voters to reelect Roosevelt in 1944, teach leadership and protest methodologies to SNYC constituents, and fight the restrictions on black access to the basic entitlements of American citizenship within the framework of the US government's democratic rhetoric. He thought about all these issues in connection with how he would work with his wife when he returned and how their love would grow through the work they did.

Jack believed that racial problems in the South were unique and planned with his wife the different ways they could work to change their home. The SNYC was a highly effective organization, he believed, but he also did not think that an adult southern Negro congress was the most practical way to work for racial justice. Still, he and Esther were getting older (when they reunited, they were thirty-one and twenty-eight, respectively), and they felt that staying with the youth congress could not be a long-term plan. In planning their postwar years, Jack suggested that they might work for the National Association for the Advancement of Colored People (NAACP). He saw that the NAACP had the potential to be pro-ductive in the South if it were administered under the proper leadership:

> Can we declare that it is impossible to transform this quantity into quality with this organization (NAACP)? Can we say that the national leadership of the NAACP is so reactionary that it would rather have the lethargic Southern enrollment that of today rather than the whole South organized as strongly under its banners with a membership as active as they now have in Detroit? The very question is absurd. Of course not! [Walter] White has long looked enviously at the SNYC "miracle workers." He has no doubt longed for such organizational talent to breathe life into the Southern section.

Jack continued, addressing the various types of organizations in the South and the sorts of leadership that could contribute to a mass movement. He suggested that he and Esther try to get jobs as regional directors for the southern NAACP and build it into a left-wing-oriented mass movement. He wrote: "The [Communist Party] in the South, strong in Negro mem-bership, a trade union movement conscious of its role of ally of the Negro people in their struggle for democratic rights, plus the [Southern Confer-ence for Human Welfare]—all would contribute toward the rapid rear-ing of a Negro people's movement in the South out of the womb of the NAACP."[61] Of course, Esther and Jack did not anticipate the sharp anti-Left turn the NAACP would take in the postwar years.

Esther's letters spent significantly less time pondering plans for the future and much more time discussing the activities the SNYC was engaged in at the moment. An average day for Esther included a full workday at the SNYC office, time with her daughter, meetings and inves-tigations, and writing to Jack. Although Jack was busy in the army, his shifts on duty were usually spent waiting for soldiers who needed medica-tions or other treatment. He had time to read and reflect, and he wrote much more introspective letters. For Esther, on the other hand, con-stant activity meant that she had more to report on and interesting sto-ries about her day to tell her husband. She offered constant updates on

SNYC developments. Her discussions of current problems affirmed Jack's emphasis on the unique context of the South. After reporting on disagreements with an SNYC member in the organization's New York office (the only northern branch), Esther wrote: "These mistakes have taught us in the South a real lesson. We'll study more and in the future not look to directions from 'up thar' for a correct policy on the South."[62]

Jack also spent substantial time thinking about the leadership and administration of the SNYC. As a founder of the organization and one of its key leaders, he had invested a lot of energy and emotion in building it. He was concerned about the other individuals who had worked hard to make the organization effective as well. For instance, when Dorothy Burnham had her second child, Jack was concerned about ensuring her continued inclusion in SNYC activities. He suggested to his wife: "Louis [Burnham] would do well to see that she shares in the glory of the brilliant new achievements of the Congress. . . . In considering your new staff appointments for Educational Director, etc., Dorothy should not be overlooked."[63] The SNYC took Jack's suggestion, adding Dorothy Burnham to its large cohort of female leaders in the war years.

The activist inclinations in Esther and Jack's letters illustrate the urgency of pragmatic black struggle in the South alongside the idealism of two black Communists who ultimately struggled toward radically restructuring the US social and political culture. The couple were situated directly in what the historian Nikhil Pal Singh calls "the intersection of state-oriented liberalism inclined to ameliorative reform and a relatively autonomous black activism inclined to acts of rebellion."[64] The couple represented the fluidity of black nationalism and internationalism, radicalism and reform that worked within the framework of the federal government, and patriotism and its limits in the context of World War II. The war also offered them a new framework for understanding the black freedom struggle in the context of global politics.

Esther and Jack's internationalism was very common among black activists of the period. Black leaders, ranging from the radical Trotskyite theorist C. L. R. James to the liberal NAACP executive secretary Walter White, believed that the ground on which America's wartime rhetoric of democracy and liberty stood was fundamentally shaky. The simultaneous oppression of black Americans at home and effort to save democracy in Europe were wholly paradoxical. Black leaders also saw the contradictions inherent in the Allies' occupation and subjugation of colonies across Africa and Asia and their concurrent struggle to liberate oppressed groups from Axis fascism.

By linking black oppression in the United States, particularly in the Jim Crow South, to the oppression of colonized peoples across the globe, leaders offered an interpretation of global conflict that resonated deeply with black Americans. Black Americans might have participated in the war through either military service or war industry employment, they might have contributed to the war effort by purchasing war bonds and appropriately rationing their goods, and they might have wholeheartedly believed that they could share in the experience of saving democracy. Participation and support of the cause, however, did not mean that they failed to critique the contradictions of World War II and fight to lessen the gap between democratic rhetoric and the undemocratic reality in which they and millions of subjugated people across the world lived.[65]

Jack's internationalism developed during his time overseas. Although black soldiers all gained new exposure to international issues through their wartime service, Jack's theoretical background and political positions gave him a different vantage point for cultivating his internationalism. It is impossible to measure the degree to which his fellow soldiers developed their own new understandings of their struggles and the world around them, but it is clear through his observations that the context of war influenced black soldiers' lives overall. In one letter, Jack noted that his barrack mates in North Carolina were "stoic peasant lads from the cotton and cane country of the deep south" to whom "a knife and fork are awesome and unfathomable tools, whose cultural level is almost primitive": "Yet . . . knowing that some will die when we go forth to apply the lessons we are learning here [they] do nonetheless elect to go forward with a confident equanimity that it is 'worthwhile' and somehow they are actors in a drama that will bring happiness to a lot of people who are 'having it tough.' They don't say what—if anything—they think is the relationship between their service and their own aspirations or that of their folks back home."[66]

Jack's letter suggests that even black soldiers from the poorest backgrounds with extremely limited education still understood to a certain degree that they were fighting for a noble cause. In spite of their unequal access to the democracy they fought for, Jack observed that his fellow soldiers felt the patriotic spirit of the war.

Jack's activist experience and intellectual viewpoints were uncommon among his fellow soldiers. The average soldier was, as the historian John Morton Blum has suggested, "a reluctant hero, a folk hero." Taken together these soldiers were "just ordinary American boys . . . friendly and enthusiastic and sensible . . . as normal as if nothing had happened."[67] The historian Gary Gerstle echoed that analysis, arguing that soldiers' understanding of what they were fighting for was grounded in a sense of loyalty to their unit. While some nationalism or some sense of common American identity came into play for them, they did not fight "for flag or country, for the Marine Corps or glory, or any other abstraction." Rather: "They fight for one another."[68] That Jack's fellow black soldiers lacked a developed understanding of American goals in war, then, was not uncommon. Yet their lack of cultural development sheds light on how the practice of segregation had systematically excluded black Americans from the very basic elements of the democracy for which they were fighting. Given this background, these men were probably even less likely to develop a sense of what the war was about than the average white soldier. Jack's observations speak to the overall power of the Allied cause, in spite of its paradoxes.

Many black Communists found the war to be a moment in which a particular political analysis crystallized. For Nelson Peery, a black Communist who served in the Pacific Theater, war and combat helped him hone and refine his racial critique. After killing a Japanese soldier in a confrontation, Peery, already a radical thinker, gained new insight on race. He told a fellow soldier that, as the event unfolded, he knew killing was wrong but that he had to find a way to justify it in his own mind. The experience made him think about racial violence at home, and he told his friend: "When they go out an' lynch somebody, or rape some woman, they know they're wrong. They know they've sinned. . . . So then, they got to pretend we're not human. . . . When I stuck that fuckin' guy—I called him a Jap bastard. If I'd thought 'soldier' or 'man,' I'd of fixed him up and got him to the field hospital." Peery continued, linking his analysis of race at home with the US cause in wartime: "It ain't right. It don't seem real. We out here killin' these people to protect something we hate. Lonnie [another soldier] getting' killed while they lynching our people in his backyard. . . . If we can kill and fight and die here, for nothing, let's keep on fighting and killing when we get back home. . . . [T]hat would be the end of lynching."[69] The reality of combat cast into stark relief the contradictions of fighting to protect, preserve, and promote the values of a segregated democracy, and, for some black soldiers, that tension elicited and helped focus a radical racial analysis that spurred postwar activism.

Once Jack was overseas, his own level of exposure to the world outside the United States changed, and he began to think about the blatant similarities between British colonialism in South Asia and segregation in the American South. He had read political articles and books in the past about the nature of imperialism, but seeing it firsthand changed the importance of the issue for him. He wrote in January 1945: "I have seen nothing in Alabama or Mississippi to equal the brutality of some of these Kiplingesque buccaneers." Jack observed that the behavior of soldiers toward the indigenous population differed significantly from that of the colonists. For the most part, American GIs were respectful of their hosts. He told Esther: "It is to the undying credit of our troops that such exhibitions have been the exception . . . rather than the rule—especially (and naturally) have the Negro troops conducted themselves well in their relations with our Indian hosts."[70] Jack had seen how black soldiers who had no exposure to the basic implements of a modern society, who were far from the sort of worldly intellectual he was, could still understand the injustices of colonialism enacted before their eyes and respond to the situation sympathetically because of their own experiences with Jim Crow.

For Jack, the war illustrated the connections between the problems of black southerners and international concerns. Jack was a well-educated and shrewd student of international politics. His letters juxtaposed black soldiers' awareness of the world around them with the stark relationship between the circumstances in colonial India and the segregated South. He elaborated on the implications of colonialism for Western Europe: "The west cannot honestly hope to attain a very high stage of democracy as long as the people of the East are held in colonial subjugation. The people of the Far East have been stirred mightily by the winds of freedom emanating from this Great War of National Liberation. This ferment can never again be contained within the framework of [antebellum] colonial possession."[71]

The nature of colonialism certainly had a powerful influence on Jack's thinking about the character of racial oppression. He believed firmly in the Allied cause in spite of America's paradoxical relationship with a war for democracy and its own black citizens. Yet witnessing British colonialism in India solidified his belief that fascism was not unique to the Axis, that World War II was truly a war to end racism regardless of its national origin. In other words, fascism and racial tyranny were global phenomena that did not stop at Germany, Italy, Japan, and Spain. Jack's experience and analysis fit squarely into the internationalist discourse among black leaders during World War II.

Jack's internationalism drew on a long tradition of black global thought, communism, and his own experiences abroad. As a couple with a young child, however, the Jacksons' international experience during World War II stands out: both partners spent time overseas during the war, and Esther went as an activist. Esther recalled of the war years: "We'd covered the world between us."[72] In 1945, SNYC leaders selected Esther to represent the organization at the World Youth Conference, sponsored by the leftist World Youth Council, in London. She spent a great deal of time in her letters discussing the sorts of issues she would promote at the conference, and her experience was shaped by the connections between the American South and the colonized world. In preparation for the October conference, she wrote a bulletin on the topic of "the colonial question" for SNYC members and councils. She drew from a wide range of sources, including her husband's experiences and W. E. B. Du Bois's 1945 *Color and Democracy*.[73] When she was at the conference, she took special interest in issues relating to struggles in colonies and became friends with two female delegates from India, Kitty Boomla and Vedya Kanuga. She spent much of her time at the conference, both in sessions and socially, with delegates from colonies.[74]

Attending the World Youth Conference was not an easy decision for Esther to make. Politically, she knew it would be an important opportunity for her, but familial concerns loomed large in her mind. With her husband overseas and a two-year-old to consider, spending two and a half months in London was not something she initially believed would be possible for her. She wrote Jack: "Alice . . . wants to take care of Harriet while I go to the WYC this summer, but 'no dice.' Not 2½ months away from both of my darlings! The first trip I make overseas, I want it to be with the *two* of you."[75] Soon thereafter, however, she wrote to tell her husband that she had decided to represent the SNYC at the conference after all. The opportunity was too important to miss.

Jack's first reaction to the news that Esther would be traveling overseas was fraught with frustration despite his radical gender politics and the pride he took in his wife's accomplishments. On June 3, 1945, he wrote: "In spite of the apparent conclusive nature and sincerity of [your statement that you would not go] it was becoming quite obvious from your letter that you had already made up your mind that it was your historic duty to make the trip and you were merely seeking to reconcile this with certain lingering sentimentalities."[76] He felt out of the loop even though he anticipated his wife's decision. She was far too talented to miss that opportunity, and he knew that she knew that. He felt excluded from the exciting changes going on in her life.

In a June 15 letter, however, Jack apologized for his sarcastic tone: "[I] just sink down in my chair in shame, with my consciousness smacking me across the face for having written you so selfish and sarcastic a letter upon first learning of your contemplated trip to London. . . . I'll deserve every reprehensible thing you may think of me for having written it. . . . [I]n spite of the bigoted, selfish first reaction, I don't hold a word of it now (my fears were the fears of Soviet girls when their lover-warriors were entering the 'wicked' bourgeois countries of Europe with their whores and jaded, tinseled glamour)."[77] The nature of Jack's reaction to his wife's news illustrates that he was constantly and self-consciously striving to be a supportive husband and to be consistent with the political values he espoused within his relationship. Additionally, in his apology, Jack placed himself into the shoes of "Soviet girls," adopting a unique gendered perspective. He did not express much concern over his wife's furlough from the traditional wifely and motherly duties: she was also a warrior, and he understood that. Still, his instinctive concern as a husband had fused with his unique gender politics, and he became a "Soviet girl" fretting about his "lover-warrior." Esther, Jack believed, did not face the same dangers as a typical woman traveling overseas by herself, but his initial reaction was that her travels were a threat to him and to their marriage.

Esther forgave her husband's first reaction, stating that she too would have preferred it if another SNYC leader could go instead. Because there was so much delay in mail delivery, much of the exchange between the couple occurred weeks after one partner or the other had already dealt with the emotions aroused by a given letter. Wartime, for a couple that wrote daily, meant that disagreements were fleeting. If Jack wrote an unhappy letter on June 3, Esther might not have been able to reply until June 17, and it could easily have been July before Jack received that reply. On June 17, Esther wrote: "By now you have my letter which explains my reaction to the *reason for* your objection to my attending the Youth Conference."[78] There was no point in holding on to frustrations (especially since Jack had penned his apology two days earlier), and Esther spent most of the letter discussing other matters.

On first arriving in London, Esther was shocked by the degree of damage. She wrote to her dear friend Louis Burnham: "You can't imagine the damage from bombings . . . until you've been here—it's horrible to see."[79] After the conference, the Soviet Anti-Fascist Youth Committee offered Esther an opportunity to join an all-female delegation from the newly founded World Federation of Democratic Youth (WFDY) on a tour of war-ravaged Europe. Fixing some of this devastation was something Esther simply had to do. Not only would the tour help her truly understand the war's costs, but she would also have an opportunity to help change things. The devastated cities the group visited included Berlin, Warsaw, Paris, and Stalingrad. In Berlin, which was newly divided into three sections, Esther and the other women in the delegation had difficulty moving between the US-occupied area and the Soviet-occupied area. Esther soon learned that the issue holding the group up was her race. Because the occupying US military was still segregated and the unit Esther witnessed in Germany was all white, the interracial delegation had difficulty moving about freely. Eventually, they were allowed to pass between sections.[80]

Once the delegation arrived in Stalingrad, Esther and the other women moved into the basement of one of the few buildings that had not been destroyed in the war. The women from different countries would

share stories, sing, and discuss ideas while witnessing the worst consequences of wartime devastation. While they were in Stalingrad, Esther
and the WFDY delegation worked as assistant bricklayers, helping rebuild
the city. Some of the other American women who toured Europe with
Esther were not married yet and were significantly younger than she was.
Esther recalled: "Some of them were a little startled that I had left a
young child."[81] Many of these women would later sacrifice either their
activist ambitions or their desires for family.

Esther had faced that very conundrum at various points in her activist career and routinely sought to create solutions when none existed. In
Birmingham, for instance, SNYC women felt frustration with the limited
availability of child care, particularly if their husbands were overseas. The
organization established youth centers and collective day cares to afford
women the time to work and have families. Sallye Davis, the mother of
Angela Davis, and others routinely watched Harriet Jackson and the
Burnham children, for instance, when their mothers were away on SNYC
business.[82] And, although she had been somewhat uneasy about leaving
the country when Harriet was so young, Esther had already established
a pattern of asking for child-care help when she needed it and left her
daughter in the care of her mother. Esther and Jack's egalitarian relationship and the connections they saw between personal and political life
allowed each partner to contribute more broadly to the black freedom
movement and the cause of democracy in World War II than could couples whose roles were shaped by traditional gender norms.

Esther's experience abroad during the immediate postwar period
helped shape the analytic viewpoint she brought to both her activism
and her marriage. Because Jack had also seen a section of the world during the war, the couple had an uncommonly broad firsthand experience
with wartime internationalism. They planned to utilize their experiences
in their postwar life. In one letter discussing plans for the postwar years,
Jack suggested that they could apply for Rosenwald Fellowships to live
and study in the Soviet Union for a year. Personal and political considerations were at stake in this potential move. Jack wrote: "We would love,
work and play in a land free of jim crow; in a land of music lovers, theater lovers and people—happy and alive . . . the kind of environment for
our daughter to become five and six years old in—when she will begin

to understand and be more or less permanently influenced by her experiences." He also suggested that living for a year abroad would be profoundly influential in their activism in the United States: "We would be
prepared to fill speaking engagements on most every country in the world
by virtue of having been there: You on Mexico, England, France, and
Yugoslavia and USSR, and I on Africa, India, China and USSR."[83] Esther
agreed that the plan was "tops" and added that the fellowship would also
help the couple's financial situation.[84] As Esther and Jack planned for the
postwar years, they knew that political activism in some form would be a
priority, but they were sure to consider their family's needs and the success of their marriage.

Jack excitedly anticipated his reunion with his wife. After a long discussion of Indian nationalism and Britain's policies in wartime India, he
wrote: "Freedom is in the air, on the march everywhere. Freedom for
me lies over there where you are—'Till locked again in your arms I will
not know freedom from all the pangs of lonliness [sic] that inhabit the
silent chambers of my being."[85] Through Esther and Jack's World War
II letters, the daily struggles against racism and the accompanying emotional victories and defeats become clear and the connections between
the context of war, European imperialism, American segregation, and the
personal dynamics of a family disrupted by global conflict coalesce. The
couple's open correspondence sheds light on the human frustrations of
life in the Deep South and the piercing psychological impact of war. For
Esther and Jack, wartime also contributed to the way in which they con-
structed their marriage and planned their future together, separated by
thousands of miles. The couple anticipated their postwar life with the
belief that the war's end would begin to fulfill the promises of democracy for black Americans. They prepared to seek out organizations and
locations where they could fuse mainstream and radical politics to affect
change, and they continually kept their family's well-being and future in
mind. Total war meant that no sector of life was untouched by global
conflict. Jack and Esther's correspondence reveals that freedom needed
to be "on the march everywhere," from the battlefield to the home, for
the sake of its own triumph in World War II.

3

The Demise of the Black Popular Front in the Postwar Period

Jack and Esther reunited in February 1946 on a dock in New York City. In a characteristic play on conventional gender roles, it was Jack who stood waiting, clad in a Stetson hat and with a bouquet of flowers, as his wife's ship from England docked.[1] He was fighting frustration, as he had returned from war with no idea where his wife was. Even though he had overcome his envy that she got to be an internationalist activist while he languished in Burma, he had to travel around the South to get information about where to find his daughter and when his wife would get back from her now-extended trip. It was not the reunion he had envisioned, but, when they saw each other, they recognized again one another's passion and commitment. Their love was infused with purpose, and they resolved to use their marriage as a tool in their activism. Following World War II, the couple immediately plunged into action in an effort to realize the goals of the Double Victory campaign. Victory abroad was complete, but the defeat of fascism in Europe and Asia did not mean that the attitudes and legal structures enforcing segregation at home would change. Esther and Jack, along with their Southern Negro Youth Congress (SNYC) colleagues, had great hope for the postwar years. They believed that the foundations for true democracy in the United States had been laid by the nation's triumph in the war.

But hope and reality were two very different things after World War II, and activists knew that the struggle for social change in the American South would be a hard one. As Jack wrote: "We've been around the world serving in an army which has been fighting tyranny, fighting for freedom, for the dignity and rights of the little people, fighting the concepts of the master race with its self-appointed power to circumscribe the lives and discriminate against other peoples. . . . We believe in [the Four Freedoms] . . . but we are not stupid."[2] Returning black soldiers were well aware that their military service did not guarantee them civil rights.

The struggle to attain democracy for African Americans at home meant that black veterans and civilians alike needed to continue to highlight the disparity between wartime rhetoric and the reality of the South while they demanded genuine change.

The postwar years included some of the most significant civil rights advancements, from the desegregation of the military to the Supreme Court rulings that white primaries were unconstitutional and that racially restrictive covenants in real estate were unenforceable.[3] Yet the era also marked a dramatic moment of transition and difficulty for black Popular Front activists as the Cold War took shape. Activists like Jack and Esther continued in their efforts to promote racial justice and carry out their vision for the postwar years, but America's diplomatic relationship with the Soviet Union changed the political backdrop and threatened the efforts of black Popular Front activists. The SNYC, too, worked to sustain a Popular Front–style mobilization in the South after the war but confronted mounting anticommunism that bolstered southern racism. Instead of capitulating to the demands of an increasingly conservative Cold War political atmosphere, SNYC leaders, including Esther and Jack, added the fight against anticommunism to their program. They believed that they were battling the threat of domestic fascism, but their fight against anticommunism highlighted their Communist connections in a nation newly overcome by Cold War fear and anxiety. Regardless, for Esther and Jack, their focus remained on the fight for racial equality, economic justice, and political liberty while they rebuilt their life together, reconnected as a couple, and grew their family after the war.

The couple saw black internationalism as crucial in creating a democratic postwar world. At the end of World War II, a progressive international youth movement burgeoned. The World Youth Council, an antifascist organization that united youths in Allied countries during World War II, organized a World Youth Conference. Delegates at the 1945 World Youth Conference in London founded the World Federation of Democratic Youth (WFDY). The WFDY united progressive youth organizations from sixty-three countries, and SNYC leaders described it as an "unofficial 'Junior United Nations.'"[4] The Left-leaning delegates of all races represented a wide variety of religions, had specific interests in sports, labor, politics, and urban and rural issues, and spanned the aca-

demic and professional spectrums.[5] Esther was one of five black US delegates and the only SNYC representative. Participants elected her along
with five other US delegates to serve on the WFDY's governing council,
and the SNYC was one of many American youth organizations to immediately affiliate with the WFDY.[6]

Every aspect of the World Youth Conference, including the building
where it was held, emphasized hope and survival amid the destruction of
war. The organizers hosted the conference in one of the buildings that
had survived the massive bombing of London. Members of the US delegation wondered whether they had any right to be optimistic about the
future amid such despair. Yet the delegates remained confident and hopeful and saw great promise in their unity. The US delegates learned that
"the problems of a 'dead-end kid' [in the United States] were inexorably
bound up with those of a Czechoslovakian child born in a concentration
camp or the child of an 'untouchable' in India." The WFDY was "the
machinery which could be used to cooperate with world youth," and
"the educational and inspirational experience of these twenty American
delegates made evident the vital need for fully utilizing this indispensable
weapon."[7] Over eight days, the conference participants molded plans to
take actions in their own countries as representatives of the program fashioned at the conference. Esther and other delegates prepared to forge the
same sense of international unity on local levels.

For Esther, the political context of the postwar years highlighted
the importance of international youth solidarity. With the advent of
the atomic bomb and the lingering memories of fascism's rampage in
Europe, the world was suspended precariously between war and peace. At
the same time, the worldwide condemnation of fascism as the Allies triumphed revealed the possibilities for a full realization of democratic ideals, freedom, and equality. Esther recalled: "There was such enthusiasm
at this conference, and young people were feeling that they were going to
make a difference in the world; that we'd won the battle against fascism
and now we're going to win some battles at home." The US delegation
saw racial segregation as a key domestic problem, and their colleagues
supported the need to fix the South's racial caste system.[8]

The SNYC maintained close ties with the international youth activist community after the founding of the WFDY. It saw that community

as a key ally in the struggles it faced at home. In spite of the Allied triumph over the Axis powers in World War II, democracy did not immediately come for blacks in the United States. In fact, white supremacist
violence increased in 1946 when African American soldiers returned from
war empowered to achieve democracy at home. Lynching had declined
steadily since the late 1930s, with fewer than five incidents every year but
1942, but in 1946 the number increased again.[9] In Monroe, Georgia, on
July 25, 1946, the World War II veteran George Dorsey, his wife, Mae
Murray Dorsey, his sister, Dorothy Dorsey Malcolm, and her husband,
Roger Malcolm, became a part of that growing number. Malcolm had
fought with his landlord a few days before and injured him, and the four
were in the car with Malcolm's landlord when they were taken by a mob
of whites and lynched. The FBI investigated but never solved the case.[10]

The lynching of the Dorseys and Malcolms occurred as the 1946
gubernatorial primary in Georgia approached. After *Smith v. Allwright*
made white primaries unconstitutional, a black preacher from Columbus
named Primus King filed suit for the right to vote in Georgia and won.
The Supreme Court refused to hear the appeal, and the 1946 gubernatorial primary was the first election in Georgia's history in which blacks
could vote. Though the lynching was not directly related to voting rights,
the Supreme Court's refusal ignited white anger and fear that the racial
status quo was evaporating. The postwar period brought about intensified white anxiety as blacks used democracy's triumph as a catalyst for
change.[11]

In this context, many American activists believed that the South
closely resembled the fascist regimes the nation had fought in World
War II. Notwithstanding the Allied victory in the war, the horrors of
fascism abroad remained in those activists' memories. The similarities
between atrocities overseas and the racial climate in the South, alongside
new restrictions on civil liberties, led many leftist black leaders to see the
South as not just segregated, Jim Crowed, or undemocratic but fascist.
Segregation in the South was not simply a way of social life. It was part
of the South's legal and political structure, enforced and supported by
the national government and given strength by the complicity of Americans across the nation. For left-wing and progressive activists, along with
some liberals, the resemblance the South bore to a fascist state motivated

a new wave of social movements. The promise of democracy's triumph forecast the coming of improved race relations in the United States, and black activists of all political persuasions saw renewed potential in the postwar years.

The SNYC continued to participate in the WFDY, and, in August 1946, SNYC education director Dorothy Burnham traveled to Paris to attend the organization's council meeting. In a speech at the meeting, Burnham detailed cases of lynching, disenfranchisement, employment discrimination, and other everyday elements of Jim Crow. She equated the situation in the South with fascism and urged delegates to pass a resolution on the situation in the South.

Delegates from youth organizations around the world listened as Burnham implored them to reject America'a portrayal of itself as a center for peace and democracy and to recognize the brand of fascism harbored in the South by politicians, police, and the Ku Klux Klan. She declared: "Perhaps the members of this Council have accepted the declaration proclaimed so often that the United States is the seat of peace and well-being. I would like to remind you that two days ago four young Negroes were lynched in our country for wanting to take part in the elections. The Ku-Klux-Klan is growing very much in the United States and this organization is perhaps one of the most powerful active fascist forces in the world."[12]

Such a clear description of racial violence in the United States directly contradicted the democratic rhetoric promoted by the US government. Burnham suggested that the WFDY council push the Truman administration to take responsibility for making democracy a reality in the United States. She urged that Secretary of State James Byrnes "cannot expect to lead the world in democracy if there is no democracy in his own country" and that "it is about time that he . . . [do] something to stamp out the Ku-Klux-Klan and the lynchings in the United States and [set] the machinery in motion which will eliminate those activities."[13]

Burnham's resolution passed easily. Delegates wondered "about this America which tells them without any humility how to run their democracies here in Europe and which yet tolerates racial oppression and brutality at home."[14] The council members at the meeting were interested in how young people in the American South were combating racism, and sending a message to the US secretary of state reflected the WFDY's global democratic agenda.[15] To fight oppression in all its manifestations included tackling disfranchisement and racist terror in the United States, which were widespread despite the nation's slogans of freedom and democracy.

Burnham's speech brought the discrepancies between American democratic rhetoric and the reality of racism and segregation in the South to the forefront of a global conversation about injustice. Also, presenting government-supported segregation as a form of fascism and an affront to freedom to a global community of activists placed the United States in a position to be held accountable for its sanctioning of racism. Burnham and the SNYC believed that international condemnation of segregation could be a powerful tool in its demise. In addition, by using America's democratic rhetoric to highlight other nations' undemocratic behavior before an international audience, the SNYC could both employ that rhetoric to the organization's advantage and expose the limitations of true democracy in the United States.[16] As Burnham's experience illustrates, the SNYC's internationalism was both connected to an effort to expand the scope of the southern struggle and a reflection of black activists' mounting disenchantment with the possibilities in the United States. The international youth movement provided SNYC activists with a means to fight for global democracy without losing focus on the struggle at home.

For Jack and Esther, fighting for global democracy implied that democracy needed to exist at the very base of the social structure of the United States: within families. Esther and Jack's vision of postwar democracy was simultaneously internationalist and personal. Jack had expanded his international lens as he talked with local activists while serving in the China-Burma-India Theater and, once he overcame his jealousy, was enthusiastic about his wife's trip to Europe. The couple's unique relationship and activist goals offered SNYC constituents an example of how to simultaneously engage in internationalist political activism and craft their personal lives after World War II. Esther and Jack had successfully reconstructed their marriage in the postwar period, worked equally and happily together, and were deeply in love. They believed that, with their commitment to working toward gender egalitarianism and their focus on fighting for black freedom, their marriage could serve as an example to other young black couples in the SNYC's network. Young black southerners who encountered them at any number of SNYC events in the postwar years learned from a pair of activists who not only had seen the world during the war but also were engaged in wide-ranging internationalist activism and grassroots organization.

Esther and Jack's experiences with postwar SNYC programs showed them that young black southerners, too, were seeking to reconstruct their personal lives and implement global democracy. Just as World War II transcended all aspects of public and private life during the previous four years, the political and social problems of the postwar period permeated people's homes and families. Young black southerners struggled to reunite their families, resettle into jobs, and recover from the psychological effects of total war, with the added complication of being consistently denied the benefits of the democracy they had defended. The SNYC made veterans' issues a primary component of its program alongside voting rights, antilynching legislation, jobs, and desegregation, all of which the organization had prioritized since its inception. Esther and Jack employed both their international experiences during the war and their transition into domestic life afterward in their campaigns with the SNYC to educate young blacks across the South.

Reconstructing gender relations within marriages became as paramount as politics for the SNYC in the postwar years. Many couples that the organization worked with continued to abide by traditional gender roles, which hindered efforts to promote women's equality. Esther recalled that wives of workers that the SNYC had been trying to unionize were often "kept so backwards that they [thought] I must have been in it because I was interested in their husbands."[17] The SNYC worked to combat this suspicion by organizing the workers' wives to assist in unionization struggles and to include all women in their vision for democracy.

SNYC leaders asserted that black women's employment rights, in particular, were a critical piece of the dream of postwar democracy. At the 1946 Southern Youth Legislature in Columbia, South Carolina, Miami Council secretary Florence J. Valentine delivered "Remarks on Jobs and Job Training for Negro Women." She connected class, gender, and race in her talk and argued that black women "were behind the noise—the hammer, the thunder, the drive." In the postwar years, black women's job security was "the best weapon against defeat at home and abroad": "Negro women need jobs . . . with no bars created because of color, creed, or sex. We, the Negro women, want jobs not only for today, but jobs forever."[18] Valentine linked domestic and international women's issues, arguing that black women's employment was fundamental to their own security and that their security was fundamental to stability at home and abroad. She asserted that black women's equal employment would increase the possibilities for peace and democracy. In 1950, the activist Vicki Garvin echoed Valentine, declaring: "Historically, it is the burning desire of every Negro woman to be free, to live and work in dignity, on equal terms with all other workers. Negro women are eager to undertake a greater role to give substance to freedom and democracy, to help build an America of peace and abundance."[19]

The SNYC lived up to its creed by providing leadership opportunities for women. Since World War II women had consistently constituted roughly half the leadership in the SNYC national office, and this was also true in SNYC clubs throughout the South.[20] The Miami club member Jack O'Dell recalled: "It was very clear that women's leadership was very prominent." He noted that women held important leadership roles in the organization and were not confined to secretarial work: "They were very much a part of the decision-making and the policy setting and the public presence of the SNYC."[21] In March 1947, *Seventeen Magazine* recognized the SNYC as an ideal place of employment for young women dedicated to social justice.[22]

Esther and Jack sought to incorporate their new international experience and their gender dynamic into their postwar activism. Almost immediately, the couple was touring the South, giving lectures at colleges, churches, and trade unions. SNYC leaders intended that the lecture series would provide young black southerners with an opportunity to understand where their struggle fit in an international fight against oppression. The SNYC emphasized Esther and Jack's marriage in flyers for the tour, describing them as a "unique and outstanding couple." A press release for the lecture series stated: "The tour is a feature of the SNYC program which emphasizes the close bond of interest which exists between American Negro youth and democratic youth throughout the world, especially in the colonial areas."[23] The lecture tour encouraged young black southerners to participate in local struggles as a component of working in solidarity with activists around the world.

Esther's experience at the World Youth Conference allowed her to illustrate that an international activist community was concerned with the experiences of young black southerners.[24] Her subsequent tour of war-devastated Europe also afforded her a unique perspective on international struggles in the postwar world. The topics she addressed on the SNYC lecture tour included "Youth Movements in Colonial Countries," "Youth's Plan for World Security," and "The World Student Movement."[25] Jack used his firsthand experience in a colonized country to address other international issues. His lecture topics included "Unrest in the Colonies—What Does the Future Hold?" "Negro Youth—Their Stake in Colonial Freedom," and "Political, Economic, and Social Developments in the Major Population Centers of the World."[26]

The lecture tour generated interest among young black southerners. As Esther recalled: "[People] in some of the smaller schools that we went to in the Southern states were almost in awe of the 'world travelers' coming back to the South to relate their experience."[27] Through the lecture tour, Esther and Jack impressed audiences with what they had learned from being abroad during the war, the interest the international youth movement took in southern struggles, and the manner in which the audiences' struggles fit into a world movement.[28]

Esther and Jack hoped to help young people struggling simultaneously for social change and family security. Just as Esther had told her husband in 1945 that their "marriage must serve as an 'example,'" the couple sought to demonstrate their successful combination of love and activism for their audiences.[29] Their world experience, political ideology, and strong marriage mirrored the SNYC's position on domestic, public, and international politics. Through their involvement with domestic and international progressive youth organizations, they offered a powerful model for young black people trying to reconfigure their own relationships while fighting for social change in the postwar world. The primary purpose of the lecture tour was to educate young black southerners about the world around them, but Esther and Jack also offered their audiences an example of a stable marriage. At the lectures, Esther recalled: "Young people were very interested and very curious about our relationship, and why we chose what we were doing in our life, and they asked questions about how long we'd been married . . . as much as anything else. . . . [T]hat was a very healthy aspect of the tour."[30] Esther and Jack understood that their relationship was part of their politics, and they knew that the model they provided of gender relations within marriage was important in conjunction with the internationalist themes of their lectures.

Esther and Jack decided to continue working with the SNYC until the 1946 Southern Youth Legislature in October, after which they would resign from the organization. As members of a youth movement who were now adults with families, personal considerations reshaped their activism as well. In reconstructing their family after they returned from overseas, Esther and Jack made decisions that they believed would improve the world for their children's futures but would also provide them with a safer present. The 1946 Southern Youth Legislature served as a defining moment in the couple's activist career. Their resignation marked for them a transition from youth to adult activism. The legislature also stood as a moment of tremendous hope before the postwar Popular Front would meet its demise in the coming Cold War.

As the Southern Youth Legislature approached, black activists were not entirely united under one banner. The historian Peter Lau writes: "While the left-wing of the New Deal coalition was to splinter from within and be ensnared and crushed by the emerging cold war, African Americans would push ahead on an agenda of democratic reform that represented a revision and extension of earlier reform efforts, not a turn away from them."[31] Esther and Jack were a part of the postwar revival of the Popular Front and, with other SNYC and left-wing activists, were explicit about their desire to unite the working class and emphasize socialist reform as the crux of the struggle for civil rights. But the Soviet Union's efforts at self-preservation during the war and the cooperation of the Communist Party USA (CPUSA) with Moscow on political issues came at the expense of American blacks. The Party drove many African Americans so far from the Communist fold that they were not willing to entertain the notion that Marxist reform could be appropriate for the United States. The postwar political situation served to deepen the already wide gulf between Popular Front black organizations and liberal groups like the National Association for the Advancement of Colored People (NAACP).

By the time the Southern Youth Legislature began, the US-Soviet wartime alliance had begun to erode. Activists from the South who participated in Communist-influenced movements during the Popular Front era found new political waters to navigate after World War II. In 1946, Winston Churchill delivered his influential "Iron Curtain" speech in Fulton, Missouri, and declared that the new threat to world peace and security came from a former ally, the Soviet Union. In the speech Churchill used the phrase "the Soviet Sphere" and provided his audience with what would become the language of the Cold War. The world was now cast into a state of "permanent prevention of war" in which "the establishment of conditions of freedom and democracy as rapidly as possible in all countries" was paramount. Churchill continued: "Our difficulties and dangers will not be removed by closing our eyes to them. They will not be removed by mere waiting to see what happens; nor will they be removed by a policy of appeasement."[32] The federal government and local administrations began to monitor activists' movements more closely as a way to avoid any tacit or overt appeasement of a potential domestic enemy. On March 21, 1947, President Harry Truman issued Executive Order 9835, which implemented the Loyalty-Security program. The program created barriers to government employment on the basis of an individual's political positions. Though the Truman administration did not see an immediate threat in government employees, creating a new security apparatus in the face of mounting fear was a politically efficacious move.[33]

The contradictions of the postwar political climate meant that the potential for progressive racial change was met with vigorous resistance among white supremacists. In the South, mob violence was a very real threat for black veterans who dared to enjoy the benefits of the democracy they had fought for abroad. This violence had international reverberations, drawing attention in particular from colonies and Soviet-influenced nations. The United States needed to portray itself as a beacon of freedom and democracy, but its own citizens were denied basic rights and safety on the basis of race.[34] As Brenda Gayle Plummer explains: "Afro-Americans could not reconcile themselves to a racially oppressive order. They nevertheless often disagreed about the best way to challenge that order."[35] Black activists saw in this context an opportunity to utilize international attention and the postwar rhetoric of freedom and equality to create true democracy at home.

For some black activists, early Cold War liberalism offered new opportunities for moderate reform. In 1946, the NAACP in South Carolina began a vast mobilization that by 1951 doubled statewide membership.[36] Around the same time, the NAACP actively distanced itself from organizations like the SNYC. The association leader Walter White declared: "The Negro wants no part of any system in which arbitrary power is vested in one man or a small clique of men . . . whether they be Communist, Dixiecrat, or any other."[37] The association accordingly purged Communist members from its ranks. In spite of the NAACP's moderate reputation, black southerners still confronted the threat of white violence for affiliating with it. The NAACP grew its membership and experienced mounting legal successes in the postwar years as it separated itself from the Left, and the far Left gradually vanished from the public eye in this era. Notwithstanding the deep divisions the NAACP sought to carve between itself and organizations like the SNYC, to segregationists any form of racial equality might well have been communism. As the Popular Front disappeared, to its most conservative and racist detractors the prominent NAACP represented the Left in the struggle for African American civil rights.

In the late 1940s, the NAACP promoted "a narrowed civil rights agenda" that included gradual reform and support of the federal government in the Cold War and emphasized its growing record of legal victories. While the association took substantial criticism for "acquiescing" to the national mood as the Cold War set in, it continued to promote "the full inclusion of black people in the political and economic life of the nation on a nondiscriminatory basis."[38] The distinctions the association drew by carefully articulating its political affiliations separated it ideologically from communism but maintained its position at the forefront of the emerging civil rights struggle.

Other political and diplomatic developments in the postwar years helped motivate social change in the United States. The Atlantic Charter and the creation of the United Nations, for instance, offered new vehicles for black activists on a variety of fronts. The historian James Meriwether writes: "[The Atlantic Charter offered] a postwar peace assuring safety to all nations and freedom from fear and want for all men. The colonial peoples of the world interpreted the principles contained within these documents to mean that democratic freedoms would come for them, too."[39] The promise of democracy for exploited and oppressed peoples across the world seemed ripe for realization.

The creation of the United Nations offered black internationalists the hope for change internationally and domestically as well. The historian Carol Anderson argues that the UN vow to promote human rights "had the language and philosophical power to address not only the political and legal inequality that African Americans endured, but also the education, health care, housing, and employment needs that haunted the Black community." In spite of the promise of human rights rhetoric, Cold War pressures forced groups like the NAACP to retreat from their emphasis on human rights because the language of universal humanity resembled communism.[40]

Not all black activists saw the United Nations as an appropriate channel for achieving rights. Some believed that it was too much a tool of superpower governments, rather than the voice of the world community. These governments would not uphold the sections of the UN Charter that did not serve their interests; they "had already violated the terms of the charter by denying democracy to their subjects."[41] And, as Mary Dudziak illustrates, the United States had a great deal of authority in determining which human rights violations would be investigated. When the NAACP introduced a petition relating human rights violations against black Americans, members of the American delegation, including Eleanor Roosevelt, quashed its efforts.[42]

Worldwide, activists confronted similar disregard and continued to fight for change. Just as African Americans had defended democracy for a nation that left them in the margins, colonial subjects across Africa and Asia fought for freedom on behalf of their metropoles in World War II. The Allied victory inspired many African and Asian leaders to push for decolonization. In South Asia, Indian leaders achieved independence from Great Britain in 1947. Colonized Africans, too, believed that they were entitled to enjoy the rewards of the system they had defended. As a soldier from the Gold Coast wrote: "We have fought against fascism, the enemy of mankind, so that all people, white or black, civilized or uncivilized, free or in bondage, may have the right to enjoy the privileges and bounties of nature."[43]

Initially, the United Nations fumbled on the issue of decolonization as the Cold War emerged. Cold War strategy and moral idealism were in conflict, and African colonies became a focal point in the struggle between capitalism and communism. Though the United States had promoted the end of British imperialism under Franklin Roosevelt, Harry Truman believed that the United States needed to acquire territories in the Pacific for military purposes. He also believed that "the USSR had to be kept out of the colonies" and "this new policy led [the United States] into closer alliance with the imperial powers."[44] Colonial territories and African independence were targets in the rivalry between the Soviet Union and the United States, the tactical locales for political planning, and the objects, rather than the agents, of UN policy. In this context, organizations like the WFDY and the SNYC united international youths not only to promote social change across the world but also to find support from one another when it was lacking from governments at home.

The international youth movement was an important theme at the 1946 Southern Youth Legislature, the SNYC's largest conference. The flyer advertising the legislature highlighted the changing international context that became so influential in the postwar years. It also addressed the problems of youths in a class context, bringing to light the emerging struggle between American capitalism and Soviet communism. The "Call to the Southern Youth Legislature" underscored the tenuous hold the world had on postwar peace. It read: "Before post-war reconstruction activities have been fairly begun and our wounds from yesterday's battles have mended, high-placed, cynical and greedy men in our country are busily engaged in plotting with imperialists of other nations to push our country into an atomic war against the Soviet Union, our ally in the anti-fascist war, and to crush the colonial peoples now battling for their emancipation."[45] The "Call" to the Southern Youth Legislature also anticipated a conference theme that connected the end of slavery in the United States to the postwar context, anticolonial movements, and the emerging struggle between the United States and the Soviet Union.

At the legislature, SNYC leaders would educate delegates about their role in the international youth movement while reminding them of their own arduous history. The leaders decorated the church where the conference was held with portraits of all the black Reconstruction congressmen in the United States.[46] The "Call" continued: "We who were one with the people of the world in the war against fascist enslavement are determined, even as they are, to succeed in reaching ever higher levels of self-government and democracy. We share with the freedom-loving youth of Europe, Asia, India, Africa and Latin America the common struggle for true democracy just as we shared with them the fight against the common enemy in battle."[47]

By connecting the recent war against fascism to the images of slavery and emancipation, SNYC leaders made the international youth movement relevant for the young people of the South. The link between current and historic oppression worldwide, coupled with the emphasis on the greed of imperialism and colonialism, highlighted the timeliness and scope of the struggle for freedom. That young people worldwide were continuing to fight forms of racial and economic enslavement after winning the war against fascism challenged the idea that democracy prevailed. Delegates to the Southern Youth Legislature learned that their fight for liberty happened in solidarity with youths across the globe.

International solidarity at the Southern Youth Legislature served a purpose for delegates and leaders alike by reflecting a larger discontent with the ways in which the US government treated racial inequality. Racism in the United States was sutured to the rhetoric of inclusive, universalistic democracy and the American system of liberal capitalism in which only particular individuals with a historic advantage could advance economically. Nikhil Pal Singh writes that the hope of equality and the American language of democracy "should be understood as performative": That is: "They seek to produce what they purport to describe. They are civic ideologies, normative and pedagogical statements that attempt to create or reinforce a particular narrative of national identity."[48] In other words, when black Americans did not succeed under capitalism, the state could remain disengaged and unaccountable because it promoted access to opportunity as universal. Yet even though, alongside idealistic universalism, American identity was built on the notion that individuals could advance by accumulating capital, institutional racism precluded African Americans and other people of color from that model by systematically denying opportunities. Even if social movements were in a stage of increased activity, the disparity between state ideology and individual experience rendered only small and symbolic advances toward social justice. By looking abroad, SNYC leaders found solidarity and support that went beyond the framework of American democracy.

SNYC leaders selected speakers for the Southern Youth Legislature to address a wide range of local, national, and international issues. While she was in London, Esther first met W. E. B. Du Bois. Du Bois was in Manchester, England, at the fifth Pan African Congress. Impressed by Esther's sharp intellect and strong leadership abilities, he became interested in the SNYC and agreed to give a talk at the Southern Youth Legislature.[49] The conference connected seemingly disparate struggles and rallied young activists to work with dedication and fervor toward massive social change. The speakers encouraged delegates to fight fascism in the South actively, keeping in mind the fact that their struggle was one component of a broad international battle against inequality and oppression. It was at the conference that W. E. B. Du Bois made his famous "Behold the Land" speech, which implored southern youths: "Regard the South as the battleground of a great crusade. Here . . . is the need of the thinker, the worker and the dreamer. This is the firing line not simply for the emancipation of the American Negro but for the emancipation of the African Negro and the Negroes of the West Indies . . . for the emancipation of the white slaves of modern capitalistic monopoly."[50]

Mobilizing the language of slavery and emancipation, the speech insisted that the delegates recognize the importance of fighting fascism and segregation in the South. It urged racial unity and collaboration among the black and white working classes to defeat injustice. It linked past and present and local and global, pointing to what Singh characterizes as "a radical democratic vision that confronted national capitalism with the 'real modern labor problem,' . . . the struggle of a racialized world."[51] "Behold the Land" reflected the SNYC's position, declaring that the "emancipation of the American Negro" would be a victory for democracy that would trigger similar victories for oppressed people worldwide.[52]

Other elements of the Southern Youth Legislature raised international awareness among the 861 young delegates and several hundred observers. Attendees represented a variety of racial and ethnic backgrounds. The three-day conference included the International Youth Night, during which Esther spoke on her experiences at the World Youth Conference. In a summary of the evening's activities, SNYC education director Dorothy Burnham described the delegates as "the youth of the South who had been hemmed in all their lives by the racial segregation existing in America": "These were the youth who were denied jobs, many of whom could not vote for their representatives in congress, these were the youth who shared the problems of the youth of all America but who had in addition the problems imposed upon Black Americans by prejudice and an economic system which demanded a scapegoat."[53]

For these young people, the challenge of thinking beyond their everyday problems presented an exciting opportunity to understand their connection to young people from "countries which were so foreign to [them]." As Burnham put it: "[Delegates] began to understand that we were not fighting this battle for freedom alone. And we gained courage and fortitude to continue our struggle. . . . [W]e know [Esther] had made friends for the youth of the South far across the world."[54]

The SNYC consistently used artistic expression to spread its liberationist and internationalist message, and the Southern Youth Legislature's International Youth Night was no exception. Art and music were particularly effective tools for reaching southerners who did not have the same level of education as SNYC leaders, many of whom had turned down academic and professional opportunities to pursue activism. As the historian Robin D. G. Kelley notes, the SNYC participated in a tradition common among Popular Front organizations that "not only recognized a unique Black cultural heritage but set upon the task of promoting 'a conscious art, rooted in the lives, the struggles, and aspirations of the vast numbers of our race.'"[55] SNYC leaders consistently opened meetings and conferences with a sing-along, held poetry readings, concerts, and puppet shows, and used the work of local black artists on all their flyers and pamphlets to create an open, comfortable, and unified atmosphere.[56] Politics expressed through arts and culture created a bond between SNYC activists of all levels of education.

The Southern Youth Legislature included a performance by the beloved musician, actor, and Pan-African social activist Paul Robeson. Robeson, who was a leader of the Council on African Affairs, a left-wing organization that had close ties to the Communist Party and advocated for African decolonization, performed on International Youth Night. After Esther's speech, Robeson began to sing. Dorothy Burnham wrote:

> It was then that he sang the songs of our America. He sang the songs of the workers and of the Negro slaves of long ago. Some of these were the songs that he had sung to the boys of the International Brigade during the Spanish Civil War. . . . A hush fell and Robeson sang songs of the youth of China, France, and the Soviet Union. . . . Our own hearts were full of admiration for this man who so loved the people of all lands, who hated tyranny wherever it existed and who this evening in a simple manner had helped us to come closer to the youth of the world.[57]

Through song, Robeson conveyed the SNYC's message of international youth solidarity to delegates in a manner that was accessible to sharecroppers, miners, students, and leaders alike. A. Romeo Horton, a Morehouse College delegate from Liberia, and Theodore Baker, a Haitian delegate, also discussed the histories of their respective countries, social and cultural circumstances, the status of youth movements, and how their struggles were relevant to SNYC youths.[58]

The surge in SNYC activity in 1946 was the group's climax before its conclusion. Just as the end of World War II generated a new sense of hope for radical social change worldwide on the grassroots level, it simultaneously created the Cold War political setting that led organizations on the Left to dissolve. As a Popular Front organization that included Communist leaders, the SNYC suffered in this climate. In part because the CPUSA had shrouded itself in secrecy during the majority of its existence, and in part because the government relied on anti-Communist propaganda to garner public support for the Cold War, the effort to vilify Communists took on a new life in the postwar years. Communists, whose perceived dedication to their political causes came at the expense of normal social and family lives, were seen not as individuals but as mere cogs in the Comintern's global machine. As the historian Ellen Schrecker put it: "[They] presumably subscribed to the same beliefs, mouthed the same slogans, and followed the same orders. The notion of a monolithic Moscow-run party was utterly crucial [to domestic politics in the early Cold War years]." Cold War propaganda also portrayed Communists as fanatics who were prone to "irrationality and even madness." In fact: "Especially among moderates and liberals, the notion that Communism was some kind of psychological disorder came to be quite common."[59] This political situation began to erode the influence of the SNYC.

Across the left side of the political spectrum, organizations either forced Communists out or faced their demise. By the end of the 1940s, the CIO, an organization that had been influential in the SNYC's early years, had expelled nearly all Communists from its ranks. As the historian Richard Fried writes, the CIO grew wary of Communist influence and believed "that to survive a hostile and conservative climate labor must put its house in order": "So it did, but not without cost. The CIO's early militance vanished, replaced by a tamed bureaucracy, still powerful but no longer dynamic."[60] In this context, the SNYC's difficulties were only beginning to mount, and Esther and Jack confronted new problems after resigning from the organization that defined their young adulthood. The couple left the SNYC in part to attempt to implement their wartime vision for a postwar South, and they began to gravitate toward new challenges.

Although the political climate was growing increasingly tense, Esther and Jack moved further to the Left. On leaving the SNYC in 1946, Jack spent a brief period as the state director of the Communist Party in Louisiana. The position was an ideal match for his politics and abilities, but he faced mounting political opposition in the state. When he got to New Orleans, he was scheduled to speak at a union meeting. At the start of the meeting, he was disrupted by "a bunch of thugs" who "beat up some of the Communists."[61] Though he was on the receiving end of the assault, Jack was arrested along with 119 others and charged with malicious mischief and disturbing the peace.[62]

After paying a fine, Jack returned to the apartment he was renting. His landlady called police that evening because she thought she had heard a burglar in the bathroom. When the police arrived, they found the yard swarming with neighbors wielding guns and clubs, and the land-lady had discovered that it was Jack in the bathroom, "breaking things." Jack, it happened, had been hiding from the mob and had thrown an ink-well through the window when he saw an angry face on the other side.[63] Esther had been preparing to join her husband in New Orleans, but this incident threw a wrench in her plans. According to an FBI informant, she reacted to her husband's difficulties by stating that the United States was "rapidly becoming fascist and the people just won't see the light."[64]

Jack had hoped that his new position as Louisiana state director of the CPUSA would allow him to lead a drive against fascism in the South, but, owing to the contradictions of the postwar years, the situation proved much more complicated than he had expected. As Robert Korstad writes: "The Cold War, the metamorphosis of white supremacy, the contain-ment of the trade union movement, and the fracturing of the political left all helped to derail . . . the broader insurgency."[65] Blacks were asking for equal treatment and access to opportunity, and poor whites, particu-larly workers, might have benefited from a leveling of the economic play-ing field. Instead, the jingoistic, anti-Communist language of the Cold War led many white workers to see the social privilege that came with their whiteness, the one advantage they could cling to that put them ahead of black workers, as an expression of patriotism. Civil rights became the political twin of communism, and white opponents of racial equal-ity could easily manipulate Cold War sentiments in furtherance of their cause. Jack's efforts to bring economic parity to union members com-bined with his race put him within arm's length of lynching.

Meanwhile, in Birmingham, the SNYC's fight for social justice was growing increasingly difficult. Though Esther and Jack had left the orga-nization after the Southern Youth Legislature, they maintained strong ties to the SNYC's leaders, particularly Dorothy and Louis Burnham. The couple was keenly aware of the overlap between the problems they faced and the SNYC's continuing struggle. By 1948, the SNYC was fight-ing the early stages of McCarthyism, and the dominant culture of anti-communism forced the organization to focus more directly on domestic issues. Early in 1948, it was placed on the attorney general's list of subver-sive organizations. Its leaders resisted the characterization by reaffirming their nonpartisan policy, refusing "to participate in the political idiocy of witch-hunting and red-baiting." The organization engaged anticommunism only by denouncing it as an undemocratic, fascist scheme.[66]

In April 1948, anticommunism and segregation pushed the SNYC further to the brink of political demise. Events at that year's Southern Youth Legislature drew national attention to the organization's supposed subversive nature and obscured its eleven years of work toward racial justice. Planning the conference proved difficult, but Executive Secretary Louis Burnham and other conference organizers were steadfast, refusing to succumb to the intimidation of local authorities and growing anticommunism.[67]

The first problem for conference organizers was finding a venue for the event. Birmingham's public safety commissioner, Eugene "Bull" Connor, who became famous for his use of fire hoses and police dogs against civil rights activists in the 1960s, threatened potential venue owners and SNYC leaders, warning of Ku Klux Klan action and police intervention. He forced Burnham to meet with him on April 26, 1948. Holding the SNYC's poster for the event in his hand, he read each line and replied: "'Young Southerners, oppressed and beaten,' 'Who's oppressed and beaten?' 'Young Southerners burned and hung,' 'Who's burned and hung?' 'Young Southerners suffering daily the injustices of the Klansman's law . . .' 'There isn't a Klan here, but there will be if you persist with this meeting!'"[68]

Connor continued to threaten Burnham with police and Klan action, contending: "Why, you're the Executive Secretary of the organization—Why, that ain't no job, you should be working in the mills or the mines. I ought to lock you up for vagrancy." Connor's attitude toward Burnham's job invoked the legacy of Reconstruction labor laws. By threatening imprisonment for vagrancy, Connor illustrated that Jim Crow included white entitlement to black labor.[69] Connor promised police action if the city's segregation ordinance was not upheld, adding that Birmingham was "not big enough for the SNYC and him."[70]

Tensions surrounding the SNYC's upcoming conference escalated sharply the following day when Birmingham police murdered the nineteen-year-old SNYC member Marion Noble. Police arrested Noble while he was standing on a street corner. They took him to a garage where they beat and shot him. It was claimed that he was shot because he was reach-

ing for a knife, despite the fact that he was handcuffed, had already suffered extensive head injuries from a severe beating, and posed no threat.
Noble died on the way to the hospital, the fifth black person Birmingham
police had murdered in April 1948.[71]

The search for a venue for the conference continued as various church leaders made offers and then withdrew them after Connor threatened them with arrest, the possibility that they would lose
their church, and Klan action. After an extensive search, the twenty-
three-year-old Reverend C. Herbert Oliver "defied the Nazi like tactics of Commissioner Eugene Connor in order that the flame of liberty
and freedom might continue to burn in Birmingham." He offered his
church, the Alliance Gospel Tabernacle, proclaiming: "This is a House
of God, not of Bull Connor. He has this city but God has this church."[72]
Oliver's assessment of Connor's brutality reflected the growing fear
among those on the Left that the new efforts to restrict political expression in the United States verged on fascism. Oliver's point reverberated
with the views expressed by the Communist Party, but his position as a
religious leader afforded him some political leeway that secular SNYC
leaders did not get.

The conference lineup represented the SNYC's firm defiance of mainstream anti-Communist politics. Idaho senator Glen Taylor, the 1948
running mate of Progressive Party presidential candidate Henry Wallace,
was scheduled to speak. Wallace, a former Roosevelt vice president, broke
away from the New Deal Democrats after he realized that his antisegregation and prounion positions, along with his alliance with Communists
and their sympathizers, were out of step with the Cold War position of
the liberal Democratic Party. He had been critical of Truman's style of
diplomacy and in 1946 was dismissed from his post as secretary of commerce for his public display of dissent. His 1948 presidential campaign
drew support from civil rights activists but was quickly characterized by
liberal Cold Warriors as too far left for comfort.[73] Taylor's Birmingham
visit was an important stop on his southern campaign tour, as the Progressive Party had earned significant respect among black activists, particularly in industrial cities.[74]

Connor and the Birmingham police surrounded the Alliance Gospel
Tabernacle on the first night of the conference to ensure that segregation

laws were obeyed. In its eleven-year history, the SNYC never complied with segregation ordinances at its events. Taylor, wanting to express his solidarity with the SNYC's cause and illustrate in the most palpable way his opposition to segregation, refused to speak before a segregated audience. After some negotiation, leaders convinced the senator to proceed. However, to avoid a confrontation with Connor, SNYC leaders plastered Oliver's church with segregation signs.

That night, Taylor arrived and attempted to enter the church through the front door, which now bore the label "Negro Entrance."[75] When a police officer instructed him to use a side entrance, he refused. The officer replied: "We have laws in this town to be obeyed!" He lifted Taylor off his feet, threw him to the lawn, and began to beat him. Police quickly arrested Taylor, Reverend Oliver, Louis Burnham, and several others. SNYC delegates struggled to raise $100 bail each for the men who had been detained.

Three days later police charged Taylor with interfering with an officer, disorderly conduct, and assault. Because of his status as a senator, the Birmingham city attorney did not charge him with violation of the segregation ordinance for fear that he could take the case to the Supreme Court, where the constitutionality of segregation would be tried.[76] Some later speculated that Taylor had set out to create a scene for campaign publicity, but the events demonstrated that the Birmingham police were determined to hinder the success of the conference.[77]

Senator Taylor's violation of a segregation law and support of a group considered subversive confirmed the nation's worst fears about communism in the upper echelons of government. His arrest signified a growing divide between the Left and the rest of the nation in several ways. First, Taylor confronted the authority of the southern system of segregation. In the eyes of the Birmingham police, he showed disregard for a way of life by attempting to enter through the black entrance. Second, his alliance with a Popular Front organization like the SNYC drew even more hostility from southern authorities. His political party invoked contempt among white supremacists and anti-Communists alike. Finally, his national status meant that his arrest had the potential to bring both these issues to the attention of a national audience. Ultimately, while Taylor's arrest might have provided an opportunity for a national reexamination of segregation, his affiliation with a leftist political party and a subversive organization prevented this.

The response of the national press to Taylor's arrest focused on the question of communism within the SNYC. Most articles noted that the SNYC was, as the *New York Times* put it, "listed in Department of Justice files as Communist-dominated."[78] This drew attention away from the issue of segregation by catering to the public's fear of communism. As anticommunism intensified, affiliation with the SNYC was a political risk that many of the organization's supporters and members decided not to take. Resignations, particularly among members of the Adult Advisory Board, grew more frequent.

The SNYC responded to the Birmingham incident by issuing a press release emphasizing the struggle between its democratic ideals, the image of democracy put forth by the US government, and the fascism of the southern system of segregation. One of Taylor's lawyers maintained: "It is not Senator Taylor who is on trial, but the city of Birmingham which is on trial before the other cities of Alabama and the 47 other states."[79] Louis Burnham focused on the SNYC's goals of social justice and opposition to the fascism of segregation. He wrote in a press release:

> Here, we are in a wilderness, whereto we have been led by the rulers of America, the Congressional hucksters of "separate but equal" "regional" education, the Kowards of the Klan, the bipartisan experts at pigeon-holing civil rights legislation. . . . In this literal police state—in this social wilderness—the weed of fascism grows rapidly and ominously. We stand in the direct path of its advance, hacking at it with a labor movement still pitifully weak, with a Third Party organization in various stages of embryonic development, with the splendid branches of the N.A.A.C.P., with the Southern Negro Youth Congress.[80]

Burnham placed direct blame for the spread of anticommunism and racism on the government, further denying that there was real democracy in the United States. The crusade against communism both at home and abroad overshadowed the SNYC's work for political liberty and racial justice and reinforced the authority of segregation in the South. The SNYC struggled against its characterization as subversive, but, amid declining support and strong opposition among white supremacist groups, it closed its headquarters in 1949.

It is no coincidence that the SNYC's demise occurred alongside the start of the Cold War and the corresponding rise in politically restrictive laws in the United States. As anticommunism gained strength, links between race, class, and political affiliation imposed themselves on the southern movement for social justice and civil rights. As the historian Robin D. G. Kelley argues: "Post-war red baiting in the South was accompanied by the rise of pro-segregationist sentiment." This was the result of racist and anti-Communist responses to black activism during World War II, job competition, and federal legislation supporting civil rights. Kelley continues: "The Ku Klux Klan, the League to Maintain White Supremacy, and the Alabama American Legion deftly appropriated Cold War language to legitimize white supremacy before the rest of the world."[81] With Glen Taylor's arrest and the demise of the SNYC, nationwide anticommunism breathed new life into the southern system of segregation.

In this moment, the rise of Cold War political repression in the late 1940s changed the shape of the black freedom movement. Although many narratives of the postwar black freedom movement argue that economic critique and radical change were swept aside in favor of moderate change that mobilized the American judicial system and legislative process, the moment itself was far more complex.[82] As Peter Lau writes: "The African American civil rights movement did not represent a turn away from the economic concerns of the New Deal era. Rather, the movement brought to the surface the limits of the New Deal era's ostensibly universal reform efforts."[83] Black leaders across the South had similar goals: legal parity, equal access to opportunity, political enfranchisement, and freedom from racial violence. Equitable economic circumstances for African Americans were implicitly connected to each of those goals.

But the means to success differed depending on where activists situated themselves on the political spectrum. As Lau argues, the NAACP under the anti-Communist Walter White adapted itself to changing national circumstances to provide for the well-being of its local branches and expelled Communists where possible. Local association leaders saw this shift as "consistent with the organization's history and the constantly shifting terrain of struggle confronted by black people in America."[84] On the other hand, the SNYC put every bit of its waning energy into reviving the Popular Front. These differences not only account for the successes and failures of two organizations; they also illustrate the ways in which the US-Soviet rivalry influenced activism at home. The events at the 1948 Southern Youth Legislature marked a key moment of transition for black activism in the United States. It was, as Louis Burnham remarked, "the end of a story, but only the beginning of battle."[85]

The growing connection between racism and anticommunism that came along with the Cold War was not specific to the South, and Esther and Jack experienced a similar set of difficulties after moving north. After Jack's tumultuous and life-threatening experience leading the Louisiana Communist Party, the family relocated to Detroit, Michigan, where Jack worked as the education director of the state's Communist Party. There, Esther and Jack's second daughter, Kathryn, was born.

Esther worked as a local organizer for the Progressive Party in Detroit. In 1949, she became an employee of the local branch of the Civil Rights Congress (CRC), an organization that included prominent Communist leaders and led struggles against political repression and racism. Jack fused his black freedom movement work and CPUSA leadership and experienced some success in labor union organization with Ford autoworkers. Nonetheless, his formal leadership position in the Michigan Party became the basis for his future legal troubles. In Detroit, the couple confronted racism and political repression from the Red Squad, a division of the local police department assigned to monitor individuals whose politics appeared subversive. In a fashion similar to the post–World War I Red Scare, local police forces upheld the goals of the House Un-American Activities Committee (HUAC) by observing and raiding suspected Party-influenced groups. Red Squads typically exchanged information with the FBI, linking national and local anti-Communist efforts.[86] In their usual fashion, Esther and Jack refused to compromise their ideals to avoid political and legal troubles.

Jack used his platform within the Michigan Communist Party to speak out against white chauvinism, both as a long American tradition and as a problem within the Party. In fact, in the late 1940s, the Party made eliminating white chauvinism one of its central projects.[87] In spite of the Black

Belt thesis and the Party's effort to be cutting edge on issues of race, whites in and around the Party sometimes slipped into ingrained patterns of racial bias.[88] In a piece for the Michigan Communist Party news bulletin, Jack combated white leftists' shortcomings on race. He noted: "A stable feature of American life, has been the oppression of the Negro people. . . . We cannot underestimate the depth of chauvinist poison which has been part and parcel of the great American tradition." In addressing the Michigan Party, he suggested that white leftists were not immune to the problem and argued that Communist goals could not be achieved "unless we can force our own Party to a consciousness to daily struggle against every manifestation of white chauvinism, against all forms of oppression of the Negro people."[89] The Party's efforts to unravel its own chauvinism suggested some self-awareness that was a distinct result of the efforts of black Communists pushing the Party to embrace wide-ranging black freedom. Jack and others in the Party were well aware that even the most progressive among white leftists had to acknowledge and overcome cultural and institutional narratives that offered them privilege, and these patterns led to some tensions between black and white Communists.

The Party's efforts on issues of race were soon eclipsed by mounting Cold War political repression. In the postwar years, the CPUSA was beginning to redefine itself as it confronted mounting national opposition. Under the leadership of Earl Browder in 1944, the CPUSA became the Communist Political Association as part of an effort to end the Party's isolation in American politics. Browder hoped this move would help "explain our true relationship with all other democratic and progressive groupings which operate through . . . the two party system" and allow Party members to "take our place in true collaboration at their side." Browder, in the midst of a US-Soviet alliance targeted at defeating fascism, argued that capitalism and communism could peacefully coexist in the United States. The transition from Party to association was not well received, and it did not last long. A scathing article by the French Communist leader Jacques Duclos along with substantial domestic criticism of Browder led Communists to reestablish the organization as a political party shortly before the war ended. After World War II, the Party expelled Browder and, under the new leadership of William Z. Foster and Eugene Dennis, attempted to rebuild itself in the wake of increasing anti-

Communist sentiment across the country. As the historian Maurice Isserman writes: "Browder's successors in the [Party] leadership found their authority strengthened in the years after 1945 by the fact that, after all, Browder had clearly been proven wrong." "Peaceful coexistence between socialism and capitalism in international relations" was not possible.[90]

As anti-Communist hysteria began to pervade all areas of public life, social activism, and cultural expression, Foster led the Party under the "five minutes to midnight" slogan. The new line emerged from the Party's expectation that there would imminently be, as Isserman put it, a "new depression, the triumph of domestic fascism, and the outbreak of war between the United States and the Soviet Union." Whether or not doom really was the Party's fate, leaders prepared for the worst and effectively sealed their fate by mounting an ideological wall of defense. Though a more pragmatic attempt to integrate the Party into American politics might have salvaged some of its credibility, the opportunities to do so were growing increasingly scarce and would conflict with Foster's leadership in any case. In turn, when the leaders Benjamin Davis, Gus Hall, Henry Winston, Robert Thompson, Gil Green, William Z. Foster, John Gates, Eugene Dennis, Irving Potash, Jack Stachel, John Williamson, and Carl Winter were indicted under the Smith Act on July 20, 1948, the defense tactics the Party took further alienated it from the political mainstream. As Isserman argues: "Foster insisted that they undertake an active defense of their theoretical and political positions, rather than concentrating on civil liberties issues. As a result, the eleven defendants [Foster was tried separately] and their lawyers wound up in long, fruitless exchanges with the prosecution over the true meaning of passages in the works of Marx, Lenin, and Stalin—a strategy that brought neither legal nor political benefit."[91] Instead of arguing that the Smith Act constituted a form of political repression that was incompatible with democratic ideals, as some leaders later did, the Party in 1948 found itself explaining its philosophy to a hostile, unforgiving audience.

During this time, Jack maintained his internationalist focus in the black freedom movement and fused that with the goals of the Michigan Communist Party. In an official statement, the organization assailed Truman's Marshall Plan and his work to implement a universal military training program. Party leaders linked the government's promotion of democratic ideals abroad to the situation confronting African Americans at home. Truman, the Party argued, sought to implement a "draft and [universal military training] so that the Wall Street monopolists and military men who control the bi-partisan government in Washington would be 'free' to dominate the world." Because the government intended to use the Marshall Plan and universal military training to preserve peace and spread democracy, "we can't make the world safe for democracy without making democracy safe for 14 million Negro people at home."[92] The Party's attention to universal military training was connected to its critique of the diplomacy Truman used with the Soviet Union in the postwar years. The critique emerged from the language of World War II by highlighting the failure to achieve one of the two victories black and progressive Americans had fought for.

While the Party faced growing criticism, harassment, and repression from the government, it linked the black freedom movement and black internationalism with a scathing condemnation of US politics and diplomacy. The statement continued: "The Soviet Union and the new European democracies are leading the march of the people towards liberation of colonies, extension of democracy and socialism. They are therefore the friends and not the enemies of the American people."[93] Whereas most Americans viewed communism and democracy as mutually exclusive, the Michigan Communist Party saw the two as inextricably linked. That Communist governments worked on behalf of colonies seeking liberation led Party leaders to perceive the Soviet Union as in the vanguard of the global black freedom movement. Party activists, who had no political clout to lose, had no reservations about praising the Soviet Union as an example of global democracy. In years to come, such support and praise for Stalin's regime would continually haunt Party leaders.

The Party traveled in international political circles and saw its movement as a reflection of a global workers' struggle for democracy. Yet the early stages of the Cold War also led some leaders to attempt to reaffirm their patriotism as Americans. After the Detroit city council set out to establish a local loyalty board that would investigate city employees, Jack issued a statement on behalf of the Michigan Communist Party. He argued that the CPUSA was composed of loyal Americans, stating: "The Communist Party of the United States can trace its direct lineal development back 130 years in the history of the American working class struggle for bread. . . . The communists in word and deed are the most loyal fighters in the defense of the Constitution and Bill of Rights against all those jackals of reaction and fascism."[94] In defending Communists' national loyalty, Jack hoped to strike a blow against the anti-Communist postwar political backlash. In combination with the changing shape of the black freedom movement in the early Cold War years, his statement urged a reconsideration of all declarations about individuals' presumed disloyalty and a reevaluation of what made a person's political views patriotic or subversive. His position was a bit unusual as it came at a moment when the Party was moving further away from declaring its loyalty to the American political system, but it offered a counterpoint to the government's efforts to cast American communism as a monolith.

Jack believed that the 1948 indictment of the twelve national Party leaders emboldened Detroit and other cities to form loyalty boards. He declared that Detroit mayor Eugene Van Antwerp "in the tax payer's employ may have gained some boldness from the courageous conduct of the puny marionette on the bench at Foley Square."[95] The indictments and the rise in government-sponsored organizations dedicated to rooting Communists out of public life solidified the perceived criminality of communism. In spite of his message of loyal American communism, Jack's activism with the Michigan Communist Party became evidence against him in his own 1956 Smith Act trial.

Though Esther Cooper's formal affiliation with the Michigan Communist Party was as a member, not as a leader, the FBI construed her work with the CRC and the Progressive Party as worthy of close investigation. It had been monitoring her activities since the early 1940s, when she was an SNYC leader. The bureau listed her occupation from 1947 to 1948 as "housewife." Esther quickly struck a balance between raising two young daughters and being involved in political organizations, but she prioritized her children. In fact, motherhood might have saved her from a political setup by the FBI. In one instance in January 1948, an informant, working in collaboration with another individual known to investigators, tried to persuade her to speak about opposition to universal military training at an event. She refused because Kathryn was barely four months old at that time and she was not yet comfortable with leaving her for a speaking engagement. Later, in March, she did speak on universal military training on behalf of the Progressive Party at a Women's Rally for Peace.[96]

For Esther, working for the Progressive Party was a part of the natural progression of her politics. Though a member of the CPUSA, she strove to maintain her political independence and was never formally part of the Party's leadership structure in the way that her husband was.[97] She was a quintessential Popular Front activist, bringing Communist ideals with her without permitting her Marxism to overshadow the goals of other organizations. Nonetheless, her association with the Progressive Party helped the FBI further impugn her politics and her family. As an organizer for the local Progressive Party, Esther helped distribute leaflets and flyers on actions the government should take on antilynching, anti–poll tax, and pro–Fair Employment Practices Committee expansion legislation. The FBI noted that Esther "was included in the setting up of a [Communist Party] Steering Committee for the affairs of the Progressive Party."[98] She also worked with local black communities to rally support for Henry Wallace's Progressive Party campaign for the presidency.

Esther and Jack's wartime hopes included building a leftist coalition across the South in the postwar years through the NAACP, but their postwar positions on foreign policy and diplomacy isolated them from the most recognizable organization of the black freedom movement. During the 1948 election, the Wallace campaign against the Democrats realigned sectors of the black freedom movement, building the distinctions between the activist mainstream and the fringe in ways that would influence the direction of the civil rights movement. NAACP executive director Walter White argued that Wallace was a dupe of the CPUSA and would never be elected in spite of his own contention that civil rights was "*the* measuring rod by which candidates . . . will be judged." In the 1930s, the Department of Commerce under Secretary of Agriculture Wallace had actively worked for integration.[99] White's effort to distance himself and his organization from the politics of the Progressive Party reflected the NAACP's embrace of Cold War liberalism more than its racial politics, and this shift left progressive NAACP activists in the lurch. Even though the NAACP attempted to purge itself of Communists, it still faced Red-baiting and repression by both HUAC and southern authorities.

Esther's FBI investigators noted that she was an NAACP member as well as a Communist and Progressive Party activist, suggesting an association among the three.[100] Notations of her membership in a variety of distinct organizations in part reflected FBI efforts to disregard the distinctions between the mainstream black freedom movement and the political Left. What the bureau's notations neglected was that individuals like Esther could, and often did, hold multiple memberships in very different organizations without there being a direct collaboration among the organizations themselves. Esther's allegiances to organizations in conflict with one another reflected her political independence.

After Wallace's defeat in the 1948 election, Esther joined the CRC and worked for it briefly before the family moved to New York City. In the wake of a changing political backdrop, the CRC filled a void in leftist black activists' political lives. In 1946, the CRC grew out of the National Negro Congress, the International Labor Defense, and the National Federation for Constitutional Civil Liberties, and the government took immediate note of the organization's Communist influence.[101] Hoping to revisit their 1930s heyday when the Party won the admiration of blacks for its role in the Scottsboro defense, Communists encouraged the CRC to "become a defense organization fashioned along similar but broader lines than the now defunct International Labor Defense." The organization focused on egregious legal assaults against African Americans, particularly cases in which black men were falsely accused of raping white women. Though its goals were similar to those of the NAACP in the larger political scheme, including its advocacy of voting rights and its fight against housing and job discrimination, its inclusion of Communists distanced it from the association. The CRC leader William Patterson tried to assure the NAACP leader Roy Wilkins that his organization was nonpartisan and urged that the two organizations should unite, but "Wilkins was not buying."[102]

The historian Gerald Horne has suggested that the CRC sought to include women in leadership roles on an equal basis with men, but, from Esther's experience, it is clear that it did not quite provide the support that the SNYC had for activist mothers.[103] Esther lamented that she missed several important meetings for the CRC because of a "lack of cooperation . . . on the baby sitting problem" and said that she had taken the post only because the other CRC leaders had offered to help.[104] By early 1949, she was one of two full-time staff members for the Detroit CRC. Campaigns she promoted through the organization included the defense of the Trenton Six, Rosa Lee Ingram, and the initial twelve Communist leaders indicted under the Smith Act.[105]

Esther saw the CRC as an outlet for her racial activism and hoped it could remain an independent political organization. Though the CRC and the Michigan Communist Party were aligned in many political scenarios, she was frustrated that "there was a lack of understanding shown by Party members on the fact that the Communist Party and the CRC are two distinct organizations."[106] By working between the groups, she likely hoped each would benefit equally from their mutual association. Esther was adept at reinforcing the Popular Front notion that an organization's association with the Party was not always subversive but could be efficacious and was sometimes even coincidental. Her complaint to the informant likely bolstered the bureau's case against the Party, reifying the image of it as a virus that overtook anything in proximity. The FBI was interested neither in distinguishing between the CRC and the Party nor in giving credence to Esther's efforts to do so.

As an individual, Esther outwardly defied the rising anti-Communist anxiety in her political expression during her time in Detroit. Her activism reflected her Popular Front–informed ability to distinguish between and navigate different organizations with similar goals. Her work also separated her political views from her husband's, although the FBI, and even, occasionally, the Party, saw her as a Communist first and a mother, wife, and activist in other organizations second. Esther and Jack had developed open and respectful lines of communication through their wartime correspondence, and, though they had differences of opinion, they did not create a deep divide within their marriage.

Cold War politics defined individuals like Esther and Jack and organizations like the SNYC, the Progressive Party, and the CRC by their proximity to the CPUSA, not by their political goals. In the increasingly tense political climate of the late 1940s, Esther and Jack decided it would be best to move to New York City, and, in 1950, they settled in Brooklyn. There, Jack planned to work full-time for the national CPUSA, and the pair planned to raise their daughters in what they hoped would be a more open-minded city. Unfortunately, shortly after moving to New York, Jack was included in the second round of Smith Act indictments. The vision the couple shared for their postwar future on that dock in New York as Esther returned from Europe was short-lived, but their determination to fight for change was unceasing. For Esther and Jack, resisting the government's efforts to paint Communist and progressive goals as subversive was full-time work ingrained in their black freedom activism and self-preservation. Their goals persisted as they encountered their most difficult political challenge: Jack's 1951 indictment and subsequent disappearance into the CPUSA's underground.

4

Family and the Black Freedom Movement in the Early Cold War Years

On June 20, 1951, Jack disappeared, and four-year-old Kathy's nightmares became reality. Her mother's hand would tighten around hers when they spotted FBI agents in dark trench coats and fedoras as they walked in their Brooklyn neighborhood. Her mother's normally pleasant Virginia accent turned harsh when she picked up the telephone and heard an unfamiliar voice. Fully suited men watching her play in the summertime proved an uncomfortable and awkward experience for Kathy. These FBI agents so terrified her when they approached her on the streets that she refused to let her mother leave her side after interacting with them.[1] She asked her mother: "They can't put little children in jail, can they?" Her big sister, eight-year-old Harriet, was tougher. She could draw strength from memories of her father that Kathy had not yet acquired. Harriet was more accustomed to the kinds of turmoil the children of activist parents faced, and she "contemptuously pointed [the FBI agents] out to her playmates."[2] Esther could not answer her younger daughter's questions about where her father went or when he would be back, most simply because she, like other wives of disappeared Communist husbands, did not know. She could only explain that he had vanished because he was trying to make a better future for his daughters and children across the country and the people in charge wanted to stop him.

Kathy quickly learned that the nation's highest law enforcement officers did not concern themselves with her protection. Rather, they were out to scare little children into betraying their families, haunt their imaginations, and let them know that, whatever their fathers had done wrong, the children would pay the price. As Esther believed: "[The agents were] particularly vindictive toward us because we're Negroes."[3] She and her family had left the Deep South in 1947, their efforts to change the racial order having been met with both a white supremacist and an anti-Communist backlash. On arriving and becoming active in Detroit, Esther had

123

witnessed the way anticommunism in a northern city shaped the experiences of its black residents, who sought to improve their political and economic conditions through union organization and protest. By the time she and her family moved to New York City in 1950 and her husband disappeared a year later, Esther fully understood the consequences of the early stages of the Cold War and McCarthyism on the black freedom movement and on her family's well-being.

Tangled notions of liberal democracy in the early 1950s resulted in the undemocratic treatment of the families of Communists and fellow travelers and had a particular influence on the way activists approached the black freedom movement. The domestic effects of Cold War politics shaped the black freedom movement specifically by shaping the family lives of black activists. For Esther and her two daughters, the early Cold War years represented an era of unparalleled fear and repression, but the injustice of the period motivated and empowered Esther to continue to work for change. Her efforts to defend her husband's political rights and protect her family's welfare were not only linked to each other but also an essential component of the black freedom movement and the activist ideology the Jacksons had developed over the course of their lives.

Esther employed the democratic idea of family and the changing black freedom movement to seek justice for her husband. In an era when images of idealized nuclear families reinforced anti-Communist liberalism, she exposed the devastating effect political repression had on her family. In addition, Jack's disappearance and the subsequent treatment of his family were symptomatic of a larger change in the struggle against racial injustice. In other words, the way in which the United States undermined the Left in the black freedom movement during the early Cold War years shaped the particular form of civil rights activism that gained popularity in the late 1950s. The Jackson family's experiences tell that story.

On June 20, 1951, Jack was indicted under the Smith Act for "conspiracy to teach or advocate the violent overthrow of the government." The Smith Act, a peacetime sedition law, was originally passed in 1940 as the Alien Registration Act. It allowed the government to pursue activists who discussed "overthrowing the government by 'force and violence'" and deport "aliens who had once belonged to an organization that advocated force and violence."[4] Instead of standing trial immediately in a potentially dangerous political climate, Jack went underground until 1956, and his family became victims of constant FBI harassment. Esther, who took her husband's last name after ten years of marriage in order to support him, led efforts for his defense by working with the Families Committee of Smith Act Victims and the National Committee to Defend Negro Leadership (NCDNL). She did not know where her husband was and had no contact with him for the five years they were apart. The period was terrifyingly uncertain, and Esther recalls that she focused on preserving stability for her daughters and fighting for her husband to survive and maintain her sanity.

Popular Front politics had reached their nadir by the time Jack was indicted. Since World War II, acting on radical ideas had become increasingly difficult in the United States. Loyalty oath programs led government employees to hide questionable political affiliations or face removal from their positions. Twelve top-tier Communist Party leaders had already been indicted, tried, and convicted over the course of 1948 and 1949. Two years later, the Supreme Court upheld their convictions in *Dennis v. United States* (1951), a ruling that prompted Jackson and others to become fugitives.[5] In Birmingham, a former center of the southern Popular Front civil rights movement, the city commission "unanimously passed an ordinance on July 18, 1950, that decreed the outlawing of the Communist Party and all liberal and progressive organizations." The ordinance was not unique to the Magic City; similar local laws gained popularity in Gary, Indiana; Peoria, Illinois; Chattanooga, Tennessee; Atlanta, Georgia; and other major and minor industrial hubs across the country.[6]

One progressive organization distributed a fact sheet emphasizing the ordinance's negative impact on civil rights organizing in Birmingham by pointing out that it was first introduced by Police Commissioner Eugene "Bull" Connor. Connor had already gained notoriety in Birmingham for his role in the demise of the Southern Negro Youth Congress (SNYC). The fact sheet connected Connor's racism to anticommunism, stating: "For the past several years police killings of Negro citizens in Birmingham has [*sic*] averaged 16 to 19 annually. . . . The Ku Klux Klan operates boldly under the umbrella of Connor's Dixiecrat protection. Connor started his tenure of office in the 1930s by attempting to stop the organizing drive of the CIO. In his recent unsuccessful campaign for governor of Alabama, he based his appeal on anti-Negro and anti-Communist prejudice. . . . It aims at giving the lynchers carte blanche."[7]

In the South, conservative forces linked the Communist Party's long effort to court black activists with the fight against Jim Crow, driving the Popular Front's civil rights organizing and unionization efforts out of business.[8] The connection between anticommunism and racism went beyond Party-influenced groups as well, forcing moderate and liberal civil rights activists to downplay any economic solution to racial problems. White supremacists equated access to equal opportunities across racial lines with communism and appropriated the new context of the Cold War to uphold segregation. While there were some radical groups that remained active, including the Southern Conference Educational Fund, organizations across the Left were weakened.[9] Coupled with the indictments of Communist leaders and the nationwide panic over any form of social critique that remotely resembled socialism, even activists who had no direct ties with the Communist Party often faded into quiet conformity.

Many histories of the effect of the early Cold War years on activists focus on individuals with loose ties to Communist-influenced organizations or on those who plainly refused to cooperate with political repression. Hollywood writers and actors, outspoken newspaper editors, union organizers, gays and lesbians, and individuals who had been involved in an array of civil rights and Popular Front activism were questioned and persecuted for their political ideals and social positions.[10] FBI director J. Edgar Hoover wrote that each of these groups was susceptible to Communist "thought control." He argued: "The result of this manipulation, as applied to diverse personalities, groups, and issues, is a tribute to the communists' deceitful skill. By this technique, using its own membership as a base, the Party today is influencing literally thousands of Americans."[11]

Hoover and the FBI also targeted people who had once been members of the Communist Party but had since withdrawn. The British immigrant Cedric Belfrage, the longtime editor of the leftist newspaper the *National Guardian,* was deported along with his ex-wife for his political beliefs and for his paper's uncompromising support for political and civil liberties. His daughter wrote in her memoir of the 1950s: "The minute anybody becomes a truly unspeakable pariah, you can bet my father's in there sticking up for them." In spite of those who believed that the *Guardian* was "a propaganda arm of the Kremlin," Belfrage and the paper were often in conflict with the Communist Party USA (CPUSA). Belfrage wrote: "[The CPUSA's] private war against us . . . was waged vigorously. . . . The going was rough with the political group that we had resolved to defend as a matter of principle, but we were surer than ever of the principle: keeping our eye on the real enemy." He was deported in 1955 for working with organizations considered subversive while he was "an alien."[12] Evidence against him included a Hollywood screenwriter's assertion that he knew Belfrage was a Communist in 1937 and that he had traveled to Russia during the 1930s on several occasions.

Others were similarly firm about their democratic right to hold minority political positions, and, while the strategy was risky and often costly, some were able to use the dynamics of the period to promote their careers. Black writers, artists, and performers saw opportunities to express their political ideals in a cultural format within the Left. As Mary Helen Washington writes: "The Left offered black writers the institutional support that they could get nowhere else in white America." She argues that black artists and writers continued to resist in the hostile 1950s and that, in spite of the legal obstacles, personal persecution, and trauma they encountered, the era was "a dynamic, exciting period of debate, a moment when the Black Left continued to work despite the pressures of the Cold War."[13] Since the Left had routinely been more open to black cultural expression than was the mainstream, its role in promoting black art as the mainstream grew more restrictive is exceptional but unsurprising.

Some members of the black Left fared better than others. Canada Lee, the black actor best known for his portrayal of Bigger Thomas in *Native Son,* died in 1952 of kidney failure. Some of his close friends and family attributed his illness to the stress of being blacklisted. He had lost some work as a performer because of his political affiliations. The *New York Herald Tribune* wrote that, while he "stoutly denied" being a Communist, he had "lent his name in the past to some organizations which appeared subsequently on the Attorney General's subversive list": "But he declared that he had done so only because they were anti-Nazi or anti-fascist groups and were 'working for the civil rights of my people.'"[14] As were those of many others who faced persecution in the early years of the Cold War, Lee's politics were similar to most progressive activists' in the Depression and World War II eras. In the 1950s, Esther and Jack endured the trauma of being targeted by the FBI but survived precisely because they remained committed to their ideals and found rare avenues for their expression.

As the historian Andrea Friedman points out, many of McCarthyism's victims were not serious, career Communists but individuals with a casual interest in an organization who might have attended a few meetings or paid occasional dues. Annie Lee Moss, a black cafeteria worker in Washington, DC, whose House Un-American Activities Committee (HUAC) inquiry was televised on Edward R. Morrow's *See It Now*, was most likely "attracted [to communism] by its social and economic justice politics." Moss, like many others who faced or feared persecution for their politics, did little beyond expressing sympathy and solidarity for ideals that she had developed during the Great Depression and World War II. By the time of her HUAC investigation, she felt it necessary to deny understanding even the basics of communism despite her prior activism with community organizations and unions. This tactic not only distanced her from the intellectual and theoretical underpinnings of a movement scorned: it pegged her as a pitiable pawn. She appeared to be not a politically empowered agent but a mere dupe who fell for an abstract promise of equality.[15] This method of responding to McCarthyism generated sympathy for the presumably innocent victims of government harassment. It also points to the extent of the fear of communism and the scope of the FBI's reach into the lives of ordinary citizens.

The Party leaders bore more guilt in the eyes of the public than did celebrities and other individuals who were simply guilty by association. After all, they were charged with violating a specific law, the Smith Act, and were seen as responsible for, as J. Edgar Hoover put it, "[trying] to poison our thinking about the issues of the day: social reforms, peace, politics, veterans', women's, and youth problems."[16] It was not difficult for Hoover, Joseph McCarthy, and others to rally support around the Smith Act. In September 1949, the Soviet Union detonated its first atomic bomb. On June 25, 1950, Soviet-equipped North Korea invaded US-backed South Korea, making the peninsula the first hot spot of the Cold War. The US military responded with a "police action" that lasted for more than three years.[17] In addition, many associated the leadership of the CPUSA with the nation's worst fear: atomic espionage. In a concrete example, the trial and execution of Julius and Ethel Rosenberg from 1950 to 1953 reminded Americans that they stood on the brink of disaster because of homegrown Communists.

Jack had become southern regional director of the Communist Party in 1949. By virtue of the fact that nearly all Party activities were outlawed and stigmatized, he and his fellow CPUSA leaders were easy targets for the government's crusade against domestic subversion. His indictment for "conspiracy to teach or advocate the overthrow of the government by force or violence," however, does not accurately characterize his position. His political ideas grew out of his upbringing, his exposure to people of varying social and economic circumstances, and his passion for the black freedom movement. He advocated changing the way the United States operated on behalf of its citizens. While his commitment to the Party in the face of some of its most disastrous political moves necessitates critique, he did not suggest force or violence as a means for unraveling the existing power structure.

As Gil Green, one of the Communist Party leaders prosecuted in the first round of trials, declared: "We were not even charged with actual teaching and advocacy, only with conspiring—that is, agreeing—to do so. And the conspiracy consisted (according to the government) of our being members and leaders of the Communist Party and believing and teaching the social theory of Marxism-Leninism." Drawing on the CPUSA's defense strategy of explaining Marxist-Leninist theory, Green argued:

As we saw it, socialism would come to this country as the end result of a long, difficult, and many sided struggle to extend democratic rights—economic, political, and social. . . . [W]e held that the victory of such a new political force could bring about major social and economic reforms aimed at so curbing the excessive power of the corporate ultra-rich that, in time, a relatively peaceful transition to a socialist society could be made. Violence had no place in our projection, though we warned of the danger that violence would be used by entrenched power to thwart the will of the majority.

The concepts that Green described do not match the charges against him. But, at the height of the Cold War, rumors about the Soviet Union's power—that the Red Army could travel through Alaska and Canada to obliterate Detroit and so on—generated such fear of communism as an ideology that none of the indicted leaders stood a chance of a fair trial.[18]

The twelve Communist Party leaders who were initially convicted under the Smith Act were awaiting sentencing when the indictments of 126 "second-string" Communist leaders came up in 1951.[19] The hostile political atmosphere intensified when the Supreme Court upheld the initial convictions in *Dennis v. United States*. The decision led the Communist Party leadership to create the "second cadre," which would operate underground and include some of the high-level leaders facing prosecution and prison. Of the initial twelve who were sentenced, only seven—Benjamin Davis Jr., Eugene Dennis, John Gates, Irving Potash, Jack Stachel, John Williamson, and Carl Winter—appeared immediately to serve their time. William Z. Foster's case had been severed from the original twelve because of his failing health. The remaining four—Gus Hall, Robert Thompson, Henry Winston, and Gil Green—went underground and were known by the CPUSA community as *unavailables*. Among the second-stringers, Fred Fine, William Norman Marron, Sidney Steinberg, and James Jackson "had not been at home when the FBI showed up."[20] They disappeared before standing trial.

The FBI launched a massive search for the missing men. News reports urged citizens "to join in the intense manhunt for the eight Communist leaders." Every democracy-loving American was "in a position to assist the FBI in locating and capturing the Red fugitives." Party leadership believed that creating the second cadre to operate underground was a viable, if difficult, alternative to having so many top leaders incarcerated. While its detractors viewed the move as confirmation that a conspiracy was under way, the Communist Party itself saw the heightened political repression as fascist. As Gil Green put it: "With the war still on in Korea, the atomic spy scare, the frenzy to outlaw the Party, we cannot exclude a further growth of reaction."[21] Putting some of the indicted and convicted key Communists into the second cadre meant that, if the remaining leadership faced indictment or incarceration in the increasingly hostile political environment, a group of experienced Party functionaries could remain in covert action.

While the Party never recovered from the McCarthy years—in part as a result of its own actions—the second cadre and their families made reasoned political moves in the McCarthy era given their situations. The Jacksons had envisioned a postwar world in which they would be able to unite the South under a left-wing, interracial, labor-oriented National Association for the Advancement of Colored People (NAACP). They imagined the Double Victory campaign would be realized through socialist-influenced economic reform, political equality, and social integration. The wartime alliance with the Soviet Union would continue, and the harnessing of nuclear power for peaceful means would allow for limitless productivity and reduced capitalist competition. It appeared to many Communists that a golden age was approaching. While they knew it would not be without difficulties, few anticipated the conservative backlash that drove so many of them underground. The second cadre and its support system of wives, children, and extended family served to keep alive some of the hope of the World War II years.

For the families of the second cadre, McCarthyism introduced an era of fear that was worlds apart from the anxiety about communism most Americans felt. The FBI waged a "war of nerves" against the families of Smith Act defendants.[22] Tactics included surveillance, harassment, subtle threats, and actual interference in family members' abilities to sustain their incomes, homes, cars, and any semblance of a normal life. The trauma thus inflicted was so profound and immediate that Kathy Jackson would later go on to write a dissertation on the psychological consequences of this war of nerves.[23] These tactics proved ineffective at information gathering and did not lead to the apprehension of any of the unavailables. But harassing family members caused psychological damage and made the FBI appear to the public to be making progress toward halting an underground army of Communists ready to overthrow the US government. Still, FBI harassment engendered substantial opposition from activist groups on the Left, and these groups were often composed of friends, family, and acquaintances of the unavailables. Esther and other activists recast questions of political affiliation and national loyalty as issues of race, gender, and class coercion that were contrary to the nuclear family–oriented language of liberal postwar democracy.

The rhetoric of family life, suburban bliss, and the comfort of traditional gender roles characterized portrayals of democracy in the early Cold War years. Divorce rates dropped along with the average age of marriage, suburbs expanded, and birth rates increased. For white Americans, an attainable suburban ideal emerged because of better mortgage opportunities, new housing developments, and widespread availability. American workers saw wages rise as the Great Depression ended, and labor unions saw success. Residential segregation, however, excluded black Americans from much of the postwar suburban dream. While black women were not represented in expressions of this new American ideal, they still had to contend with the cultural expectations for women and with aspirations for middle-class normativity.[24]

The government also employed these new gender constructions in its ideological war on communism. In 1956, FBI director J. Edgar Hoover declared that in the fight against "crime and communism . . . there are no careers as important as those of homemaker and mother." This assertion was rooted in a solidly middle-class analysis, as it assumed that mothers could afford not to have a career other than homemaker. Vice President Richard Nixon echoed that sentiment in 1959 during his "Kitchen Debate" with Soviet premier Nikita Khrushchev when he stated that America's effort "to make easier the life of our housewives" was a common and democratic ideal across the globe.[25] Targeting the suburban middle class's gender ideals became a simple way for politicians to gain support for their side in a complex ideological struggle.

In the eyes of law enforcement and the mainstream public, Jack and his comrades' political ideologies overshadowed their family devotion. How could these men, who had abandoned their families and fled from justice, share any democratic ideals with average Americans, whose capitalist consumption represented their political stance and their family values? Jack's alleged crime and disappearance were portrayed as a heinous assault on democracy, and his family became a unique tool in both the FBI's pursuit of him and his defense. Although his family did not see or hear from him for nearly five years, the FBI left no member of the extended Jackson and Cooper families alone. In spite of the federal government's emphasis on nuclear families as a line of defense against the Soviets, the FBI's work actively undermined the presence of family commitment and values in Communist nuclear families.

The FBI's strategy of perpetual harassment was intended to force family members to admit contact with a fugitive or force the fugitives out of hiding to spare their families any psychological trauma. Or perhaps it was believed that tormenting children would turn families against the unavailables, breaking their loyalty by implicitly suggesting that the fugitives were, themselves, disloyal. Keeping in close proximity to the families of unavailables illustrated to the public that the FBI was being persistent in its quest for the missing Communists. Yet many family members of the unavailables protested these tactics, first, because they were both unable and unwilling to inform on their loved ones and, second, because the tactics were plainly unjust. Esther, like many other Smith Act victim family members, believed that political ideals and the future of her family were intimately connected. Jack's disappearance was not a question of family versus political party. Instead, the Jacksons viewed the move as necessary in the face of mounting persecution and justified the turmoil their family endured by arguing that they were creating a better world for their daughters to live in.

The FBI spent nearly $1 million a year maintaining staff to tail Smith Act families. Agents regularly forced their way into homes, intimidated neighbors, and destroyed their victims' abilities to maintain jobs. In one instance, Fred Fine's six-year-old son Larry was targeted in his classroom. Agents followed the family all the time, taking photos and forbidding them any privacy. One day, Larry Fine's principal came into his class with an FBI agent and asked the teacher to point the child out. His mother, Doris, commented: "As if they didn't know what he looked like! They took enough pictures of him this summer—yes, and his playmates too—they had him afraid to go out of the cottage where we were staying. Maybe they went to his classroom because they expected to find his father under his desk! No, they just wanted to frighten him some more." She continued: "They think they can break us down this way and make us tell them where our husbands are. As if we knew!" Agents used intimidation tactics with adults connected to these children as well. Smith Act children were routinely denied admission to summer camps because camp administrators feared an FBI presence would frighten other children.[26]

The FBI also inflicted financial difficulty on the wives of second cadre members. Lillian Green faced harassment at work and in her everyday life. The FBI also contacted her car insurance company, which subsequently canceled her policy. Without insurance, Green saw little point in keeping the car and decided to sell it for some much-needed income. The FBI caught wind of the potential sale and intimidated prospective buyers, and, when Green finally brought someone to see the car, "she found a large spoke imbedded in a tire."[27] She could neither keep nor sell the car.

Beyond these covert tactics, the FBI used outright threats. For Green, the threat came when she was looking after her three children and her brother's two children at a summer cottage. FBI agents entered the cottage, and, after Green implored them to leave, they refused, saying: "We don't use guns much . . . but sometimes a man we're hunting gets shot. Now you wouldn't want that to happen to your husband, would you?"[28] Jack's mother, Clara, received a similarly threatening call from FBI agents. After telling them repeatedly that she did not know where her son was, agents pressed harder. "Supposing your husband were to drop dead tonight, how would you get in touch with your son to let him know?" they asked.[29] While they did not directly threaten to harm James Jackson Sr., the menacing call itself suggested to Clara Jackson that the FBI might go to even greater lengths to ferret the fugitives out of hiding.

In response to FBI harassment, the families of the unavailables formed the Families Committee of Smith Act Victims. The organization was composed predominantly of women whose husbands faced prosecution, and they worked, as the sociologist Deborah Gerson notes, "to give financial, material, and emotional assistance to the children and spouses of the Smith Act victims and the prisoners themselves." Gerson argues: "The Families Committee resisted state repression with a strategy that made use of the valorization of family. The alliance between patriotism and familialism was challenged by women who pointed to the state as the destroyer of family freedom, security, and happiness." Gerson also suggests that the Families Committee provided Communist wives and mothers with an opportunity to become more politically empowered by taking hold of their families' fates.[30]

The historian Kate Weigand's work on the CPUSA and the women's movement points to a gap between the lives of Party wives and Party gender ideology. While the CPUSA's position on "the Woman Question" called for gender equity and opposition to male chauvinism, many Communist men had difficulty treating their wives as equals. After the war, when the Party began to discuss the Woman Question further, Party women believed that they would make strides in achieving their liberation. However: "The demanding realities of family life during the postwar baby boom quickly brought many young Communist women to the realization that as wives—and especially as mothers—their ability to participate in the political and social life of their Party was actually more restricted than before."[31] Nonetheless, in an atmosphere of escalating Cold War tension, some Party women found an avenue for activism in caring for families and within the confines of normative gender roles. The establishment of the Families Committee transformed the ideas of maternal responsibility into a liberating political force for Party women.

Race also gave meaning to Esther's political activism on behalf of her family. The historian Ruth Feldstein writes that, in the 1950s, it was "through [the] rendering of politics as personal and psychological that the 'good' and 'bad' mother—black and white—did political work in the reconfiguration of liberalism." Esther confronted cultural expectations that required a good black mother to be a loyal wife, a patriotic citizen, emotional, and active on behalf of her race.[32] These ideals conflicted in her situation. She could not be construed as simultaneously patriotic and loyal to her husband, who had fled the justice system. She could not exemplify patriotism and remain active on behalf of her race through organizations that supported her loyalty to her fugitive husband. Her children needed a mother who was strong and composed, not effusively emotional. Esther navigated the cultural requirements for a black wife and mother as a victim of government harassment and as an activist who fought for a United States that embodied its own rhetoric of democracy.

The FBI's assault on the Jackson family was not only contrary to the "valorization of family" but also a hindrance to many other progressive movements. For the Jacksons, the Communist Party offered a path to racial justice and had long been an essential component of the black free-dom movement. Though Esther acknowledged the importance of the postwar civil rights advancements organized by the NAACP, she also saw her unique family circumstances as indicative of widespread setbacks in progressive movements.

Esther's increasingly distant relationship with mainstream civil rights organizations like the NAACP was shaped by the early Cold War years. The NAACP never worked with the CPUSA on an organizational level and never sought to radically overhaul the government. The Scottsboro case offers one stark illustration of the conflict that existed between the two groups as early as the 1930s. The NAACP and the leftist organiza-tions also clashed over the handling of other, similar incidents in the late 1940s and the 1950s. For example, Willie McGee was charged with rap-ing a white woman in 1945, the white woman he was having an affair with having claimed rape after her husband discovered the relationship. The left-wing Civil Rights Congress (CRC) came to his defense, and the NAACP steered clear of the case. The Supreme Court refused to hear his appeal, and he was executed on May 8, 1951. The Martinsville Seven, another group of young black men, were also executed in 1951 for rap-ing a white woman. Again, it was the CRC and not the NAACP that mounted the men's defense, but they had confessed to police officers, and the case was unwinnable. In 1951, W. E. B. Du Bois and the CRC leader William Patterson issued the report "We Charge Genocide" to the United Nations, noting the Martinsville Seven and many other black men who were subject to racial violence, lynching, and unjust executions in the United States.[33] The NAACP took a far more tepid and cautious approach to these situations, choosing to focus on legal challenges to segregation instead. The organization's national prominence nonethe-less drew black activists from a wide array of political positions, including Communists.

In the 1930s, the NAACP advocated policies that would benefit poor people of all races. Concern with issues of poverty aligned it politically with the CPUSA but also connected it with many federal New Deal pro-grams, reflecting its long-standing pattern of working within existing political structures. In other words, the situation created by the sheer eco-nomic despair of the Great Depression required solutions that addressed the issue of poverty, and a wide array of organizations, along with the federal government, responded to that need. Rather than championing its position as one of interracial working-class unity like Popular Front organizations did, the NAACP advocated its policies as integrationist. The distinction illustrated that it saw African Americans not "as part of an exploited working class . . . [but] as an oppressed racial minority."[34] Many black activists saw powerful, promising, and effective elements in both the NAACP and the CPUSA, and the Popular Front had allowed them to engage ideas from both organizations in ways that suited their goals.

In the postwar years, the NAACP needed to distinguish itself from the Left. It was part of many progressive activists' résumés, but in order to keep functioning as a liberal organization it followed suit with the government's embodiment of Cold War liberalism. It had always distanced itself from Communist ideas and embraced the distinctions between itself and the CPUSA, but never was it more important to highlight those differences than in the early Cold War years. Its recent purge of Communists from its ranks highlights that division. As the McCarthy era took hold, black activists who had worked toward civil rights in the Popular Front years needed to choose between groups that incorporated Marxist influence and groups that worked within the existing political system, like the NAACP. The path between no longer existed.[35] When Jack went underground, Esther saw his absence and the assault on his Communist political ideals as detrimental to the black freedom movement. While the NAACP's postwar achievements were significant, she believed that the greatest opportunity to defend her husband and the struggle for racial equality existed in groups that fought the dominant political rejection of communism instead of embracing it.

To Esther, the FBI's tactics were an assault on an ideal of American family and on the black freedom movement. Joining forces with the Families Committee and the NCDNL, Esther created through her work a nexus between the two movements. The black freedom movement in the early Cold War years and the movement to protect the families of persecuted activists could not have been more relevant to one another, and, in highlighting this, Esther illustrated the contradictions between the federal government's enforcement of civil rights and its pursuit of political fugitives. The time and money that the FBI devoted to harassing Smith

Act families in the name of democracy were counterbalanced by the federal agency's limited resources when it came to enforcing equal justice, a powerful symbol of that very democracy. The investigation of the murder of the civil rights leader Harry T. Moore provides a case in point. Esther demonstrated the contradiction between the FBI's inconsequential Moore investigation and its constant harassment of her family. In the process, she attempted to connect the welfare of her children with the advancement of the black freedom movement.

On Christmas night in 1951, after the Florida state NAACP leader Harry T. Moore and his family had gone to sleep in the small town of Mims, an explosion rocked the household. It was loud enough to be heard four miles away. The bomb had been placed underneath the house by members of the Ku Klux Klan, and Moore and his wife died of injuries sustained in the blast, Moore that same night on the way to the hospital, his wife a day after his funeral. Though the explosion jolted neighbors out of bed, bombings had become a common occurrence in Florida in 1951. Between August and Christmas of that year, twelve separate bundles of dynamite had delivered "the Florida Terror" to a black housing project, synagogues, Catholic churches, a black high school, and a white-owned ice cream shop, to name a few. Any individual or group that fought for social justice, racial equality, or progressive change in Florida came to fear the Ku Klux Klan's retributive violence.[36]

Most people who commented on the murder agreed that Moore's role in the defense of three young black men accused of raping a white woman was the impetus for the bombing. In a 1949 incident that would prove to be just one example in an ongoing pattern of police violence stemming from racial tensions, a Groveland, Florida, seventeen-year-old white girl alleged that four young black men had abducted and raped her. A doctor who examined her declared that her accusations were false. One of the accused, Ernest Thomas, fled the scene and was shot over a week after the incident. The three remaining young men were known as "Florida's Little Scottsboro," and their case drew national attention. The white community in Groveland rioted in the aftermath of the rape charge, burning black neighborhoods and attacking their residents. Moore led efforts to rally the nation around the Groveland Boys and to quell the violence, arguing: "Incidents like these play right into the hands of the communists. . . . [W]e cannot successfully defend ourselves against communist propaganda unless we subdue such undemocratic practices as the recent mob violence in Lake County."[37] The Groveland three were quickly convicted by an all-white jury, but the Supreme Court ordered a new trial on procedural grounds.[38] On November 6, 1951, Sheriff Willis McCall shot two of the defendants on their way to the retrials, bringing the tension surrounding the case to new heights. In response, Moore implored that McCall be suspended and indicted for murder.[39]

The attention Moore received for his vocal critique of the Groveland situation paled in comparison to the attention given to his murder. For a short while, the entire country was in an uproar. The international press editorialized on the murder. The violence in Florida became a tool for North Korean soldiers, who used racial injustice in the United States to interrogate and break down black prisoners of war. Eleanor Roosevelt acknowledged: "The harm it will do to us among the people of the world is untold."[40]

For the FBI to get involved in the case, proof was needed that the murder was a product of the violation of Moore's civil rights or that state or county officials had been involved. Without such proof, J. Edgar Hoover hesitated to intervene but quickly realized that the FBI's reputation was on the line. Hoover, who preferred to work by the book, needed to set aside his reservations in order to appease a public on the verge of outrage. Initially, two agents arrived on the scene, and, eventually, a dozen agents set to work on the case. For Hoover, "a civil rights case with tremendous political and public relations repercussions" meant that jurisdictional concerns needed to be set aside in the interest of solving the case.[41] Its official presence did not mean the FBI was visible in the community, however. Although twelve agents were officially assigned to the case, one researcher who visited the area noted: "No FBI agents were to be found in the community."[42]

Harry T. Moore's murder occurred at a distinct moment in black freedom movement history. Moore rose to prominence in the late 1930s, becoming the Brevard County NAACP director in 1934, organizing the state NAACP conference in 1941, and becoming the paid state executive secretary in 1946. In 1944, he organized the Progressive Voter's League (PVL), which served as an unofficial political offshoot of the NAACP geared at voter registration and black political empowerment. Although Moore was moderate in his own political practices, he earned the respect of groups like the SNYC. The persecution he confronted for his political activities resembled the anti-Communist persecution that activists further to the left also faced. In 1946, he was fired from a teaching job because he was "a trouble maker and negro organizer."[43] After a while he also faced substantial opposition from the national leadership of the NAACP for his endorsement of Democratic political candidates and his allegedly divisive politics in the PVL. The NAACP held him responsible for the drop in membership in Florida and ousted him as its leader a month before his murder.

At the time of the murder, the black freedom movement was in a period of transition, moving toward the liberal position that would characterize the civil rights years. The Popular Front had clearly met its demise, and the modes of acceptable protest were changing. Though Moore was no Communist and not even a fellow traveler, his outspoken, uncompromising style was more dangerous than the NAACP could bear to risk. His significant power in Florida's black community symbolized a potential for change that Florida whites needed to quell. The repression of black leadership in the early 1950s occurred in tandem with the increasing momentum of the anti-Communist backlash. In Florida, as in much of the South, there was a coalition between these two movements. Anticommunism and segregationism went hand-in-hand.[44] While Moore's political positions tended to be more aligned with liberalism, his death generated solidarity across what remained of Left and radical political organizations. His murder inspired a response from the CRC, the CPUSA, the Socialist Workers Party, and the American Labor Party.[45] For organizations facing political persecution, his death symbolized the decline of civil and political liberty.

The FBI was a quiet presence in Mims after the murder. National NAACP executive secretary Walter White investigated as well, and he offered the leads he discovered to the FBI. The bureau made little information public and eventually faced severe criticism for its inability to apprehend the killers. At the 1952 NAACP convention in Oklahoma City, delegates passed a resolution singling out the FBI for its failure in the Moore case, asserting that it was "almost invariably unable to cope with violent criminal action by bigoted, prejudiced Americans against Negro Americans." In the face of this criticism, the FBI apprehended several Orlando Klan members, who were indicted on June 3, 1953, for a variety of terrorist acts, but "no mention was made of the Moore bombing except for the fact that it had been investigated." The defendants' lawyer, a Klansman, argued the jurisdictional issue, and the indictments were dismissed on January 11, 1954. The Moore case faded from memory.[46]

For Esther, who found herself in the summer of 1951 without her husband's financial and emotional support and with no idea when he would return, the FBI's failure in the Moore case was especially noteworthy. Never the type of woman who feared independence, she secured a part-time job and set out to enroll four-year-old Kathy in nursery school. Kathy was admitted to Cleveland Day Nursery in Brooklyn, but within two months she was expelled because her mother allegedly had "undisclosed sources of income."[47] Esther was unable to ascertain the source of this allegation and could only assume that the FBI agents who had hounded her family since June were to blame. She wrote: "Unable to locate their father, the FBI has decided to take it out on the children and wife."[48] In a letter to the editor of the otherwise unidentified *Union,* she connected her family's harassment to the Moore situation in Florida:

A month has passed and still no arrests in the Christmas night murder of Mr. and Mrs. Harry T. Moor [*sic*]! A month in which the authorities say an investigation is still taking place yet nothing of significance has been issued by the FBI or the Department of Justice. . . . Why are they so silent? Is it because they are busy elsewhere hounding the families of those very people whose life has been devoted to the things Harry Moor stood for—justice, equality and freedom? . . . This F.B.I. which utilizes great power and authority to hound young Negro children finds no funds or manpowers to unearth the killers of my people![49]

The school expulsion generated attention from the black press as well. The journalist James L. Hicks of the *Baltimore Afro-American* printed a front-page article on the issue, referring to the FBI's failure in the Moore case. He argued: "It looks like some of those eight FBI boys frittering away their time trailing innocent four-year-old children down the streets of Brooklyn could be more profitably employed tracking down bomb-throwing killers in the everglades of Florida."[50]

Because Esther could maintain the job she had only by putting Kathy in day care, the suggestion that she had unreported income was baseless. The Cleveland Day Nursery officials refused to allow her to appeal the expulsion. In response, she wrote to the editor of the *New York Daily Compass*, stating: "Since keeping [Kathy] in nursery school is the only way I have been able to seek and find employment, the effect of this expulsion order can only be interpreted as an attempt to starve the family and deny the children a chance at a normal life."[51] As with the denied entrance to summer camps for other Smith Act children, Kathy's expulsion from nursery school was a part of the FBI's efforts to disrupt the families of the unavailables more than a concerted effort to "get its man."[52]

Until Esther took her story to the public in January 1952, the New York Welfare Department flatly refused to help the family. But, on hearing the appalling story of a child's persecution by the FBI, Esther's allies sprung to action. The Families Committee of Smith Act Victims organized a response to Kathy's expulsion, highlighting the connection between political repression and racism.[53] The group sent a delegation of eighteen people to discuss the situation with John H. Lewis, community relations director of the New York Welfare Department, who, as Peggy Dennis and Sophie Gerson, leaders of the Families Committee, noted, informed the group that Kathy's case "would be decided without prejudice of color, race, or political belief." Dennis and Gerson continued: "The father of little Kathy Jackson is Dr. James Jackson, noted Negro Communist leader, who is being sought by the FBI. . . . [J. Edgar] Hoover's cloak-and-dagger men, in their fruitless efforts to locate the father, have held as virtual political hostages the two small daughters and the wife of Dr. Jackson. . . . Mrs Esther Jackson, as a young Negro woman, had with difficulty found a suitable job and her continuance in that position is contingent upon her daughter's maintenance in a nursery school—a facility not easily available to a Negro child."[54]

The Families Committee argued that the Welfare Department's initial refusal to intervene "can leave no doubt that the issue of 'color, race or political belief' is very much in evidence in the shocking discrimination and victimization of the Jackson family."[55] After substantial protest from the community, educators, social workers, family, and friends, Esther and the Families Committee convinced the Welfare Department to stay the expulsion order indefinitely on January 30.[56]

The connection between race, Kathy's expulsion, the Moore murder, and the victimization of Smith Act families offers a window into an important moment in the history of the black freedom movement. Historians have often perceived the early 1950s as a transitional period in black activism as the movement was restructuring itself around new political circumstances. McCarthyism and the Cold War surely shaped the fight for black freedom. The FBI and HUAC did extraordinary damage to the protest models that were seeing success during the Popular Front years, and the accusation of subversive activity drove many activists from the front lines. Historians have also noted similarities in protest strategies between groups like the Student Nonviolent Coordinating Committee in the 1960s and the SNYC in the 1930s and 1940s, so the appearance of a gap in the struggle during the McCarthy years fed the notion that there was an opportunity dashed by political repression, a period in which radical fighters for black rights were least partially silenced.[57]

But, by expanding the narrative of the black freedom movement beyond the trends and approaches that would become mainstream civil rights, the early 1950s included vibrant black political expression in a range of arenas. Many on the Left fought the trauma of political persecution, racial violence, and suspicion while they continued to promote black freedom. As James Smethurst and Mary Helen Washington have each pointed out, black leftist artists and writers continued to work during the early 1950s, building on and contributing to a tradition of literary black nationalism. Smethurst identified a bridge between the black Popular Front's remnants and the black arts movement of the 1960s and 1970s. He writes that, from the late 1940s and the early 1950s, "relatively stable intellectual and artistic institutions by alliances of leftists, former leftists, nationalists, and Left nationalists" eventually "radicalized civil rights workers who had become impatient with Cold War liberalism."[58] Washington has argued that black artists and activists were persistent in the early 1950s and that, while leftists felt the effects of Cold War persecution, they continued to generate ideas and publish work that would provide an artistic and ideological milieu for later black freedom activism.[59] Paul Robeson's weekly newspaper *Freedom* commenced publication in 1950 and survived until 1955.[60] *Freedom's* network included people like Louis Burnham and the author Lorraine Hansberry and provided the foundation for *Freedomways,* which Esther, Burnham, and the Du Boises would establish in 1960. These activists complicated the narrative of civil rights in the United States and the broader black freedom movement not only because their work dispels the notion of a break in movement activity but also because they contributed in ways that offered a framework for later civil rights work without shying away from their radicalism.

In the late 1940s and the 1950s as well, significant developments foreshadowed the coming of Black Power and the surge in black nationalism in the late 1960s. Malcolm Little joined the Nation of Islam while in prison and changed his name to Malcolm X. The Nation of Islam drew on the ideology of black empowerment and self-sufficiency that Marcus Garvey and the Universal Negro Improvement Association had promoted, eschewing the push for integration. The Nation of Islam argued that, as Manning Marable explained, "registering to vote or mobilizing blacks to petition the courts, as the NAACP did, was a waste of time." Malcolm embraced the group's religious and racial views, fought for his rights to practice Islam in prison, read black history, and honed his political acumen.[61] Over the same period, Robert F. Williams, a staunch promoter of armed self-defense, was experiencing a radical political coming of age in New York and North Carolina. A veteran who returned from war and both went to work in a factory and enrolled in college, Williams began writing and eventually published an article in *Freedom* calling for militancy in the South. According to Timothy Tyson, Williams argued in 1952 that young black people should become the vanguard of a movement for "Negro liberation, the dignity of the Negro race." He wrote: "[Southern black college students] should be the most militant agitators for democracy in America today. They have nothing to lose and all to gain." He also flirted with communism and other leftist ideologies but forged his own influential political path.[62]

While the Cold War decline opened the door for moderate and liberal civil rights groups to make progress, the leaders of the Popular Front black freedom movement did not simply stop acting because they faced

FBI harassment and public scorn. It is important to examine their continued activism in the early Cold War years because the experiences of individuals like Esther offer insight into how the movement changed. The work of black leftist activists in the early 1950s demonstrates how the radical economic agenda of the Popular Front became obscured: families needed to refocus their attention on immediate issues of political liberty and freedom from harassment. The intersection of personal and political life was never more obvious than in this era, when Esther's activism centered on protecting her family from political persecution and racial discrimination. Understanding the ways in which the Jacksons' family life changed within a shifting international political context between the Popular Front years and the civil rights years sheds light on the changing nature of the black freedom movement. It offers a new look at how the seeming decline of one portion of the movement can really be understood as a harbinger of the rise of another.[63]

In addition to working with the Families Committee, Esther drew her dedication to her family together with her devotion to the black freedom movement by working with the NCDNL. After President Harry Truman's secretary of labor Lewis Schwellenbach proposed outlawing the Communist Party, individuals and groups with some CPUSA ties formed the NCDNL in 1947. The group responded with a petition, urging that Truman instead outlaw segregation and lynching. Over twelve black newspapers ran the petition, which boasted the signature of Paul Robeson. When the initial twelve Party leaders were indicted in 1948, the NCDNL emphasized the situations of Henry Winston and Benjamin Davis as particularly important assaults on the black freedom movement. It characterized the Smith Act as "a menace confronting the Negro people."[64]

Though its primary goal was to defend persecuted black Communists and fellow travelers, the NCDNL deemphasized Party affiliation in favor of highlighting the larger struggle against racism. At an address in Detroit on April 30, 1953, the Reverend Edward D. McGowan, the NCDNL chairman, told the National Fraternal Council of Churches at the Bethel African Methodist Episcopal Church USA that the attack on black leadership "by the forces of reaction is an attempt to curb the mounting struggle of our people for dignity and full citizenship." Making reference to the NAACP's political position in the postwar years, he continued: "And so we must, by concerted action, foil the attempt of those forces that would discredit the real leaders of the Negro people and substitute those who dare speak only as their masters please."[65]

McGowan defended New York City councilman and Communist Party leader Benjamin Davis but did not draw explicit attention to communism. Davis was elected to the city council in 1943, by the system of proportional representation, and again in 1945, succeeding Adam Clayton Powell Jr. Part of his appeal was his position on racial issues. He also garnered support because of the wartime alliance between the United States and the Soviet Union, which, as the historian Gerald Horne argues, "allowed [his] message to be heard by less-prejudiced ears."[66] Davis was ousted from his council seat after his 1949 Smith Act conviction. McGowan argued that Davis voters in New York City "did not seem to question his politics" but rather knew that "he was fighting for a better way of life for the Negro people."[67]

In fact, Horne notes, Davis had significant support among the clergy. The Reverend Ben Richardson, for example, discussing Davis's quest for the council seat, declared: "[The CPUSA] approximates what Jesus stands for [more] than any other group."[68] Similarly, in his speech McGowan appealed to his religious audience, drawing not on common perceptions of godless communism but on Christ's sacrifice so that his followers could live "according to the dictates of [their] own conscience rather than being told by a religious hierarchy what [they] must think, speak, believe."[69] In all, the NCDNL leadership offered its audiences a way of understanding the repression of black political leadership that appealed to a wide set of moral, religious, and political values while neither crediting nor dismissing the CPUSA.

Esther remained uncompromising in her belief that her husband had a democratic right to his Communist political affiliation and that his absence was a severe blow to the black freedom movement. Through the NCDNL, she wrote a pamphlet titled *This Is My Husband: Fighter for His People, Political Refugee* that was first published in April 1953 and reissued in two additional printings later that same year. In the thirty-six-page pamphlet, she made her most persuasive case for the intersection of the struggles of Smith Act victim families and the black freedom movement, all the while fusing her romantic love for her husband, her family's welfare, and their political goals.

Esther began *This Is My Husband* with a brief statement on her emotional suffering, but she situated her pain in the context of the connections between politics and romance, setting the tone for the pamphlet: "It is a hard thing to confine oneself merely to making words about one's beloved upon whose face one has not looked for what seems an eternity of time. I want so much to have now his warm comradeship; to hear again from his lips those winged words of exciting promise as he would give voice to his confident dreams of a free and bountiful new life for the world's humblest peoples."[70] On the cover, a photograph of Esther and her daughters highlighted Jack's absence. While the pamphlet focused on how the violation of Jack's civil liberties damaged the black freedom movement, Esther wrote as a wife and mother. This emphasis mobilized the moment's focus on family as a defining American ideal. Just as she did with the Families Committee when Kathy was removed from day care, Esther understood that her defense of her husband would be stronger if she underlined her loyalty and her familial devotion. She quickly detailed the FBI persecution her family experienced, again contrasting her situation to the bureau's desultory handling of the Moore case.

The narrative takes Esther's political perspective, drawing on her background as a Popular Front activist in the process. This strategy downplays the CPUSA itself, wisely distancing Jack from the Party's dogmatism even as his right to adhere to it is defended. Esther focused on Jack's broad commitment to black freedom because her audience would likely consist of individuals in the NCDNL's reach. This approach showcases Esther's political savvy alongside her commitment to her husband's defense, her dedication to the black freedom movement, and the effect of McCarthyism on her marriage and family.

The pamphlet highlighted the impact the Smith Act had on black activists. Referring to the Supreme Court's upholding of the act in *Dennis v. United States*, Esther quoted the black lawyers Earl B. Dickerson and Richard E. Westbrooks as arguing that "the inevitable effect of the Supreme Court decision on the Smith Act is to undermine, if not destroy, effective protest with regard to government practices and policies inimical to the welfare of Negroes." Dickerson and Westbrooks suggested that the

Smith Act intimidated black activists to the point of silence by prosecuting high-level black Party leaders. They also suggested, as did Esther, that government attacks on communism and Communist-influenced protest nourished the economic disenfranchisement of poor and working-class blacks who had been empowered by the unionization efforts of the Popular Front years. Jack's indictment, then, was an outright assault against attempts to build "a nation in which the workers will toil to enrich *themselves* and not a small set of exploiting industrialists, a nation in which poor farming folk will own the land they till."[71]

This Is My Husband offered readers a portrait of Jack as a real person and not simply some Communist subversive blindly taking orders from Moscow. It highlighted the growth of his political perspective within the context of his Richmond upbringing. Jack was raised by highly educated parents, and he was afforded opportunities that many of his friends were denied, but his exposure to extreme poverty within his community led him to apply Marxist theory to practical change. Esther mobilized her husband's upbringing in his defense, invoking the poor people of Richmond and arguing that the "soul-killing drudgery of their toil and sufferings, yet ever-hopeful spirit and striving for better things . . . inspired him to write, to speak, to join in and to lead struggles in their behalf." She invited readers to understand how a young boy's exposure to the dramatically different opportunities for white and black, poor and privileged people in a neighborhood would lead to the development of a Marxist political perspective. She wrote: "Whatever the power, the effect, or influence of my husband's ideas upon the future conduct of the masses of people in this country in general and the South in particular, no sensible person can believe that it requires the dictates of some foreign Communist leader, living or dead, to have caused him to advocate a program of social reforms."[72]

By situating his attraction to communism in the context of an impoverished, exploited black community, Esther was asking her audience to see her husband as a rational, thoughtful man, not a cold political mouthpiece for a distant tyrant. Jack, she argued, was not an unfeeling Soviet dupe; rather, he was a compassionate man who sought to end the struggle and suffering of economically disadvantaged people, particularly those whose circumstances grew out of the South's racist culture.

Jack was also a patriot, Esther argued. She reprinted several of his World War II letters and speeches in the pamphlet. Her intention was to demonstrate his enthusiasm for the United States and his honorable service in the China-Burma-India Theater of war. In his letters, Jack explored the implications of segregation for black soldiers returning in the context of a victorious democracy. Toward the end of the war he expressed enthusiasm that the goals of the Double Victory campaign would be realized, asserting: "It seems to me, the SNYC and other Negro and progressive organizations in the South should build the organizations in such large numbers to take the offensive against the Ku Klux Klan and for the fulfillment of the Four Freedoms promised, which is so long overdue." Esther asked: "Are not these the words of a true leader of the people, loyal to the best that is in America?"[73] While Jack was a Communist, his military service showed that he was also a true American willing to fight for democracy, she argued.

In using these letters, Esther also demonstrated that her husband's communism needed consideration in the context of a US-Soviet alliance during the war. One letter highlighted Jack's perspective on the new atomic technology and offered one Communist's view on widespread access to nuclear knowledge. Jack wrote: "The application of the atomic bomb principle to industry may constitute a means for the revolutionary development of the formerly economically backward countries and for the speedy reconstruction of war devastated countries."[74] While the spread of atomic energy became a highly contentious issue during the Cold War, Jack's letters offer insight into the perspective of a Communist who was not bent on destroying the United States but determined to increase productivity and introduce equality worldwide.

Many of the individuals persecuted in the early Cold War years came under attack for their wartime politics. Esther's use of her husband's letters showed that there was no black-and-white divide between communism and patriotism, that the political context in a given era shaped forms of popular protest and political perspective. Though many others who were persecuted had abandoned their wartime beliefs by the time they came under attack, Jack's war letters illustrated that communism could be a part of American patriotism, particularly in the context of the US-Soviet wartime alliance. His adherence to his politics did not ebb and flow with changing diplomatic relations, and he believed that the framework of US democracy afforded him a right to believe unpopular ideas. Esther illustrated that his views emerged from a combination of circumstances grounded in his Richmond upbringing along with the Depression-era emergence of antifascist politics. She also employed the letters as a way of illustrating how Popular Front activists envisioned the postwar world and how starkly their vision contrasted with the reality they confronted in the early 1950s. She understood that she was defending views that were despised in the American political landscape, but she forcefully argued for her husband's right to hold them.

Esther never accepted the charge that her husband had committed a crime by acting on his political convictions and defended his right to seek ideas for change from thinkers in other countries, including Lenin and Stalin, citing a long tradition of relying on international influences to reformulate and perfect American democracy. Reports of tyranny in the Soviet Union were growing more frequent, and, though many Communists held out hope that the reports were rumors and political propaganda, Esther phrased her reference to Stalin carefully. She did not deny that his ideas had influenced her husband, but she did not believe that the Soviet leader's words were a precise reflection of her husband's politics. She instead argued that Jack had a right to read, interpret, and adapt the ideas of even the most unpopular political figure and that doing so did not make him the mirror image of a tyrant.

Esther asked: "Should that search for answers to the most burning problems of every Negro and every worker stop at the continental borders of the United States? Concede this and our nation will soon become a benighted wasteland of 'super patriotic' bigots." She noted the exchange of revolutionary ideas between the United States and France and argued that the spirit of change abroad inspired Thomas Jefferson to refine the democratic ideals in the early republic. She contended that Frederick Douglass drew strength for the antislavery cause in the United States from Britain's abolitionist movement. And she wondered what made her husband's efforts to advance the cause of racial justice through the ideas of non-American thinkers so different from those of earlier heroes in American history: "Today Congress would deny us the rich heritage of peoples of other lands. . . . That these ideas have been adopted in other lands simply indicates that mankind, facing common problems, eventually arrives at common answers."[75] In other words, the United States had entered a distinct political phase in which it stubbornly insulated itself from broad ideas from outside its physical and ideological borders to the detriment of the black freedom movement and efforts to create economic parity and security among workers.

Smith Act persecution was thoroughly intertwined with antiworker and antisegregation movements, and Esther saw that connection at work in her husband's situation. She argued that Jack and the other unavailables "acted in the great tradition of Frederick Douglass and the abolitionists who defied the Fugitive Slave Law of 1850 . . . and chose to carry on their fight as 'fugitives' rather than obediently surrender their cause to the jailers of liberty." Likening the early Cold War years to the antebellum period in American history, she argued that black leaders, "whether they are Communists, non-Communists, or anti-Communists, . . . are being persecuted as 'dangerous subversives,' threatened, jailed, deported, lynched."[76] Her husband's and his comrades' freedom, she believed, would advance the cause of democracy, equality, and liberty for the economically and racially oppressed in the United States.

This Is My Husband closed with a declaration of pride in the efforts of the unavailables to promote and secure true democracy. Esther asked friends and family not to offer her their pity for her plight but to fight on behalf of the persecuted men and women in order to preserve true American ideals. She declared: "I have the wonderful satisfaction of knowing that my husband has labored to find a path that will lead my people and all those who are heavily burdened into an age of peace and security."[77] The freedom of her family, the freedom of black citizens, and the freedom of the nation relied on her husband's ability to work in concert with an international movement of progressive thought and radical activism.

Jack's disappearance and Esther's effort to protect her daughters and defend her husband show how Cold War experiences like that of the Jacksons helped propel the shift from Popular Front–driven organizing, with an emphasis on labor, unions, and economic equality, to the liberal civil rights movement that emphasized social and political rights. The Jacksons' political and personal experiences reflect the changing struggle for racial justice. Because the Jackson family felt the immediate, personal impact of anti-Communist laws and the icy relationship between the United States and the Soviet Union, the nature of their activity in the black freedom movement changed. The Cold War isolated black leftists from the struggle, resulting in political shifts within the black freedom movement and diluting the influence of the Left. But, in spite of their harassment and isolation, the couple never disappeared.

Esther regularly reassured her daughters by explaining that their father was trying to make the United States a better place for them to live, as Americans, as black children, and as representatives to the world. As a mother, Esther believed that creating a better world for future generations meant being politically engaged on behalf of her family and on behalf of oppressed groups across the world. It was not enough to be a mother protecting her children from daily harm if they would become adults in an unjust world. The Families Committee of Smith Act Victims and the NCDNL allowed Esther's work toward changing the world and protecting her family to go hand-in-hand.

5

The Communist Party USA
and Black Freedom in the 1950s

At a 1957 meeting of the top leadership of the Communist Party USA (CPUSA), Jack recorded detailed notes of the proceedings. The conversation centered on the crisis in Little Rock, Arkansas, where nine black children attempted to integrate the city's Central High School and met soldiers with bayonets, hostile white civilians, and a state government dead set on maintaining segregation. CPUSA general secretary Eugene Dennis suggested that Little Rock foreshadowed the type of resistance blacks would confront in their struggles, then stated that the Party should work to induce the packing and automobile industries to "initiate actions and solidarity rallies in Detroit and Chicago." Interspersed with other comments on Little Rock and the emerging civil rights movement in the South were notes on unionization efforts across the country. Meeting participants discussed the theoretical connections between efforts to advance and unite the working class and the civil rights struggles in the South. But to Jack the conversation seemed mired in his comrades' ideas about what others should be thinking, not plans for concrete action that would directly benefit the children putting themselves on the dangerous front lines in the South.[1]

Jack was a devoted, lifelong Communist committed to Marxism-Leninism, the labor movement, and the ideological links between different struggles, but his position as a prominent black leader in the South during the 1930s and 1940s afforded him a different perspective on Little Rock. While his comrades debated whether and how they could work to convince the labor movement that it should be involved in the southern civil rights struggles, he had one picture fixed in his mind. To him, nothing spoke more profoundly of the sacrifice and courage of the Little Rock Nine than the image of Elizabeth Eckford, alone in a mob of angry white Arkansans. In a side note to himself, he wrote: "Show them [the] picture of [Elizabeth] Eckford. Challenge them. Measure their effort by hers." He jotted down an idea for a book: "Dear Elizabeth—compilation of letters to newspapers from Americans on the Little Rock events." To Jack, getting the labor movement, the Communist Party, and the rest of the nation concerned about civil rights was as simple as showing them that "the measured trod of children's small feet in the South have [*sic*] set a new pace and standard for the determined struggle to secure an equality of freedom for all citizens."[2] The Party's ideals were in the right place, but its frequently complicated analysis obscured how pressing the realities of the civil rights movement were. Jack knew that there was little use for complex Marxist theory and Party paternalism when it came to on-the-ground crises and change in the South, and he devoted himself to helping the Party act with that in mind.

Cold War liberalism shaped the 1950s civil rights movement and the CPUSA. The connection between the movement and the Party during these years was complicated by US politics, foreign policy, and domestic culture. Both the CPUSA and the black freedom movement worked to re-create themselves in the wake of a shifting US-Soviet relationship. The Popular Front's demise in the postwar years led to the CPUSA's decreased influence on the black freedom movement, and the Party drifted back from the front lines of the struggle. Still, understanding the link that the Party worked to maintain offers insight into how the civil rights movement functioned, where its support came from, and how activists from across the political spectrum adapted to the mainstream civil rights ideas of the time. As the Party's southern regional director, Jack was one of the CPUSA's highest-ranking leaders with experience working on civil rights. His connections and insight not only helped the Party shape its position on the situation in the South during the 1950s; they also served to maintain some links between the CPUSA and the black freedom movement during a time when the relationship between the two was tenuous.

The CPUSA faced its most difficult period in the 1950s. The Smith Act alone was enough to drive many members from the Party, and maintaining any influence while operating underground proved a challenge. The FBI's psychological assault on Party members and their families forced the organization to divert resources to the protection of wives and children and away from many of the efforts for social change it had emphasized in the past. The domestic trials the organization confronted proved daunting and understandably difficult to surmount.

But these challenges were not limited to repression within US borders. On February 25, 1956, Soviet premier Nikita Khrushchev delivered a lengthy address to the Twentieth Congress of the Soviet Communist Party in which he revealed to a stunned audience the horrors of Joseph Stalin's brutal regime. The CPUSA learned of the address in June, just six months after its underground operatives had reemerged. Faced with a series of complex questions about how to proceed, the CPUSA's top leaders came into conflict with one another. The debate followed the same line it had in the immediate postwar years over whether the organization should distance itself from the Soviet Union, adapt its program to fit more securely into the American political milieu, or move further to the left in an effort to distinguish communism from Stalinism. In all this conflict, the Party became unable to function effectively. Party members and leaders who had weathered the difficult McCarthy years began to leave the organization, a reaction to their deep disappointment in having been a part of a group that had touted a leader who, it turned out, was truly the tyrant he was rumored to be. Throughout this era, the CPUSA needed to adapt itself not only to the changing national political climate but also to the prevailing worldview of the Soviet Union. Leaders clashed over these issues. Despite what it perceived as a moral victory when the McCarthy era waned, the CPUSA would never recover and never regain the influence it boasted in the Popular Front era, in part because echoes of McCarthyism persisted, and in part because it failed continually to make palpable connections with the activist mainstream.[3]

The tumultuous aftermath of Khrushchev's revelations resulted in a period of intense conflict for the remaining Party members. Despite renunciations of growing factionalism, the Party's leadership remained divided among three prevailing points of view. John Gates argued that the CPUSA required substantial reform. He suggested deleting the phrase *Marxism-Leninism* from the Party's constitution and acknowledging that the revelation of Stalin's crimes had had a "liberating effect on world Communism" and that the American public should be reassured that the CPUSA was indeed reforming itself to fit better within its own national context. William Z. Foster, on the other hand, advocated strengthening the Party's attachment to Marxism-Leninism and focusing on the "general world crisis of capitalism and the certainty of serious repercussions of it in the United States." Eugene Dennis stood squarely between Gates and Foster, arguing for unity and for Marxist goals to be "grasped scientifically and applied creatively in accord with the concrete conditions of our country and the needs of the American working class."[4] The three wisely avoided the appearance of condoning Stalin's crimes but fell short when it came to crafting a Party line that was accessible and appealing beyond the reach it already had. Jack aligned himself most closely with Dennis. His reaction to Khrushchev's revelations was similar to his position on communism's applicability to civil rights: that Communists needed to consider contexts and employ theories in a flexible and pragmatic, not a dogmatic, way. He fought to keep separate the ideological foundations of communism and what he now understood to be Stalin's misinterpretation of them.

The CPUSA lost much of its legitimacy in the 1950s amid the turmoil.[5] Its membership declined dramatically, and it suffered a crisis of credibility. But it had certainly not disappeared from the public eye: it continued to hold conferences and work with Communist nations across the globe to try to rebuild itself; it also continued to draw criticism and inspire fear throughout the ongoing Cold War period. In 1962, its remaining leaders again faced the threat of jail time when they declined to register as foreign agents under the McCarran Act. In 1968, Charlene Mitchell ran as the CPUSA's candidate for president of the United States; she was the first black woman to run for the office.

Over the course of the civil rights movement, critics and white supremacists regularly equated civil rights leaders, organizations, and participants with Communists. While such accusations manipulated people's fears in the politically tense Cold War, they were grounded both in the CPUSA's long tradition of supporting the black freedom movement and in the frequent criticism that Communists used and duped African Americans. Many older civil rights leaders did come out of the Popular Front, but most had vanquished their Communist ties. For instance, Bayard Rustin, who had been a Communist in the 1930s but severed ties with the Party during World War II, had a positive rapport with Johnson White House officials, even as Martin Luther King Jr.'s influence declined.[6] But, by the

1950s, open Communists were all but banished from mainstream civil rights organizations. Both Walter White and Roy Wilkins of the National Association for the Advancement of Colored People (NAACP) distanced themselves from activists associated with the Popular Front and openly questioned the motives and involvement of Communists at all levels of the civil rights movement. Martin Luther King Jr. was quiet about his Communist friends, and, while he accepted their support, he did succumb to pressure to dismiss them publicly.[7]

In the traditional civil rights narrative, the lingering traces of McCarthyism shaped the way civil rights leaders devised their tactics. Some Communists and former Communists were involved in the movement, but the ideology of the movement itself explicitly differed from Communist ideology. The CPUSA's experiences in this period illustrate how a struggling political organization sought to resurrect itself. Jack saw civil rights as the Party's biggest hope, as just the sort of cutting-edge movement that could help revitalize the CPUSA. The civil rights movement drew Jack's primary interest in racial justice to the forefront of Communist discourse. And, while the Party was unsuccessful in rebuilding itself as part of the civil rights vanguard, its efforts to revise its program offer insight into the ways in which communism and civil rights overlap and diverge.

Conflicts around the Khrushchev report and McCarthyism stunted the CPUSA's civil rights efforts. The Party often seemed out of step with the civil rights movement in the 1950s, but its problem did not stem from its intentions. Its heart was in the right place: it stuck by its long advocacy of racial equality and justice and continued to offer expressions of solidarity to the organizations heading the movements in the South. Jack and other leaders worked to steer its interest in and influence on the civil rights movement in a productive direction. They pushed not only to make the Party relevant to the civil rights movement but also to make the civil rights movement a key component in the Party's success during a challenging period.

The difficulties the Party faced in its civil rights efforts were three-fold. First, it lacked a concrete plan of action to help in the civil rights movement as it emerged. Beyond expressions of solidarity, it failed to take tangible steps toward getting involved in grassroots struggles. This problem directly resulted from its second serious set of dilemmas in the

1950s. Between McCarthyism, legal problems, and Khrushchev's revelations about Stalin's brutality, the CPUSA was paralyzed. The leaders who weathered all these difficulties and remained involved in the Party discussed the structure of the organization at immense length, but initiating any real action to get involved on the ground was nearly impossible. This paralysis was certainly a result of internal conflict, but it was also linked with an unfavorable public image. A significant reality for the Party in its civil rights efforts was that the open participation of Communists was unwelcome among many of the top organizations involved in the movement. Communism's rapid fall from grace after the Popular Front years meant that its inclusion had the potential to taint the activities of organizations like the NAACP, the Southern Christian Leadership Conference (SCLC), the Montgomery Improvement Association, and others.

Nonetheless, black Popular Front activists operating in the 1950s did not necessarily dismiss wholesale the economic perspective Communists had brought to the movement simply because the Party went out of vogue. The analysis of the civil rights movement that Jack conducted while he was underground and after his reemergence and trial offers insight into the changing influence of the CPUSA on the black freedom movement. Throughout the 1950s, Jack worked to hone his expertise on race and labor relations in the South in order to allow for the most practical employment of communism.

Because of his indictment in June 1951, Jack's work in the early 1950s took place in the Party underground. From 1951 until late 1955, a significant part of the Communist Party operated within what it referred to as *the second cadre*. These leaders were classified in three categories, as Junius Scales recalled: "deep freeze," a sort of "brain trust" of experienced leaders; "deep, deep freeze," people who would abandon their lives and live in hiding ready to assume leadership if the Party's crisis worsened; and "operative but unavailable," leaders who kept some contact while they traveled about in hiding, contacting the other two categories of operatives.[8] Under the direction of the Party, hundreds of Communists and sympathizers across the United States quietly slipped from their daily lives into the underground. As a result of McCarthyism's long reach, most of these individuals still remain unknown, and their history is difficult to trace. They changed their names, raised their families, worked regular jobs, and were on hand in the event that the CPUSA needed them. Some of these people housed and protected the indicted leaders, and some hardly had any contact with the Party at all. Bunny Devine, whose family slipped into the second cadre, led the quiet life of a middle-class housewife in Bridgeport, Connecticut. She gave birth to a daughter while she was underground and had to change her daughter's name when the family reemerged. She did not know whether or when her family would be called on to provide assistance or leadership. They never were.[9]

Party secrecy and the legal implications for individuals who aided the second cadre mean that there is limited historical record of the CPUSA's covert operations. It is nearly impossible to trace individuals' time underground and verify their precise positions and activities. As a black fugitive from 1951 to 1955, Jack was in a more precarious position than were his white counterparts. Finding suitable housing for him and Henry Winston, another African American, proved challenging for the Party. As Gil Green noted: "If they lived in Black ghetto communities, which were subject to far more rigorous police surveillance, accidental discovery was obviously a greater possibility. . . . Yet if Winston or Jackson were to live with white families, they would be trapped indoors."[10] Jack spent some time in the Midwest, and he may have visited the South. The Party member Charlene Mitchell once hosted him in St. Louis, Missouri. He also spent some of his time on a farm in upstate New York, where locals knew him only as "Crazy Joe." None of his family members had any contact with him, but he was able to get occasional updates on them through the CPUSA's complex network of individuals linking the underground to those living out in the open. At one rally, a man approached Esther and handed her an envelope that contained her husband's wedding band and watch. Esther later recalled that the incident was frightening: she did not know who the man was, and there was no note in the envelope. She tucked it away and hoped for the best, guessing that it was Jack's way of letting her know he was OK. While there is a dearth of sources on Jack's time underground, it is still possible to understand the development of his intellectual perspective on the civil rights movement and the CPUSA. He continued to influence leftist thought on these matters by writing articles under the pseudonym Charles P. Mann (or "CP Man").[11]

That the second cadre remained elusive proved enormously frustrating to the FBI even though it sought to deny the effectiveness of an underground Communist Party. In his 1958 work on communism in the United States, *Masters of Deceit,* FBI director J. Edgar Hoover presented readers with a brief statement on the impact of the second cadre on the CPUSA. In his assessment, the CPUSA was almost completely disabled by the outcome of *Dennis v. United States* (1951). By moving to underground operations, "the Party in protecting itself spent energy, time, and money that otherwise would have gone into agitation and propaganda." It was "weakened and largely immobilized in its underground haunts."[12] Hoover's analysis credits the Supreme Court's ruling in one case with the dissolution of the CPUSA but makes no mention of his own organization's frenzied, expensive, and largely unsuccessful efforts to dismantle the second cadre. He was particularly embarrassed when the fugitives surrendered voluntarily. When Gil Green's surrender was announced, he scrawled, "This makes us look silly" over the text of the memo he received.[13] Hoover believed that the Party was rendered nonfunctional by the Smith Act trials, an assertion that contradicted his own contention that it remained a dangerous menace to the United States. On the other hand, CPUSA general secretary Eugene Dennis suggested that the second cadre had scored some successes against Cold War authorities.[14]

The black freedom movement underwent profound changes during the McCarthy era as black Popular Front leaders shifted their focus to fit the political context of the time. Indictments of prominent black Party leaders illustrated the dual perils of anticommunism and segregationism. While economic equality and interracial working-class solidarity had been the rallying cry of the Popular Front, the nationwide attack on Communist activities and ideas meant that the main thrust of efforts to attain racial justice moved away from labor and unionization and toward social, cultural, and political rights. Many historians cite the demise of the Popular Front as the key moment when the CPUSA's influence in other social movements vanished. Robert Korstad argues that postwar Red-baiting "[narrowed] the range of ideas and leaders on which the movement could draw": "The black challenge of the 1950s and 1960s came to be understood as a single-issue attack on Jim Crow and not as a more broad-based critique of racial capitalism."[15] While it is important to acknowledge that the movement away from labor marked a transition in the black freedom movement that left some economic issues unaddressed, the goals of mainstream civil rights did include long-term economic progress.[16] For the activists of the Popular Front years, staying active presented challenges that changed the shape of social movements in the United States. The emphasis in some circles began to center on protecting civil liberties and the families of the indicted leaders; in others, Popular Front black freedom work gave way to liberal civil rights.

For the Jackson family, these two shifts were linked to one another. While Esther focused on illustrating how her husband's disappearance and legal difficulty were direct assaults on her family and the black freedom movement, Jack was able to continue quietly commenting on civil rights discourse, at least within the Party's limited reach. His unavailability afforded him certain freedoms that would have been impossible had he not disappeared. Party leaders who went to prison were unable to write as extensively and unrestrainedly on political issues as were those who went underground. As Peggy Dennis wrote of her husband's imprisonment: "A special ruling was made in Washington that . . . none of Eugene Dennis' [prison] letters could be published or quoted in public, and that he could not comment specifically on the Communist Party or 'communism.'" Had he done so, he would have faced solitary confinement and the revocation of his correspondence privileges.[17] And, while Jack was surely concerned with his family's well-being, he also believed that his decision to avoid prison was beneficial to his children's futures, and he strove to make the most of his time out of the immediate spotlight.

The Party leaders who remained above ground continued to rely on and express their appreciation for Jack's sacrifice. In a statement, they wrote: "We say to Comrade Jim Jackson, elected leader of the Party in the South and driven into hiding by the bankrupt US bourgeoisie—wherever you may be—you should know we are making good use of the legacy you have left us . . . and thus your leadership still guides us." The CPUSA statement suggests that the second cadre's influence was not diminished by their unavailability. Party leaders who were in hiding had left intellectual support for the aboveground operatives. The Party also sought to support Esther and her two daughters and assured Jack: "Your family is now ours."[18]

In his disappearance, Jack embodied the stereotype of Communists as functionaries who put the Party before everything else, including their families. He justified the move with his belief that the Communist agenda would build an ideal world and that his absence would contribute to a greater good. He had attempted to live by the ideals of the Party since he joined. When his older daughter was born, he was not inclined to start a college fund for her because he believed that the Communist agenda would win out by the time she would need it.[19] But, by going along with the "signal to the Party membership that its leadership considered the situation so dismal that they were preparing for illegal conditions," through his actions Jack also contradicted his real-life effort to commit to an egalitarian household.[20] Shared obligation for child rearing and housework was not an option when Jack was underground. Esther made use of her status as a wife and mother in this period, mobilizing both her adherence to normative roles and her plight as an essentially single mother to fight for justice for her husband. In the early 1950s, the demands the Party made of its leaders and members to uphold and fight for its ideological agenda contradicted the implementation of some of those ideals on the ground.

Jack continued to function underground as a prominent Party expert on the issues black Americans were confronting throughout the 1950s. He covertly reported on and analyzed the major developments in the black freedom movement during the Party's period of great tumult. Gil Green, who saw him several times while the two were unavailable, recalled that he continued to function as southern regional director from 1951 to 1955. He wrote: "[Jack's] style of work was not all that different. Conditions in the South even prior to the witch hunt had never made possible the open functioning of the Party. . . . Even in the best of times, [Party] organizers worked in the South at their peril."[21]

The Party's formal position on the black freedom movement and its actions often differed. Jack worked to make that position more tangible and relevant to the rapidly growing movement in the South. In 1959, he was a key contributor in revising the CPUSA's position on the Negro Question, which the Party formally revisited for the first time since the 1928 advent of the Black Belt thesis.[22] The Black Belt thesis had become the source used by many of the Party's critics to suggest that Moscow was merely using American blacks to promote Soviet communism in the United States. Although the official Party line prioritized class issues, arguing that class encompassed race, and while many Party leaders were not immune to white chauvinism, American Communists were unequivocal in their support of the notion of racial equality.[23] Jack's effort to reform Party policy on civil rights was an attempt to correct the notion that the Party cared only to use African Americans for its own ends as well as an expression of unwavering solidarity with the integration efforts in the Deep South.

While Jack was in hiding, he worked on evaluating the Party line and the efforts black Americans were making in the South in order to allow the CPUSA to uphold its reputation as a frontline fighter for racial equality. The key points in all his writing emphasized the notion of the civil rights movement as a struggle that was distinct from, but required the support of, the CPUSA. As a Party centrist, he believed that the CPUSA would benefit from adapting itself to the changing US political discourse and offering full support to civil rights organizations. His earlier work with the Southern Negro Youth Congress (SNYC) allowed him to see the emerging civil rights movement as a mass struggle that the Party could assist but should not co-opt. Though he was a part of the upper levels of Party leadership, Jack did not take a dogmatic position on civil rights in this period. He believed that the oppression in the South required a people's movement and that the movement should reflect the needs, desires, and ideas of black southerners, not Party hard-liners.

Jack's time underground provided him with the opportunity to develop his knowledge of the issues in the South, hone his position, and ultimately shape Party policy on the civil rights movement. Some of his writings during these years emphasized how black efforts to obtain civil, social, and political rights in the South fit squarely within the Party's class analysis. Other works focused exclusively on how the Party should adapt its position on the Negro Question to fit the times. Jack also produced a number of short pieces in which he sought to illustrate how his own legal troubles reflected the changing black freedom movement. These describe his devotion to communism as a manifestation of his core commitment to the struggles of politically, socially, and economically disenfranchised African Americans. They invoke his personal history and his dedication to his family as crucial factors in his political life. Once he reemerged, his research while in the second cadre was crucial to his articulation of the 1959 revision of the Party's position on the Negro Question.

While his ideas and his leadership of the Southern Regional Committee had reach within Party circles, Jack had very little influence, if any, beyond that. He and Ed Strong, as Junius Scales recalled, always hoped to rebuild Party membership in the South, which had dwindled more precipitously than elsewhere because of the combination of McCarthyism and segregationism. The pair became focused on membership numbers and "set about their task with more passion than reason . . . because they . . . had known the exaltation of giving inspirational leadership to hundreds of Negro youth." Scales wrote that Jack and Strong "were both generals without much of an army" who "had invested their talents and aspirations in the Party after the war and found themselves isolated." And, as a result of finding himself "hunted and politically impotent," Jack grew increasingly authoritarian within the Party's underground network. The postwar political turn was tragic and devastating for him. Even Scales, who found him arrogant and did not particularly like him, felt sympathy for him in this context.[24] He was a youth leader who saw success with the SNYC and, after misreading the way political winds in the United States were blowing, was now a member of a discredited organization who sacrificed everything to save it. In this light, Jack offers a portrait of an activist who was trying to make sense of changes as they happened. He made choices and alliances that ultimately diminished his potential for widespread, mainstream influence, and he alienated some comrades like Scales, but he also showed deep commitment to his own convictions and his cause. In the underground years, he wrote and worked to save the Party, and saving the Party was essential to keeping sane in the midst of what surely brought about intense emotional turmoil.

In 1952, Jack began writing a piece under the pseudonym Charles P. Mann titled "Universal Suffrage . . . the Gauge of the Maturity of the Working Class." Shortly before this, a few members of the second cadre met in Chicago and organized a plan to continue activity covertly. They submitted proposals to the CPUSA's national board, which agreed to allow the unavailables to write articles for *Political Affairs* using pseudonyms. Because the security and protection of the second cadre were paramount for its continued ability to fulfill its purpose, it is likely that the pseudonyms under which the unavailables wrote were unknown to most of the aboveground leadership.[25] In addition to allowing the unavailables to remain active, writing under pseudonyms gave them anonymity and afforded them the opportunity to critique Party practices. For men who had given up their family lives and devoted themselves to fighting what they saw as American fascism, it was increasingly important that they were able to express their views on Party policies and shape the organization to serve their interpretation of the nation's needs. Jack's drafting of "Universal Suffrage" reflects the development of a burgeoning civil rights movement over the course of the 1950s and illustrates how his view on political rights for black Americans related to CPUSA interests.[26]

The first version of "Universal Suffrage," drafted in August, emphasized the impact of mass voter disenfranchisement on the upcoming 1952 election. Jack argued that Adlai Stevenson and Dwight D. Eisenhower's campaign measures to increase the electorate and register new voters were insincere. Voter registration efforts did not mitigate the impact of the candidates' lack of attention to the South's poll tax system. Anti–poll tax legislation had bounced around the House of Representatives and the Senate to no avail in the mid-twentieth century. Southerners, ranging from liberal politicians to Popular Front organizers and civil rights organizations, had lobbied to end the tax, which made voting cost prohibitive for poor and working-class blacks and whites.[27] Jack's essay connected Communists' concerns for the working class and the rights of black southerners: "Spokesmen in both the Stevenson and Eisenhower entourage have been exhorting the people about their 'laziness and indifference' to the necessity of registering to vote. . . . Yet, not one word has passed from their lips in support of enabling measures to enforce the constitutionally proclaimed but historically denied right of those men and women of voting age among the ten million disenfranchised Negroes in the South."[28]

In a footnote, Jack estimated that in the South 95 percent of potential black voters and, because of the policies enforcing the poll tax system, 65 percent of potential white voters were disenfranchised. Yet he avoided arguing that the mass disenfranchisement of poor and working-class whites and blacks was exclusively a class issue. Instead, he pinpointed racism as the source of the problem, suggesting that disenfranchised white voters were mere collateral damage from Dixiecrat efforts to limit the political agency of black southerners.

The essay detailed the undemocratic nature of the South's electoral process. Jack argued that the absence of black voters resulted in unrepresentative government. He pointed out that, although Mississippi's first district had 122,826 potential voters, Representative John Rankin, a notorious racist, "was elected to Congress in 1950 by only 8,994 votes, his Republican opponent receiving a mere 730."[29] Voter turnout was just 8 percent of the potential electorate. That particular election was particularly egregious in the eyes of African Americans and American Communists because Rankin's politics defined the link between anticommunism and hard-line segregationism. Rankin was also a proud anti-Semite, and he opposed House Un-American Activities Committee investigations of the Ku Klux Klan.[30] Because he was elected by such a tiny portion of the individuals of voting age in his district, there was, Jack argued, no way he could truly represent the public interest. The example of this election, alongside other southern elections, led Jack to liken the United States to South Africa, which had "disfranchised so many people in so many 'free elections,' for so long a time and still [has] the gall to proclaim itself a democracy!"[31]

Jack compared Rankin's election to Adam Clayton Powell's in New York City and William C. Dawson's in Chicago in 1950. Pointing out that Powell won 35,233 votes of 55,491 cast and that Dawson won 69,506 of 112,585 votes cast, he contrasted the lack of voter participation in the South with the "stubborn and oft times heroic struggle of the Southern Negroes for possession of that elemental badge of citizenship— the right to vote." He argued that, along with educational and moral requirements, poll taxes were the primary cause for the disproportionately low numbers of voters in the South. In a state like Alabama, where the poll tax was cumulative, a "forty-five year old person seeking to cast his or her first vote must pay $36.00 [roughly $316.00 in 2014 terms] for the privilege . . . [making] voting a prohibitive luxury for the millions of working people and farmers whose incomes are notoriously the lowest in the country."[32] By highlighting the racial politics of this system's primary beneficiaries, Jack illustrated that class exploitation was a product of racism in the South's electoral system, not the other way around.

In addition to discriminatory voter registration requirements, Jack noted that the Ku Klux Klan offered the region its most effective method for disenfranchising black voters. He argued that Harry and Harriette Moore's assassinations in 1951, along with the shooting of Maceo Snipes in Georgia in 1946, were prime examples of the Klan's effective "organized terror against would-be Negro voters."[33] He called on Communists to assist in the black struggle for the ballot in any way possible, arguing: "Every really popular movement of the people for democratic reforms—no matter how elementary the demands—is pregnant with the seeds of enormous possibilities for favorably altering the social forces in the direction of sweeping progressive advancements for the working class, the Negro masses and all democratic classes of people."[34]

Jack focused on how black efforts for political rights and against racial violence were relevant to the activism of other progressives, not how communism or other leftist movements were important in the lives of black southerners. This distinction offers insight into how he employed communism in his own political life. For him, it was a relevant and vital means to achieving social and economic justice for all. But he believed that black southerners were the primary agents of change in their own lives and were capable of making informed political decisions. By encouraging Communists and other progressives to lend their support to and act with black southerners, Jack was attempting to move activist discourse away from the notion that Communists were out to take advantage of African Americans. Instead, he argued: "Communists . . . above all others must appreciate and energetically fight for such a partial democratic reform as this: first of all because it is right, and just, and would represent some measure of dignity to an outrageously oppressed people."[35] In other words, Communists should join with and follow other social movements, including the black freedom movement.

Jack's disappearance into the Communist underground represented one way in which Cold War tensions shaped the black freedom movement. His political affiliation, along with his approach to racial justice movements, drove him further from the mainstream. Meanwhile, black freedom movement tactics shifted, in part as a response to the Cold War. In nearly every major civil rights crisis that emerged in the mid- and late 1950s, the image of democracy that the United States projected abroad was compromised. The United States could hardly promote American ideals abroad when it failed to implement them at home. As the historian Mary Dudziak argues: "Domestic racism and civil rights protest led to international criticism of the U.S. government. International criticism led the federal government to respond, through placating foreign critics by reframing the narrative of race in America, and through promoting some level of social change." Social change in the beginning of the Cold War was influenced by the "need for reform in order to make credible the government's argument about race and democracy."[36] Cold War civil rights reforms emerged from embarrassment and image consciousness, rather than a purist vision of social justice. The United States could not continue to promote itself as a democratic nation if the Soviet Union could criticize and mock its racial caste system.

Black activists in the South saw an opportunity for mass action as McCarthyism began to fade and the international political climate demanded that the United States embody the democracy it promoted. Over the course of the mid-1950s, African Americans would see the beginnings of school integration in the South, along with the rise of major organizations and leaders who would fully reshape racial politics in the United States. In December 1955, Rosa Parks agreed to allow the Montgomery, Alabama, NAACP to use her arrest for refusing to comply with segregation laws on a city bus to kick-start a boycott and fight transportation segregation. The Montgomery Improvement Association and the SCLC emerged from the Montgomery bus boycott and found in the Reverend Martin Luther King Jr. a charismatic leader.[37] Black activists, under King, proved through nonviolent tactics that "the philosophy of Thoreau and Gandhi can triumph."[38] In this context, Jack's efforts to keep civil rights discourse at the forefront of the Party program while in hiding is one component of the impact that Cold War politics had on the black freedom movement.

Jack continued to develop his understanding of the problems black southerners confronted throughout his time underground. In March 1955, writing as Charles P. Mann and Frederick C. Hastings, he and Henry Winston published an article in *Political Affairs* called "For a Mass Policy in Negro Freedom's Cause" that criticized the Party for being out of step with the growing civil rights movement and called on the CPUSA to revise its approach to black freedom. In hiding, the two men found an opportunity to push the Party to make a tangible difference in its approach to civil rights. If the Party could become a part of the growing momentum around civil rights, it might find a path back to political relevance. The piece did not shape the civil rights movement itself, but the arguments Jack and Winston made in it suggest their frustration with their isolation after four years in hiding. If Jack's disappointment with the circumstances that led him underground illustrated to him the effects of his commitment to the Party, his writings highlight how he sought to make his time underground worthwhile. He continued to fight for the cause not only because he believed in it but also, in part, because he had sacrificed so much to save it. He and Winston offered an extensive policy proposal for bridging the divide between civil rights and the Party. As black Communists with southern roots who were indicted, in hiding, and facing prison, they were particularly interested in how the Party positioned itself in relation to a movement in which they were each personally invested.

Jack and Winston contested Communist claims that the civil rights movement needed more of the Party's influence and that the Party's failure led the "Negro masses to be taken over by the bourgeois reformist leaders." Though it may have frustrated Roy Wilkins, the NAACP's anti-Communist executive secretary, they praised the NAACP's efforts for school desegregation and applauded the steps black Americans took to mobilize the organization. They argued: "The N.A.A.C.P. is viewed by the Negro people as their own organized mass weapon which has won important battles for them in recent years." Nonetheless, they criticized the NAACP's leaders, calling them "reformist supporters of the white ruling class" who only follow the tide of protest, rather than initiating it, in order to "remain the leaders of the Negro people." If the NAACP had not followed the will of the people toward increased militancy, Jack and Winston suggested, "the initiative and leadership exercised by the Communists and the Left would have resulted in the whole Negro liberation movement being organized and led by the working-class ideology and leadership of our Party." Instead, they argued, the masses of poor, disenfranchised, and segregated blacks in the South were seeking practical leadership, and, in spite of its moderate reputation, the NAACP had become a vehicle for radical change.[39]

"For a Mass Policy in Negro Freedom's Cause" was published shortly after *Brown v. Board of Education* (1954).[40] Jack and Winston lamented the slow steps toward true desegregation in public schools and argued that Communists should be involved in helping implement the ruling on the ground. Taking an unnamed fellow Communist to task for suggesting that "Left Centers," or leftist groups working to influence mass movements, would provide a solution to the problems facing black southerners, they suggested: "The historic and heroic fight to implement the Supreme Court decision on outlawing school segregation and the fight to extend the right to vote and equal representation are such movements and struggles already involving millions."[41] The Party did not need to ignite a struggle if one already existed, and such an idea distracted Communists from becoming fully involved in a momentous movement. The primary goal, according to Jack and Winston, should have been to get involved with the organizations already working toward complete school desegregation, instead of pondering how to win the black masses over to a Communist-run organization working toward the same end.

"For a Mass Policy in Negro Freedom's Cause" called on Communists to correct their flawed approach to the black freedom movement by reinvigorating Popular Front–style involvement. Jack and Winston agreed that looking only to the 1930s, when Communists exercised considerable influence in the black freedom movement and were a more popular organization, was wrong-headed and ignored too much of the current context. But they acknowledged that a similar approach to the current movement could effectively win the hearts and minds of the black southern masses *and* contribute to the mounting victories in civil rights struggles. They concluded: "If our Party enters with both feet into the mass movement of the Negro people without losing its own identity and more advanced ideological and political program, then it can begin to regain rapidly its lost influence and leave its decisive mark on the future of the movement."[42]

Further, the pair implied, the Party's isolation from the civil rights movement was in part a product of the fact that it viewed "bourgeois reformist" organizations like the NAACP as the force to be conquered. Though Jack and Winston believed that the true enemy of racial justice was obvious, they made a point of reminding their audience that resistance to change in the South was powerful. Highlighting the surge of white citizen councils, states' rights associations, the "National Association for the Advancement of White People," the "National Association to Defend the Majority of White People," and the "Defenders of State Sovereignty and Liberty," they argued that the "reign of terror against the Negro people" required immediate attention. They noted that, even though the CPUSA characterized the NAACP as "reformists" who pandered to the white ruling class, to white supremacist organizations there was no distinction between Communists and moderate black activists who advocated for desegregation.[43]

Jack and Winston illustrated to the Party that the white citizen councils in Mississippi "[applied] economic pressures to 'trouble-makers' [who advocated] compliance with the Supreme Court decision." White supremacist organizations used foreclosure, credit denial, and other threatening and violent tactics to accomplish their goals, and black Mississippians who had made it out of poverty risked severe danger if they were not quiet about their politics. Jack and Winston applauded NAACP efforts to provide financial support to business owners, homeowners, farmers, and workers who risked their livelihoods to defend civil rights. They argued that the "unity displayed in Mississippi by all classes of Negro life cannot but inspire the entire democratic camp." They also noted that the NAACP and black leaders in Mississippi were "developing a new form of struggle, 'the economic boycott' as their answer to the economic terror of the white bankers, merchants, and plantation owners."[44]

The situation in Mississippi deteriorated in 1955 in response to *Brown.* According to the NAACP leader Amzie Moore, white supremacists killed seven blacks that year. Among them, the Reverend George Lee and Gus Courts, organizers of the Belzoni, Mississippi, NAACP were murdered after they filed suit against a local sheriff who refused to accept poll taxes from potential African American voters. In August, Mississippi's pattern of racial violence gained national attention with the murder of the fourteen-year-old Chicago boy Emmett Louis Till. Till, visiting an uncle in Money, Mississippi, over the summer, was unfamiliar with the particularities of Jim Crow. Though he was aware of racial separation, he was not versed in the gendered rules of segregation. He was kidnapped, beaten, and shot, his weighted body thrown in the Tallahatchie

River, after a white woman in a convenience store reported that he had spoken to her inappropriately. His death, along with the trial of his killers and his highly publicized open-casket funeral, catalyzed the start of the civil rights movement across the South, including the Montgomery bus boycott.[45] Although Jack and Winston reemerged and began to confront their own legal problems at the precise moment the Montgomery bus boycott began, their praise for the Mississippi leaders discussing boycott plans indicated that they would have expressed support. They closed the portion of their article on school desegregation by urging the Party to "end our isolation and weaknesses which flow from the past underestimation of this question."[46]

Ending Communist isolation from the growing civil rights movement was Jack and Winston's dominant theme. Their article drew on their personal commitment as black southern Communists and likely provided both of them with a way to maintain their psychological stability in the wake of an exceptionally traumatic period. It expressed general agreement with the Party's goals but offered extensive criticism of the CPUSA's ideas for how best to become involved. The pair vehemently disagreed with a fellow comrade who "mechanically shouts 'working-class hegemony' and politically places his main emphasis not on the struggle to unite the Negro people as a people but on sharpening up the differences within [their] ranks."[47] Instead of further fragmenting the American Left, they asserted, Communists needed to bring their radical ideas quietly to the front lines of the mounting struggles across the South. Unity among the masses would prevail over a splintered movement with similar goals but different means.

"For a Mass Policy in Negro Freedom's Cause" did not simply allow Jack and Winston to articulate a position on the CPUSA's involvement in the black freedom movement. Publishing under pseudonyms in *Political Affairs* allowed them to continue to participate in Communist discourse in a period of censorship, repression, and fear and thus to feel active in their underground isolation. Such writings made no impact on the civil rights movement. But, while they had little reach beyond the Party itself, the idea that discourse could continue within the Party during a period of crisis meant that the people who sacrificed their normal lives to go underground did so for an organization that at least attempted to live up to

its ideals. Jack and Winston pushed the Party on civil rights from underground because doing so was a way to actively create the Party they were
fighting for. Their work also formed the foundation for the Party's position on the Negro Question after the second cadre emerged.

In addition, though a great deal of vociferous debate occurred regularly in the pages of *Political Affairs,* Jack and Winston had greater
liberty to critique their comrades and the Party writing as Mann and
Hastings than they might have had writing under their own names. Jack's
pseudonymous writings served a dual function for the Party as well. His
pieces allowed for the outward appearance of solidarity from within Party
ranks, for the unavailables seemed completely behind the Party line. But,
because his anonymity allowed him to express his opinions openly, *Political Affairs* contradicted the common assumption that Communists were
of one mind, following a single policy coming from Moscow.

After nearly five years in hiding, Jack emerged from the second cadre
on Friday, December 2, 1955, turning himself in at the federal courthouse building in New York City. On learning of his surrender, US Attorney Paul W. Williams told the *New York Times* that Jack was "one of
the most dangerous Communist conspirators in the United States." The
Times article also noted that he was "the Party's top organizer in the
South" and that his surrender was a critical step in ensuring the security of the United States.[48] The attention to Jack's supposed threat to
the United States, along with his role in the South, illustrated the extent
to which the Communist Party's potential position in the emerging civil
rights movement was truly a national issue. Whereas black religious leaders, local business owners, domestics, and moderates in the South could
ask for their rights and ruffle only the feathers of those whites most resis-
tant to change, the specter of a Communist asking for the South to sacrifice its traditions made the whole nation nervous.

Jack was the second unavailable to surrender in one week's time.
Fred Fine had surrendered two days before, and William Norman Marron was expected to emerge sometime in the following week. Both the
federal government and the CPUSA saw the surrenders as victories, and
both interpreted their victories as triumphs for the ideals and goals of
the United States. The government claimed success because the surrenders proved that a conspiracy existed, the threat was real, and the dan-

ger had been quelled. On the other hand, William Z. Foster, the Party's national chairman, issued a statement that argued: "Communists fight for the democratic rights of all and seek to advance their socialist ideals openly in the American marketplace of opinion." He asserted that the surrenders of Fine and Jack were "an expression of confidence in the rising democratic strength of the American people."[49] In other words, the Soviet Union's new leadership, the Senate's censuring of McCarthy, and a more stable international political climate made the likelihood of a fair trial better in 1955 than it had been in 1951.

Still, the trial would not be an easy fight. Jack, like his wife, saw his legal situation as a reflection of the struggles black Americans consistently faced when they became politically active. On his surrender, he issued a statement at the courthouse in which he contrasted the attention his political views received with the injustices millions of blacks across the South confronted daily: "While the Mississippi lyncher-murderers of the Negro child Till go unpunished and 'Councils' of white supremacy racists (by overt criminal acts of shooting, floggings, and burnings) terrorize Negroes who seek to exercise their elementary rights of citizenship encounter no opposition from the federal law enforcement authorities, innocent men and women are indicted, tried and imprisoned like common criminals because of ideas they are alleged to harbor in their minds!"[50]

Having furthered his analysis of the changes happening in the South during his time underground, Jack consistently contextualized his defense in the burgeoning black freedom movement. As his wife contrasted the FBI's uneven investigations of her family and violent acts in the South, he compared Smith Act proponents to the white supremacists in the South who adamantly resisted change.

Jack had the strong representation of Charles T. Duncan, a Harvard-educated black civil rights attorney. Duncan, along with his associate council, Frank Reeves, participated in the NAACP's efforts in *Brown v. Board of Education*.[51] By selecting attorneys who were a part of the civil rights movement and represented a more moderate strain of political thought than he did, Jack set himself apart from the other defendants. His choice of representation reflected his view that his trial was not just a fight against political repression. It was also inextricably linked with the black freedom movement. As a black Communist with a long history in the struggle for racial justice, he attempted to illustrate that he was an independent-minded participant in a larger movement, not just a hard-line follower of Soviet doctrine.

His trial included moving testimony from his elderly father and a letter of support from Ralph Bunche, his former supervisor from his work under Gunnar Myrdal. W. E. B. Du Bois also testified, called by the defense as a character witness. The prosecution asked Du Bois if there was "any organization or conference that I have referred to so far that in your opinion had no Communist participation." He replied: "That's too general a question. I don't know. Besides, I don't see how anyone can determine whether or not there is Communist participation. . . . I can't look out in this audience and say whether there is or not. I don't recognize Communists by their faces or their dress." The court questioned whether Du Bois meant that he could not identify Communists in the courtroom, dismissed the nuance of his statement, and proceeded to interrogate the eighty-eight-year-old activist and scholar's statement, suggesting that he was no more than a confused old man. Du Bois was palpably irritated at prosecution attempts to dilute his complex analysis of socialism and force him to identify the Communists in the room. Du Bois stuck to the distinction he had made between having knowledge of an individual's political reputation and his own firsthand knowledge of an individual's actual affiliations, to the frustration of the prosecution and the court.[52]

Prosecutors worked to be very specific about the charges against Jack and his codefendants. Although there was ample opportunity to incite fear in the jurors with just the idea that a true threat of violence existed, they distinguished the charges from acts of violence. They argued that conspiracy was threat enough: "The intent of a defendant to knowingly and willfully participate need not be proved by direct evidence but, on the contrary, may and indeed generally must be inferred from all of the facts and circumstances." The prosecution suggested that intent could be inferred from the mere fact that the defendants had an awareness of the consequences of their conspiracy.[53] The defense sought to establish that communism did not inherently advocate or imply that violence was necessary, challenging the notion that Communists were automatically un-American. After eleven hours of deliberation, a jury of eight men and four women found Jack and his comrades guilty.[54]

At the sentencing stage, Jack made another attempt to prove himself a compassionate, thoughtful activist whose politics would benefit the masses. He grounded his statement to the court in his upbringing and the development of his political consciousness alongside the injustices of the Jim Crow South, drawing on the burgeoning civil rights movement rather than focusing solely on Communist dogma. He argued: "The freedom of choice in associates, the freedom of choice of membership in an association, are freedoms particularly dear to the Negro people. Involved is the essence of the right to pursue and secure relationships with other Americans in order to further our advance toward genuine equality and to realize our stature as free American citizens."[55]

Although most black Americans, Jack asserted, "hold no brief for the Communist Party's program of socialism," the history of slavery, segregation, lynching, and disenfranchisement would lead them to believe in his "right to pursue the struggle for their rights through this political party." Black Americans would, he suggested, "want the doors of political alternative left open to facilitate a greater responsiveness to their needs and demands on the part of the Democratic or Republican Party of their current choice." He also characterized his own communism as "a social science . . . and not . . . holy scripture."[56] Jack appealed to potential judicial appreciation for the emerging civil rights struggle in the nation, hoping that he could help the court make sense of communism's appeal. Also, his aging mother made an emotional plea for clemency on her son's behalf.

Jack received a two-year sentence and was released on $20,000 bail to prepare for his appeal. While the appeals process was beginning, the Supreme Court determined in *Yates v. United States* (1957) that, under the Smith Act, "advocacy, to be criminal, must be of some future *action*, rather than of the desirability of believing something," thereby severely limiting the scope of the *Dennis* opinion. The *Yates* decision affected nearly ninety Communists who were either convicted or awaiting prosecution.[57] Jack's case was among the convictions that were reversed.

When the ordeal of his trial, sentencing, and appeal was over, Jack's key priority was reconnecting with his family. Jack, Esther, and their daughters all felt a strain after five years of separation and two years of trials and uncertainty. Jack barely knew his daughters. When he returned, Harriet was thirteen, and Kathy, who had been a toddler when he left, was eight. While he waited for his bail to be arranged, Jack wrote Kathy a letter that expressed both a strong sense of paternal devotion and an awkward unfamiliarity with her. He had seen her recently and complimented her on her appearance and maturity. He told her: "You speak with grown-up words and ideas. I am so proud." He was writing to a child who probably regarded him as a near stranger, but he was confident that he could get to know her. He wrote: "We will all have a good time together. There will be so many things you will have to tell me—about your trips to camp, to school, the Christmas play and everything."[58] If Jack had gone to jail instead of disappearing, he would have been able to communicate with and thus know his daughters as they grew up. But, on the Party's directive, he sacrificed the stability of his home life to fight political repression. While he justified the move with big-picture thinking about ultimately creating a better world for his daughters, he and his family paid a heavy price.

Esther recalled that it was a big struggle to put the family back together. Between the underground years and World War II, she had lived independently for roughly half her marriage, and the unique uncertainty of the recent separation made her feel equipped to continue as a single parent to her two daughters. She loved, missed, and supported Jack and fought tooth-and-nail for his freedom, but day-to-day life, accommodating one another's quirks and patterns and readjusting to the flows of a household with two adults, was difficult. Esther was used to doing everything on her own, and Jack's return resulted in annoyances and bickering and both partners questioning whether the marriage could survive. Esther had to break the habit of making all the decisions about the girls' schooling, extracurricular activities, and social calendar without consulting anyone. She recalled that she and Jack were both determined but that the period was exceptionally difficult.[59]

In addition to their shared desire to work things out, Esther and Jack also felt a sense of obligation to their extended families. Esther's mother and Jack's parents had been so helpful during the underground years, putting the needs of Esther and the girls ahead of other obligations. They had suffered FBI harassment and had sacrificed to support Jack during his trial. As Esther recalled: "We were so fortunate and grateful. . . . [W]e wanted to support them and thank them and we couldn't put them through any more." As a couple, they agreed that the pressure of reestablishing their marriage went beyond just the two of them, and they resolved to reconnect for the broader benefit of everyone who had endured the underground years with them. They also drew on their community of friends: Ed and Augusta Strong and Dorothy and Louis Burnham all lived nearby, and Esther described the community as "a little commune" of people who had shared similar experiences. The families worked together to help one another readjust.[60]

Commitment to one another and a desire to rebuild their life together for their families and their community was important, but it took more than that to help the pair rekindle their deep connection to each other. Esther and Jack decided to take the family on a cross-country driving trip to work on their marriage. During the trip, they drove through the South. Revisiting their old home was helpful in making them feel normal again. By the late 1950s, the civil rights movement was growing more and more visible across the South, and, for Esther and Jack, it was exciting and inspiring. It also brought them back to the space and circumstances under which they first fell in love. As Esther recalled: "It was a new phase of the struggle and we wanted to be part of it. It really helped unite us."[61] For Esther and Jack, the black freedom movement was, and always had been, central to their marriage and their romance. Their love for one another was ignited in the SNYC, and the burgeoning civil rights movement gave it fuel when it was running on empty.

As Jack reconnected with his family, the Left remained in turmoil. Jack dove headfirst into insisting that the CPUSA develop a pragmatic approach to the civil rights movement. He also hoped that mainstream civil rights organizations would open themselves more to Communists, their ideas, and their comradeship. He had long been critical of the NAACP's opposition to communism and argued in a letter to Roy Wilkins that suggestions that the CPUSA "had some diabolical interest . . . and some Machiavellian intrigue afoot to 'infiltrate, subvert, and take over'" were pure nonsense. He attempted to explain that "all such rumors are the inspired products of the fevered brains of the foes of Negro-white unity for civil rights and of the NAACP." Communists wanted to participate in and support NAACP activities "in conformity with the practices, procedures, and specific objectives prescribed by their respective host."[62]

But most Communists and moderate black activists did not agree with Jack on the current compatibility of the NAACP and the CPUSA.

Still, Jack believed that striving for some form of reciprocal relationship could only help salvage the CPUSA from the difficulties of the 1950s and broaden the NAACP's appeal to encompass a wider political spectrum. The first step, for Jack, was to assure the NAACP that, while vocal, Communists were not out to take over the organization. As he and Henry Winston argued in "For a Mass Policy," he also believed that the Communist Party needed to move beyond the limitations of its dogmatic approach to the black freedom movement, accept that civil rights workers had forged a mass movement without its help, and offer assistance and solidarity before criticism. The school integration crisis in Little Rock, Arkansas, offered him an opportunity to lead the CPUSA in the direction he believed was most appropriate.

On September 9, 1957, after Arkansas governor Orval Faubus called in the national guard to prevent nine black children from entering Central High School, the Communist Party issued a statement on the Little Rock events based on a report Jack had written. Though the statement was uncompromisingly militant and forceful, nearly all Communist rhetoric was noticeably absent. The statement urged that Faubus's actions merited indictment because he was a "criminal at large not alone because he has ordered over two hundred armed soldiers to menace young Negro children with loaded guns, tear gas and fixed bayonets, but, in doing so he has organized a military *force* committed to *violence* against a branch (the judiciary) of the federal authority of the United States Government."[63]

In the statement, the Party acknowledged the supremacy of the US Constitution and legitimized federal policies in the face of state-level defiance. In fact, the CPUSA's position was not substantively different from that of the NAACP on the crisis. The two organizations differed in style but on little else.

The main difference between the CPUSA's position and that of the NAACP was one of public persona. While the CPUSA had little to lose by issuing a militant statement, the NAACP attempted to be more diplomatic in public. It was, after all, responsible for the legal proceedings in the situation and was ultimately on the side of the federal government. The organization was also much closer to the thick of the crisis than was the CPUSA and needed to be cautious in order to protect the safety of the children. In a letter to Adam Clayton Powell, Roy Wilkins noted that he could not comment "in language suitable either for the stationery of the N.A.A.C.P. or the ears of a Baptist clergyman" on his reaction to the Little Rock situation. He wrote: "I have great difficulty in speaking calmly about the role of President Eisenhower in this whole mess. He has been absolutely and thoroughly disappointing and disillusioning from beginning to end. . . . [P]erhaps he did not want to get into a fight on behalf of the Negro but he didn't do anything when the authority of his own Federal Government was challenged." Eisenhower had, according to Wilkins, "abdicated leadership in a great moral crisis."[64] The Party agreed, calling the White House's behavior "double talk, procrastination, evasion, and buck-passing" as children confronted the aggression of soldiers and "wild-eyed racist mobsters."[65]

The Party also slipped out of character and meandered into religious territory. It compared Eisenhower to Pontius Pilate, condemning his "inaction while high officials invoke mobs to menace the lives and liberties of Negro school children."[66] Wilkins had also mocked Faubus, who, on learning that the national guard would be removed from Central High School, declared: "Now begins the crucifixion." Wilkins wrote: "What baloney, I thought to myself. The governor was not Jesus. Defying the Supreme Court was no ministry."[67] The Party's statement centered first on expressing its outrage at the crisis, but the language it used evoked an image of the CPUSA as an organization that could appreciate and support movements without necessarily bringing in its own agenda. Class struggle was wholly absent, and trade unions were mentioned only once, alongside churches, schools, and civic organizations as an example of a popular form of leadership. At the behest of leaders like Jack, the Communist Party took care to present itself to the civil rights movement as a colleague, not a superior or an adversary.

Once Eisenhower deployed the 101st Airborne Division to guide nine black teenagers through the halls of their high school, the Party issued another statement written by Jack that called for "continued action." The September 23 statement applauded the president's overdue effort to counteract the mob in Little Rock but insisted that the crisis itself, along with Eisenhower's hesitancy and the ever-looming specter of continued violence, should become an impetus for the federal government to initiate further change. Jack argued: "The action of the government at Little Rock must not become simply a single shot expedient. Little Rock cannot be a halfway house for the government to rest its case against the insurrectionary southern segregationists." While it was the most newsworthy civil rights event of 1957, the Little Rock crisis was not isolated. The Party argued that, even though the violence had subsided, the incident indicated that southern racists would fight bitterly against change and that the federal government provided the only opportunity for "broad new measures of law enforcement." Eisenhower's action, according to Jack, "open[ed] the way to a great victory for human rights and democracy over the slave-time remains of Jim Crowism."[68] Jack saw the outcome of the Little Rock crisis as an opportunity to call for the expulsion of Dixiecrat congressmen and the criminal indictment of Faubus. These steps would not only offer racial justice to southern blacks, who would have new access to opportunity in the absence of racist politicians creating the laws, but also punish Jim Crow's perpetrators.

Jack's statement on September 23 went slightly further than the September 9 statement in its overt expression of communism, but the Party's traditions and agenda remained primarily a backdrop to the civil rights emphasis. In these statements, Jack had accomplished what he argued for in "For a Mass Policy." Instead of an attempt to recruit civil rights workers under the Communist umbrella, he set the concerns of activists already organizing as the top priority. He suggested that AFL-CIO unions take out two-inch solidarity ads in the *Arkansas State Press* in order to assist the paper's publisher, Daisy Bates, who was also the NAACP leader at the forefront of the struggle. As the crisis ensued, the Arkansas White Citizen Council intimidated the *State Press*'s advertisers, and the newspaper was losing money and influence owing to people's fears of retribution.[69] Jack sought to bring the labor movement closer to the civil rights movement but kept his emphasis on civil rights. He employed Communist interests when they were relevant or when they would serve to draw the attention of other Communists, but he never wavered from his stance that the civil rights movement needed the unequivocal support of the CPUSA without self-interested ulterior motives.

In seeking to connect the Party more concretely to the civil rights movement, Jack found in Little Rock a situation that perfectly evidenced the need for pragmatism over theory. Perhaps because he was a father reconnecting with his two daughters after nearly five years of separation, and perhaps because he saw his own children in the stoic faces of the Little Rock Nine, his writings for the CPUSA on Little Rock emphasized that the main protagonists in the crisis were children. In an October 1957 essay entitled "Children Challenge Bayonets at Little Rock," he argued that the Little Rock Nine were the most crucial factor in their own survival: "In counterpoint to the animal-like exhibitionism and brutal, cowardly conduct of the white supremacist mobs, the undaunted and fearless Negro school children won the compassion, admiration, and gratitude of all decent-minded people everywhere. . . . With heads erect, backs unbowed, fearless and unafraid, proud of their place of honor . . . the unfailing steps of Negro youth have set a new pace for all those who struggle on the frontiers of social progress and a new and lofty standard of courage for all its fighters to emulate."[70]

In addressing a Communist audience that often bypassed practicality to dissect the theoretical roots of an issue, focusing on the pathos of the real-life confrontation between young teenagers and armed soldiers at a public high school allowed Jack to present his analysis in a way that bridged the gap between ideology and practice. For him, the civil rights movement had the potential to offer the Party the occasion to get involved in a momentous struggle to realize democracy in the United States. As the Khrushchev report forced the CPUSA to reckon with its loyalties, its theories, and its agenda, Jack saw civil rights action as a path toward redemption for all the groups that had been harmed or diminished by the events of the early Cold War years. If unions, leftist political parties, and black freedom movement organizations could unite behind civil rights, they could "help rout anti-Negro racism from our national life . . . opening wide the doors to great new initiatives of struggle to advance, under the leadership of the working class, along the whole social frontier."[71] Keeping focused on the ways in which the Party could help the civil rights movement provided sustenance for Jack's communism during the difficult 1950s, but he would never again hold the sort of influence in the black freedom movement that he had in the SNYC years. Instead, his work grew more intellectual in focus, and he concentrated his efforts on making the Party into an organization that could contribute to civil rights. His 1959 "Resolution on Theoretical Aspects of the Negro Question" drew his interest in the civil rights movement to the forefront of CPUSA discussions.

While arguing that a practical approach to civil rights merited attention, Jack also sought to reshape the CPUSA's theoretical approach to the movement. In an address to the Party at its major conference in 1959, he insisted: "As vitally necessary as it is to come to grips with and resolve in the interest of clarity and sound orientation the fundamental theoretical problems . . . of the Negro people's freedom cause—the urgent, pressing tasks of the living moment are not unrelated or irrelevant considerations in the correct achievement of this work."[72] The Party's political location on questions of race could not remain static or separate from contemporary context. As he had argued before his sentencing, Jack saw Marxism as a flexible, changing, growing science that needed to encompass the rest of the changing political world.

Jack's address outlined the reaction and resistance to the civil rights movement and built the framework for the CPUSA's discussion. He anticipated the Eighty-Sixth Congress's filibuster in 1960 over civil rights legislation, addressed the "over 200 state laws against the constitutional rights of the Negro people to equal, unsegregated education," and argued that black trade unions needed a bigger role in the movement and that black Americans needed wider political representation in local, state, and federal positions. He made note of the opportunities available to the CPUSA and the civil rights movement to unite and initiate major advances, but he remained critical of black leaders who had an "addiction to the dope of the ruling class propaganda against the communist and communism."[73] He also argued that white progressives should promote civil rights "in their white communities . . . among the white masses" and that white Communists needed to avoid "paternalism and discourtesy towards Negroes that manifest themselves in any degree within the ranks of our party." After noting the international movements toward ending colonialism and the lingering legal "hang-overs from McCarthyism," he urged his comrades to consider theory's practical application. The Party's discussion, he reminded his audience, should center not on "how to compress the phenomena of the Negro people's movement in the US into a single given Marxist category" but on "how to use the total science of Marxism-Leninism to serve the cause of Negro equality and freedom."[74]

In its discussion of the Negro Question, the Party acknowledged that its position was outdated and long overdue for revision. Although it noted that the improved status of African Americans was one reason to revise the Black Belt thesis, it also recognized that the idea of a "nation within a nation" did not necessarily fit the United States as well as it might have the Soviet Union. The changing racial culture in the United States was in part due to the post–World War II migration to the North and West and in part due to improvements in the economic, social, and political position of African Americans. Still, the Party noted that, in spite of these improvements, black Americans continued to face significant disadvantages in the areas of education, job availability, and political and economic status. Racists still murdered blacks who asserted their rights, and blacks "remain[ed], very definitely, the 'second-class citizens' of our country . . . changed only in degree by the many democratic gains the Negro people have won during the past quarter-century." The Party also recognized Jack's point that Marxism could not be applied dogmatically to the racial context of the United States. It noted the "tragedy that our movement did not welcome [the] skepticism" of Communists who "sensed . . . that our slogan of 'self-determination in the Black Belt' [was] patently alien to the American scene" and lamented that the debates the Party currently engaged in could have happened years earlier.[75] In acknowledging that its position on the Negro Question needed to be flexible in order to suit the rapidly changing times, the CPUSA opened itself to continual debate on race throughout the 1960s.

Between 1959 and 1960, the Party underwent a restructuring of its leadership to accommodate both its decrease in membership and shifts in its approach to the world around it. Its policies reflected a desire to be at the cutting edge of American politics alongside an effort to fit into the larger political milieu.[76] The CPUSA selected Jack as the new editor of *The Worker*, and he used that role to present the civil rights movement as the Party's central focus. As the Party rebuilt itself after the disastrous 1950s, Jack's pragmatism in his approach to the link between the CPUSA and civil rights proved to be a crucial tool.

As the CPUSA moved into the 1960s, its position on the civil rights movement would continue to be a rallying cry and a source of debate internally as well as cause for criticism from both its pro– and anti–civil rights detractors externally. The civil rights movement forced it to engage in an important evolution of its racial politics, but that evolution was also linked to its own predicament in the 1950s. With Southern Regional Director James Jackson discreetly probing its position on race alongside the emerging civil rights movement during the early 1950s, its development relied on the work of its second cadre leadership. And, while the Smith Act indictments and the national anxiety over communism changed the shape of the black freedom movement, the CPUSA also began to change its approach to social movements and theoretical questions. After the second cadre reemerged, the Party—facing legal difficulties and the fallout from the Khrushchev report—began work to reinvent itself in the public eye without sacrificing its fundamental values and core ideology. Although its increased openness to change during this era did not help it regain the status it boasted in the Popular Front years or allow it to make inroads in the civil rights movement, its internal evolution reflected an organization that still saw itself as vital and still sought allies and relevance. Jack, deeply entrenched in both movements, continued to navigate, analyze, and define the link between communism and civil rights, and the 1960s would allow him to do so with his wife at his side.

The Jackson family. *Left to right:* Alice, James Sr., Clara, Jack, and baby Clara. James Sr. is holding baby Clara. ca. 1920. From the personal collection of Esther Cooper Jackson.

James E. Jackson Jr., around age three, experimenting with his father's pharmacy equipment. ca. 1917. The mortar and pestle remains in the family. James and Esther Cooper Jackson Photographs, Tamiment Library, New York University, box 1, folder 1.

Jack, age sixteen, in his Boy Scout uniform. ca. 1930. Jackson Photographs, box 1, folder 1.

Esther Irving Cooper at work in Washington, DC. ca. 1910s (?). From the personal collection of Esther Cooper Jackson.

Esther, at approximately age three. ca. 1920. From the personal collection of Esther Cooper Jackson.

Esther, second from the left, with friends at Oberlin College. ca. 1934–1938. From the personal collection of Esther Cooper Jackson.

The Southern Negro Youth Congress welcomes Paul Robeson to its conference in Tuskegee, AL. 1942. Esther is facing Robeson. Jackson Photographs, box 2, folder 47.

Jack in Burma. ca. 1945. Jackson Photographs, box 1, folder 3.

Esther while Jack is away. ca. 1944–1945. In her hand is the photo of the couple featured on the cover of the book. From the personal collection of Esther Cooper Jackson.

Esther, in back row, center, as part of the all-female World Federation of Democratic Youth delegation, working as a bricklayer in postwar Stalingrad. 1945. From the personal collection of Esther Cooper Jackson.

Southern Negro Youth Congress poster advertising Esther and Jack's postwar speaking tour. 1946. From the personal collection of Esther Cooper Jackson.

PRESENTING:

Two of America's Foremost Youth Leaders

In A

Vital, Provocative Joint Lecture

You Can't Afford to Miss!

James E. Jackson, Jr.

Esther Cooper Jackson

SUBJECT:

"WAR OR PEACE---WHICH WAY AMERICA?"

SPEAKERS:

James E. Jackson, Jr.
Past Educational Director, Southern Negro Youth Congress; writer, lecturer, expert on Colonial problems, outstanding Youth organizer.

Esther Cooper Jackson
Executive Secretary, Southern Negro Youth Congress; Member of the Governing Council, World Federation of Democratic Youth; Just returned from England, France, Germany, Soviet Union.

Protesting police brutality in Detroit, Michigan. ca. 1948–1949. Jack is walking, third from the left. Jackson Photographs, box 1, folder 13.

Esther participating in a Detroit demonstration to support Smith Act defendants, including Carl Winter. ca. 1948. Jackson Photographs, box 1, folder 13.

Jack, W. E. B. Du Bois, and Esther. 1958. From the personal collection of Esther Cooper Jackson.

Left to right: Augusta Strong, W. E. B. Du Bois, and Esther at a *Freedomways* gathering. ca. 1961. From the personal collection of Esther Cooper Jackson.

James Baldwin and Martin Luther King Jr. before King's speech titled "Honoring Dr. Du Bois" at the *Freedomways* Du Bois centennial celebration. 1968. From the personal collection of Esther Cooper Jackson.

Jack with Ho Chi Minh in North Vietnam as part of a Communist Party USA delegation. 1968. Jackson Photographs, box 1, folder 10.

Esther speaking at the dedication of the Du Bois Home Site in Great Barrington, MA. 1969. From the personal collection of Esther Cooper Jackson.

Angela Davis and Jack at the Communist Party USA national convention. 1979. From the personal collection of Esther Cooper Jackson.

James Jackson's sixtieth birthday party. 1974. Jack is speaking at the podium. Seated, *left to right:* Chris Alston, Pete Seeger, Mary Kaufman, Henry Winston, and Gus Hall. In the backdrop is Hugo Gellert's portrait of Jack. Jackson Photographs, box 1, folder 12.

Esther and Jack at Long Island University, Brooklyn, after Esther received an honorary degree. 2003. From the personal collection of Esther Cooper Jackson.

6

Radical Journalism in the Civil Rights Years

Although part of Jack's purpose in the Communist Party's underground from 1951 to 1955 was to create a more democratic world for his daughters to grow up in, he missed out on the day-to-day life of a father. When he emerged and settled his legal troubles, he and his wife knew that renewed stability and support for their daughters would be paramount, and they worked to present themselves as a united front. When Kathy, now in the sixth grade, brought home history homework in 1958 that glorified the South's redemption after Reconstruction, the Jacksons took immediate action. Writing jointly, the couple penned a letter to her teacher that excused their daughter from the assignment and argued: "Is it for my daughter, a Negro child, to join in the authors' gladness that 'the white people got control once more.' . . . Indeed, there is a direct chain of historic linkage between the KKK against Negroes in overthrowing Reconstruction and the conduct of [Governor Orval Faubus] to assault the constitution and drive little Negro children from school doors in the South."[1] Though Esther and Jack had lived together briefly before World War II and in Detroit before the McCarthy period, Jack's emergence from the second cadre allowed the couple to build a new home life in which their gender egalitarianism, family devotion, and political ideals would keep them together.

Part of the couple's reunion involved finding new career paths that would contribute to their family's security and express their political ideals. Jack remained a part of the Communist Party USA (CPUSA) leadership and became the editor of its newspaper, *The Worker*, in 1959. Esther was a founder and the managing editor of *Freedomways* magazine, a quarterly journal of the black freedom movement. The years the couple spent apart during World War II and the 1950s helped set the foundation for their independent and often different editorial perspectives in the 1960s. Through *The Worker* and *Freedomways*, Jack and Esther found individual career paths that allowed them to adhere to their ideals, engage with the black freedom movement, and live comfortably together with their daughters after nearly two decades of intermittent separation and political upheaval. Working to promote the civil rights movement gave their marriage much-needed sustenance as they put their family back together. Their editorial positions created the essential connection they needed between their activism and their love and family life. That connection built their marriage, and after the 1950s their independent editorial and activist careers served as an expression of renewed family stability.

As *The Worker*'s editor, Jack emphasized the civil rights movement as a cause the CPUSA should support without imposing its own agenda. He offered favorable editorials on civil rights triumphs, criticized the economic roots of racism in the United States, and advocated for criminal indictments of politicians, police, and civilians who violated the civil rights of blacks across the nation. His editorials offered an analysis of race and civil rights in the United States that was much further to the left than that of any mainstream newspaper. This was in part because the CPUSA was not burdened by the need to retain public favor, as its ideological opponents did not typically subscribe to the paper unless they worked for the FBI. Rather, Jack and other Communists believed that, by offering an analysis that showed support for civil rights and reflected the Party's ideas, *The Worker* could help the CPUSA win back some support. The Party did see an uptick in membership by the end of the decade, but the success of the strategy was quite limited. By offering the Party's support to the civil rights movement, a cause that was uniquely rooted in American democratic ideals, Jack hoped to demonstrate that Communists were a vital part of national political discourse, patriotic in their own right, and willing to back movements without the direct involvement of the Soviet Union. *The Worker*'s predecessor, *The Daily Worker,* suffered in the McCarthy period, but the Party resumed its publication as a weekly in the late 1950s. In the 1960s, a midweek *Worker* was added, and, after Jack's tenure, the paper merged with *The Daily World,* then became *The People's Daily World,* and, finally, *The People's Weekly World.* The paper's reach is difficult to assess because an unknown number of subscribers included undercover agents seeking to undermine the Party's efforts, but the Party worked steadily to reestablish its reach in print.

Jack was inexperienced in the field of editing, so on becoming editor of *The Worker* he signed up for an editing course at New York University. He planned to revamp the newspaper, hoping to reestablish it as a daily periodical. Busy with his editorial work, he wrote to his friends John and Margrit Pittman: "The new duties have kept my feet to the fire and my head in a whirl. . . . I think already we have some improvements in political content." John Pittman was a black Communist originally from Atlanta who became a newspaper editor in California. He married Margrit Adler, a German-Jewish refugee and fellow Communist. From 1959 to 1961, the pair lived in Moscow as correspondents for the Party's newspapers. Jack expressed his appreciation for the Pittmans' news stories and promised to "use them better and catch up," then directed the couple to the paper's stories about the South, which "is really jumping these days . . . the big story stateside."[2]

Communism was an important part of Esther's individual political identity, but dedication to her political ideals did not come with the same organizational commitment to the CPUSA as did her husband's. After joining the Party in 1939 with some hesitation that membership would compromise her political independence, Esther used her political affiliation as just one path toward achieving her objectives. Though she never formally left the Party, she became inactive after the McCarthy years.[3] She had a number of reasons for this decision, including news of the 1956 Khrushchev report on Stalin's brutality and some exhaustion after the challenges she confronted while her husband was underground and stood trial. After spending a few years trying to figure out how best to support her family and maintain her activism, she joined forces with W. E. B. and Shirley Graham Du Bois and founded *Freedomways* magazine.

Freedomways afforded Esther a new kind of independence. Though she and her husband built their marriage around the notion of women's equality, her past activism and careers had been intertwined with her relationship with her husband. In the 1960s, after decades of turmoil, her independent career represented her ability to express her politics in a forum that was not directly connected to her husband's work or political predicaments. *Freedomways* became a path for her to promote and live out her gender ideology, politics, and activism. The magazine represented her political identity as a Popular Front activist, and, in selecting the range of articles that *Freedomways* published, she displayed her position on the growing black freedom movement in its pages.

The periodicals provided an ideal forum for the Jacksons to continue contributing to the black freedom movement as seasoned, experienced activists who could offer guidance and lessons from earlier struggles. *Freedomways,* in particular, strove to represent all the segments of the black freedom movement, including liberal civil rights, black nationalism, cultural expression, and internationalism. Though its primary purpose was to promote the Party's positions and goals, *The Worker* attempted to illustrate that the Party's views on black freedom were not all that different from those of the civil rights movement. It offered frequent analysis of the ways in which capitalism and class exploitation perpetuated racism in the United States, providing an angle on the civil rights movement that mainstream news outlets avoided. It also highlighted the ways in which political repression similarly influenced both the Party and the civil rights movement.

These two publications illustrated that, while the Cold War restricted more radical forms of activism in the United States, dedicated leftists continued to challenge conventional thinking and engage with civil rights discourse. The Jacksons' lives reveal that Cold War anticommunism influenced the direction and methods of the civil rights movement in the 1960s but did not prevent Communists from contributing to the broad ideological struggle against racial injustice in the United States. Between the two publications, Esther's and Jack's editorial roles highlight the continuity from the Popular Front to civil rights and the places where their individual activism overlapped and diverged. Though the civil rights movement had a complicated relationship with the left wing as the Cold War restricted US activism, the Jacksons' editorial work points to a more fluid collaboration among activists across the political spectrum. Both *The Worker* and *Freedomways,* along with other periodicals including the *National Guardian,* championed civil rights as the movement gained momentum, and both were on the perimeter of the mainstream news media because of their left-wing orientation. As editors, Jack and Esther maintained their activism by calling attention to forms of racism in the United States, from the most egregious to the subtlest, reporting on efforts at resistance, and analyzing the political, social, and cultural systems governing race relations in the United States.

Freedomways grew out of Paul Robeson's newspaper *Freedom,* which ran from 1951 to 1955. *Freedom* published the work of black artists and intellectuals and offered a rare leftist political commentary in the early 1950s. It suffered in the context of the Cold War, particularly given the difficulties that Robeson confronted as anti-Communist sentiment increased, and it ceased publication after four years.[4] The *Freedomways* organizers began planning shortly after Jack's reemergence. Esther worked with Southern Negro Youth Congress (SNYC) veterans Ed Strong and Louis Burnham until Ed died of cancer in 1957 and Louis died of a heart attack in 1960. After Louis's death, Esther and Shirley Graham Du Bois assumed the editorial responsibilities and spent a year fund-raising and planning. They established an editorial philosophy based on intellectual independence and did not rely on "big foundation money," which "meant more people participated and supported the journal."[5] The journal's staff and contributors celebrated its debut in April 1961 at the Hotel Martinique in New York City.

Freedomways reached a wide range of individuals, from former Popular Front activists and New Dealers, to young activists working from the grass roots in the South, to international universities and organizations. As Jack O'Dell wrote to the Student Nonviolent Coordinating Committee (SNCC) leader Diane Nash Bevels in 1967: "FREEDOMWAYS now has some circulation in 40 states as well as Mexico, Canada, the West Indies, and the leading universities in Africa."[6] Among the magazine's subscribers were the Southern Christian Leadership Conference (SCLC) leader Fred Shuttlesworth, the Africanist scholar Basil Davidson, Indian prime minister Jawaharlal Nehru, the Reverend Jesse Jackson, and a range of college and university libraries. In 1964, the Congress of Racial Equality (CORE) and Council of Federated Organizations (COFO) activist Michael Schwerner wrote to Esther regarding a community center COFO was working to establish in Meridian, Mississippi. The community center included a library, and Schwerner requested ten free copies of *Freedomways* because "[it] is so pertinent to the work that is being done here in the south."[7] By 1968, *Freedomways* had around five thousand paid subscriptions. Some of its special issues, including one commemorating the life of W. E. B. Du Bois, sold around fifteen thousand copies.[8]

As editors of *Freedomways,* Esther and Graham Du Bois outlined its purpose in the first issue. They situated themselves as a key link between an older generation of activists and the new civil rights workers. The journal's primary goal was to provide a forum for discussion, and the editors stated: "FREEDOMWAYS is born of the necessity for a vehicle of communication which will mirror developments in the diversified and many-sided struggles of the Negro people. It will provide a public forum for the review, examination, and debate of all problems confronting Negroes in the United States."[9]

Esther and Graham Du Bois emphasized that the journal had no formal connection with any organizations or institutions and no specific political ties. Instead: "[It] offers all of us the opportunity to speak for ourselves."[10] The noted writer James Baldwin, a member of the *Freedomways* editorial board, juxtaposed art and politics when he wrote: "Its in-depth coverage and analysis of important developments on African and Asian continents, its poetry, short stories, art and photography make FREEDOMWAYS a most complete magazine."[11] For Esther, *Freedomways* offered a means for her to continue her Popular Front–style activism in a forum that made a distinct contribution to the black freedom movement.

Freedomways strove to represent the desires and goals of African Americans across the nation of varying political perspectives. As the editors stated: "Those who commit themselves to its support become patrons only of a publication and an editorial policy designed to provide an open forum for the free expression of ideas. Sponsors of the publication will assume no responsibility for the particular views of any of its contributors; nor will contributors be constrained to abide by any editorial preference or bias of the publishers or editors."[12] In her role as managing editor, Esther "shaped [the journal's] intellectual direction and was the energy behind it."[13] The journal's style of wide-ranging, open political expression mirrored the activist style Esther had honed since the late 1930s. Though Esther remained with the magazine for its twenty-five-year duration, *Freedomways*' other editors changed periodically and included, at one point or another, the scholar John Henrik Clarke, the artist Margaret Burroughs, the activist Jack O'Dell, the philosopher Angela Davis, the poet Keith E. Baird, the cartoonist Brumsic Brandon Jr., the novelist John Oliver Killens, the activist W. Alphaeus Hunton, the editor George B. Murphy, the librarian Ernest Kaiser, and the activist Jean Carey Bond.

The magazine received some grant money but operated on a small budget of subscription funds and the proceeds of fund-raising efforts. At *Freedomways* fund-raisers, well-known actors and musicians loaned their talents for public events, and artists contributed works for greeting cards and auctions.

Freedomways reflected its editors' desire to maintain intellectual independence as the US-Soviet conflict shaped public life and political expression. In the 1960s, the Cold War continued to influence daily life as tense global events consumed American politics during the Kennedy and Johnson administrations. Politicians kept up efforts to restrict political activism aimed at altering the racial status quo.[14] But, in the absence of widespread McCarthy-style witch hunts, many of the early domestic anxieties of the Cold War had subsided, and the United States adjusted to the state of perpetual diplomatic conflict. As a new generation began to dominate the civil rights movement, young activists who had not weathered the difficulties of McCarthyism were increasingly bold and eschewed some of the caution that their elders had been conditioned to embrace.

The movement's increasing momentum as the 1960s approached was in part a result of the successes in Montgomery and Little Rock and in part a response to the continued resistance to change and the violent white backlash it produced. While organizations like the SCLC, SNCC, CORE, the Fellowship of Reconciliation, and the National Association for the Advancement of Colored People (NAACP) worked for the common cause of equality and freedom for African Americans, as more individuals got involved and brought new perspectives to the table the movement's ideological scope widened.[15] In particular, younger activists from the North as well as the South came to the civil rights movement with new ideas about leadership. While the SCLC and the NAACP operated with a hierarchical, clear leadership apparatus and used charismatic figures to inspire and instruct the southern masses, the student organizers of SNCC promoted "group-centered leadership." SNCC's style encouraged anyone who wanted to lead to do so, and "the role of spokesperson rotated among all those who desired to serve."[16]

SNCC's organizers were less hesitant to push the boundaries of acceptable political discourse than were their elder counterparts in the SCLC and the NAACP. Their organization never adopted a provision against Communist participation, unlike most activist organizations in the Cold War years. Because SNCC emerged after McCarthyism had essentially dissipated, its young organizers honed their activist ideology without the same fears that had hounded their older colleagues in the movement. The organization embraced political inclusiveness as a key component of its mission. Just as their Popular Front counterparts had done a generation earlier, SNCC leaders recognized that their goals did not always require a uniform political or ideological method and that activists across the South worked in distinct local and regional contexts. As the historian Clayborne Carson has written, SNCC was "typically less willing than other civil rights groups to impose its ideas on local black leaders or to restrain southern black militancy." It ventured into what for the civil rights movement was uncharted territory, including rural Mississippi, and its experiences on the ground pushed it toward a "secular, humanistic radicalism" and eventually Black Power.[17] To segregationists, however, SNCC radicalism differed little from that of such liberal organizations as the SCLC and the NAACP as all worked to change the racial status quo and chip away at the states' rights defense of legalized racial terror.

Freedomways emerged as the civil rights movement was growing and splintering. The expanding ideological breadth of the movement in the early 1960s presented a unique opportunity for its editors to draw on their activist backgrounds in the 1930s, 1940s, and 1950s. Connected to Communists, liberals, artists, intellectuals, politicians, and activist leaders, *Freedomways* drew contributors of varying ideological and political perspectives and broke down barriers between the left and the middle of the black political spectrum. From the vantage points of a number of organizations that may have had disagreements with each other, it offered a forum for conversation, debate, and political expression. While not everyone it approached embraced the opportunity to publish in a venue that embraced the far left of the political spectrum, its pages presented the ideas of activists and thinkers in juxtapositions that would have been unlikely elsewhere.

In striving to present an array of perspectives on the black freedom movement, *Freedomways* collected the work of individuals without heavy editorial commentary, allowing readers to assess the sides of debates for themselves. These debates encompassed liberal, socialist, and nationalist views, and *Freedomways* hoped to represent them all. This was especially true, as the literary scholar James Smethurst has written, "once the civil rights movement and the rise of Black Power had blunted Cold War divisions and taboos within the African American community a bit."[18] The novelist John Oliver Killens once described the magazine's editorial point of view as "black nationalist with a socialist perspective," though the journal regularly included contributions from liberal writers who advocated integration.[19] In fact, as the historian Ian Rocksborough-Smith argues, the Popular Front background of *Freedomways*' editors led them to emphasize coalitions and embrace radicalism, and the magazine worked to demonstrate continuity and promote cohesion among movement eras and organizers. He notes: "*Freedomways* editors could assume an intermediary role between the Du Bois and Robeson generation and younger activists like John Lewis and Julian Bond of SNCC—in effect, creating a dialogue that reconciled the leftist ideals of past decades with the black freedom movement of the early 1960s." *Freedomways* staff members highlighted radicalism and militancy within the existing civil rights movement in the 1960s, illustrating their support and gratitude for the organizers' uncompromising integrationism.[20]

A key debate in the early 1960s black freedom movement evolved between black nationalists and civil rights advocates, and *Freedomways* worked to build a bridge between the two. Black leaders clashed over how best to solve the centuries-old problem of racial oppression in the United States. Martin Luther King Jr. promoted civil rights and nonviolent integration and, in the public view, represented the movement's moral core. He declared: "Through nonviolent resistance the Negro will be able to rise to the noble height of opposing the unjust system while loving the perpetrators of the system."[21] King won the support of white liberals and credibility with politicians and had significant success in achieving national attention for civil rights. For African Americans, nonviolence offered empowerment, and integration brought gradual and pragmatic results. King's brand of integrationism, alongside his charisma and eloquence, earned the admiration of the *Freedomways* staff, Jack, and other older black freedom activists, even in instances where their ideological principles differed.

Nationalists like Malcolm X offered a separatist alternative, arguing that African Americans needed their own nation and had the right to defend themselves against white violence. Malcolm drew on the work of Robert F. Williams, the Monroe, North Carolina, NAACP leader, when he argued in favor of self-defense. Williams wrote: "In a civilized society the law is a deterrent against the strong who would take advantage of the weak, but the South is not a civilized society; the South is a social jungle."[22] Malcolm X echoed that sentiment in criticizing King's emphasis on morality, arguing: "Tactics based solely on morality can only succeed when you are dealing with a people who are moral or a system that is moral."[23] Black nationalism afforded African Americans autonomy and control over their own fates and communities. Whites did not embrace black nationalism as they did nonviolence in part because it undermined white engagement with civil rights causes, and even sympathetic whites felt threatened by separatist ideology. As contrasting viewpoints, integrationism and nationalism embraced similar fundamental goals, including political and economic liberty for African Americans, but mobilized different tactics and envisioned divergent outcomes. In addition to linking older generations of activists and young civil rights workers, *Freedomways* envisioned connections between various threads of the movement, in part by situating civil rights and black nationalism within a global conversation about black freedom.[24]

The relationship between nonviolence and nationalism grew more important and visible in the domestic sphere as national politics began to influence civil rights. When Lyndon Johnson became president, he took on John F. Kennedy's civil rights agenda and made it a priority. Johnson, a Texan, had sway with southern Democrats, was persistent, and insisted on the passage of civil rights legislation. In 1964, he signed into law the Civil Rights Act, legislation that had been initiated by Kennedy the previous year. In the past, civil rights legislation fell short of guaranteeing full equality under the law and included a number of compromises conceived to appease southern politicians. This time, the legislation had a much further reach, outlawing segregation in public spaces and schools and establishing the Equal Employment Opportunity Commission. The act, coming from a Democratic administration, began a massive shift of southern voters to the Republican Party, strengthening the wave of conservatism that would come to dominate American politics. A year later, Johnson signed the Voting Rights Act following the momentous Freedom Summer and Selma civil rights campaigns.[25] Esther and Jack celebrated these victories in their respective arenas, but their experience and political perspectives illustrated that the road to full equal justice wound on. They also recognized that other areas of the black freedom movement made cogent points and offered perspectives that suggested that these victories were incomplete.

The Civil Rights and Voting Rights Acts were major civil rights gains, but they did not solve all the problems blacks confronted on a daily basis. In the North, de facto segregation and racism created a situation in which African Americans were more subtly denied opportunities, and, in the absence of a movement targeted at such oppression, frustration began to mount. Federal laws ensuring that Jim Crow was no longer a legal way of life had little meaning in areas that had no segregation laws to begin with. In northern cities in particular, a pattern of residential segregation dating back to the New Deal and job discrimination resulted in the concentration of poverty among African Americans. In addition, many majority black urban areas experienced daily conflicts with local white police forces.[26] For *Freedomways,* these developments called attention to the importance of sustaining and encouraging coalitions across the black freedom movement.

In 1964, Harlem and the Bedford-Stuyvesant neighborhood of Brooklyn erupted in protest. Racial tensions between white police officers, white landlords, and black residents in Harlem and Bedford-Stuyvesant had begun to boil over by 1963. The strife in Harlem first centered on high rents for squalid living conditions. In comparison to rental rates in other parts of New York City, Harlem's cost of living was exorbitant, and inattentive white landlords who lived in other areas let buildings deteriorate. Jesse Gray, a local activist, led residents in a rent strike. In November 1963, Gray organized a fifteen-block protest in which residents brought both live and dead rats to a hearing in civil court. The goal of the theatrical protest was to highlight unsanitary infestations consuming overpriced Harlem apartments.[27]

Tensions continued to mount in 1964 as black nationalist sentiment rose and conditions festered. On July 16, 1964, an off-duty white police officer named Thomas Gilligan shot a black fifteen-year-old named James

Powell. Ten days of racial violence ensued as white police officers bloodily beat protestors, including Gray, who called for "100 skilled revolutionaries who are ready to die" to engage in "guerilla warfare" and orchestrate "a black takeover of the city."[28] The conflict in Harlem spilled over into Bedford-Stuyvesant, a neighborhood whose own tensions had been brewing for years.[29] In 1965, a few days after passage of the Voting Rights Act, a rebellion consumed the Watts neighborhood of Los Angeles. Over the next several years, similar uprisings took place across urban industrial centers, including Newark, New Jersey, and Detroit, Michigan. Though most of the casualties of the rebellions resulted from police action against black protestors, the violence and destruction associated with the uprisings altered public perception of the black freedom movement.

As riots in the North overtook nonviolent southern protests in the headlines, white news reporters struggled to explain the shift. National reports offered oversimplified summaries of the events with little analysis of the conditions that produced them. As Gene Roberts and Hank Klibanoff have written: "Blacks complained that television portrayed the militancy of black power without explaining that it could be regarded as an understandable reaction to persistent white racism; they said that television was 'simplistically' focusing on the violence and mayhem of the riots without devoting equal time to the underlying problems of urban blacks."[30] In part, national coverage of urban rebellions in the North catered to white audiences who had fled the inner cities for the suburbs since the postwar years along with whites who tentatively remained in the cities, and reporters were unable to make the frustration blacks felt about their circumstances palatable for their audiences. *Freedomways* and *The Worker*, in contrast, focused on the root causes of the uprisings and offered a counterpoint to national coverage.

As northern blacks expressed their frustrations through violence, southern blacks continued to confront the lingering problem of white racism. In 1966, James Meredith decided to walk alone from Memphis, Tennessee, to Jackson, Mississippi, "against fear" of segregation, racism, and continued disenfranchisement. Meredith was known for his attempt to enroll at the segregated University of Mississippi in 1962 and the resulting civil rights crisis that led white students to riot and resulted in two deaths. On the second day of his march against fear, an unemployed white man from Memphis named Aubrey James Norvell shot and injured him.

In response, civil rights leaders from SNCC, the SCLC, and CORE vowed to continue the march. The marchers faced belligerent white troopers on the road, and in Greenwood, Mississippi, SNCC chairman Stokely Carmichael was arrested. Frustrated by resistance to the march, and increasingly disillusioned by white liberals and the Johnson admin-istration, Carmichael offered a new slogan for the black freedom move-ment. He told his audience in Greenwood: "This is the twenty-seventh time that I've been arrested. I ain't going to jail no more. The only way we gonna stop them white men from whuppin' us is to take over. What we gonna start sayin' now is Black Power!"[31] Carmichael's frustration and new declaration resonated with his audience and with African Ameri-cans across the country and kick-started a shift in SNCC and CORE as those organizations began to embrace black nationalism and self-defense strategies.

While Martin Luther King Jr. and the SCLC "represented an unwill-ingness to wait for racial justice," Carmichael's cry "portrayed the impa-tient face of political anger." King kept the Black Power movement at arm's length but recognized that the ideology behind it represented the needs of the black masses. He differed with Black Power advocates on the point of self-defense, staunchly advocating nonviolence, but embraced the idea that blacks would "realize deliverance only when they have accu-mulated the power to enforce change." While the mainstream news media reported that the new "Black Power" slogan was "a racist philoso-phy" and a "distorted cry" and looked to leaders like King to quell fears, King did not denounce Black Power or Carmichael.[32]

Black Power embodied political, ideological, social, economic, and cultural goals. As the historian William Van Deberg writes: "Black Power is best understood as a broad, adaptive, cultural term serving to connect and illuminate the differing ideological orientations of the movement's supporters."[33] Black Power advocates saw little hope in integration and believed that blacks should take control of their communities to fight racism, police brutality, and discrimination. President Johnson, whose passion for domestic issues took a back seat to his commitment to the unpopular Vietnam War, appeared increasingly unable to produce lasting, fundamental change to the structure of race relations in the United States. In this regard, national politics and diplomacy aided the rise of Black Power ideology because they fostered frustration with slow civil rights implementation and again juxtaposed the government's concern with democracy abroad and its failure to support its black citizens at home.

Run mainly by older activists like Esther who had encountered, participated in, and shaped an array of approaches to black freedom, *Freedomways* interpreted the rise of Black Power as another iteration of a broad, encompassing struggle that was not solely about mainstream civil rights. The magazine "offered a form of black radicalism that reconciled issues of cultural autonomy and leftist radicalism with mainstream initiatives in the electoral and legislative spheres."[34] Alongside articles by moderate and radical grassroots activists, artists, and writers, it published the work of African and Caribbean leaders. Contributors like Kwame Nkrumah of Ghana, Julius Nyerere of Tanzania, and Cheddi Jagan of Guyana were at the helm of a long international freedom movement that was deeply entangled in Cold War diplomacy. They offered political commentary on socialism, capitalism, and democracy in Africa and the Caribbean, the US-Soviet conflict, and the independence of their nations. Former Popular Front activists, Communists, and others on the left offered radical critiques of US capitalism, commentary on the civil rights struggles in the South, labor, and artistic work. In this respect, the editors chose to draw on internationalist and nationalist traditions that had origins in earlier periods and offered far-reaching implications and instruction for current movements. *Freedomways* was more likely to highlight ways in which these seemingly new developments in the black freedom movement in fact drew on longer traditions that had been obscured by history than it was to explicitly take one side or another in a given debate. More moderate civil rights leaders, including Whitney Young of the National Urban League and the Reverend Milton Galamison, a Brooklyn community leader, also contributed, representing more centrist perspectives. As managing editor, Esther incorporated a range of viewpoints on civil rights into the magazine, which resulted in a quarterly that tilted further to the left than mainstream discussion of the civil rights movement.

Most national newspapers and magazines sought to present the civil rights movement to national readers as an epic struggle against a clear evil, highlighting white violence against nonviolent protesters. They described the efforts of civil rights activists as patriotic demonstrations that reflected American ideals and portrayed the movement positively. In contrast, regional southern media outlets regularly reported either that Martin Luther King Jr. was a Communist or that he supported communism. Press attacks on his alleged subversion bolstered the white South's efforts to brand all those who fought racism as Communists. Occasionally, the Associated Press would pick up these stories, giving them national distribution. In one instance, a story that linked King, SNCC, the NAACP, and the SCLC to the Southern Conference Educational Fund, a Left-leaning organization that had weathered the McCarthy era, was printed in the *Jackson (MS) Advocate,* picked up by the Associated Press, and reprinted in the *Jackson Clarion-Ledger* under a headline reading "M. L. King Linked to Red Front." A state representative read the article aloud on the floor of the House of Representatives. That article and others like it bolstered FBI director J. Edgar Hoover's crusade to unveil King's allegedly hidden Communist inclinations, and the bureau regularly distributed similar stories. Some of those articles were printed in the North as well, including in the *Long Island Star-Journal.*[35]

King and other civil rights leaders had a number of important connections to Communists and former Communists, but the meaning of those connections was veiled by the mere fact that they existed. The Kennedy administration, the FBI, and the right wing viewed any connection to communism as a threat.[36] Linking communism to civil rights allowed reactionary southern whites to believe that the civil rights movement was not only contrary to their way of life but also fundamentally un-American. The Kennedy administration was nervous about civil rights leaders' Communist connections, and its response to those connections validated reactionary whites on a national scale.

Realistically, however, black leaders in the 1960s would have been hard-pressed to establish connections with leaders of an older generation who were not, in one way or another, linked with the Popular Front. Some distanced themselves from those connections, including A. Philip Randolph, who led the National Negro Congress during the Popular Front years. Martin Luther King Jr.'s father attended the SNYC's 1944 conference in Atlanta.[37] And, while many of the older civil rights leaders in the 1960s were ardently anti-Communist, including Whitney Young and Roy Wilkins, their organizations took on the task of balancing complicated local needs, national politics, and their own ideologies. As the historian Jonathan Holloway has written, local NAACP chapters in the 1930s "worked cooperatively with labor and were developing a mass base": "The association was aggressively working to secure equal pay for equal work."[38] While McCarthyism and its legacies influenced the black freedom movement in the United States by quieting leftist activists who had Communist connections in the 1930s and 1940s, a clean break between one era and another did not result.

Civil rights leaders did not exclusively pander to Cold War ideology, even when they espoused anti-Communist political perspectives and did not believe that completely restructuring the US economy was a necessity. In spite of liberal rhetoric that promoted integration as a social and legal, not economic, issue, integrationism incorporated the fight against job discrimination, equal access to resources, and achieving middle-class ideals. The distinction between the civil rights era and the Popular Front years was the way in which economics manifested. Liberal civil rights leaders could hardly promote middle-class ideals without addressing the issue of poverty, and they did so. Popular Front activists tackled similar issues but did not see middle-class status as the necessary outcome.

Another tension in the 1960s that had roots in the Popular Front era was that between civil rights activists and labor leaders. After unions purged their ranks of the leftist and Communist organizers who had promoted interracial working-class unity as an essential element of the labor movement, a broad-based coalition between labor and civil rights grew increasingly unlikely. As the historian Robert Korstad writes: "Throughout the 1960s, the FBI and white supremacist groups kept up a drumbeat of pressure by taking every opportunity to tar a new generation of activists." Red-baiting and racism led to an "absence of radical, union-based leaders and institutions" in the civil rights movement.[39] The complicated relationship between labor and civil rights created conflict in Party leadership as well. Jack wrote to Party chairman Gus Hall: "Some seem to think that being pro-labor means that Negro workers have no right to challenge the assumptions of special privileges and preferential status in hiring, promotion and apprenticeship prerogatives of white workers. Such a position is anti–Negro workers' interests. That which is anti-Negro *is* anti-labor."[40] In other words, the Cold War context of the 1960s made union and civil rights collaboration politically challenging, even if it was not impossible.

Postwar Red-baiting reinforced white supremacy by equating efforts to improve the condition of the working class, both black and white, with communism and made labor's role in the 1960s civil rights movement all the more complex. Blacks were almost wholly absent from craft unions in the mid-1960s, and, as the historian Michael Honey explains: "The merger of AFL and CIO unions beginning in the midfifties further muted the distinctive interracial presence that industrial unions once provided, placing whites in an increasingly dominant position within the labor movement." Though black workers continued to participate in unions to protect their rights as workers, the decline of interracial solidarity within unions meant that labor organizations were no longer a source for civil rights activism. Unions like the AFL-CIO and the United Automobile Workers (UAW) provided civil rights efforts with funds and political support, but unity among black and white workers on the ground was increasingly difficult to forge.[41]

Nonetheless, it is important to acknowledge the presence of labor within the broad civil rights network and the weight of work as an essential component of the fight for justice. After all, the famous March on Washington for Jobs and Freedom grew out of the labor leader A. Philip Randolph's long-term vision for economic and racial equality. Walter Reuther's UAW endorsed the March on Washington, and King had long recognized that the vast majority of grassroots activists in the civil rights movement were also laborers. As Honey notes, the Montgomery bus boycott was driven by "working-class foot soldiers, especially women," and King "demonstrated the powerful affinity he felt with poor and working people who propelled these movements." King was conscious of the ways in which economic critique riled anti-Communist critics, but he stood firm and "pushed many unionists to fuse their support for civil rights and labor rights into an even broader social agenda."[42]

In such a context, defining the line between mainstream labor and the Communist Left was paramount. The presence of labor in the civil rights movement and at the March on Washington was one thing, but Communists remained a source of anxiety. For instance, on August 27, 1963, as blacks and whites from across the nation traveled to the National Mall, the *Baltimore News Post* journalist David Sentner worried that some of the attendees would infect the whole of the civil rights movement with insidious Communist ideas. Sentner had received word that Communists, including Jack, on behalf of *The Worker,* planned to use "Trojan horse methods in an attempt to exploit" the march for their own sinister benefit. The Party, Sentner wrote, had "issued detailed orders to its membership to 'discreetly' bore within the movement," in spite of the march organizers' clear instructions to keep away.[43] Jobs and economic aspirations, then, were acceptable within the broad civil rights coalition, but ideologies that promoted economic restructuring remained taboo. The CPUSA's failed effort to be a part of civil rights, alongside the movement's attempt to attract labor, highlights the complexity and nuance of the role of economics, poverty, and employment in 1960s civil rights struggles.

Economic concerns were nevertheless an important and unavoidable component of the civil rights movement. As the range of essays in *Freedomways* demonstrates, black leaders remained interested in economics, poverty, and labor exploitation as fundamental causes of racial inequality even as the Cold War led people to shy away from fighting for a change to major economic systems. With editors like Esther who planted their activist roots in the Popular Front years, *Freedomways* did not disregard economic issues. The magazine showed no trepidation in openly presenting economic concerns in spite of the Cold War's repressive atmosphere. A number of articles focused on the economics of racism came from leftist activists like the former SNYC member, dismissed SCLC leader, and Communist Jack O'Dell.[44] But liberals including National Urban League director Whitney Young, the Illinois NAACP leader Lester Davis, and the Reverend Milton Galamison also contributed articles that analyzed poverty, labor inequality, and residential segregation as key forces driving the civil rights movement.

In the 1962 summer issue of *Freedomways,* Whitney Young contributed an article based on a speech he gave to the National Conference of Social Welfare in New York City titled "What Price Prejudice? On the Economics of Discrimination." Young argued that poverty contributed to "family disorganization" among African Americans, an academic theme that gained traction following the publication of E. Franklin Frazier's *The Negro Family in the United States* in 1939.[45] Widely known for his ability to get economic backing for the National Urban League from major corporations, Young offered a pointed critique of capitalist consumption as a source for the social and familial problems of African Americans. He framed his argument by outlining the significance of poverty in American culture: "What does being without money mean in a society whose values are highly materialistic, whose consumer production everywhere displayed are without precedent, and where the acquisition of everything in that society, both tangible and intangible, requires money? In these terms it means little food, little housing, little health, little education, little culture, little status, and little citizenship."[46]

Young did not argue that capitalism was the source of the problems poor black families faced; rather, he argued that, without access to capitalist accumulation and consumption, African Americans had limited contact with the economic resources that would define their citizenship. The distinction between capitalism as the problem and access to capitalism's benefits as the problem represented the key difference between the role of economics in the Popular Front and its role in the civil rights years.

Young argued that the black father who was unable to find suitable employment was "made to feel inadequate, not because he lacks love and affection, intelligence or even a grey flannel suit, but because in a society that measures him by the size of his paycheck he just doesn't stand very tall." As a result, the black mother needed to find employment as well and become "a major breadwinner—if not the only breadwinner of the family [who] assumes roles and responsibilities far beyond her ability to perform any of them too well." Young argued that as black families struggled to compete for the means to full citizenship—stable, adequate housing, full employment, and access to amenities—the circumstances that resulted produced "broken homes, delinquency, drop-outs, crime, illegitimacy, and other social disorganization."[47] In the midst of the Cold War, when any critique of capitalism could become a source of government harassment and southern conservatives sought to connect economic and racial protest to an effort to undermine the government, Young's *Freedomways* article pointed out that black family life was tied to capitalist society and full American citizenship. In fact, by presenting the image of a normative nuclear family as something that African Americans aspired to but fell short of because of economic disparities, Young reinforced cultural values in the Cold War United States.

Other activists used *Freedomways* to make arguments that connected economic disparities to the civil rights movement in the early 1960s as well. Jimmy McDonald, a CORE activist, wrote about his experiences as a freedom rider in 1961. CORE initiated integrated bus rides through the South in that year to test the Interstate Commerce Commission's commitment to enforcing the Supreme Court's ruling in *Boynton v. Virginia* (1960), which formally desegregated bus terminals in the South. The freedom riders met violent white resistance at a number of stops in the South, including a firebombing in Anniston, Alabama. Riders were beaten and jailed. CORE's commitment to nonviolence clashed with the excessive violence of white supremacists and created a crisis that required federal intervention, a tactic that activists relied on throughout the civil rights movement.[48]

In the middle of the freedom rides, the Kennedy administration called for a cooling-off period to let tensions subside before the bus trips resumed. In his *Freedomways* article, McDonald argued that the freedom rides had a significance that extended beyond integrated bus terminals. Asserting that job discrimination was a significant source of strife and that it reinforced inequality in social and political life, he wrote: "We do not want our women to have to work for the white women because our men are denied the right to a well-paying and challenging job. We are tired of being porters with college degrees." He also assailed trade unions in the South, arguing that they "have made very few and very weak attempts to organize a full civil rights program, even within the limited framework of the union."[49] Efforts to attain equality across the South by integrating social spaces symbolized broader change for African Americans. By fighting for equal access to bus terminals, lunch counters, and schools, civil rights workers were also fighting for equal access to opportunities for jobs, housing, and middle-class life. In demonstrating the lengths to which whites would go in order to maintain the racial status quo in a space as ordinary and transitory as a bus terminal, the freedom riders offered a clear image of Jim Crow's ferocity and highlighted the potential for even more extreme violence as African Americans fought for comprehensive equality.

In the issue that followed, Lester Davis, an Illinois NAACP member, contributed an essay suggesting that the NAACP needed to embrace the militancy of organizations like SNCC and CORE. In the midst of sit-in movements, freedom rides, and boycotts, the NAACP had consistently provided legal counsel and leadership but, as Davis argued, turned "a deaf ear to the demands from the membership for more internal democracy and a militant direct mass action program to implement legal victories."[50] Davis discussed the recent history of the NAACP, pointing to the expulsion of the Monroe, North Carolina, chapter leader Robert F. Williams as a turning point.[51] He highlighted the NAACP's response to the freedom rides as a way of understanding how the organization lagged behind the civil rights vanguard. He quoted NAACP chairman Bishop Stephen Gill Spottswood as saying: "The dramatic exposure of segregation practices and of law enforcement procedures is useful in awakening a complacent public opinion among white and colored Americans, but to suggest that its function goes much beyond that is to confuse a signal flare with a barrage. . . . [W]e are too old in the ways of the long struggle that has engaged our fathers and forefathers not to realize that wars are won by using every available military resource and not by the employment of raiding parties."[52]

For the NAACP to stay relevant to the civil rights movement, Davis argued, it needed not only to engage with more militant organizations but also to become a more militant organization. The NAACP was an essential part of the long black freedom movement, but it was clear to Davis that the association had fallen behind in the wave of civil rights activity. He argued that it "must change with the time or be destroyed by it."[53]

To Davis, the NAACP had a clear and simple choice to make. It could either change or stay the same. In changing, it would need to elect more young leaders, implement more militant and radical programs, and focus on fighting for all-encompassing equality in the South rather than gradual legal change that fostered slow implementation. An inherent component of the fight for comprehensive equality in the South was an analysis of the ways in which whites attained and amassed power. Davis wrote: "The entrenched wealth of the South will never agree to a change which must ultimately destroy the basic source of their wealth. Similarly, few leaders of any organization will readily agree to changes which can destroy their positions of power and influence. All change is radical, be it chemical, political, or social. No matter how gradual the prelude, there must come a point in which what was yesterday, is something else today."[54]

In Davis's assessment, the reason behind the slow pace of integration in the South was that whites maintained economic power by keeping a firm grip on their social and political supremacy. Their power to segregate social spaces and disenfranchise poor blacks contributed to their ability to keep better jobs, acquire a better education, and accumulate more wealth. Inequality did not start or stop with segregation in public spaces, but fighting to integrate them would go a long way toward more sweeping change. Davis's analysis illustrates how economic concerns shaped the situations African Americans in the South confronted on a daily basis. By arguing that wealth equaled power and that whites controlled wealth, Davis explained racial politics in the South in a way that would not have been out of place during the Popular Front years.

Because *Freedomways* published a wide range of viewpoints, it inspired debate and faced ideological conflicts. Ralph Ellison declined to contribute in 1964 because of philosophical disagreements with its editors and contributors, declaring: "If I appeared in your journal it would constitute an act of opportunism on the part of both of us."[55] Virginia Durr clashed with Esther over the magazine's inclusion of black nationalist contributors and its nearly all-black editorial board. At its inception, *Freedomways* emphasized the ideas, culture, and identity of African Americans. Though it published the work of whites, Latinos, and international contributors of all racial backgrounds, the editorial board was almost exclusively black throughout its existence, with the exception of John L. Devine, an art editor.[56] As James Smethurst writes: "Esther Cooper Jackson and the board of the journal were generally much more open to the whole ideological spectrum of the Black Power movement . . . and adamantly insisted that African Americans run the journal."[57]

Virginia Foster Durr was an Alabama native who was raised in a wealthy household and deeply enmeshed in early twentieth-century racial culture. When her family lost a significant portion of their fortune in the Great Depression and she was exposed to integration as a student at Wellesley College in Massachusetts, her social and political views began to change. She married Clifford Durr, an attorney who became involved in New Deal politics, and her views on race evolved further. The Durrs were active in the Southern Conference for Human Welfare (SCHW), a Popular Front organization, and were engaged in the civil rights movement as liberal integrationists. As black nationalism began to dominate the movement, Durr became increasingly frustrated at what she perceived as the rudeness and racism of civil rights activists. As the historian Patricia Sullivan writes: "[Durr] was sensitive to the depth of black grievances against whites, but her experiences in the movement had raised her expectations about the capacity of black Southerners to act upon the democratic ideal and create a political environment free from the stigma of race prejudice."[58]

Durr found the change in the civil rights movement jarring and in 1966 wrote to Esther about it. The two were not close friends but were familiar with one another from their days with the SCHW and the SNYC. Esther's mother also knew Durr in Washington, DC. Durr wrote of her admiration for the elder Esther Cooper's social circle, proclaiming: "I am sure no ladies ever were more ladies, had better manners or more social graces." She then asked Esther for advice. Referring to growing antiwhite sentiment among young black activists, she wrote:

> So today when I run into the deliberate, planned, and really dreadful rudeness of some of the people in the "movement" I get a shock and also I get angry and resent it. People tell me I should simply overlook it as the hatred and contempt was always there and is just now coming out, but I think this seems very patronizing indeed. I never had to make any excuses for your mother and her friends, in fact I am sure that they would have felt these kinds of manners to be as inexcusable as I do. . . . I don't want to be provincial or simply "Southern" but I am simply flabbergasted by it. Do you have any advice?[59]

Esther responded by sending issues of *Freedomways* with the intent that Durr might better understand the perspectives of the young people in the movement and the frustrations racism fostered. Durr subscribed and continued to write to Esther.

In 1967, Durr expressed her interest in *Freedomways* but warned that she would not overlook any sign of a favorable approach to separatist tendencies in the magazine. She asked Esther for advice again, this time using firmer and more frustrated language:

> I still would like to know how to treat these outbursts of racial hatred that occur with increasing frequency, directed against "whitey," The White Man, Whites etc. etc. I not only think it distracts people from the real problems of our society but is also self defeating as I do not think the Negro community can win its battles all alone, and without any white allies at all. . . . I do not now intend to excuse it and forgive it and swallow it and say "Lo! The Poor Black Man, we must be kind and forgiving to him since he has suffered so," and treat him like a retarded child.

She continued: "So be prepared for battle if I find [this attitude] in *Freedomways*."[60] Such frustration highlights the importance of generational change in the civil rights movement. Durr kept in touch with Esther, providing her thoughts on the magazine's articles and editorials, at times raising contentious points and reacting negatively to what she perceived as black nationalism. Esther maintained her position that *Freedomways* should include a range of viewpoints and reflect the changes in the movement.

Yet Shirley Graham Du Bois did not think the magazine went far enough in promoting Black Power, noting that the other editors were "so busy on 'peaceful coexistence' that they are wholly on the side of Martin Luther King."[61] In the 1960s *Freedomways* provided more printed space to integrationist, nonviolent leaders and internationalists. With the exception of a poem published in 1966, it made little mention of Malcolm X. Though it did not extensively cover his activity, several of its editors and contributors, including John Henrik Clarke, contributed to the founding of his Organization of Afro-American Unity. *Freedomways* also offered little coverage of the emergence and activity of the Black Panther Party, despite the organization's prominence in the late 1960s black freedom movement.[62] Nonetheless, it continued to work to promote dialogue among various strains of the black freedom movement. As Ian Rocksborough-Smith writes: "The magazine's editors went beyond the mainstream of the civil rights movement in advocating a more radical integrationism that took into account anticolonial struggles and sought an associated transformation of American society."[63] The editors recognized how a global freedom movement was reflected in strains of the domestic movement, and, by the 1970s, the magazine was promoting more and more black nationalism in its pages. One of the most significant spaces in which *Freedomways* built coalitions among politically disparate groups was in coverage of the literary and artistic expression of the black arts movement.

Freedomways offered a number of black artists, poets, and writers the opportunity to publish their work as the black arts movement burgeoned in the 1960s. The movement emerged alongside other postwar artistic movements, including avant-garde theater and Beat poetry. Through artistic expression, it "negotiated the ideological climate of the Cold War, decolonization, and the re-emergent civil rights movement, particularly the black student movement," and built the foundations for black studies programs.[64] In this regard, *Freedomways* made significant contributions to black nationalism, providing up-and-coming artists and writers with a forum in which to display their works. In embracing the literary scenes of Harlem, Chicago, and other American cities along with the work of artists in the decolonizing world, the magazine's editors wove art and politics together, juxtaposing the work of liberal integrationists with that of nationalist artists and writers. They were determined that, as the actress and contributor Ruby Dee wrote, "literature, poetry, drama, and music could contribute to liberation struggles."[65]

Freedomways featured works by the Pulitzer Prize winners Gwendolyn Brooks and Alice Walker, the art of Charles White, Romare Bearden, Tom Feelings, and Elizabeth Catlett, and the essays of a range of political and social figures, including international politicians and artists. The magazine's New York circle was deeply involved in the city's black literary scene and supported the work of the Harlem Writers Guild, the black artist and activist organization On Guard for Freedom, and Umbra, a poetry collective. Esther and other *Freedomways* organizers attended readings and raised funds for Umbra, whose members included Tom Dent, Askia Touré, and George Coleman. Umbra embraced *Freedomways* as well. It is likely that Umbra's connection with *Freedomways* and Esther facilitated the printing of some of the collective's poets in *The Worker*, which "did not publish a lot of serious poetry at that time."[66]

Freedomways also featured the work of the Harlem Renaissance writers, including Langston Hughes and Zora Neale Hurston, in an effort to remind "readers of the distinguished heritage of a progressive black political art."[67] It juxtaposed the work of young and old artists, offering its readers a sense of black cultural history and emphasizing continuity and memory as important components of the black freedom movement. The Harlem Renaissance poet and playwright Arna Bontemps published a tribute to Langston Hughes in the magazine in 1968. Bontemps, who bore a physical resemblance to Hughes, recalled an incident where he was confused with Hughes and wrote: "I considered this my official welcome, under mistaken identity, into the Harlem literati."[68] By illustrating the generational continuity of black cultural and literary expression, *Freedomways* used art to promote a political message that highlighted international solidarity and "[bridged] the divide between the civil rights mainstream and the more radical articulations of international black cultural autonomy."[69] Just as its editors, like Esther, brought Popular Front ideals to the new political context of the 1960s, the magazine's artistic contributions offered readers an expression of radical black cultural politics that could coexist with a message of integration. This point in particular tied Esther and the *Freedomways* staff to the legacy of the SNYC and *Cavalcade*, which had fused black politics and cultural expression.[70] Through *Freedomways*, then, Esther was not only promoting the expression of the African American cultural heritage; she was also drawing on a tradition of doing so that she had participated in and built decades earlier.

A number of noted writers and artists contributed political tomes to the magazine, highlighting themes like gender as important components of cultural expression. In a 1966 essay on black women and literature, the author Sarah Wright argued that black women "in spite of economic enslavement in various forms . . . are both readers and writers."[71] The writer Alice Childress expressed a similar sentiment, linking the stereotypes of black women in literature with the absence of major black political and social figures in history classes: "Have you seen us in any portrayal of the Civil War? *Gone With the Wind* is not our story. And our history is not gone with the wind." Referring to stereotypes of both noble and dysfunctional black women, she wrote: "It seems a contradiction for a woman to be degraded . . . by popular opinion which was shaped and formed by [the] law, and yet also take her rightful place as the most heroic figure to emerge on the American scene, with more stamina than that shown by any pioneer." But she expressed hope for the future of black women in literature, arguing that activists who were invested in the black freedom movement would offer truer representations, that, as political change altered black women's social status, stereotypes would evaporate.[72]

African nationalism and black internationalism were significant themes in *Freedomways* as well, and the editors used both art and political articles to express them. In 1962, the jazz percussionist Max Roach contributed an especially poetic essay called "Jazz." He opened with the *Encyclopaedia Britannica* definition of jazz and suggested that it overlooked the genre's cultural roots. "Jazz," he argued, "is an extension of the African chants and songs . . . an extension of the pain and suffering of those long, and too often, destinationless trips across the Atlantic Ocean, deep in the holes of those dark, damp, filthy, human slave ships . . . of the Black artist being relegated to practice his or her craft, even today, under these intolerable, too similar conditions."[73] The blues singer Abbey Lincoln wrote of "the female African American in music": "Her songs tell of a way of life, of the joy and pain of being Black in racist America. Her portrayals of life's experiences are functional and act as 'equipment for living.'"[74] Articles on African American music highlighted the idea that black cultural expression could not be divorced from a long history of racism and exploitation and that the essence of particular art forms was uniquely rooted in an African American past.

Nationalism as a political ideology also found a home in the pages of *Freedomways*, in spite of the magazine's lack of coverage of Malcolm X's movement. In a special issue titled "Harlem: A Community in Transition," the magazine published articles by authors with opposite viewpoints on black nationalism, reflecting Esther's editorial view that multiple activist styles could contribute to a broad black freedom movement. The Reverend Milton Galamison and the Nigerian scholar E. U. Essien-Udom offered two points of view on nationalism as it related to the context of urban uprisings.

When rioting spilled from Harlem into the Brooklyn neighborhood of Bedford-Stuyvesant in 1964, the Reverend Milton Galamison, a community leader, offered an analysis of the strife. The black proportion of the population in Bedford-Stuyvesant had mushroomed from 20 percent to 90 percent between 1930 and 1957, a result of suburbanization, white flight, and residential segregation. The neighborhood confronted dilemmas caused by white business owners, police officers, and landlords who were largely neighborhood outsiders. Galamison compared the situation to colonialism: "The hospital in which I am born, the apartment in which I live and the cemetery in which I am buried are owned and controlled by commuter circuit riders whose allegiance lies in another world which I cannot visit, not even in my dreams. The masters of my destiny are faceless foreigners who find my community a satisfactory place to make a living but not a very satisfactory place to live."[75]

Though such a colonial situation had the potential to foster a sense of nationalism, Galamison did not see such a trend developing in Bedford-Stuyvesant. A moderate, he was highly critical of nationalist movements and condemned "existing Negro separationist movements as the biggest Uncle Tom movements in the country." He went on to criticize black nationalists in the North who concerned themselves with southern problems, citing their misdirected energy as a cause for strife in Brooklyn.[76]

Offering a counterpoint to Galamison's antinationalism, Essien-Udom underscored the importance of recognizing the variations among different types of nationalism and analyzed the historical development of nationalism as a political ideology. In so doing, he sought to dispel the myth of a "monolithic 'angry' black mass" of nationalists conspiring to undermine the government. Such a pattern of thinking, he argued, "obscures issues and tends to divert public attention from the deplorable conditions of the masses of Negroes": "[It] explains away the legitimate protest of the oppressed against an unjust social situation, and helps to mask the absence of long-term self-help and 'uplifting' programs for the social and cultural elevation of the masses of Negroes." To counter this, he provided a history of African American cultural politics, highlighting nationalism as a form of community development in the face of oppression. He also drew comparisons between Harlem nationalism and African nationalism, arguing that "the liberation of Afro-Americans in Harlem . . . ultimately lies in understanding, appreciation, and assertion of [their] Afro-American and African cultural heritage."[77]

As a representation of Esther's political development, *Freedomways* highlighted the potential for unity among activists and groups with different viewpoints, contributed to a vital surge in African American cultural expression, and carved out a political space that prioritized freedom of expression over the restrictions the Cold War placed on the press. It illustrated that Popular Front radicals were active contributors to the civil rights movement. Stylistically it straddled the line between an academic journal and a popular journal, and as such it offered sophisticated political articles, art, and literature that would appeal to ivory tower elites and grassroots civil rights activists alike. As a *Freedomways* editor, Esther contributed to a "complicated matrix of political and cultural radicalism" that linked black art, social movements, and politics.[78]

The Worker, on the other hand, had a specific political affiliation and represented the goals of the Communist Party. While Esther's role at *Freedomways* was to curate a forum for other writers and intellectuals, Jack used his role as *The Worker*'s editor to promote his own ideas for the Party. He used the paper as a way to show Party support for civil rights and how the Party grappled with many of the changes in the black freedom movement. The urban rebellions in the North, starting with Harlem in 1964, offered fertile ground for Communists to promote a class-based analysis of racial strife. Jack's basic analysis of the Harlem riots did not substantively differ from that offered by *Freedomways,* but his style, political perspective, and intended audience shaped his articles. He emphasized the contrast between black youths, who were arrested, criminalized, and feared for lashing out against oppression, and those white youths who ran wild but were considered merely "juvenile delinquents."[79] He argued that both the police and the press treated young blacks far more harshly solely on the basis of their race. He felt that race and class could not be separated in CPUSA analysis, and he linked the concentration of poverty among urban African Americans to the racial context of the rebellion.

In his articles Jack called for the criminal prosecution of the authorities perpetrating violence against Harlem residents. Echoing Galamison's colonial analysis, he argued that the police constituted an "invasion army of hundreds." He asserted that Harlem needed services, autonomy, and political and social equity, not more police officers, as the Republican presidential candidate Barry Goldwater had suggested.[80] He wrote: "[Helping Harlem involves] a massive program in the areas of re-housing the ill-housed, mass education in skills for modern employment of the under-employed and the unemployed; it requires a development program for tens of thousands of new jobs inside and outside of the community through an influx of business and industrial establishments."[81] By advocating increased access to the benefits of capitalism in an exploited community, he weighed theoretical race and class questions against people's real-life needs.

Jack attempted to promote a pragmatic response to the problem, and, while some of his analysis aligned with Galamison's, he was also sensitive to nationalism as a response. In drafting some of his analysis, he wrote: "Black nationalism is essentially a reaction to, a response to white nationalism."[82] His understanding of nationalism as a rational response, however, did not mean that his specific political views aligned with those of nationalists. As he explained to one of his daughters in 1967, he believed that the uprisings were "not the 'revolution'" but that they were "smoke signals." He argued that people in Detroit and Newark who rioted in 1967 had found that "there is an alternative to strangling to death in the slums of this land . . . to take from those who have [wealth and resources]." In a solidly class-based analysis, he noted that a number of looters in many of the rebellions were white.[83] Given this observation, it is clear that he appreciated black nationalism as a realistic response to racial poverty, but his interpretation of the urban rebellions of the late 1960s was a solidly Communist one. Though black nationalism was often a product of urban strife, he saw the clashes as struggles between poverty and affluence and used that to mobilize an argument for class unity.

When northern uprisings and dissatisfaction with the slow pace of change in the South led to calls for Black Power throughout the nation, the CPUSA struggled with how to interpret and approach this new political development. The rising tide of nationalism and separatism produced a conundrum for Party leaders, who had gone to great lengths to mod-

ernize their stance on racial issues in 1959 by stepping back from separatism and removing the Black Belt thesis from their program. The Party
rejected what it viewed as an outdated and unproductive political ideology for African Americans, but it remained convinced that the black freedom movement was the best inroad for regaining political status in the
United States.

Instead of summarily dismissing Black Power, Party leaders like Jack
tried to articulate a position that both reflected CPUSA ideas favoring
integration and provided support and understanding for urban blacks
whose nationalism was a product of inequitable social and political institutions. On September 4, 1966, Jack published an editorial titled "Negro
Unity and Negro-White Unity Are Needed for Freedom Power." He
argued that Black Power was a rational response to oppression but that,
without the participation and support of whites and particularly white
labor, it would accomplish little. He wrote that Black Power was "a struggle against all manifestations of racist indignities, for recognition and
respect for the cultural, material and ethnic contribution which Negro
Americans make to the national culture and history of the country." In
that regard, he offered the Party a rationale for the new development in
the black freedom movement. Still, he argued: "It is necessary to win
broad strata of the white masses to active participation in the struggle for
the freedom rights of the Negro people."[84] Jack and the Party worked to
contribute to a growing discussion of Black Power by offering guidance
and promoting a specifically Communist viewpoint.

In a 1966 pamphlet titled *The Meaning of Black Power,* which was
reprinted from an article in *Political Affairs,* Jack provided a more extensive interpretation of the new political movement that he targeted at Communist readers. He explained the origins of the concept of Black Power,
along with its current usage: "There is a general agreement among Negro
spokesmen today that the chant, 'Black Power,' is reflective of a determination on the part of the Negro freedom movement to build up a maximum strength of united action in all situations in which Negroes are the
preponderant number in total, to create local bases of political power and
economic strength, and thereby transform their isolated ghettoes into
positions of influence, of 'Black Power.'" Aware that Black Power was
overtaking liberal integrationism as the advance guard of the black free-

dom movement, Jack attempted to square it with the CPUSA's 1959 Resolution on the Negro Question. He argued that the Party had in fact articulated a Black Power position when it stated: "The struggle for the rights of the Negro people is not merely a 'civil rights' fight, it is a political struggle for the power to secure and safeguard the freedom of a people . . . for a just share of representation nationally; it is a struggle for majority rule in those localities where Negroes are the dominant people in the population."[85]

But Jack and the Party were unable to reconcile their advocacy of integration and class unity with the separatism Black Power leaders advocated. In a 1966 *New York Review of Books* article titled "What We Want," Stokely Carmichael outlined the reasons he advocated nationalism: "Only black people can convey the revolutionary idea that black people are able to do things themselves. Only they can help create in the community an aroused and continuing black consciousness that will help provide the basis for political strength."[86] Carmichael developed that position further in his 1967 work with Charles Hamilton, *Black Power: The Politics of Liberation*. Carmichael and Hamilton outlined what they meant by the term *institutional racism* in that work, arguing that the structural and systematic oppression of African Americans precluded full participation in national life: "Black people are not in a depressed condition because of some defect in their character. The colonial power structure clamped a boot of oppression on the neck of the black people and then, ironically, said 'they are not ready for freedom.'"[87] Nationalism, they argued, was a natural response to a situation comparable to colonialism, and efforts at integration were futile in a context with such unbalanced racial power. Jack, however, considered black leaders who promoted black nationalism as a response to white supremacy "poorly informed . . . and demagogic" and argued that Black Power should not be invoked as a nationalist response to racism.[88]

Suggesting that such invocations led the press and the public to view the black freedom movement in sensationalized and distorted ways, Jack argued that Black Power needed to be understood and represented as a struggle for political, social, and economic equality. He believed that calls for self-defense were a reasonable response to oppressive violence and an important component of African American history but that they should not evolve into calls for blacks to "organize their own policing system to counter the violence of racists and police." Instead, he argued, while white police officers and the mainstream legal system had "committed 'the deeds most foul,'" the federal government still had a responsibility for "securing the lives and property of Negroes, while protecting them in the full exercise of their constitutional rights to a non-segregated participating share in public affairs anywhere in this country."[89] As Jack and the CPUSA saw it, Black Power offered a path to political authority where African Americans constituted a majority, but it should not be the sole force for black freedom in the United States.

The Meaning of Black Power sheds light on the CPUSA's struggle for relevance in the 1960s. Black Americans, Jack argued, "are victimized by class exploitation," and their struggle should "be viewed as a specialized part of the general class struggle of the jobless and working poor against the reign of the monopolists."[90] To Jack's mind, socialism included Black Power but did not disconnect blacks from the rest of the nation in terms of political structures or economic opportunity. He believed that socialism had the potential to connect an array of race- and class-based social movements and lead them to victory.

While the popular push of the black freedom movement included an element of the Party's earlier position on African American freedom, Communists, it seemed, were consistently unable to get the timing of their ideas about race right after the Popular Front years. In spite of its support for moderate and liberal organizations like the NAACP, and in spite of its commitment to supporting the rights of African Americans to construct their own mass movements without interference, the CPUSA failed to make a tangible impact on the growing black freedom movement. Its connection—both real and perceived—to the Soviet Union, along with the FBI's continued effort to connect it with a range of social movements, led black freedom organizations of varying political positions to turn a cold shoulder toward it.[91]

Anticommunism remained an obstacle for the Party as it sought to promote racial justice as well. Despite the fact that McCarthy's widespread and arbitrary style of anticommunism had faded, the CPUSA and its newspaper still represented a fearful idea, and *The Worker* came under anti-Communist fire. The McCarran Act, passed in 1950, required all

Communist Party members and affiliated groups to register as foreign agents with the federal government. While the government mobilized the Smith Act in the early 1950s to indict Party leaders, the McCarran Act was the subject of a decade-long judicial debate over its constitutionality. In 1961, the Supreme Court upheld the act as constitutional, despite arguments that it violated the Fifth Amendment.[92] The exposure that registering would bring, federal officials believed, was necessary because Communists had become adept at hiding their political affiliations. Eisenhower's attorney general, Herbert Brownell, wrote that Communists "no longer use membership cards or other written documents which will identify them for what they are."[93] Penalties for failure to register as foreign agents included a five-year prison sentence and fines of $10,000 for each day past the deadline it took Communists to register. In early 1962, Jack, along with other *Worker* publishers and supporters, was summoned before a grand jury for failure to register under the McCarran Act.

Jack and *The Worker* anticipated the challenges of the McCarran Act in the early 1960s, as other Communists had been summoned for failure to register. In an editorial in March 1961, Jack wrote that restricting the civil liberties of unpopular political organizations was "a challenge to every fighter for peace and democracy, for decency and progress, not just to Communists." He warned that limiting the freedom of Communists to espouse and advocate their political ideals limited the freedom of all citizens in a democratic society.[94] He ridiculed the act in an editorial that ran on February 11, 1962, after he and other *Worker* employees were summoned: "Allegedly, the men and women connected with *The Worker* are being brought before the grand jury in order to establish a relationship between *The Worker* and the Communist Party. . . . The relationship between *The Worker* and the Communist Party is no deep, dark mystery or secret affair. It is a proud relationship. . . . Any telephone book will show that *The Worker* and the Communist Party occupy premises in the same building."[95]

Jack argued in a series of articles that the McCarran Act's assault on *The Worker* was antithetical to a democratic society, which thrived on a free press. His editorials pointed to the conflict created by Cold War–driven efforts to stifle the Left while white supremacist assaults on racial democracy went unchecked.

Following this theme, Jack linked the McCarran Act to the black freedom movement, illustrating the connections between Cold War political culture and civil rights. Just as he and his wife had done during the 1950s, he questioned the effort of the United States to promote itself as a beacon of democracy abroad while it condoned racism at home. The predicament that SNCC activists confronted in Albany, Georgia, struck a chord with him and led him to draw parallels between his situation and theirs. Freedom riders traveled through Albany in 1961 and ignited a wave of SNCC-organized protest in the area. The activists met with fierce local resistance, and the Kennedy administration made little effort to aid civil rights workers. "As long as Albany's police chief Laurie Pritchett gave the public appearance of arresting Black protesters without excessive force," Washington kept its distance. More than one thousand protesters were arrested in Albany, and any police brutality that occurred happened behind closed doors. The situation illustrated to Martin Luther King Jr., who was arrested three times in Albany, the need for direct confrontations between activists and segregationists to ensure that the government would have to intervene.[96]

After roughly four hundred black protestors were jailed in Albany in 1962 for demonstrating solidarity with the freedom riders, Jack published an editorial urging the federal government to act. He offered a stinging critique of Attorney General Robert F. Kennedy's passive attitude toward civil rights struggles: "The attorney general has found no words or means to uphold the lives and liberties of Albany, Georgia's Negroes, the victims of mass police lynch terror. And this is the man who so blatantly has proclaimed his intention to enforce 'as the law of the land' the patently fascist and unconstitutional McCarran Law which would imprison the Communists."[97]

Jack argued that the timing of the McCarran Act and the mass jailing of civil rights activists was not coincidental. The First Amendment, guaranteeing free speech and a free press, the Fourteenth Amendment, guaranteeing equal protection under the law, and the Fifteenth Amendment, guaranteeing the right to vote, were entwined, and an assault on one would threaten them all.

The Albany situation reverberated for Jack at home, too. Harriet, the older Jackson daughter, had followed in her mother's footsteps and was a student at Oberlin at the time. She attended the World Youth Conference in Helsinki that summer and, after traveling through Eastern Europe, proposed to her parents that she might stay abroad and postpone the completion of her studies to live in the Soviet Union. Jack was proud that his daughter was enthusiastic and politically engaged, but he believed her energy was misdirected. He cited the civil rights movement as a reason for her to return, arguing:

> Morally, I don't think it's a good year for advanced thinking young people to LEAVE our country: have you not read of the mass heroism of the children of our people in Albany, Georgia during these weeks—where one out of every four teen agers, and one of every twenty Negroes in Albany have been jailed (many brutally beaten) in a great new stage that the de-segregation struggle has entered upon? Oberlin students, youth of the Nation and the world should be rallied to support these youth who are contributing their young bodies to the solution of a great problem of our time.

Jack told his daughter that she would be expected to return to the United States to develop "the capability to give something, to render some service in exchange for what you would receive by living and studying in the Soviet Union, Cuba, or elsewhere."[98] He argued that the civil rights movement at home was intimately connected to the Cold War and that this context offered Harriet unique opportunities for political engagement in the United States.

As a black Communist, Jack believed that government efforts to undermine the CPUSA through the McCarran Act could easily extend to young black activists fighting for civil rights. Because southern politicians mobilized anticommunism to uphold segregation, the act was yet another tool they could use to rein in civil rights activity. As the historian Ellen Schrecker writes: "Almost every [southern] state had its own little [House Un-American Activities Committee] clone or registration statute modeled on the 1950 McCarran Act. Several states even outlawed the NAACP. . . . Southern investigators usually took on civil rights activists."[99] The *Baltimore Afro-American* editor and *Freedomways* supporter

George B. Murphy wrote a letter to another editor that connected Jack's predicament and the issue of race in the United States. He noted: "This is the first time that the U.S. government has acted in this manner in connection with an editor of a newspaper since 1837 when Elijah P. Lovejoy, was enjoined, as the editor of an Abolitionist newspaper. . . . The fact that Mr. Jackson is a Negro (again proving that there is no area of American life where the Negro Question does not appear sooner or later as a matter of central importance) gives further significance to this case." Murphy asserted that Jack's case was of special importance to the freedom of the black press in particular. His letter suggested a pattern of First Amendment violations when a free press threatened the racial status quo in the United States. Because Murphy was the editor of a mainstream black newspaper, his support for Jack demonstrated that the issue of racial discrimination remained important, regardless of political affiliation.[100]

The connection between the McCarran Act and southern judicial efforts to halt civil rights activism was not lost on young activists either. One freedom rider who was jailed in Monroe, North Carolina, John C. Lowery, wrote to Jack about the similarities in their circumstances.[101] When the freedom riders were leaving New York City, Jack attempted to interview Lowery. Lowery wrote to Jack: "I was startled to learn you were from *The Worker,* but even more so to learn that you had been 'thrown out' of a C.O.R.E. press conference." After being arrested in Monroe, Lowery expressed his "sympathy" with Jack's "situation" and that of his "party," noting apologetically: "My own situation prohibits me from openly and vigorously fighting for our civil liberties."[102] Though the McCarran Act threatened to bring yet another separation into the Jacksons' lives, Jack managed to avoid jail as legal debates over the act continued.

Given his position as the editor of a newspaper under anti-Communist fire, Jack vigorously condemned the Kennedy administration. Unlike many Americans, he saw little romance in the American version of Camelot and instead saw an administration whose "ruthless energy in carrying out [its] commitments to Big Business against friend or foe is matched only by [its] lassitude, timidity, and cynical sleight-of-hand deceptiveness when it comes to honoring [its] constitutional obligation to . . . secure the 20 millions of Negro citizens their . . . equal civil rights." He noted that, while Coretta Scott King reported that her husband was having trouble breathing in the four-man Albany jail cell that he shared with fifteen other jailed blacks, Jackie Kennedy was "cavorting on skis churning-up a cooling ocean spray" in Hyannisport.[103]

But, while Jack remained critical of the Kennedys' capitalism, aloof approach to civil rights, and affluent lifestyle, he held out hope that the president had the potential to create the change he had promised during his campaign.[104] His editorials reflect his disappointment in Kennedy's inability to handle a civil rights situation without compromising with racists like Albany's Laurie Pritchett and Mississippi governor Ross Barnett.[105] He wrote to Kennedy regarding the Albany situation and received a reply from Lee C. White, an assistant to the president's special counsel. In an effort to placate Kennedy's critics on the issue of civil rights, White wrote that the administration hoped that "the Negro citizens of Albany will have the opportunity to discuss with members of the City Commission the various issues which have given rise to the demonstrations that have occurred in Albany."[106] In response to the situation in Albany, Jack wrote in an editorial: "[Kennedy] dons the garb of commander-in-chief when the reactionaries call him from Berlin or Southeast Asia, [but] speaks hesitatingly through the mouth of the Department of Justice attorneys when the rights of the Negro people are flouted."[107]

Jack was frustrated that a president who had a theoretical and ideological commitment to equality was so hesitant to enact justice in the face of a crisis, but he nonetheless hoped that Kennedy would create change. By June 1963, he praised Kennedy for an uncompromising speech addressing civil rights. The speech, which came on the heels of the Birmingham crisis, declared that civil rights violations represented a "moral crisis" and proposed a civil rights act that would outlaw segregation in public spaces. Kennedy professed: "We cannot say to ten percent of the population that you can't have that right, that your children can't have the chance to develop whatever talents they have; that the only way that they are going to get their rights is to go into the streets and demonstrate. I think we owe them and we owe ourselves a better country than that." Jack wrote: "The president made an important stride toward the redemption of his neglected responsibility to give positive leadership to securing the rights of Negro American citizens."[108]

In spite of Kennedy's shortcomings, his assassination on November 22, 1963, shook even his staunchest critics on the left. The next day, *The Worker* ran a set of articles under the banner headline "DEFEND AMERICA! Punish the Assassins, Unite for Democracy!" Jack's editorial argued that Kennedy's assassination was "the long deliberated and planned-for deed of the fascist minded forces of the political ultra-Right and the Segregationists with their vested interests in maintaining the racist oppression of Negroes at any cost." The term *ultra-Right* encompassed organizations like white citizen councils and other segregationist groups; the Minutemen, an anti-Communist paramilitary organization; and the John Birch Society, a right-wing anti-Communist organization. Jack urged Communists to "join with all patriotic citizens in pledging to redouble our work for the realization of all lofty democratic visions which President Kennedy articulated at various times."[109]

But Jack's calls for unity against the "ultra-Right," who, in his view, bore responsibility for the assassination, were met with similar calls from the Right for unity against communism. On December 16, 1963, the *New York Times* printed a full-page ad from the John Birch Society that described Kennedy's alleged assassin, Lee Harvey Oswald, as a Communist. About three weeks earlier, the society had contributed to a similar advertisement in the *Dallas Morning News* that "characterized the late President Kennedy as a Soviet stooge, 'a Communist,' a traitor to his country." Jack did not neglect to note the inconsistency of the society's position in his editorials. He wrote, for example: "Yesterday they dubbed Kennedy a communist, today they try to make Oswald a communist, but their real target remains the same—the destruction of the people's liberties on their way to a fascist society." He noted that the allegation of Oswald's communism originated with former congressman Martin Dies, who once "described Shirley Temple when she was a child movie star as 'a Communist.'"[110]

Jack likened the right wing to the perpetrators of racial terror and segregation. He noted: "THE TIME HAS COME, for the government and the people to sharpen vigilance against the brazen conspirators of the ultra-Right . . . the John Birch Society and the segregationists of the White Citizens Councils." To the John Birch Society, *Communist* was a convenient term for its enemies, useful in mustering fear of and contempt for them, but to Jack it was not a name to be thrown around like a school-yard taunt. He defended communism as a specific political ideology with a history, goals, and an organization whose members had suffered for their ideals. His editorial assailed the Birch Society, calling its attempt to place blame for the Kennedy assassination on Communists "a frenetic effort . . . to foster a [lie]."[111]

Jack and the CPUSA also underscored the significance of Dallas, a southern city, as the location. It was clear to Party leaders that Kennedy's death in the South was connected to segregationists' opposition to his civil rights goals, and they likened the brutality and public nature of the assassination to a lynching. In a statement issued in late 1963, it was asserted that the assassination was "the poison fruit of the brutal reign of terror which has enveloped the South, intimidating not only the Negro people but white democratic citizens as well, murdering not only Medgar Evers, but William Moore."[112] The statement reaffirmed the Party's commitment to democratic causes and its opposition to segregation and attempted to offer answers to questions about and analyses of the assassination that were politically compatible with its position.

Freedomways took a similar position on the Kennedy assassination, mourning the loss with the nation and offering a political analysis linking the assassin with racist lynch mobs: "In joining millions of our countrymen in mourning [the president's] death, we are not unaware of the climate of violence and barbarism which took his life, and the [lives] of many others in the south during 1963. William Moore, the Baltimore mailman, slain in Alabama; Medgar Evers, slain in Mississippi; the six children, slain in Birmingham, Alabama; and the President of the United States, slain in Dallas, Texas. It would be a tragic mistake for the people of our country to fail to recognize the pattern of reaction symbolized by these murders."[113]

Freedomways also examined the murder of the alleged assassin, Lee Harvey Oswald, who was shot in the basement of the Dallas courthouse two days after Kennedy's assassination. The editors again highlighted a pattern of "southern justice," arguing that the murder of Oswald "fits an all too familiar pattern of southern police work." Southern law enforcement officers, the editors argued, "found it more convenient to have the accused person dead, than to have him alive and given a fair trial as the Constitution provides."[114] In both *The Worker* and *Freedomways,* the Jacksons offered analyses of the Kennedy assassination that reflected their political ideologies, their commitment to civil rights, and their efforts to demonstrate that the political left wing did indeed include democratic ideals.

Through *Freedomways* and *The Worker,* Jack and Esther found individual niches that allowed them to remain engaged in the black freedom movement in the civil rights era. The couple negotiated new space as civil rights and Black Power changed the racial status quo in the United States. The successes of liberal civil rights proponents and the bold new radicalism that emerged in the 1960s reshaped the possibilities for activism in the black freedom movement. Jack and Esther used their editorial positions to remain relevant and provide exposure for and analysis of the black freedom movement. Their editorships allowed them to continue to hone their distinct activist ideologies: Esther and *Freedomways* offered a range of ideas to create a conversation about black freedom, and Jack's role with *The Worker* allowed him to promote his distinct view of the Party's relationship with civil rights. The couple spoke through their publications both as individuals and as members of a generation whose activism inspired and supported the civil rights movement. The Cold War had changed their lives and the black freedom movement, but it did not change their passion for participation or their commitment to social justice. In the 1960s the Jacksons were newly able to work independently, adapt to changing times, and devote themselves to each other and to the struggle for equality and social justice, and they would continue this pattern of work through their retirement.

7

Freedomways, the Communist Party USA, and Black Freedom in the Post–Civil Rights Years

In November 1974, nearly one thousand Communists, black activists, and a variety of other leftists gathered at the newly built Hilton hotel in New York City to celebrate Jack's sixtieth birthday. The folk singer Pete Seeger performed and told stories of his travels through the South in the 1940s. The South Carolina civil rights activist Modjeska Simkins gave a speech in which she reflected on her experiences with Jack when they were both active in the Southern Negro Youth Congress (SNYC). The attorney Mary Kaufman, one of the youngest prosecutors at the Nuremberg trials and a defender of Communists in the 1950s, spoke, as did Communist Party USA (CPUSA) chairman Gus Hall. On the stage was a floor-to-ceiling portrait of Jack by the renowned Communist artist Hugo Gellert, made especially for the occasion. The gathering was a who's who of twentieth-century leftist activism, with attendees reflecting Jack's wide-ranging and complex political background.

At this happy event, Jack spoke about his personal life and career. He provided a lively narrative of his family's past, filled with history and humor. He noted that his paternal grandfather did not marry or become a parent until he was sixty, when the slaves in Richmond were finally liberated. Recalling his upbringing, he thanked his parents for "their contributions to the cause of our people's emancipation from poverty, illiteracy, disenfranchisement and discrimination over the span of a full lifetime." Most of all, he also paid tribute to his wife:

> On this very public occasion, I want to express a deep private appreciation—of love and esteem—for my wife Esther, who has been so important a part of all of my endeavors during the past third of a century; and, if some of those efforts have proven

meaningful and of value, no small credit is due to Esther for her comradeship and help, patience and endurance. Of course, she does a much more important work than merely being my wife; she is a . . . confidant of scores of writers and opinion-makers in broad areas of Afro-American literature, culture and thought.[1]

Jack adored and respected his wife, not simply because she had been an encouraging and supportive spouse in the face of enduring political turmoil and his most important political ally, but because she was, in her own right, worthy of admiration. In fact, by the time of Jack's sixtieth birthday party, Esther's activist career had eclipsed her husband's, and she was central to *Freedomways,* one of the couple's most enduring legacies.

In the years following the passage of the Civil Rights and Voting Rights Acts, Esther and Jack remained committed to the fight for black liberation and the promotion of Marxist ideals. As a couple, they supported one another's work, but they also continued to nurture their independent careers. Both kept race as a central focus in their work, but Esther, much more than Jack, remained on the cutting edge of the black freedom movement. In the years after the height of the civil rights movement, *Freedomways* provided critical analysis of national and international issues, gender, art, literature, and history, promoting the development of the black arts and black studies movements and keeping current with trends and shifts in the fight for racial equality. Esther, along with her *Freedomways* colleagues, held on to a Popular Front–style approach, wherein contributors from a broad range of political persuasions could publish work. But the journal also changed with the times, reflecting and centralizing aspects of black nationalism and Black Power, promoting black studies, and advocating for peace with an internationalist framework as those tendencies came to the forefront of the movement. The magazine's twenty-five-year run offered Esther the opportunity to link her earlier experiences and activism to a project that had a profound influence on black intellectual life.

By the time of Jack's party, Esther had run *Freedomways* for nearly a decade and a half. She managed a journal that was launching artistic and literary careers, offering sharp analysis of political, social, and academic writing on race, and reaching audiences around the world. The journal, and the staff that published it, represented a salient link between generations of black freedom activists of varying political perspectives. Its contents offered a glimpse of its managing editor's personality and political methods. Esther had always approached social movements with a deep sense of nuance. Her work reflects a style that prioritized fluidity and connection, rather than divergence, between various strains in the black freedom movement. In this respect, *Freedomways* had the ability to capture and juxtapose an array of political ideas, promote black art and cultural production, and recognize the urgency of preserving and disseminating the history of the long black freedom movement. As the culmination of her activist career, *Freedomways* allowed Esther to create a legacy that offers insight into race politics in the latter half of the twentieth century and into her own life story. Her approach changed as the dominant political and social contexts changed, and it was her political maturation in the Popular Front that opened her to the different ideas and perspectives managing *Freedomways* would bring into her work.

In the decades after the 1960s, traces of the Popular Front endured, but the CPUSA no longer inspired it. Instead of uniting with other movements, the Party remained mired in internal conflicts and committed to a scientific interpretation of Marxism-Leninism as it worked to win influence. By the 1980s, it was out of step with mainstream and even leftist American political life. In the period of the Old Left, Communist and non-Communist activists alike had embraced working-class solidarity as a central ideology and worked in coordination with CPUSA policies. At the same time, the Party opened itself, particularly in the Popular Front years, to participation among activists who did not embrace its entire program. It saw the period as its benchmark for success and clung to the idea of its popularity within the Old Left, even as it struggled with new social, political, and cultural challenges and showed reluctance to opening itself up again. The New Left, on the other hand, rejected the authoritative stance the Party had taken, and, while it accepted aspects of the Party's economic theories and programs, its hierarchies and centralization were unappealing. Unlike Cold War–era liberals and anti-Stalin leftists, however, the New Left did not adopt strict anticommunism. And, as part of a reaction to 1950s suburban complacency, it viewed the middle class as the sector of society that could become the vanguard for change.

By the late 1960s, the Party and the New Left shared some similar values but were not aligned in their approaches to activism.[2] Nevertheless, Jack, as a prominent Communist leader, worked hard to present CPUSA ideas more broadly and seek ways to expand the Party's influence. Part of this he did by connecting his work with Esther's, but for much of the period he used his energy to explain Communist doctrine and apply Marxist-Leninist solutions scientifically to contemporary social and political affairs.

At sixty, Jack remained committed to the CPUSA. Having completed his tenure as editor of *The Worker* in 1969, he became the Party's international affairs secretary and also served as the director of the Party's political bureau and its education director. In 1974, he embraced his forty-four-year Communist Party membership and declared: "If I am anything, I am a man of the Party." Outlining the philosophy that had sustained his commitment to the organization over decades, he explained: "The [Communist Party] is the collective mind [and consciousness] of the working class. Our vanguard party is a structured part of the working class of our country whose destiny it is to finally free the people from all manner of misery, exploitation and discrimination, and to play a leading role in ushering in a new order of social human relations—socialism. Our country needs our Communist Party."[3] While his commitment to the Party did not prevent him from offering nuanced political analysis, given the Party's vastly diminished presence at the margins of American politics, Jack failed to reach as wide an audience as possible.

This shift from pragmatic, approachable analysis to dense rhetoric fit squarely into the shifting political and social context of the period. The Party emerged from the McCarthy era in an understandably defensive mode. It spent much of the 1960s in an effort to revive and defend its relevance and, in some arenas, saw success. Membership increased. Sectors of the black freedom movement embraced communism and Communist-influenced ideas, especially the Black Panther Party. But, rather than following a strict Party line, such leftist groups cherry-picked ideas from Marxism-Leninism, Trotskyism, Maoism, and other philosophical influences. Jack and the CPUSA expressed frustration that the acceptance of pieces of Communist doctrine diluted their deliberate, specific program of Marxism-Leninism. The use of piecemeal Communist doctrine by sectors of the Left led Jack to promote a much more rigid Party doctrine than he had in the past. Instead of interpreting the appeal of Communist and socialist ideas to the Left as a sign of an increasing degree of social acceptability, the CPUSA drew even further back from the mainstream in an effort to promote its program as a cohesive, complete body that should not be dissected.[4]

As a couple, Jack and Esther also reached a new stage during this period. Harriet and Kathy became adults, and Jack and Esther continued to focus on their independent careers. They were on individual trajectories in the freedom movement, and, while their ideologies did not always align perfectly, they continued to support one another and defend each other in the face of criticism. In these years, Esther's career took center stage as *Freedomways* became a significant part of the black political and cultural tradition. With the journal, Esther found a new space for her activism that illustrated the continued utility of her Popular Front experiences, but her success existed outside of the Communist Party. On the other hand, Jack's dedication to Marxism-Leninism tied him closer to the Party. And, as the Cold War and the black freedom movement were changing, his Party work took top priority. As a couple, they worked as a united front even when their independent careers led to political divergences, and, at times, they created and nourished bridges between their respective endeavors.

In the post–civil rights years, the couple's gender politics remained consistent. Jack's long support for his wife's independence placed him at the tip of the growing feminist movement. By the late 1960s, second-wave feminists highlighted the intersections of personal and political life, fighting for equal pay, an end to employment discrimination, day-care and maternal support, and sexual liberation. Many aspects of the feminist movement drew on the work of female Communists in the 1930s, 1940s, and 1950s who crafted an argument that acknowledged the distinct oppression women encountered. However, as a lingering effect of McCarthyism, many of these feminists had distanced themselves from Old Left work on the Woman Question. This resulted in a new feminist movement that picked up on problems that appeared to have been unattended to since the women's suffrage movement. As Kate Weigand points out, there were significant differences between second-wave femi-

234 JAMES AND ESTHER COOPER JACKSON

nism and the Communist position on the Woman Question, particularly related to issues of motherhood and sexuality, but there was also overlap on many core ideas. Weigand writes: "The modern movement's vocabulary for expressing its ideas, its emphasis on the political nature of women's so-called personal problems, its use of women's history to inspire women and to gain support for their ongoing struggles, and its efforts to build feminist unity in the face of women's differences all flowed from the Old Left."[5] Many Communist women and men had long engaged in efforts to eliminate male chauvinism from their ranks, struggled to build egalitarian households, and called attention to ways in which gender discrimination perpetuated racial and class divides.

In 1977, Jack gave a lecture and participated in a question-and-answer session during which he linked the Party's position on the Woman Question with other forms of oppression. He told the audience: "Some things are more decisive and though a person may be doing some general good work . . . if they are carrying the stench of racism in one pocket, or male supremacy in the other, then it's necessary to isolate that person or he'll louse up the whole environment."[6] Jack's position on the Woman Question reiterated his long-standing view of the role of gender in his own life. He and his activist cohort had long promoted women's leadership and made consistent efforts to combat chauvinism within their organizations and their households.

Jack's marriage to Esther remained a point of interest for observers, and, because the couple were activists, their relationship offered the audience a useful case study for seeing a gender ideology in practice. In response to a question about his own marriage, Jack pointed out that he was "half of an all Party couple with distinctive functions." He noted that he worked directly with the Party and characterized Esther's role as "mass work." While he did not call attention to the fact that Esther had stopped participating in formal Party activities after the McCarthy era, he pointed out: "A sustaining factor [of our marriage] is our ability to have a sense of humor." He also offered his audience a glimpse of humanity, pointing out that an egalitarian marriage was not always easy to execute perfectly. He acknowledged that periods of separation and the unpredictability of daily life made turning an ideal into a reality complicated. "You cannot logically, like the textbook formula," he stated, "pattern form and reform

relationships in such a way that will come out balanced . . . on the necessary chores."[7]

Jack also pointed out that Esther's politics were an essential piece of
their philosophy on their relationship. He and Esther were committed
to the tenets of Marxism first, he explained, and it was that commitment
that bound them to one another. He recalled: "My wife was a Communist before I met her and was quite committed to what she was about.
. . . [O]ur prior marriage, so to speak, . . . was to the Party and the goals
of Marx and Lenin. And there were no illusions on that count that if we
had to choose . . . she on her part would choose Marx and Lenin over
me. . . . I would also over her." He noted that this commitment explained
his choice to go underground and to be apart from his family during
other periods. His intermittent absences did leave Esther with the lion's
share of typically female work, including child rearing, housework, and
the financial strain of what was essentially single parenthood. He rationalized his absence by putting it into the context of his broader Communist
goals: his philosophical embrace of gender egalitarianism and Party ideology meant that he had to abandon his share of responsibilities within
his marriage to fight for a bigger cause. He explained that, in "a reward-
ing, exciting and productive life . . . the hardships are a part of the thing."
The couple was not "preoccupied with the trivia of personal acquisitions
or the trivia of life" but committed to having "confidence in what we are
about."[8] Jack's reflection on the role of communism and his marriage
offered an example of a man who experienced the effects of feminism and
Marxism as they played out in his life.

Esther agreed with this characterization of her marriage. By the 1970s,
the couple had been reunited for a longer stretch than the combined
duration of their periods of separation, but their individual political alliances had changed significantly. As a couple, Esther and Jack had worked
through their difficulties and evolved as individuals, but they continued
to respect one another's careers. Esther's managerial role at *Freedomways*
meant that, as Jack had stated, her work was in a different arena. The pair
had built the foundation of their marriage on a shared commitment to
"change the wrongs of capitalism," uniting over their politics and developing their knowledge of the world together. When Esther began to distance herself from formal Party activities in the late 1950s, Jack supported

her choice to make a contribution elsewhere. Esther recalled that, while her political ideology had not changed, some Party functionaries questioned her commitments and criticized Jack for his wife's choices but that Jack defended her. Esther had long honed a sense of political autonomy, and Jack recognized that her absence from formal Party functions did not compromise her convictions or her ability to create change.[9]

Jack's capacity to respect his wife's convictions even though she left the Party offers an illustration of his own gender ideology in practice. Since the days of the SNYC Jack had challenged himself on the Woman Question and recognized women as equal contributors in the struggle. This attitude applied to his marriage. Jack viewed Marxism-Leninism as a science and believed that the Party's process of debating, enacting, and abiding by policy until an opportunity to debate arose again was an effective approach to activism. And, while he abided by Party policy in his activism, he was more likely to deviate from the Party line when it came to supporting his wife's independence. When Party members questioned her activities, particularly when *Freedomways* offered a forum for activists in the black freedom movement who supported nationalism and other ideas rejected by the Party, he viewed any attempt to control his wife's work as male chauvinism. After rebuilding his marriage in the post-McCarthy years, it is clear that Jack was, in some instances, willing to prioritize his marriage over the Party. Perhaps he realized how much he risked losing in the underground years, but he mobilized Party positions creatively in order to assert that his defense of his wife reflected his loyalty to the Party. Even as he grew more dogmatic ideologically, he was able to mobilize his interpretation of the Communist position on the Woman Question to fight assertions that he ought to rein in his wife's deviation from the Party line. The couple's ideological commitment to female equality worked out of necessity during their periods of separation, was challenged after they reunited, and was put into practice thereafter.

In the post–civil rights years, Jack's most significant political contributions remained his intellectual work on race, but, in this period, he also linked those ideas in prolific writings on imperialism, world liberation, and peace. For three weeks in May 1968, he visited North Vietnam as part of a CPUSA delegation. It was one of his final major endeavors as editor of *The Worker*, and, on the trip, he became the last American reporter to interview Ho Chi Minh. His report on Vietnam for the Party had reach beyond the organization, particularly in other leftist circles, and the war was one area where his work overlapped closely with Esther's work through *Freedomways.* His report on Vietnam for the Party drew attention beyond the small CPUSA audience, linking agendas with a range of social movements in the United States.

Jack observed that, on every leg of the trip, people inquired about the peace movement in the United States, the black freedom movement, American and CPUSA politics, the upcoming presidential election, and American perceptions of Vietnam. In his report, he juxtaposed the violence of war with the resilience of ordinary Vietnamese people, noting that, when he left, people had gathered to "celebrate the victory of the 3,000th 'Johnson,'" or the shooting down of a US plane. This event led him to reflect on his upbringing in the segregated South, noting that the government that created segregation was the same "ruling class that invented nuclear bombs." Characterizing the Vietnam War as a "war of genocide; a war of destruction to fulfill [the] strategic objective of seeking victory in this war of aggression . . . to convert South Vietnam into a special colony; to use it as a military base for its further economic penetration and control of markets in the East," he celebrated the Vietnamese people's "revolution in defense of revolution."[10]

As a Communist Party leader, Jack took a view of Vietnam that underscored an anti-imperialist outlook, focusing on a critique of US and South Vietnamese infringement on North Vietnamese sovereignty. While much of the US liberal mainstream did not embrace the same critique, the Vietnam War was the focus of protest and mass opposition. The most visible segment of the antiwar movement was the student Left, but by 1968 the nation was increasingly war weary. Body counts were skyrocketing, the US government had lost much of its credibility, and an end seemed nowhere in sight. Earlier that year, the North Vietnamese military and the Vietcong had escalated efforts to push the US military out of the country, inaugurating the Tet Offensive. While the offensive was pushed back—a significant military victory for the Americans—Tet also provided a psychological victory for the North Vietnamese. Americans were bombarded with images of violence and death on their televisions, intensifying antiwar sentiment at home. Within the context of the antiwar movement, Communists were one part of a broad coalition. As the historian Van Gosse has written, opposition to the war in Vietnam brought together a "fractious collection of veteran pacifists, youthful draft resisters, former [Students for a Democratic Society] organizers, radical scholars, Trotskyists, and traditional Communists."[11] This shaky alliance reflected the breadth of late-1960s social movements, signaling a change in the influence Cold War anticommunism had on activists. Jack and Esther were a natural part of this diverse group.

By 1968, leftist movements in the United States were garnering significant media attention. Antiwar, free speech, feminist, anti-US, anti-Soviet, and black freedom protests swept the nation and the world as students sat in and fought for academic freedom, racial, gender, and class equality, and global peace. The traditional tactics of the civil rights movement were overcome as racial upheavals consumed northern cities. Activists ranging from Stokely Carmichael to Martin Luther King Jr. recognized that the Civil Rights and Voting Rights Acts had not fulfilled a promise of equality in the United States and that new tactics were necessary. Integrationism gave way to black nationalism, and a focus on economic inequality took center stage as black leaders tackled new problems after the end of legal segregation. And, on April 4, 1968, Martin Luther King Jr. was assassinated in Memphis, Tennessee, after coming to the city to aid striking sanitation workers.[12]

King's assassination was fresh in Jack's mind when he left for Vietnam. Just a year earlier, King had given an important speech on Vietnam. In "A Time to Break the Silence," which was reprinted in *Freedomways*, he argued that the war in Vietnam was "a demonic destructive suction tube." It drew resources away from the war on poverty and drew young black men from their homes "to guarantee liberties to Southeast Asia which they had not found in Southwest Georgia or East Harlem": "So we have been repeatedly faced with the cruel irony of watching Negro and white boys on TV screens as they kill and die together for a nation that has been unable to seat them together in the same schools." King roundly condemned the US government for misleading the public and asserted that the West's misguided values not only took an incorrect approach to solving the world's problems but also facilitated the growth of Marxism around the world. He stated: "It is a sad fact that, because of comfort, complacency, a morbid fear of Communism, and our proneness to adjust to injustice, the Western nations that initiated so much of the revolutionary spirit of the modern world have now become the arch antirevolutionaries. This has driven many to feel that only Marxism has the revolutionary spirit. Therefore, Communism is a judgment against our failure to make democracy real and follow through on the revolutions that we initiated."[13]

This speech put on display the antiwar views of the most popular mainstream civil rights leader. By embracing antiwar activism, linking it with the black freedom movement, and offering a critique of the US government's hypocrisy and deception, King illustrated a dramatic shift in political activism in the United States.

The speech also marked a turning point for King, whose alliances with Communists and fellow travelers, including Jack O'Dell and Stanley Levison, had previously resulted in FBI surveillance. By 1968, King appeared to be done distancing himself from Communists and showed a commitment to offering a measured, thorough analysis of a wide range of political issues. At a *Freedomways* reception marking W. E. B. Du Bois's one hundredth birthday, he gave an address titled "Honoring Dr. Du Bois." The event, which took place on February 23 at Carnegie Hall in New York City, featured Pablo Neruda, Pablo Casals, James Baldwin, and other intellectual, political, and cultural luminaries. The *Freedomways* staff invested itself in the preservation and commemoration of Du Bois's legacy and sought throughout its twenty-five years to remind its readers of his intellectual, political, and social contributions.

King offered a heartfelt appreciation of Du Bois. He praised him for seamlessly combining scholarly achievement and political militancy in his intellectual work and activism. He also highlighted his radicalism:

We cannot talk of Dr. Du Bois without recognizing that he was a radical all of his life. Some people would like to ignore the fact that he was a Communist in his later years. It is worth noting that Abraham Lincoln warmly welcomed the support of Karl Marx during the Civil War and corresponded with him freely. In contemporary life the English speaking world has no difficulty with the fact that Sean O'Casey was a literary giant of the twen-

240 JAMES AND ESTHER COOPER JACKSON

tieth century and a Communist or that Pablo Neruda is generally considered the greatest living poet though he also served in
the Chilean Senate as a Communist. It is time to cease muting
the fact that Dr. Du Bois was a genius and chose to be a Communist. Our irrational obsessive anti-communism has led us into
too many quagmires to be retained as if it were a mode of scientific thinking.[14]

While the speech might have generated more fodder for King's staunchest critics, like his speech on Vietnam it also suggested to audiences that
Cold War divisions in the civil rights movement were unproductive and
fruitless. King's political evolution was reflected in the broader politics
of the late 1960s, when activists from across the left side of the political spectrum increasingly forged new alliances. The injustice of the Vietnam War laid the groundwork for new critiques of the government, and
King's two speeches showed that a more open attitude toward communism stemmed outward from the antiwar movement into other areas of
political activism. His speech on Du Bois was one of the last ones he made
before his assassination and was printed in *Freedomways* posthumously.[15]

In the same issue of *Freedomways* that included "Honoring Dr.
Du Bois," the editors mourned the loss of King. In the editorial "Farewell to 'A Drum Major for Justice and Peace,'" the editors urged mourn-
ers to continue King's Poor People's Campaign by going to Washington,
DC, pressing for an end to income inequality, and fulfilling what they
argued should be King's lasting legacy. They did not express surprise at
the assassination because King was one of "a long list of men, women,
and children who have suffered martyrdom in our Movement." They
argued that, if the same recognition, national mourning, and outpour-
ing of sympathy had happened five years earlier when Medgar Evers was
assassinated, three years earlier after the murder of Jimmy Lee Jackson,
or when students were massacred on campus in Orangeburg, South Carolina, in January 1968, King might have survived to continue his work.
They declared that the "icy 'condolences'" President Johnson offered
and Vice President Hubert Humphrey's "politically hustling platitudes
about nonviolence" were inadequate and reflective of a government that
stood idly by and allowed violence to persist. They noted: "It was Dr.

King who, in his famous Riverside Church speech against the war in Vietnam, stated, 'The American Government is the greatest perpetrator of violence in the world today.'"[16]

It was King's final speech, delivered on April 3, 1968, in Memphis, that most inspired Jack's reporting on Vietnam. King offered an eerily prophetic address on the day before his death. After highlighting the urgency of the sanitation workers' strike, he traced his path through the civil rights movement, noting the threats he had encountered and his awareness that he was a persistent target. He urged audiences to go on without him to create the United States they desired. He stated: "I may not get there with you. But I want you to know tonight, that we, as a people, will get to the Promised Land."[17] Jack wrote that he felt as though he had been through a similar experience in Vietnam: "I too have been to a mountain of revolutionary inspiration. I know from these 24 days in Vietnam the infinite regenerative creative capacity of ordinary people— plain people, peasants, workers, to do deeds of heroism." He continued: "Yes, after Martin talked of human heroism and human capability, here in a confrontation of David and Goliath, was a nation of heroes who started with spears and self-made guns, who have fought and have defeated the mightiest military force the world has ever known, U.S. imperialism."[18] In Vietnam, Jack witnessed a triumph of his ideology: imperial power decimated by the will of regular people who believed in the strength of their unity.

The opportunity to have a conversation with Ho Chi Minh was one of the most noteworthy events of Jack's visit to Vietnam. Honored that the Vietnamese leader took the time out from leading a nation at war to meet with the CPUSA delegation, Jack recorded and passed along greetings from Ho to the Party. Ho praised the peace activism in the United States and acknowledged, as Jack noted, "the Negro people, the black rebellions in our cities . . . with wonder and amazement and deep appreciation": "He said, 'objectively you pursue your own goals, and correctly so, but objectively it aids our cause.'"[19] Ho's interest in black urban rebellion points to connections between the efforts of the North Vietnamese and freedom movements around the globe. Ho commended the tactics to promote racial change in US cities without, it appeared, consideration of the CPUSA's opposition to black nationalism. Where the Party had criticized urban strife as reactionary and out of step with Marxist-Leninist philosophies, Ho highlighted its revolutionary properties.

Jack was also especially impressed by the gender ideology of communism in practice in Vietnam. "In the South," he noted, "the role of women is symbolized by the deputy commander of the armed forces who recently won the Lenin Prize." Referring to Nguyen Thi Dinh, a female general who won significant victories in 1967 against the US and South Vietnamese forces, Jack explained that there was in Vietnam a "mass movement of the women," who worked as equal participants in intellectual and military life. He held North Vietnamese Communist women in high esteem and, in keeping with his position on the Woman Question, did not consider their military activity a deviation from prescribed gender roles. He regarded them as fighters doing heroic work for their cause, and, other than making a brief note of their sex, he reflected only on their status as revolutionaries.[20]

Jack's visit to Vietnam afforded him an opportunity to highlight links between the CPUSA's goals and the broader New Left program of action in the United States.[21] While the Party remained isolated into the late 1960s and the 1970s, opposition to the war in Vietnam was one avenue for coalition building and forging connections. Jack was not unusual within the Left in his visit to Vietnam: other leftist figures, including the Student Nonviolent Coordinating Committee (SNCC) leader Diane Nash, the actress Jane Fonda, and the Students for a Democratic Society leader Tom Hayden, also made visits to North Vietnam during the war and used their experiences to promote antiwar activities. Nash even published reflections on her trip in *Freedomways*.[22]

Vietnam also offered Esther and the *Freedomways* staff opportunities to build analytic bridges. Between its Old Left ties and its support for New Left and black freedom organizations, *Freedomways* provided analysis of the situation in Vietnam that linked foreign policy, black freedom, peace, and a critique of the US government. Its editorial staff condemned US policy in Vietnam from the beginning of the conflict, and, as the fighting intensified, the journal offered important critiques that, like King's speech and Jack's analysis, tied the war to broader social issues in the United States and the world. The summer 1971 issue offered an analysis of the recently published Pentagon Papers, which had leaked the secret history of Vietnam, revealing the depth of the government's deception about its role in the war. The information contained in the Pentagon Papers was used as evidence that the United States promoted a colonial foreign policy that diverted attention from the problems of urban poverty, wage stagnation, and global racial equality. Vietnam was, the editors declared, an ominous cloud that warned of more conflicts to come.

The editors argued that the persistent US involvement in Vietnam was part of an "assumption that America is the Great White Hope, whose mission in the world is to preserve colonialism and capitalism in the name of 'freedom and democracy.'" They compared President Richard Nixon's program of Vietnamization, in which South Vietnamese troops would begin to take over the fighting as US troops withdrew, to political efforts to manage racial strife at home. Nixon's position on racial tensions was part of a broader colonial mind-set, and *Freedomways* drew a distinct link between economic policies, black freedom, and war. "As the 'new look' in foreign policy," the Pentagon Papers editorial explained, "it is merely an extension of 'benign neglect'[23] so in evidence on the domestic scene today. Yet the Administration is careful to protect the $77 billion military budget and announces plans to increase it to $80 billion next year even while wages are frozen, which for millions means wages frozen at the poverty level." *Freedomways* argued that the government allocated funds for war and, in so doing, fueled economic and racial inequality at home. This meant that the United States replicated a policy that resulted in urban decline and applied it to new contexts. Blacks and victims of the Vietnam War were all considered colonial subjects.[24]

The *Freedomways* editors also explored the relationship between the Vietnam War and the US military presence in East Africa, further developing their argument that the war was tied to a larger colonial agenda that resonated with black history. In 1952, Eritrea, a former Italian colony, was designated as a semiautonomous state within Ethiopia. Ten years later, Ethiopia formalized Eritrea's status as a province, stripping the region of its autonomy. Eritreans formed the Eritrean Liberation Front to fight for independence and drew key support from the Soviet Union. US officials were concerned that the proximity of Ethiopia and Eritrea to the Middle Eastern states would ignite a regionwide Cold War conflict. In 1971, the government of Ethiopia, which the *Freedomways* editors characterized as "ancient but politically antiquated," requested arms from the United States to fight the Eritrean Liberation Front.[25]

The *Freedomways* editors argued that the presence of three thousand military advisers in Ethiopia and Eritrea was part of "a now all too familiar pattern." They expressed concern that the US position on Eritrea and Ethiopia was a path to "another 'Vietnam.'" Fearing a repeat of Vietnam in East Africa, they suggested that Nixon's "Executive Agreement" to train a counterrevolutionary force in Eritrea to fight the Eritrean Liberation Front reminded them of "a similar type of agreement which overthrew Reconstruction a hundred years ago and led to a blood-bath in the Southern States." They expressed confidence that the Congressional Black Caucus would keep the public abreast of US policy in Africa and called for troop withdrawals from Africa and Asia, the channeling of money from the defense budget to urban rehabilitation, and wage increases for the working poor. They closed by encouraging collaboration among activists, stating: "These are the common-ground issues which can unite the Freedom Movement and the Anti-War Movement in action."[26] For the *Freedomways* editorial staff, the Pentagon Papers, along with their own broad critique of the Vietnam War, revealed overlapping narratives of injustice stemming from US domestic and foreign policy. This connection presented an important opportunity for activism.

Freedomways and the Party intersected on other issues as well, giving Jack and Esther periodic opportunities to collaborate. This mutual support also fostered continued connections among members of the Old Left and the new generation of radicals fighting for change. When the philosophy scholar and activist Angela Davis found herself facing legal trouble in 1970, the CPUSA and *Freedomways* jumped to her defense. The Jacksons had a long history with Davis. Her mother, Sallye Davis, was active in the SNYC, and Harriet and Angela had been playmates as small children in Birmingham. Davis had already garnered significant public attention after her appointment to the faculty at the University of California, Los Angeles (UCLA), came under attack by the University Board of Regents because it disapproved of her publicly affirmed Communist Party affiliation.

Davis returned to the public spotlight shortly after her contract renewal was denied by UCLA. She became a central activist in the fight for the Soledad Brothers, a group of prisoners accused of murdering a guard at California's Soledad Prison in January 1970. One of the Brothers, George Jackson, and Davis established an intimate correspondence, and Davis became close with the Jackson family. Jackson had become an outspoken and poignant critic of the injustices in the prison system, particularly as they pertained to race.[27]

Frustrated at the Soledad Brothers' legal predicament, George Jackson's seventeen-year-old brother Jonathan orchestrated a hostage situation involving prisoners from San Quentin Prison in a Marin County courtroom on August 7, 1970. The teenager's ill-conceived plan was an effort to free the Soledad Brothers. Jonathan Jackson, three San Quentin prisoners, and the judge died in the subsequent hail of gunfire. Attention turned back to Davis when news broke that the guns Jonathan Jackson brought into the courthouse were registered in her name. She would be charged with aggravated kidnapping and first-degree murder. She disappeared, and FBI director J. Edgar Hoover responded by placing her on the FBI's Ten Most Wanted list. She was arrested in New York City on October 13, 1970, and extradited to California for trial.[28]

Davis's ordeal was one of only a few instances in the 1970s and 1980s during which the CPUSA captured national attention. Party leaders set out to defend Davis and simultaneously disassociate themselves from the violence of the courthouse scene. In what appeared to be the resurrection of its Scottsboro strategy, the Party worked to generate public support. Doing so was not difficult, as Davis was charismatic, charming, and well spoken. She did not appear to be an unhinged radical; she was professorial, of middle-class background, and appealing to whites and blacks alike. Ultimately, the Party's defense was successful, and Davis was acquitted in June 1972. Though it was central to the success of the trial, the Party could not capitalize on that fact and faded back into obscurity. The historian Earl Ofari Hutchinson posits that, when white and black Party members bickered over how to plan Davis's defense and promote her cause, they were rehashing unresolved "internal Party battles against 'white chauvinism' in the 1930s and 1950s." These conflicts carried over beyond her acquittal. Part of the success of her defense rested in supporters' ability to connect with her views on racial issues rather than with her political views, which diminished the presence of the Party itself in the cause.[29]

Jack and Esther counted themselves among Davis's most ardent supporters. As a Party leader, Jack offered a defense of Davis that combined her intellectual work and political affiliation with her position in the black liberation struggle. In the speech "Three Philosophers: Frederick Engels, Herbert Marcuse and Angela Davis," delivered at the International Scientific Conference in Berlin in November 1970 as Davis was awaiting extradition from New York to Los Angeles, he ranked her intellectual work with that of the philosophical luminaries. He linked her dismissal from UCLA to her legal predicament and argued: "She is an honest scholar and dedicated partisan of the freedom aspirations of her people—the segregated, racially persecuted, super-exploited, discriminated-against Black folk of Alabama, the South, and our nation. She is a philosopher in transition from Marcuse to Marx and Lenin." He also took the opportunity to explain how communism informed Davis's activism and proved her innocent: "Neither police agents-provocateurs nor the old peddler of philosophical 'revolutionary' junk will succeed in putting Angela Davis in the 'trick bag' of the anarchists. Angela Davis is a *Communist* and the demand of the masses will set her free. As a Communist, the commitment of Angela Davis is to the reasoned revolutionary science of Marxism, not to the nihilist tactics of anarchy."[30]

Jack was clear: Communists claimed to promote a nonviolent approach to political change and believed in the will of the masses to enact a just program. His scientific approach to the doctrine of Marxism-Leninism allowed him to clarify distinctive aspects of Davis's politics. As he had in his own statement before sentencing in 1956, he attempted to distill the meaning of communism for a fearful public in the hope that offering a better understanding would make Davis more sympathetic and understandable.[31]

Freedomways likewise offered Davis and the CPUSA support. It published an editorial on Davis's predicament in the second issue of 1971. The editors did not mention Davis's Communist affiliation. Instead, they focused on comparisons between her persecution and that of other political prisoners. They declared that she was "innocent of the monstrous crime of conspiracy to commit murder" and indicted California governor Ronald Reagan, Nixon, and Hoover for crafting the charges. "Her death is being sought," they wrote, "at the same time that a Lt. [William] Calley, found guilty of brutal murders against innocent Vietnamese people,[32] is hailed as a hero by the Nixon government." In further comparisons, they noted that Bobby Seale and Erika Huggins, members of the Black Panther Party, had success fighting criminal conspiracy charges in New Haven, Connecticut. They also pointed out that Davis joined a long line of prominent black figures, including the boxer Jack Johnson, Du Bois, and Paul Robeson, in representing a pattern of political harassment. *Freedomways* focused on race, rather than political affiliation, in its appeal on Davis's behalf. It reflected both the journal's effort to create political unity without emphasizing specific affiliations and the Party defense's effort to ensure that Davis's communism did not impede her ability to relate to potential supporters.[33]

Once Davis was acquitted, Jack celebrated in an article for the *World Marxist Review.* He acknowledged the substantial role she had played in her own defense and highlighted the triumph of the strategy to make her predicament relatable beyond her communism. He wrote: "Though the monstrous dimensions of the frame-up hoax against Angela Davis were laid bare in the courtroom . . . it nevertheless came as a surprise to many, if not most, that a jury of all white people in the 'middle class' community of San José could side with the victim in defiance of . . . the arm-twisting pressures of Governor Ronald Reagan's forces and those of President Richard Nixon." To Jack, the verdict suggested that middle-class non-Communists were fed up with the political establishment and frustrated at the extent of criminal persecution and that Davis's victory represented a changing tide. Ordinary people, he believed, would unite and organize against "the most powerful and arrogant and cynical of the world's imperialist ruling circles."[34] In Davis's triumph, Jack recognized victory for both the CPUSA and the *Freedomways* approaches to the problem.

However, his optimism proved unfounded. Unable to sustain its momentum, the Party receded from the public eye. While the leadership kept the fight alive, internal strife and an inability to connect with broader public sentiment inhibited efforts to win support. Hutchinson writes: "Communist Party members were like athletes running a race backward—congratulating themselves for outdistancing other runners as they watched their backs recede into the distance. But like the errant runners, Communists would still maintain their illusion that victory was in sight."[35] While Party general secretary Gus Hall even launched presidential campaigns in 1980 and 1984 with Angela Davis as his running mate, the CPUSA garnered little attention. Jack continued to write, speak, travel, and participate in Party affairs as a key leader until the end of the Cold War, but the impact of his work was weakened by the Party itself. In the 1960s, 1970s, and 1980s, the Party was in fact stronger than it had been in the immediate aftermath of the McCarthy era but had, on average, only around ten thousand members.[36] As an organization, the CPUSA was unable to manage dissent from within, and, if controversial topics were not open for debate, members either kept quiet or left. Given the other organizational options for leftist activists, the Party remained relatively tiny.

Jack's work, published for a CPUSA audience, received some attention in *Freedomways*. The editor Ernest Kaiser offered glowing reviews of Jack's books *U.S. Negroes in Battle: Little Rock to Watts* (1967) and *Revolutionary Tracings in World Politics and Black Liberation* (1974).[37] And, in 1974, Jack returned the praise in the face of Party criticism of the journal. In the third quarter of that year, the journal published a special issue titled "The Black Image in the Mass Media." Articles covered topics ranging from black women's roles in entertainment, to the perpetuation of racist stereotypes in film and television, to notable black figures in media, to the use of media to represent both black history and black roles in American history.

The Party member Sumner Jones expressed disapproval of aspects of the journal in the December 7, 1974, issue of the *Daily World*. In three columns, Jones, a regular contributor and photographer for the Communist newspaper, criticized the *Freedomways* editors for what he believed was a lack of a cohesive Marxist-Leninist point of view in the media issue. Jack immediately delivered a reply, urging the Party to issue a corrective to Jones's review. He offered a glowing response, stating: "These wonderfully readable, down-to-earth, issue-concerned articles lay bare the hidden hand of racism manipulating the dials of the TV and radio transmitters of the nation. At the same time, they indicate the direction for seeking solution of the problem, of turning the media into an awaited means of bringing the peoples of our nation together along with the peoples of all nations, for peace and progress and happiness."[38] The *Freedom-*

ways issue included a brief editorial presenting the view that the articles the editors had collected represented a wide range of opinions on many media-related problems and could speak for themselves.

After providing a summary of selected articles, Jack praised not only the content of the journal but also the editorial approach in offering an array of opinions for readers to parse. He was baffled by Jones's "odd assumption of embattled contradiction between the editorial position and the offerings of the writers." He urged the Party to apologize for the misguided review and stated that Jones's insistence that the editors and contributors must represent a unified view could "result in the breakdown of all united front formulations, and one-for-all, all-for-one coalition[s]." He accused Jones of being "eager for ideological combat" and suggested that his review did a disservice not only to *Freedomways* but also to the Party's efforts to maintain its friendships with other organizations.[39] With this statement, Jack demonstrated loyalty to his wife's Popular Front perspective even as he remained a committed voice for the Party. He recognized that Esther's ability to reach a broader audience with *Freedomways* was one point of connection the Party had beyond its own boundaries. His appreciation of the value of that connection showed subtlety in his understanding of his own activism. In the 1970s, the Party was small, isolated, and convinced of the merit of its program, but Jack illustrated the importance of maintaining connections with broader networks.

As *Freedomways* provided a forum for authors and artists who had a range of viewpoints, members within the network and beyond disagreed at times with the perspectives and the individuals printed in the quarterly. The author Alice Walker published some of her first work in the journal and served as a contributing editor from 1974 to 1985. While Walker was a central part of the *Freedomways* network, her work generated controversy, both within the journal and beyond. In keeping with his and Esther's view that activist organizations did not always have to be perfectly aligned on every issue, Jack offered a scathing critique of Walker's 1982 *The Color Purple* and the subsequent 1986 Steven Spielberg film. (The review appeared in the Communist publication *Political Affairs.* *Freedomways* had ceased publication in 1985, though its staff and supporters hoped it would resume publication after a brief hiatus.) As support for his opinion, he cited two *Freedomways* reviews offering similar condemnations of Walker's most well-known work.

Jack disapproved of Walker's image of the victimization of black women because, he argued, she crafted it at the expense of black men. He cited Maryemma Graham, a professor and contributor to *Freedomways* who also wrote a harsh review of Walker's work. Graham argued that Walker offered too narrow a view of male supremacy and racism, urging readers to consider the structural sources of both varieties of oppression.[40] Jack concurred, insisting that *The Color Purple* was "the grossest slander of a people, whose men and women have fought side by side to create, defend, and advance the opportunities and well being of the nuclear family, against merciless, oppressor ruling classes, first of slave masters, then plantation overlords, and now capitalist exploiters and landlords." Accusing Walker of attempting to amass wealth using shock value, he suggested that her success should be measured not by her profits but by the consequences of her work. He also drew on Loyle Hairston's 1984 *Freedomways* essay "Alice in the Mainstream," which argued that "these Afro-American writers who are eager to achieve literary and financial success in the mainstream had to leave behind the rich tradition of social commentary which informs the best literature this and other societies have produced."[41]

In the firmest critique he offered, Jack compared *The Color Purple* to D. W. Griffith's *Birth of a Nation,* the 1915 feature that glorified the Ku Klux Klan by mobilizing vile racial stereotypes. He argued that Spielberg's rendition of Walker's novel was "designed to foster feelings of white superiority, to surface racist prejudices and portray Black people as impossible alliance partners and class brothers." He continued: "This century, already approaching its end, offers the spectacle of an exceptionally talented writer, Alice Walker, herself an Afro-American, supplying the novel for a film, *The Color Purple,* whose psycho/political effect, and indeed function, adds to the burdens of Black people. It refuels the torch of racial prejudice." In closing his review, Jack encouraged Walker to look to her fellow *Freedomways* editors and supporters for an example of how to use a public voice to make responsible contributions and serve her cause. "Talent brings with it social obligation," he wrote. "It is not forgivable to ignore this obligation."[42]

Jack's response to the Party review of *Freedomways* and his critique of *The Color Purple* linked concerns about black representation in popular entertainment. His comment on Jones's review points to his support for Esther's vision for *Freedomways* and her evolving approach to her activism in the face of Party criticism. When fellow CPUSA members dismissed work outside their own tight-knit circle, like the *Freedomways* issue on the media, for offering a range of viewpoints without specific comment, he argued that it was their prerogative and their right to do so. And he continued to express appreciation for *Freedomways'* insistence on positive black representation in the media by citing the negative reviews the journal published of one of their own contributing editors' work. When Walker's presentation of African Americans in *The Color Purple* replayed stereotypes and did damage to racial uplift and class solidarity, he did not hesitate to censure her, and neither did her *Freedomways* colleagues. Their disapproval of *The Color Purple* offered one example of the range of perspectives that informed *Freedomways.* Even a contributing editor was subject to disapproval within the pages of the journal when her work presented an opportunity for a critical response.

As her commercial success was on the rise, Walker expressed in correspondence with Esther that she did feel some estrangement from the *Freedomways* staff toward the end of the journal's run. A drawing of Walker had appeared on the cover of the same issue that included Graham's review of *The Color Purple,* and Walker focused her sense of alienation on the cover itself. The sketch, which was done from a photograph that Walker included in the correspondence, was one of three drawings of writers that graced the cover, and Walker disliked it. She wrote to Esther: "I cannot understand why you would permit such an obviously malicious caricature unless, of course, it represents your point of view. . . . [I]t *is* an unkindness, insensitivity to another's feelings, an act, I think, of hostility."[43] She did not comment on the review itself, only on Esther's editorial role in selecting cover images. Nonetheless, she continued to consider Esther her closest confidant at the journal, and, when Esther planned to retire in 1985, Walker requested that she be removed from the list of contributing editors, stating: "Yours is the only heart I feel in touch with at the magazine."[44] The letters highlighted Esther's central role in managing the journal and keeping the peace through the force of her own personality.

As the managing editor of *Freedomways*, Esther was the glue that held the publication together. While the staff remained fairly consistent over its twenty-five-year run, Esther was always at the center. She coordinated fund-raising efforts, kept the financial records, managed the subscription lists, planned issues around special topics, recruited contributors, kept tabs on authors, mediated conflicts, and ensured that the journal went out on time. The work was overwhelming, and, by the end of her twenty-five years in the role, the *Freedomways* organizers were unable to find another person willing to take on the scope of her responsibilities. Not only did she have the administrative skill set to keep the journal going, she also had a wide and deep network of friends, colleagues, and other connections to draw from to keep *Freedomways* vibrant, varied, and at the forefront of political and cultural commentary.[45]

At the culmination of her activist career, Esther noted that her work at *Freedomways* would have been impossible had she not gained experience as an organizer with the SNYC in Alabama and the Civil Rights Congress in Detroit. A prominent figure in both organizations, she had demonstrated female leadership and never questioned her ability to manage all aspects of *Freedomways*. The journal included other prominent female leaders throughout its run, including Jean Carey Bond and Ruby Dee. Angela Davis, Margaret Burroughs, Alice Walker, Shirley Graham, Dorothy Burnham, and others also played significant roles.

As a woman running a journal with a broad reach in the black freedom movement, Esther did encounter some male chauvinism along the way. She recalled feeling that some men, including Jack O'Dell, a contributing editor whom she had known for decades, were uncomfortable with the idea of a woman in charge. She attributed this unease to the fact that, in spite of his history with the SNYC, O'Dell had more recently worked in male-centered civil rights organizations like the Southern Christian Leadership Conference and with prominent male leaders like Martin Luther King Jr. and Jesse Jackson.[46] In a 2003 interview, O'Dell acknowledged how organic and prominent women's leadership had been in the SNYC and indicated that he embraced it.[47] But Esther's sense that she had to earn respect in her leadership role, even among people she knew well, reflects the fact that male chauvinism was not a dead issue and that women in the movement still felt that their gender meant that their leadership might be questioned. It also illustrates the intersectionality of Esther's racial and gender experiences. Her interpretation of O'Dell and other men's reactions to her leadership suggests that she remained conscious of the ways in which male privilege operated. Under her stewardship, *Freedomways* affirmed the significance of women within the black freedom movement in spite of the movement's male-dominated image.[48]

Freedomways emerged in a period when the push for women's equality was gaining momentum. Of course, for Esther the notion of female leadership was nothing new. With the support of her SNYC cohort in the 1930s and 1940s, she took the role of executive secretary, was unanimously elected to represent the SNYC at the World Youth Conference, and led important campaigns against violence and injustice. She recalled that black Communist women were at the helm of conversations about the interrelationship of race, class, and gender, even ahead of white Communist women. She also noted that, when the feminist movement emerged, she was reminded of conversations, debates, and triumphs for women that she had participated in decades earlier.[49] While most of her time was consumed by *Freedomways,* she paid attention to the growing movement and considered herself a pioneering feminist. In her role at *Freedomways,* any struggle to win respect as a female leader and promote women's issues seemed to her familiar territory. She recognized that work for women's equality was ongoing and used *Freedomways* to offer new directions in the conversation and raise awareness of earlier struggles.[50]

Freedomways published a wide array of articles on the intersecting issues of race and gender throughout its twenty-five-year run. It commemorated International Women's Year in 1975 by including articles on women's issues in each issue.[51] Opening the year, the editors explained that International Women's Year was a necessity. Black women's distinct battles in the United States were important within the international women's movement, within the black freedom movement at home, and within the entire domestic women's movement. The editors wrote: "To our Black, Puerto Rican, Chicana, Native American sisters, and our white working-class sisters here in the United States; to our heroic sisters of Africa and Latin America, of Asia and especially of Vietnam; to our progressive sisters everywhere, we extend our solidarity with your struggles; we join our fate with yours in recognition of the fact that your victories are our victories, that our liberation once gained will not be secure until yours is fully consolidated." They declared that black women's liberation and freedom from oppression for women across the globe were interdependent and intertwined. Acknowledging that each group faced distinct problems, they advocated unity alongside appreciation for each group's unique struggle.[52]

Highlighting black women's distinct struggle was an important goal for *Freedomways* as well. For example, Esther's SNYC colleague Augusta Strong reflected on the black radical tradition in the United States. Foreshadowing what would become a dominant historiographic trend for the civil rights movement, in 1967 she penned an article titled "Negro Women in Freedom's Battles" that highlighted the central role black women played in freedom struggles over the course of American history. Using Rosa Parks and the Montgomery bus boycott as a framing device, she argued: "It is an interesting circumstance that a woman and a women's committee gave the impulse to this new revolution of our day. . . . Despite the image that has been kept alive in the public mind of the Negro woman as a patient matriarch or carefree harlot, there are countless stories, far more dramatic, of their role as inspirers, instigators, collaborators, and as leaders in the cause of freedom." She then explored black women's roles from the pre–Civil War period through the Popular Front freedom struggles, highlighting poets, antislavery activists, educators like Mary Church Terrell, radicals like Claudia Jones, and ordinary women like the mother of the Scottsboro defendant Haywood Patterson. She wrote of heroines "whose names may be known only locally or transitorily, but whose labors have speeded all the many movements toward freedom."[53] In crafting her argument, Strong encouraged her readers to consider both the significance of women in freedom struggles and the significance of their absence from traditional narratives. "Negro Women in Freedom's Battles" illustrated that black women were part of a distinct feminist tradition that was not broken into waves that ebbed and flowed but was continuous as long as black women faced sexism and racial discrimination.

Just as they worked to ensure that the long history of black women's activism was not forgotten, Esther and the *Freedomways* staff focused on preserving a broader black radical tradition. Their hope was to promote a history that transcended the popular narrative of the civil rights movement as beginning with the Montgomery bus boycott and ending with the passage of the Civil Rights and Voting Rights Acts. This presentation ignored the Popular Front and earlier efforts at dismantling Jim Crow. *Freedomways* played a significant part in seeking to restore older strains of black activism to their rightful place in African American history.

By the start of the 1970s black history was undergoing a renaissance that spawned a controversy over who could legitimately write this history. While historians like Du Bois, John Hope Franklin, and Herbert Aptheker had emphasized black voices in historical narratives, the practice gained increasing academic legitimacy as the New Left, black nationalist, and black arts movements took hold. Yet a new generation of black scholars seemed to abandon earlier integrationist viewpoints. And, according to the historian Peter Novick, they "aggressively challenged the claims of any whites to speak authoritatively on *their* past." In one instance, a young white leftist historian named Robert Starobin faced a humiliating response to a paper he presented at Wayne State University in 1969. The historians Vincent Harding, Sterling Stuckey, and Julius Lester ridiculed him for reading slave letters in dialect rather than in his own voice, left the talk dramatically, and did not afford him the opportunity to defend his work. Lester later claimed that he had been sympathetic to Starobin's efforts but believed that blacks had an urgent call to reclaim their own history. The incident illustrated that an earlier trend in history that Stuckey described as "an age of belief in white deliverers" had subsided and that a black claim to the black past had emerged.[54] That this took place in the late 1960s and 1970s was no coincidence. The rise and decline of the civil rights movement and the emergence of black nationalism coupled with a dramatic rise in postwar college and postbaccalaureate education resulted in ripe opportunities for black students of history to merge academic interests, contemporary cultural concerns, and activism.

By the late 1960s, black studies, Chicano studies, women's studies, and other identity-based fields began to emerge at colleges and universities across the nation. Black nationalist and artistic movements had a prime role in promoting these programs and insisting that the academy make space for them. The historian Martha Biondi describes the "unifying principle" of black studies programs as "the innovation and legitimacy of a 'Black perspective'" that "aimed to unmask the pretense of universalism in Euro-American intellectual thought and teaching." Some white scholars with an abiding interest in race and integration saw the emphasis on a black perspective as "little more than racial essentialism," but scholars who embraced black studies continued to find space and legitimacy in academic settings.[55] Much of this work occurred at the impetus of student activists who felt marginalized in predominantly white academic settings, studied black philosophers and political thinkers, and organized study groups around the concept of honing a distinct black intellectualism on campus. Student Black Power advocates and black nationalists pushed for a curriculum that reflected their experiences and perspectives. As James Smethurst has written: "Even the most ambivalent or hostile present-day African Americanists . . . must admit that their place in the academy was largely cleared for them by the activist nationalism of the 1960s and 1970s—however narrow that nationalism might seem to them now (or seemed to them then)."[56] *Freedomways* showcased black intellectual and cultural viewpoints and promoted the idea that black scholars and activists should have a venue for exploring, analyzing, and sharing intellectual and cultural insights.

Freedomways supported and promoted black studies. Esther recalled fondly: "Not surprisingly, some of the earliest research into Black history—which was eventually to be the basis of Black Studies departments in schools and universities—appeared in *Freedomways*."[57] Of course, earlier scholars and journals, *Cavalcade* among them, published research on black history and offered historical context for understanding race and the freedom struggle in the United States. Some of the work done during the SNYC years was even reprinted in *Freedomways*. In the early 1970s, however, Esther's assessment of early research on black history zeroed in on the new approaches to this work that increasingly came out of the academy. Scholars like Vincent Harding, Sterling Stuckey, Mike Thelwell, and others pioneered new approaches that gained growing legitimacy, highlighting the influence of the postwar college boom and the black freedom movement on academic research. In this respect, *Freedomways* bridged the gap between scholarly and popular publishing.

The journal's editors strove to ensure that the trails blazed by earlier activists and thinkers were not forgotten, and they welcomed the prerogative to be particular about who crafted those narratives. They planned a number of special commemorative issues to ensure that prominent black activists, artists, and thinkers, including Du Bois, Paul Robeson, Lorraine Hansberry, and Charles White, received the attention due them. Esther and her *Freedomways* colleagues also honed a specific vision for how that history should be told. As a result of this effort, in the late 1960s *Freedomways* found itself embroiled in a controversy about the protection of black radical traditions that persisted through the mid-1980s.

In 1967, the novelist William Styron published the Pulitzer Prize–winning *Confessions of Nat Turner.* He offered a fictionalized account of Turner that characterized him as inept, insane, complacent with his enslavement, and having a complicated sexuality. While a number of prominent American literary critics and cultural figures, both black and white, praised the narrative and argued that Styron had the leeway to craft Turner as he saw fit, many African Americans found the portrayal disturbing, insulting, and potentially dangerous. In 1968, the *Freedomways* editorial board member and longtime member of the black Left John Henrik Clarke edited a 120-page compilation of responses titled *William Styron's Nat Turner: Ten Black Writers Respond.* The volume included the analytic works of the *Freedomways* contributors Vincent Harding, Mike Thelwell, Ernest Kaiser, Alvin Poissant, Loyle Hairston, Lerone Bennett, Charles V. Hamilton, John Oliver Killens, and John A. Williams. In general, these critics agreed that *The Confessions of Nat Turner* created a caricature that relied on racial stereotypes and an inadequate history of the slave experience.[58] Esther too concurred that Styron's novel offered a racist image of Nat Turner.[59] And the sentiment of the *Freedomways* writers who contributed to the volume was in harmony with the black studies movement.

The authors published in *William Styron's Nat Turner* each condemned Styron's reliance on stereotypes rather than documents to create a fictional Turner. They also agreed that, by writing a novel based on historical events, Styron had a responsibility to frame Turner accurately. The essays offered the same refrain: Turner's legacy as an empowered, messianic, freedom-loving individual was destroyed by Styron's misrepresentation, and the book's popularity shaped mainstream views of black history in damaging ways. But they offered varied ideas about who should have the privilege of writing black history and historical fiction. They did cite the white Communist historian Herbert Aptheker's in-depth *American Negro Slave Revolts* throughout the book and credited Aptheker for his ability to relate the experiences, perspectives, and motivations of enslaved people in his histories.[60] Nevertheless, they considered Styron's whiteness as part of his problem and questioned the ability of white authors to offer a black perspective.

Vincent Harding suggested that it was not possible for a contemporary white southern novelist to write accurately from the perspective of a black slave. He lamented white critical praise for the book as well, arguing: "Our sorrows . . . are compounded by the host of critics who have joyously proclaimed that Styron has finally done the impossible—entered starkly white into a black man's skin and mind—and has in the course of his impossible feat created a major work of American fiction. (That these critics have been—with one significant exception—also white is, of course, part of our unspeakable dilemma. That *they* should be called upon by journals and reviews to decide when successful penetration of blackness has been accomplished is another parable of our pain.)" Harding transferred his disappointment with the critical praise to Styron himself, suggesting: "Perhaps we must now say with charity that it is likely too much to expect a white, twentieth-century American novelist to be able to conceive of the world of a black, Old-Testament-type messiah."[61]

John A. Williams did not share the same view. He stated: "I do not believe that the right to describe or portray . . . the lives of black people in American society is the private domain of Negro writers. . . . Indeed, works by white writers on black people are considered to be more palatable to the nation at large than similar works by black writers." Strong convictions, solid intentions, and honesty were, to Williams, the attributes that would qualify an author of any background to write an African American's story, and his objection was that he did not think Styron met any of those standards.[62] Harding, Williams, and the collection's contributors demonstrated that, for black readers, reviewers, students, and intellectuals seeking authentic representations in history and literature, an author's race could be a significant, but not necessarily decisive, factor in a work's reception.

Whereas Styron's novel won awards, *William Styron's Nat Turner* drew criticism and controversy. On September 12, 1968, the historian

Eugene Genovese dismissed the work in the *New York Review of Books* as "nonsense" that revealed "the thinking of intellectuals in the Black Power movement."[63] He painted the contributors as people averse to integration and trapped in a black nationalist mind-set. Several scholars responded to Genovese's review. The historian Anna Mary Wells wrote: "Professor Genovese's contention that black Americans should be grateful to Styron for having rescued their hero from oblivion even though he has perverted him in the process seems to me equaled only by the argument of slaveowners that blacks ought to be grateful for slavery because it enabled them to have instruction in the Christian religion." Mike Thelwell, a contributor to the collection, wrote: "It is the responsibility of the black scholar of this generation to pull out, articulate, and define the form and meaning of [the] past in ways that have never been done. This is our particular responsibility since we appear to have the freedom to do this and have it recognized—which was denied to other generations of black men."[64] While the contributors to *William Styron's Nat Turner* did not uniformly claim that blacks should have the sole prerogative to write or imagine black history, they did suggest that their distinct vantage point made them obligated to offer unique insight, nuance, and empathy.

Freedomways again tangled with Genovese in 1974 when it published a scathing review of his famous history *Roll, Jordan, Roll: The World the Slaves Made.*[65] Earl Smith's "Roll, Apology, Roll!" argued that Genovese's account was inaccurate and that it "virtually wiped away" black struggle, offering "a proprietary class view of southern history, racist in context." He accused Genovese of "trying to stifle the fact of the unity of resistance to the barbaric slave system." He continued: "These contemporary rationalizations are in line with the current crisis in capitalism, which needs this racist history to continue its super-exploitation of Black people."[66] It is not a far reach to read Smith's review as a response to Genovese's review of *William Styron's Nat Turner*, just as Esther and the *Freedomways* staff saw the reaction to Clarke's volume as an insult that displayed the racism in some white historians' intellectual purview.[67]

The review of *William Styron's Nat Turner* that had the most significant impact for *Freedomways* and the journal's associates was written by the historian Martin Duberman for the *New York Times*. Duberman praised Styron and suggested that Clarke's volume could damage efforts to create racial equality in the United States: "This is a depressing volume—for those who believe the past can and should be protected from the propagandists, for those with lingering hope that the races in America can be reconciled, for those who have regarded the blacks as a saving remnant that might help our country become something better than what it has been." He further argued that it was a "more recent myth" that "blacks in this country could somehow transcend the destructive racism that permeates our culture, that they, unlike the whites, might somehow avoid distorting the past as a way of inciting one half of mankind to hate the other."[68] Duberman's response to *William Styron's Nat Turner* reflected the complex issues at play in historical representation in the late 1960s. Black intellectuals promoted the idea that their claim to black history was rooted in their own experience, perspective, and access to interpretations that most white scholars disputed. White scholars such as Genovese and Duberman, however sympathetic to racial equality, viewed this new historiography as nationalistic, wishful thinking, and perhaps a form of reverse racism.

As managing editor of *Freedomways,* Esther promoted the idea that African Americans had a special claim to black history, that their interpretations of it would be valuable in highlighting black cultural contributions and empowerment and in generating social change. While *Freedomways* was intended as a journal for a range of political perspectives and contributors, by the 1970s the editors focused on providing a forum mainly for black authors that fit squarely into the expanding black arts and black studies movements. The journal's increasing embrace of a black nationalistic and internationalist perspective in the 1970s reflects its effort to reflect, engage, and influence the evolution of the black freedom movement. In the 1960s, it had infused civil rights integrationism with Popular Front ideals. But, as the context shifted and the victories of the civil rights era increasingly appeared incomplete, it made space for black academics, activists, politicians, and artists to publish work that reflected the more radical mood of the black Left. This shift was not without consequences, and, just as ardent black nationalists faced criticism for their philosophy, *Freedomways* experienced blowback and became embroiled in conflicts.

One long-running instance in which *Freedomways* found itself at the center of a controversy revolved around the journal's 1971 commemorative issue on Paul Robeson. Robeson, who died in 1976, lived the last years in his life in obscurity, having never completely recovered from the stain of the McCarthy era. He was active in *Freedomways* circles, but, beyond keeping his connections with the Old Left, he faded from the black freedom movement vanguard. Just as they did with Du Bois, the *Freedomways* editors felt an urgency to keep Robeson's legacy alive. The issue included an array of tributes from luminaries like the Kenyan leader Jomo Kenyatta, the actress Lena Horne, the authors Alice Childress and Tom Dent, the Indian leader Jawaharlal Nehru, and the comedian Dick Gregory. Articles addressed Robeson's socialism, his undergraduate education at Rutgers University, his athletic background, his cultural philosophy, and his internationalism. The poets Nikki Giovanni, Edward Royce, Richard Davidson, and Gwendolyn Brooks offered poems in Robeson's honor, and the contributing editor and journal librarian Ernest Kaiser provided a bibliography of works by and about Robeson. *Freedomways* also published parts of the issue in a book titled *Paul Robeson: The Great Forerunner* that went through six editions.

The issue offered an unflinching look at Robeson's political development and his range of perspectives, and some essays teased out the black nationalistic aspects of his political development. In one essay, titled "Paul Robeson's Cultural Philosophy," Sterling Stuckey argued that, in the 1930s, the actor, activist, and scholar had developed a black nationalist critique of race relations in the United States and in black Americans' relationship with Africa. He stated that Robeson's "most enduring and profound influence, despite all of the efforts to silence the man and to blot his example from our minds, will very likely be a result of his heretofore largely unknown intellectual achievements." He explained that Robeson came to view African Americans as "a race without nationality." Robeson, he argued, believed that black Americans experienced psychic suffering at the hands of white supremacy but felt no commonality with Africans. Robeson attempted to offer black Americans a way to connect with African ancestry while acknowledging their distinct experience. He explored African music and linguistics and suggested that African Americans could take cultural inspiration from Africans.[69]

Stuckey explained that Robeson hoped to "[dispel] the 'regrettable and abysmal ignorance of the value of its own heritage in the Negro race itself'" by undertaking a comparative study of linguistic development. As Robeson compared African languages to European and Asian languages, he also began to appreciate the significant African cultural retention within black American communities. Stuckey wrote: "The dances, songs and religion of the black man in America . . . were the same as those of his 'cousins' centuries removed in the depth of Africa, 'whom he has never seen, of whose existence he is only dimly aware.'"[70] Stuckey's work was a potent reminder that black nationalism was a long, enduring tradition, not a phenomenon new to the late 1960s. It offered one important angle on Robeson's multifaceted contributions.

Other essays took different approaches to Robeson's legacies. In "A Rock in a Weary Lan'," Jack O'Dell argued for the centrality of Robeson's contributions to black history before the civil rights movement took shape. His essay offered younger readers instruction on the methods and goals of the freedom movement in the 1930s and 1940s. O'Dell fused the emerging field of black studies with a narrative of the Popular Front and explained Robeson's role in the interracial Left during the Depression and World War II years. He described the methods and ideals of Popular Front organizations like the SNYC and labor unions and explained that, in the Depression, the movement for black freedom shifted "away from the nationalist-separatist trend of the 1920s, as represented by the Garvey movement, to the class struggle organizing trend": "Black and white workers got together, and that was power." He emphasized Robeson's close relationship with the SNYC, "the organization which, in a historical sense, was a forerunner of SNCC."[71]

O'Dell also gave special attention to Robeson's internationalism, which provided his supporters "a special link . . . to an understanding with the peoples of Africa, Asia and the growing socialist world community." Reminding scholars to acknowledge Robeson's contributions, he suggested that historians of African American life could do more: "Contemporary writers and publishers of Black History texts and social studies materials who leave brother Paul out of the story are not writing *our* history. Let us be abundantly clear on that point. Nor was he just a singer and actor deserving a few lines of passing reference as some of the 'better' black studies materials would have us believe."[72]

O'Dell declared Robeson the predecessor to Martin Luther King

Jr. and pushed the proponents of black history to incorporate his leftist thought, his Popular Front connections, his internationalism, and the impact of anticommunism on the historical memory of his contributions into the field of black studies. His article was an attempt to mobilize the principles of the Old Left to influence black studies. It reflected *Freedomways'* determination to keep the traditions and influence of the past alive while it itself adhered to the current movement.

Freedomways editors like O'Dell and Esther, whose position as managing editor gave her a substantial role in soliciting, selecting, and printing articles, did not abandon their Popular Front outlook even as the journal moved more squarely into the realm of black nationalism. In the early 1970s, the growth of black studies presented an opportunity for using the current black nationalist momentum to commemorate and recognize the radical Popular Front past. Stuckey's and O'Dell's articles illustrated that Paul Robeson could exemplify multiple movements, and *Freedomways* provided a forum to display the range of his influence. But the particular link between Robeson's earlier articulations of an Afrocentric philosophy and the context in which the *Freedomways* tribute to him emerged did draw some criticism. Some white supporters of the Popular Front did not see how emphasizing black nationalism would restore the interracial coalition that had challenged racism in the 1930s and 1940s. The former Southern Conference for Human Welfare activist and integrationist liberal Virginia Durr was among them. Durr, as noted in chapter 6, kept in contact with Esther and continued to read *Freedomways* even though she found it frustrating. She had worked with Robeson in the 1940s Progressive Party and, as an ardent integrationist, found the shift toward Black Power and black nationalism in the late 1960s unsettling. This view shaped her interpretation of the Robeson issue of *Freedomways.*

Durr wrote to Esther on May 6, 1971, to register her dissatisfaction with the Robeson issue. She acknowledged that aspects of the tribute were "beautiful," but she found herself angry and troubled by the racial demographics of the contributors, all of whom were African American. While *Freedomways* was not always an exclusively black publication, it was a journal dedicated to the black freedom movement, and African Americans did contribute the majority of the journal's contents throughout its twenty-five years. In response to the Robeson issue, Durr wrote: "As one of the WHITE people who worked with him in the Progressive Party and who considered herself at least a friendly acquaintance . . . I cannot help but say that I think it does him a *great* injustice." Durr's frustration with *Freedomways'* representation of Robeson aligned both with her distaste for black nationalism and with her background in Popular Front inter-racial coalitions that she thought could transcend the issue of race. As Erik Gellman has acknowledged, white leftists in the late 1940s "began to show the limits of their interracialism and civil rights advocacy." Many whites, including the novelist Howard Fast, viewed Robeson as "a world citizen," someone beyond race.[73] White progressives like Durr at times naively dismissed his blackness as a central component of his identity as an activist and a performer. They conveniently overlooked his own periodic black nationalist work, which Stuckey had located in the 1930s.

Frustrated that white members of Robeson's large interracial network were not included in the issue, Durr chided Esther:

> What is the matter with youall, Esther? I really cannot understand it at all, you are more racist in my opinion than George Wallace and go on and get mad, I think it is such a bad tactic and such a bad atmosphere and such a very bad psychological attitude that I will have to run the risk of losing all of your approval to say that I think the present path that is being pursued by the Black leaders and by the Black Movement is fatally wrong and doomed to fail-ure and also to weakening the whole progressive movement. . . . [T]o blame the whole oppression of the Black people on "white-ness" is so absurd and so illogical and so ridiculous.[74]

While Durr's anger and frustration were palpable in the letter, her cri-tique also reflected a feeling of alienation from a movement to which she felt she had contributed and hoped to continue to support. Her reaction projected her feelings about the expulsion of whites from SNCC and the Congress of Racial Equality, along with the development of Black Power, urban conflict, and black nationalism in the late 1960s, onto *Freedomways*. The presence of an analysis like Stuckey's, which focused on Robeson's early nationalistic and Afrocentric intellectual work, became conflated with what she had continually termed in other correspondence about

Freedomways as a "hate whitey" movement.[75] Her reaction disturbed both Esther and their mutual friend George B. Murphy, who received a similar letter. Murphy lovingly and graciously encouraged Durr to rethink her response, question her own privilege and internalized racism, and reflect on the journal editors' prerogative to print the articles they selected.[76]

Durr continued to receive *Freedomways* until 1979, when she finally declared: "I cannot bear to read it. It makes me weep. . . . [T]he greatest disappointment of my life has been the splitting of the Civil Rights Movement."[77] That Esther responded to Durr's painful letters illustrated that she had an investment in holding her broad coalition together. Not every critical letter to *Freedomways* received a patient and measured reply, but, in spite of her disagreements with the journal, Durr had long ago earned Esther's respect. On March 30, 1979, Esther wrote to Durr to question her interpretation of the journal's perspective: "First, I must say that the *Freedomways* that you write about and the one that I am associated with cannot possibly be the same magazine. We have never been a part of a so-called 'hate whitey' movement and have had an international point of view about the relationship of the Afro-American struggle to the struggles of the world's oppressed." She explained that *Freedomways* was indeed an interracial effort, and she made note of several of the white leftists on the staff. She also pointed out that her daughter Harriet had married a white man, who was an important and welcome part of their family. She did acknowledge that *Freedomways* was a predominantly black publication because black writers found "so few outlets for their work."[78]

The exchange reflected Esther's insistence that interracial coalitions were important but that providing the rare forum for black intellectuals to disseminate their work in the 1970s was an urgent and vital project. For Durr, black nationalism was a frustrated reaction to slow progress that was ultimately unproductive; it alienated former allies and left her feeling that her contributions were rejected. She did not believe that the absence of white voices would result in a vibrant multiracial democracy; rather, she argued that the shift in the black freedom movement was a fatal one. Esther, on the other hand, saw opportunities to promote the work of scholars and artists whose voices might otherwise be lost. In *Freedomways,* validating and promoting the work of people marginalized by more mainstream outlets was a foundation for cultural transformation. The backdrop of black nationalism provided new space for black scholars to engage in the intensive, focused study of the experiences, perspectives, and voices of black people. By providing space for the ideas of black writers, Esther and the *Freedomways* staff were laying groundwork for a new type of dialogue about race that incorporated fresh analysis.

Esther had an opportunity to articulate her views on black claims to black history in the early 1980s when the ghost of the *William Styron's Nat Turner* controversy resurfaced. A conflict over the authorship of Paul Robeson's official biography brought Duberman, Esther, Paul Robeson Jr., and other members of the *Freedomways* circle into battle. *Freedomways'* focus on the legacy of Paul Robeson represented the staff's interest in ensuring that the Old Left had a place in American history, as its commemorative issue and subsequent publications illustrated. The conflict gave Esther a chance to express her position as an editor, a friend of Robeson's, and a black freedom advocate in the post–civil rights years.

Robeson's legacy was closely guarded by his son, Paul Jr., who held his father's records and provided access to them when he deemed that a scholar would make an appropriate and accurate contribution. He was sensitive to the allegations that his father was a political dupe and that, in the context of the Cold War, scholars had dismissed his activism in the McCarthy period. He wanted to see his father's contributions celebrated, not tarnished by Cold War anticommunism, and he became a vocal commentator on the attributes and shortcomings of works on his father's life.[79] In 1978, the historian Philip Foner published an edited collection of Robeson's speeches and writings entitled *Paul Robeson Speaks*. The nearly five-hundred-page compilation included selections from Robeson's football days at Rutgers through his death in 1976. It contained pieces from *Freedomways*, including Robeson's tribute to Du Bois at a *Freedomways* event. In response to the publication, Robeson Jr. issued a press release that he copied to Esther. He described the volume as "fundamentally lacking in the required scholarship and breadth of material . . . an unrepresentative and distorted picture of both the essence and the development of my father's thought and action." He also accused Foner of printing material copyrighted by the Paul Robeson Estate, the Paul Robeson Archives, Inc., and *Freedomways*.[80] His particularity about the claims to his father's legacy became a sticking point, not just for Foner, but for the *Freedomways* staff.

Earlier, Paul Robeson Sr. had enlisted Lloyd L. Brown to write his official biography, and the two signed a contract that gave Brown access to Robeson's records after his death. Brown, a journalist close to *Freedomways*, had a long history of collaboration with Robeson, dating back to Robeson's journal *Freedom*. He had also written a novel titled *Iron City*, edited the *New Masses*, and helped Robeson write *Here I Stand*.[81] He knew Robeson well and had a vision for the biography. While Brown's contract expired seven months after Robeson died in 1976, he also had a contract for publication with Knopf that was valid until 1982 and included access to the records. Between 1976 and 1982, Brown experienced a series of calamities, including a broken back, that inhibited his progress on the biography, and, in 1982, Knopf terminated the contract. Subsequently healthy and motivated to resume the project, Brown informed Robeson Jr. that he would need access to his father's archival collections "to fulfill the last writing assignment given to me by him."[82] Robeson Jr. denied the request.

The reply shook Brown and the *Freedomways* circle to the core. Robeson told Brown that, while he was pleased to hear that he was in good physical shape and prepared to resume work on the book, it had been five years since the expiration of his contract with his father. In that time, he, Robeson Jr., had taken sole control of the Paul Robeson and Eslanda Robeson Collection and "developed the strong conviction that an in-depth authorized biography of Paul Robeson should be done." Not willing to wait and hope for Brown's improved health, he had signed a contract with Martin Duberman, who would write an "authorized 'life and times' biography of Paul Robeson."[83]

Duberman's stinging review of *William Styron's Nat Turner* fourteen years earlier had not faded from memory in the *Freedomways* circle. Brown exclaimed that it was "unbelievable that Paul, Jr. . . . could have come to a decision so contemptuous and insulting to Black writers, historians and scholars—indeed, to all black Americans—and to the memory of Paul Robeson himself." Duberman's defense of Styron's "monstrous accusation that the mass of black slaves did not yearn for freedom" would, he argued, color his interpretation of Robeson, who was "reared and guided by a runaway-slave father. . . . *Paul Robeson's whole life and development was a flowering of his people's resistance to enslavement and their struggle for full freedom.*" Brown continued: "Just as Styron's best-selling slander cried out for outraged protest by spokesmen for the people he had wronged, this unprincipled arrangement with Styron's defender ought to be denounced by all who believe that the fight for the truth about black history is a fight for our people's rights today. . . . I do hope and pray that others who are concerned with the legacy of Paul Robeson—a legacy that belongs to every one of us—will not take such an insult in silence. Paul Robeson never did."[84]

In his statement on Robeson Jr.'s selection of Duberman as the authorized biographer, Brown highlighted the connection between the representation of black history and the freedom movement as it existed in 1982. As the fight for civil rights became a memory and African Americans sought new ways to push for an end to their oppression, a black claim to black history was a viable and essential tool.

Esther concurred with Brown that Duberman's selection as a Robeson biographer was insulting and inappropriate. In 1983, Duberman nervously wrote to her, noting that other people had turned down his requests for interviews. Robeson Jr., he explained, told him that she "did have serious objections, but would 'probably' agree to talk with me." He had completed significant portions of the archival research but still needed the personal insights of Robeson's close confidants, colleagues, and friends and recognized that, without those interviews, his manuscript would be inadequate. "The bottom line is simple," he wrote. "I stand in urgent need of your unique knowledge and insights if I am to write Paul Robeson's history with the comprehensiveness it demands. The responsibility is awesome. To meet it, I must win the confidence of that small circle of people like yourself able to provide the right direction."[85] The letter did not acknowledge the Styron controversy, nor did it mention specifically any of the objections Esther and others had to Duberman's role. It asked only for an opportunity to meet to ascertain whether Esther could trust him enough to grant an interview.

Esther said no. She was perplexed by his letter and concerned that even sending a response could be interpreted as cooperation, but she believed that she had to explain her refusal. She wrote:

I can only say that I am weary and intolerant at this late date of white authors becoming the authoritative source of giants in Black history. There are many Afro-Americans, dedicated, trained and talented, who in this racist society never have the resources or leisure to pursue their dreams—not for travel, research or writing. And there are many such people who knew Paul Robeson.

This is not to say that a white person is incapable of producing a worthy historical work about a Black personality or period. I have questions about your selection as the person to do the "authoritative" Robeson book.

She indicated that she had problems with his 1963 play *In White America* and reminded him: "You came to the support of author William Styron when ten Black writers criticized the racist nature of the book *Nat Turner.*"[86] The issue of Duberman's whiteness was secondary to his record of scholarly interpretation, and, to Esther, his role as the Robeson biographer was part of a too-familiar historical pattern of whites unseating blacks who sought the opportunity to write their own history.

Esther's refusal to grant Duberman an interview reflected the fact that, as black studies emerged and transformed the analytic frameworks of African American history, the identity of authors mattered.[87] Black scholars, who had had limited access to academic outlets because of centuries of slavery and Jim Crow, found new doors opening for them and new opportunities to claim control over the way African American history was told. Certainly, many liberal and leftist white scholars also wrote transformative African American history in this period, as Esther acknowledged, but the quality of their work did not always shield them from challenges to their ability to make intellectual and emotional claims to the black experience.[88] As Sterling Stuckey wrote in a 1971 essay: "White historians as a group are about as popular among black people as white policemen."[89] While white historians embraced new perspectives and methodologies in crafting African American history, they also had to overcome the hurdles to building trust among black readers, who remained suspicious because of earlier white scholars whose works reinforced racist views. In this precise context, *Freedomways* prioritized black authorship because it gave black scholars access to a broad international audience, offering a venue that was otherwise not widely available and reflecting the influence of black nationalism in intellectual life. Esther's insistence that Duberman was an inadequate Robeson biographer was a reflection of her managerial perspective at the journal, her investment in black access to black history, and the racial politics of the period.

Indeed, in one of its biggest accomplishments, *Freedomways* gave a number of black writers and artists vast exposure, and their popularity increased as a result. It helped launch the careers of Alice Walker, Nikki Giovanni, Audre Lorde, Brumsic Brandon Jr., and many others. As Michael Nash and Daniel Leab have written: "African-American authors had many more and much better paying outlets for their work than had been available a generation earlier."[90] Many went on to publish much more extensively in mainstream periodicals. It was a triumph that reflected the achievement of one of the journal's goals, but the spread of the authors' voices across a range of periodicals made the journal itself less unique. In some respects, the successes of the authors foreshadowed the journal's end. Associate Editor Jack O'Dell wrote in the journal's final editorial: "Over a quarter century [*Freedomways*] has been both advocate and defender of the idea that the momentum towards freedom and social emancipation is irreversible, that the freedom agenda is non-negotiable."[91] In its twenty-five years, *Freedomways* influenced and reflected black culture, civil rights, artistic movements, and academic study and supported and promoted widespread efforts for change.

By 1985, the ideological and political controversies that animated *Freedomways* would ultimately be shoved aside by practical business problems. The editors had poured endless time and energy into the journal and could no longer keep pace with technological changes and fiscal demands. In the last few years of its existence, editorials reminded readers that they were running short on funds.[92] The editors encouraged readers to sign up new subscribers, held fundraisers, sold greeting cards designed by artist contributors, and limited the length of the volumes. None of this was enough to keep *Freedomways* afloat. Esther, whose responsibilities ran the gamut of journal production, was sixty-eight years old and ready to retire. The staff could not find a replacement willing to take on her range of duties, particularly given that the journal's business methods were out of date. In the mid-1980s, computerization was transforming publishing, and *Freedomways* simply could not keep up. When the journal folded in 1985, its staff and contributors hoped to revive it, and subscribers wrote to register their disappointment, but *Freedomways* never resumed publication.

By the end of the Cold War, Jack and Esther had prepared for new directions in their lives. Well into their seventies, they showed no signs of slowing down, but both did formally retire from public work. After *Freedomways*, Esther continued to manage the journal's lingering correspondence, accepted speaking engagements, continued to promote the preservation of African American history, and offered guidance to young scholars researching her experiences, organizations, and friends. Well into her late nineties at the time of this writing, she has continued to earn recognition around the city for her efforts, including awards in the field of journalism, an honorary degree, and, in 2014, an award from Barnard College celebrating her 1940 master's thesis on domestic workers.

Jack retired from the Communist Party in 1991 in the wake of another ideological crisis at the end of the Cold War. His departure was marked by bitterness. After over sixty years in the Party, Jack found himself with no retirement package and wrote a frustrated letter to the CPUSA's national board in which he detailed his lifelong commitment and disparaged the Party's direction. He described the turmoil he endured for the Party: "I have worked the shop worker's equivalent of two lifetimes in the several assignments given by the Party. . . . I have an equity invested in this party, my life and some part of that of my most loved ones." He urged the organization to "extricate itself from its cocoon of vainglorious pretension and judgmental pontification about the ways others should solve the problems of their current crisis circumstances, and seriously address our own." The letter accused the Party of hypocrisy in not living up to its ideals and positions, failing to give its most dedicated functionaries a "just and fair retirement package."[93] Like Esther, he continued to serve in retirement as a resource to audiences newly curious about the long history of the American Left.

The ways in which Jack and Esther navigated the black freedom movement in the post–civil rights era ensured that their legacies would not be forgotten. Both were activists who did not simply appear in a particular context and disappear when the moment was over but were committed revolutionaries who changed, at times for the better and at times for the worse, adapted, and grew as movement dynamics shifted and politics transformed. James and Esther Cooper Jackson had devoted their lives to fighting for a better world. Their love sustained them through their fight for racial equality and social justice, and their activism enhanced their devotion to one another.

Conclusion

Esther and Jack in American History

Esther and Jack never stopped fighting for change, but it was surely frustrating for them to see their lives fade into obscurity as civil rights history emphasized the more mainstream movements of the 1950s and 1960s, and they went to great lengths to change that. Scholars wrote to them frequently, but it was in the late 1980s that the historiography began to shift. In 1989, Robin D. G. Kelley, whose groundbreaking *Hammer and Hoe: Alabama Communists in the Great Depression* was set for publication the following year, wrote to Esther to ask for feedback on the parts of the manuscript that addressed the couple's experiences. He also made a note of the dearth of serious historical inquiry on the Southern Negro Youth Congress (SNYC), pointing to Johnetta Richards's dissertation, "The Southern Negro Youth Congress: A History," as the lone exception. He promised "to persuade one of my sharpest, most progressive graduate students to write a dissertation on the SNYC, and hopefully it will become a serious book."[1]

Esther did not plan to wait for a graduate student. In 1990, she wrote a grant application for a manuscript titled "Like the Dew They Covered Dixie," a history of the SNYC. She described the organization as "the blank chapter" in civil rights history and argued that it was too important to remain blank because the organization "ploughed and seeded" the "harsh soil" that ultimately produced access to civil rights for black southerners. The history she planned to write, she argued, would reveal how the SNYC "did so much to prepare the way for . . . the decade of the 60's, the King Decade."[2] The proposal made a strong argument for the importance of preserving the SNYC's history, and Esther's investment in that project was clear. In the years since, the SNYC has become an important piece of the black freedom movement's story, shaping scholarly work on the Popular Front years, the influence of communism on civil rights, the personalities in the organization, and the time line of black freedom in American history.[3]

While "Like the Dew They Covered Dixie" never materialized, Esther and Jack found other opportunities to ensure that their own story would be told. At Harvard University's W. E. B. Du Bois Institute, the National Endowment for the Humanities has sponsored summer programs to provide educators with instruction on the long black freedom movement. Run by Patricia Sullivan, Henry Louis Gates Jr., and Waldo Martin, the program offers participants insight into the parts of civil rights history commonly left out of mainstream narratives. As often as they were able, Esther and Jack served as featured speakers, giving college instructors the tools to disseminate a more complex story of black freedom in the United States, with an emphasis on the SNYC. On August 11, 1995, Patricia Sullivan wrote to the Jacksons to thank them for their participation, noting that they, along with Dorothy Burnham, "expanded the horizons of many college and university teachers who had not known that history, and deepened the understanding of those of us who did."[4] The couple's life together increasingly drew attention from the community and beyond: in 1996, the Benjamin Banneker Academy for Community Development honored them by naming its library the "Esther and Jim Jackson Freedom Way Library."[5] Esther and Jack have received honorary degrees and awards from journalistic associations, community organizations, and cultural institutions as well.

Part of preserving their own legacy included ensuring that other black Left legacies would not be lost. Just as she had during the *Freedomways* years, Esther continued to push to celebrate W. E. B. Du Bois and Paul Robeson. In 1996, she worked with the W. E. B. Du Bois Foundation's New York office, helping raise money to commemorate Du Bois's work and inspire further activism.[6] She was also involved in the movement to preserve Du Bois's birthplace in Great Barrington, Massachusetts. In 1998, she spoke at the Paul Robeson centennial celebration in Boston alongside historians and artists.[7] The Jacksons provided primary source material from their lifetime of work, including rare photographs, to documentary filmmakers, historians, and archives. In assessing their life together, the influence of their work on the narrative of American history is not insignificant. The couple made immense efforts to shape and define the story of the black freedom movement, both in their activism and in their support to scholars. And, as these efforts make clear, the connection between the history that scholars write and the ongoing process of ending racial inequality is deeply intertwined. In particular, Esther's work through *Freedomways* captured and disseminated the story of the black Left, offered insight and inspiration for black freedom activists, and provided a model for scholars to understand the multifaceted story of the fight for racial equality in the United States.

Esther and Jack were products of their generation: they were raised in talented-tenth families that expressed concern for the underprivileged and the poor; they came of age during the Great Depression and discovered that capitalism produced class strife and inequality; and they learned harsh lessons about the realities of Jim Crow from life in the South. The Popular Front defined their political coming of age. Though they maintained their Communist ideals well beyond the Popular Front years, their politics evolved as they adapted to changing political times.

As black activists, the Jacksons devoted themselves to the notion that US democracy needed to extend to all citizens and that segregation, job discrimination, racial violence, and political disfranchisement were antithetical to a democratic way of life. They chose activist outlets that fit their Communist and Popular Front political views and made significant contributions to the black freedom movement. As SNYC leaders, they sparked change in the South and offered models for activism that civil rights workers drew on in the years that followed. The activist Debbie Amis Bell grew up around SNYC members and later joined forces with the Student Nonviolent Coordinating Committee (SNCC). She recalls: "When people say 'snick,' I always think first of the Southern Negro Youth Congress and Jim and Esther Jackson. . . . Without that movement in the 1930s and 1940s, SNCC and the civil rights movement of the 1960s would not have been possible."[8] The activist and scholar Angela Davis grew up in Birmingham during the SNYC years and echoed that sentiment, stating: "We have two . . . 'SNICKS'—a SNCC and a SNYC."[9]

While the Jacksons were surely important trailblazers, clearing a path for the civil rights activists who would see success in the decades that followed, their lifetime of activism was significant in its own right. Their accomplishments were important to the people whose lives were improved as a result, and the threats they faced and survived proved the

immediacy and urgency of their work. They approached the black freedom movement with distinct outlooks, responded in unique ways to
political dilemmas, and continued in their activism even when their political ideologies and affiliations were out of step with the mainstream. In
choosing communism, Esther and Jack did not deal themselves an easy
hand. Since the Bolshevik Revolution in 1917, the United States sought
to contain communism at home and abroad, and the Jacksons placed
themselves in the crossfire. As the Cold War took shape in the middle
of the twentieth century, the relationship of the United States with the
Soviet Union had repercussions for domestic social movements and activists. The Depression and the US-Soviet alliance during World War II created space for activists on the left to simultaneously embrace Communist
ideals and fight for democracy. For many of those individuals, the start
of the Cold War turned their political lives topsy-turvy. A number disas-
sociated themselves from their leftist pasts, but some, like the Jacksons,
adhered to their political ideals and argued that holding an unpopular
political opinion was a democratic right.

The Jackson family faced tremendous political and personal consequences as a result of their commitment to communism. The anxiety surrounding Jack's Smith Act trial was difficult for his aging parents. And,
as chapter 4 illustrated, the pressure of the McCarthy years on the Jackson daughters was immense. Kathy and Harriet did not become lifelong
activists, but they made contributions to social justice. Harriet attended
Oberlin College, followed by Columbia University's journalism school,
and she became a journalist and political speechwriter. Kathy graduated
from Goddard College and earned a Ph.D. in psychology at Temple University. Her dissertation, "Trauma Survivors: Adult Children of McCarthyism and the Smith Act," analyzed the influence of political persecution
on the mental health of children of McCarthy victims and explored the
long-term consequences of that trauma on their lives.

Because the Cold War's impact on the Jacksons was so thoroughly
personal, the couple's experiences offer a window into why and how the
black freedom movement changed. The choice to fight anticommunism
in some ways distanced Esther and Jack from the immediacy of the black
freedom movement. In other ways, however, their decision to promote
racial equality from a Communist perspective kept them involved in the

black freedom movement. That they were not a part of the civil rights mainstream after the demise of the Popular Front did not mean that they were no longer a part of the larger struggle for racial equality. As they got older and their individual and family needs changed, they were able to promote the movement from their own perspectives by offering reflections, interpretations, and forums for discussion. They recognized that their contributions were individual components of a multifaceted struggle for racial justice in the United States, that debate was important, and that coalition building would create the unity needed for change.

The Jacksons' life together illustrates the importance of understanding the consequences of political and diplomatic shifts for individuals and families as defining features of social movements. The black freedom movement evolved alongside the emergence of the Cold War, and, as the Jacksons' experiences show, changes in personal and family circumstances were a part of that shift. Leftist critique of capitalism and racism became less effective in the early Cold War years because many of its proponents faced profound personal consequences because of their political beliefs. Esther and Jack understood how to be effective as activists owing to their experiences during the Popular Front era, but they also adapted to changing circumstances. When Jack was indicted in 1951 and vanished and Esther was left not only to fight her husband's political repression but also to raise her daughters and defend them against frightening FBI surveillance, the couple could no longer stand on the front lines of the black freedom movement. Their experiences were emblematic of a shift in leftist activism across the nation. The political situation in the early Cold War years drew radical black activists away from the forefront of the black freedom movement and to the front lines of another cause: their own political liberty.

Nonetheless, the Jacksons' struggle against a political system that marginalized them as activists and threatened their family's well-being did not prevent them from prioritizing the black freedom movement. On the contrary, the couple believed that their political repression, family security, and democratic rights were woven into the broader goals of the African American freedom struggle. Again and again, they found support from and solidarity with black activists across the political spectrum, and, though many black activists were ardent anti-Communists, the Jacksons were connected to them in the fight against racial injustice. Esther and Jack's new roles in the 1960s were the product of their early Cold War predicament but also the result of generational shifts in the black freedom movement. As a younger generation took over as the movement's vanguard, older leftists took on new positions as guides, confidants, and resources.

And, although activists in the civil rights years did not advocate for the same kind of economic change that the Jacksons had during the heyday of the American Communist movement, the same economic issues, including job and housing discrimination, access to social services, and poverty, remained central concerns for civil rights activists. The Cold War did not reshape mainstream activism in a vacuum. It reshaped mainstream civil rights activism precisely because it had a profound impact on the lives and families of black radicals. Esther and Jack's lives demonstrate the impact it had on the long black freedom movement.

The Jacksons were a couple who collaborated over the course of a marriage that lasted for sixty-six years. They were not perfect. They made difficult choices, took profound personal and political risks, and sacrificed significantly to participate in the black freedom and Communist movements, and those choices are worthy of attention, recognition, scrutiny, and empathy. Jack's decision to go underground and then stand by the Party after the revelations of Stalin's atrocities complicates his legacy, but it also provides an opportunity for understanding how individuals navigated a changing world, committed to their principles, however unpopular, and fought for change in unique ways. Jack had a blind spot for the Soviet Union and accorded it and its leaders an analytic lens that he did not apply to US injustices. The Soviet atrocities and the Communist Party's response to them tarnish the legacies of committed social justice activists who, like Jack, did not renounce their communism in the midst of the Cold War. Jack was under no obligation to do so, and he justified his commitments over the course of his career through his writings, speeches, and analyses. It remains important to take the words, ideas, and actions of these activists seriously and to understand where they are coming from, how they prioritized their commitments, what nuance they applied to their interpretations, and how they weighed the good and bad not only of the United States but also of the Soviet Union and other nations in a rapidly changing world.

Esther and Jack offer a story of love that was forged on a hard, unconventional path. They each brought a commitment to activism to their marriage, and part of their compatibility was built around that shared obligation. Making contributions to the black freedom movement provided the energy in their romance, and their activism was so central to their marriage that removing it from the equation would have been like removing a limb. They were an activist couple, but, even when they collaborated, they were individuals who brought unique ideas to the table, argued, compromised, and had faith in one another's ability and perspective. Jack was a lifelong Communist, and Esther was committed to Communist ideals but not to the Party itself. Their individual differences and their collaboration provide a pathway for understanding how gender and culture influence couples who are politically engaged. Esther and Jack agreed a lot, and that was certainly a foundation of their compatibility. But they also affiliated differently, and we cannot hold one accountable for the other's choices or actions. They made significant contributions, both as a couple and individually.

The Jacksons' romance was not the stuff of fairy tales but a real, human love that was messy and complex. Over sixty-six years of marriage Esther and Jack faced hardships, experienced moments of doubt, and made active decisions to persist through their most trying moments together. They did not function in unison all the time, and they spent half of their first fifteen years of marriage apart from one another. There were periods of passionate, sentimental, flowery love letters and times during which they grew so comfortable being alone, particularly in the underground years, that they wondered whether they could make it together. The difficult moments illustrate that their marriage took intentional effort. They wanted to stay together, and they always found the way back to their love for one another.

On June 21, 1945, James Jackson had written a letter to his wife that would prove prophetic. He told her:

> Dear darling, in these torrential days, with all of the demands they impose upon those of us who are conscientious in our sense of responsibility to our generation and that of children to come, nonetheless do not overburden yourself with too great a load

of these "things that must be done." Above all do not brood and "worry-worry" about them. Laugh; relax; sleep soundly; eat heartily; rest; exercise your body. This struggle is our way of life. We must not consume ourselves in a single crisis. The battle will be long, and we must be strong and healthy and happy in the fight in order to endure and win.[10]

Jack died on September 1, 2007, at the age of ninety-two, with his wife and daughters at his side. James and Esther Cooper Jackson had devoted their lives to fighting for a better world. Their love sustained them through their fight for racial equality and social justice, and their activism enhanced their devotion to one another. Seven years after Jack's death, in 2014, Esther reached her ninety-seventh birthday and continues to fight for social justice.

Acknowledgments

Every book is nourished by the input, support, love, critique, and encouragement of many people. I am grateful for this collaborative process and for the community I have built while writing this book. This work, of course, would never have happened without James and Esther Cooper Jackson's life of activism and support for this project. The opportunity to listen to their stories, look at all the papers that had been hidden away in their home, and get to know them over the years shaped my career and my life. The Jacksons were enormously gracious biographical subjects. They supported my efforts and gave me the space to craft my own interpretation of their experiences. They also put me in contact with friends and colleagues, and I had the good fortune to speak with Dorothy Burnham, Bunny Devine, Julian Houston, Jack O'Dell, Thelma Dale Perkins, Norma Rodgers, and Percy Sutton, among others.

Jonathan Holloway first put me in contact with the Jacksons when I was an undergraduate. At Mount Holyoke College, Mary Renda, Holly Hanson, and Daniel Czitrom encouraged my research, provided critical feedback, and helped to shape me as a writer and researcher. Grants from the Almara Fund at Mount Holyoke facilitated the earliest research. For all of them I am immensely grateful.

This support continued at Rutgers University. Deborah Gray White, Mia Bay, Nancy Hewitt, Minkah Makalani, Donna Murch, and Jan Lewis provided intellectual guidance over the course of my graduate career and helped the project along. Robert Korstad, of Duke University, also provided important feedback at various stages. Steven Lawson, my graduate school adviser, continues to be an amazing mentor. He has read every version of this work more than once, offering essential insights and raising important questions. I am immensely grateful for his generosity and his friendship. At Rutgers, I entered a warm, collegial, vibrant community of graduate students, and our conversations helped develop this project in important ways. I benefited enormously from the friendship and support of John Adams, Marsha Barrett, Vanessa Holden, Allison Miller, Lesley Doig, Chris Mitchell, Rebecca Tuuri, Jacki Castledine, and Katie Lee.

At St. Francis College, this project was supported by a faculty research grant. I am also exceptionally lucky to have the advice, encouragement, solidarity, and collegiality of my St. Francis community. I am especially grateful for the friendship and support of Eric Platt, who generously read parts of the manuscript at the very last minute, Scott Weiss, Emily Horowitz, Ian Maloney, Jen Wingate, Nickie Phillips, Timothy Houlihan, Julio Huato, and Paddy Quick. Edwin Mathieu, Robert Allende, Yvette Sosa, and Kathy DiTrento provided essential help at important moments. I am also happy to work with wonderful students, including my research assistant, Elizabeth Peralta.

I am thankful for the hard work of the archivists and support staff who processed the Jackson Papers at New York University and who facilitate scholarly research in their library, especially the late Michael Nash, Peter Filardo, Sarah Moazeni, and Kate Donovan. The staff at the Moorland-Spingarn Research Center, including Jo-Ellen El-Bashir and Ida Jones, has also been accommodating and helpful. At the University Press of Kentucky, Anne Dean Dotson and Bailey Johnson have made the process of publishing this book as smooth and pleasurable as possible. Erik Gellman's thoughtful, detailed comments on the full manuscript were indispensable.

I am also grateful for my family and friends, who asked how things were going often enough to keep me moving forward: Joe, Laura, Kyle, Becky, Anne, Russell, Jen, and Ellen. My parents, Zdzislaw and Carol Rzeszutek, always pushed me to achieve my goals and encouraged me throughout this long process. Words cannot express my gratitude for their love and support. Krista Haviland has been at my side since 2001 and gave me enormous patience, love, perspective, humor, and reassurance through all the stages of this project. Her partnership made this book possible. Our kids, Milo and Zora, have been a constant source of amazement, laughter, and fun. They inspire me every day. This book is dedicated to the memory of my grandparents, Wojciech and Maria Rzeszutek and Roland and Phyllis Bibeault.

Portions of chapters 2, 4, and 5 appeared previously in Sara E. Rzeszutek, "'All Those Rosy Dreams We Cherish': James Jackson and Esther Cooper's Marriage on the Front Lines of the Double Victory Campaign,"

American Communist History 7, no. 2 (2008): 211–26, which was reprinted in *Red Activists and Black Freedom: James and Esther Jackson and the Long Civil Rights Revolution,* ed. David Levering Lewis, Michael H. Nash, and Daniel J. Leab (London: Routledge, 2010), 41–55. I thank *American Communist History* and Routledge for permission to reprint this material. The journal's Web site can be found at http://www.tandfonline.com.

Notes

Introduction

1. Esther Cooper Jackson and James Jackson, interview with author, December 12, 2002, Brooklyn, NY.

2. Patricia Sullivan, *Days of Hope: Race and Democracy in the New Deal Era* (Chapel Hill: University of North Carolina Press, 1996); Glenda Gilmore, *Defying Dixie: The Radical Roots of Civil Rights, 1919–1950* (New York: Norton, 2008); Robin D. G. Kelley, *Hammer and Hoe: Alabama Communists during the Great Depression* (Chapel Hill: University of North Carolina Press, 1990); Robert Korstad and Nelson Lichtenstein, "Opportunities Found and Lost: Labor, Radicals and the Early Civil Rights Movement," *Journal of American History* 75, no. 3 (December 1988): 786–811; Robert Rogers Korstad, *Civil Rights Unionism: Tobacco Workers and the Struggle for Democracy in the Mid-Twentieth-Century South* (Chapel Hill: University of North Carolina Press, 2003); Jacquelyn Dowd Hall, "The Long Civil Rights Movement and the Political Uses of the Past," *Journal of American History* 91, no. 4 (March 2005): 1233–63; Steven Lawson, "Long Origins of the Short Civil Rights Movement, 1954–1969," in *Freedom Rights: New Perspectives on the Civil Rights Movement,* ed. Danielle McGuire and John Dittmer (Lexington: University Press of Kentucky, 2011), 9–38; Erik Gellman, *Death Blow to Jim Crow: The National Negro Congress and the Rise of Militant Civil Rights* (Chapel Hill: University of North Carolina Press, 2012).

3. Penny M. Von Eschen, *Race against Empire: Black Americans and Anticolonialism, 1937–1957* (Ithaca, NY: Cornell University Press, 1997), and *Satchmo Blows Up the World: Jazz Ambassadors Play the Cold War* (Cambridge, MA: Harvard University Press, 2004); Mary Dudziak, *Cold War Civil Rights: Race and the Image of American Democracy* (Princeton, NJ: Princeton University Press, 2000); Thomas Borstelmann, *The Cold War and the Color Line: American Race Relations in the Global Age* (Cambridge, MA: Harvard University Press, 2001); Brenda Gayle Plummer, *Rising Wind: Black Americans and U.S. Foreign Affairs, 1935–1960* (Chapel Hill: University of North Carolina Press, 1996); Patricia Sullivan, *Lift Every Voice: The NAACP and the Making of the Civil Rights Movement* (New York: New Press, 2009); Eric Arnesen, "Civil Rights and the Cold War at Home: Postwar Activism, Anticommunism, and the Decline of the Left," *American Communist History* 11, no. 1 (April 2012): 5–44.

4. George Lipsitz, *A Life in the Struggle: Ivory Perry and the Culture of Opposition* (Philadelphia: Temple University Press, 1988), 13.

5. Erik S. Gellman and Jarod Roll, *The Gospel of the Working Class: Labor's Southern Prophets in New Deal America* (Urbana: University of Illinois Press,

2011), 4. For more on biography, see Richard Hobbs, *The Cayton Legacy: An African American Family* (Pullman: Washington State University Press, 2002).

6. Wilson Record, *The Negro and the Communist Party* (Chapel Hill: University of North Carolina Press, 1951), and *Race and Radicalism: The NAACP and the Communist Party in Conflict* (Ithaca, NY: Cornell University Press, 1964); Harold Cruse, *The Crisis of the Negro Intellectual* (New York: New York Review of Books, 1967); Theodore Draper, *The Roots of American Communism* (New York: Viking, 1957). For further discussion of this perspective and more recent historiographic debate, see Theodore H. Draper, "American Communism Revisited," *New York Review of Books*, May 9, 1985, 32–37, and "The Popular Front Revisited," *New York Review of Books*, May 30, 1985, 44–50; Paul Buhle, James R. Prickett, James R. Barrett, Rob Ruck, et al., "Revisiting American Communism: An Exchange," *New York Review of Books*, August 15, 1985, 40–44; Harvey Klehr, *The Heyday of American Communism: The Depression Decade* (New York: Basic, 1984); Irving Howe, *The American Communist Party: A Critical History, 1919–1957* (Boston: Beacon, 1957); Harvey Klehr, John Earl Haynes, and Fridrikh Igorevich Firsov, *The Secret World of American Communism* (New Haven, CT: Yale University Press, 1995); Eric Arnesen, "No 'Graver Danger': Black Anticommunism, the Communist Party, and the Race Question," *Labor* 3, no. 4 (Winter 2006): 13–52; John Earl Haynes, "Reconsidering Two Questions: On Arnesen's 'No "Graver Danger"': Black Anticommunism, the Communist Party, and the Race Question,'" *Labor* 3, no. 4 (Winter 2006): 53–57; Martha Biondi, "Response to Eric Arnesen," *Labor* 3, no. 4 (Winter 2006): 59–63; Carol Anderson, "'The Brother in Black Is Always Told to Wait': The Communist Party, African American Anticommunism, and the Prioritization of Black Equality—a Reply to Eric Arnesen," *Labor* 3, no. 4 (Winter 2006): 65–68; Kenneth R. Janken, "Anticommunism or Anti–Communist Party? A Response to Eric Arnesen," *Labor* 3, no. 4 (Winter 2006): 69–74; Eric Arnesen, "The Red and the Black: Reflections on the Responses to 'No "Graver Danger,"'" *Labor* 3, no. 4 (Winter 2006): 75–79, and "Civil Rights and the Cold War at Home"; Alex Lichtenstein, "Consensus? What Consensus?" *American Communist History* 11, no. 1 (2012): 49–53; Dayo Gore, "'The Danger of Being an Active Anti-Communist': Expansive Black Left Politics and the Long Civil Rights Movement," *American Communist History* 11, no. 1 (2012): 45–48; Judith Stein, "Why American Historians Embrace the 'Long Civil Rights Movement,'" *American Communist History* 11, no. 1 (2012): 55–58; Robert H. Zieger, "Déjà Vu All over Again," *American Communist History* 11, no. 1 (2012): 59–62; and Eric Arnesen, "The Final Conflict? On the Scholarship of Civil Rights, the Left, and the Cold War," *American Communist History* 11, no. 1 (2012): 63–80.

7. Ralph Ellison, *Invisible Man* (New York: Random House, 1952); Richard Wright, *Black Boy (American Hunger)* (New York: Harper & Bros., 1945).

8. Ellen Schrecker, *Many Are the Crimes: McCarthyism in America* (Boston:

Little, Brown, 1998); Arnesen, "Civil Rights and the Cold War at Home"; Lichtenstein, "Consensus? What Consensus?"; Gore, "'The Danger of Being an Active Anti-Communist'"; Junius Irving Scales and Richard Nickson, *Cause at Heart: A Former Communist Remembers* (Athens: University of Georgia Press, 1987).

9. Kelley, *Hammer and Hoe;* Mark Naison, *Communists in Harlem during the Depression* (New York: Grove, 1984); Gerald Horne, *Black Liberation/ Red Scare: Ben Davis and the Communist Party* (Newark: University of Delaware Press, 1994); Maurice Isserman, *If I Had a Hammer . . . : The Death of the Old Left and the Birth of the New Left* (New York: Basic, 1987); James R. Barrett, *William Z. Foster and the Tragedy of American Radicalism* (Urbana: University of Illinois Press, 1999); Albert Fried, ed., *Communism in America: A History in Documents* (New York: Columbia University Press, 1997); Schrecker, *Many Are the Crimes;* Maurice Isserman, *Which Side Were You On? The American Communist Party during the Second World War* (Middletown, CT: Wesleyan University Press, 1982); Timothy Johnson, "'Death for Negro Lynching!' The Communist Party, USA's Position on the African American Question," *American Communist History* 7, no. 2 (December 2008): 242–54; Earl Ofari Hutchinson, *Blacks and Reds: Race and Class in Conflict, 1919–1990* (Lansing: Michigan State University Press, 1995); Cedric J. Robinson, *Black Marxism: The Making of the Black Radical Tradition* (London: Zed, 1983); Marc Solomon, *The Cry Was Unity: Communists and African Americans, 1917–1936* (Jackson: University Press of Mississippi, 1998); Erik S. McDuffie, *Sojourning for Freedom: Black Women, American Communism, and the Making of Black Left Feminism* (Durham, NC: Duke University Press, 2011); Kate Weigand, *Red Feminism: American Communism and the Making of Women's Liberation* (Baltimore: Johns Hopkins University Press, 2001); Dayo Gore, *Radicalism at the Crossroads: African American Women Activists in the Cold War* (New York: New York University Press, 2010); Mary Helen Washington, *The Other Blacklist: The African American Literary and Cultural Left of the 1950s* (New York: Columbia University Press, 2014).

10. Nell Irvin Painter, *The Narrative of Hosea Hudson: His Life as a Negro Communist in the South* (Cambridge, MA: Harvard University Press, 1979), 29.

11. Benjamin J. Davis, *Communist Councilman from Harlem: Autobiographical Notes Written in a Federal Penitentiary* (1969), 2nd ed. (New York: International, 1991), 217. For more autobiographies and memoirs of black Communists, see Hosea Hudson, *Black Worker in the Deep South: A Personal Record* (New York: International, 1972); Harry Haywood, *A Black Communist in the Freedom Struggle: The Life of Harry Haywood,* ed. Gwendolyn Midlo Hall (Minneapolis: University of Minnesota Press, 2011); and Nelson Peery, *Black Fire: The Making of an American Revolutionary* (New York: New Press, 1994).

12. Painter, *The Narrative of Hosea Hudson,* 15.

13. Kelley, *Hammer and Hoe.*

14. Naison, *Communists in Harlem.*

15. John Egerton, *Speak Now against the Day: The Generation Before the Civil Rights Movement in the South* (New York: Knopf, 1994); Robert Cohen, *When the Old Left Was Young: Student Radicals and America's First Mass Student Movement* (New York: Oxford University Press, 1993).

16. Lipsitz, *A Life in the Struggle*, 230.

17. Works on twentieth-century marriage include Elaine Tyler May, *Great Expectations: Marriage and Divorce in Post-Victorian America* (Chicago: University of Chicago Press, 1980); Nancy Cott, *Public Vows: A History of Marriage and the Nation* (Cambridge, MA: Harvard University Press, 2000); and Stephanie Coontz, *Marriage, a History: How Love Conquered Marriage* (New York: Penguin, 2006). Works focusing more explicitly on race include Anastasia Curwood, "Three African American Marriages in the World of E. Franklin Frazier, 1932–1967" (Ph.D. diss., Princeton University, 2003); and Eleanor Alexander, *Lyrics of Sunshine and Shadow: The Tragic Courtship and Marriage of Paul Laurence Dunbar and Alice Ruth Moore: A History of Love and Violence among the African American Elite* (New York: New York University Press, 2001).

18. Alexander, *Lyrics of Sunshine and Shadow*, 132–40 (quote 135).

19. Martin Summers, *Manliness and Its Discontents: The Black Middle Class and the Transformation of Masculinity, 1900–1930* (Chapel Hill: University of North Carolina Press, 2004), 187.

20. See Eric Foner, *Reconstruction: America's Unfinished Revolution, 1863–1877* (New York: Harper & Row, 1988); Jacqueline Jones, *Labor of Love, Labor of Sorrow: Black Women, Work, and the Family, from Slavery to the Present* (New York: Vintage, 1985); Michele Mitchell, *Righteous Propagation: African Americans and the Politics of Racial Destiny After Reconstruction* (Chapel Hill: University of North Carolina Press, 2004); and Kevin K. Gaines, *Uplifting the Race: Black Leadership, Politics, and Culture in the Twentieth Century* (Chapel Hill: University of North Carolina Press, 1996).

21. There is some evidence to suggest that couples with more leftist politics strove for more egalitarian marriages, but it is difficult to gauge how often these couples withstood the pressure to conform to more normative gender roles. Esther Cooper Jackson believes that the Strongs and the Burnhams would have had long-lasting, successful marriages like hers had Ed Strong and Louis Burnham survived. Strong and Burnham both suffered from sudden illnesses and died at young ages. Some discussion of married radicals exists in Kelley, *Hammer and Hoe*.

22. Coontz, *Marriage, a History*, 20.

23. Esther Cooper Jackson, interview with author, September 25, 2002, Brooklyn, NY; Dorothy Burnham, interview with author, January 23, 2003, Brooklyn, NY; Kelley, *Hammer and Hoe*, 206–7.

24. Esther Cooper Jackson, interview with author, March 15, 2006, Brooklyn, NY.

25. Weigand, *Red Feminism;* Erik S. McDuffie, "Long Journeys: Four Black Women and the Communist Party, U.S.A., 1930–1956" (Ph.D. diss., New York University, 2003); Jacqueline Castledine, "Gendering the Cold War: Race, Class and Women's Peace Politics, 1945–1975" (Ph.D. diss., Rutgers University, 2006); Kelley, *Hammer and Hoe;* Elaine Tyler May, *Homeward Bound: American Families in the Cold War Era* (New York: Basic, 1999); Joanne Meyerowitz, ed., *Not June Cleaver: Women and Gender in Postwar America, 1945–1960* (Philadelphia: Temple University Press, 1994); Ruth Feldstein, *Motherhood in Black and White: Race and Sex in American Liberalism, 1930–1965* (Ithaca, NY: Cornell University Press, 2000); K. A. Cuordileone, *Manhood and American Political Culture in the Cold War* (London: Routledge, 2005); Andrea Friedman, "The Strange Career of Annie Lee Moss: Rethinking Race, Gender, and McCarthyism," *Journal of American History* 94, no. 2 (September 2007): 445–68.

26. Kelley, *Hammer and Hoe,* 207.

1. Jack and Esther's Paths to Activism and Each Other

1. James E. Jackson Jr., interview with author, December 12, 2002, Brooklyn, NY.

2. Esther Cooper Jackson, *This Is My Husband: Fighter for His People, Political Refugee* (New York: National Committee to Defend Negro Leadership, 1953), 22.

3. Michael McGerr, *A Fierce Discontent: The Rise and Fall of the Progressive Movement in America, 1870–1920* (Oxford: Oxford University Press, 2003), xiv.

4. Ibid., 192–94.

5. William H. Chafe, *Civilities and Civil Rights: Greensboro, North Carolina, and the Black Struggle for Freedom* (Oxford: Oxford University Press, 1980), 8.

6. McGerr, *A Fierce Discontent,* 188.

7. David Howard-Pitney, *The African American Jeremiad: Appeals for Justice in America* (Philadelphia: Temple University Press, 2005), 104.

8. Joy James, *Transcending the Talented Tenth: Black Leaders and American Intellectuals* (New York: Routledge, 1997), 20.

9. McDuffie, "Long Journeys."

10. Family History, James and Esther Cooper Jackson Papers (hereafter Jackson Papers), n.d., Tamiment Library, New York University, New York, NY, box 1, folder 13.

11. Summers, *Manliness and Its Discontents,* 6.

12. Cooper Jackson, *This Is My Husband,* 10.

13. Upward mobility, along with uplift ideology, offers an important framework for understanding African American aspirations in the early twentieth century. As the historian Kevin K. Gaines argues: "Although the racial uplift ideology of the black intelligentsia involved intensive soul-searching, ambivalence, and

dissension on the objectives of black leadership and on the meaning of black progress, black opinion leaders deemed the promotion of bourgeois morality, patriarchal authority, and a culture of self-improvement, both among blacks and outward, to the white world, as necessary to their recognition, enfranchisement, and survival as a class." In other words, the embodiment of cultural and social ascendance would afford African Americans the status necessary to attain full citizenship. See Gaines, *Uplifting the Race*, 3. Other works addressing racial uplift ideology and the black middle class in the Progressive and Depression eras include Deborah Gray White, *Too Heavy a Load: Black Women in Defense of Themselves, 1894–1994* (New York: Norton, 1998); David Levering Lewis, *W. E. B. Du Bois: Biography of a Race, 1868–1919* (New York: Henry Holt, 1993); Summers, *Manliness and Its Discontents;* Mitchell, *Righteous Propagation;* Victoria W. Wolcott, *Remaking Respectability: African American Women in Interwar Detroit* (Chapel Hill: University of North Carolina Press, 2000); and Marlon Ross, *Manning the Race: Reforming Black Men in the Jim Crow Era* (New York: New York University Press, 2004).

14. Elsa Barkley Brown and Gregg D. Kimball, "Mapping the Terrain of Black Richmond," in *The New African American Urban History,* ed. Kenneth W. Goings and Raymond A. Mohl (Thousand Oaks, CA: Sage, 1996), 66–115, 85. For more resources on black Richmond, see Elsa Barkley Brown, "Womanist Consciousness: Maggie Lena Walker and the Independent Order of Saint Luke," *Signs: Journal of Women in Culture and Society* 14, no. 3 (Spring 1989): 610–33; and Jane Dailey, Glenda Elizabeth Gilmore, and Bryant Simon, eds., *Jumpin' Jim Crow: Southern Politics from Civil War to Civil Rights* (Princeton, NJ: Princeton University Press, 2000).

15. Brown and Kimball, "Mapping the Terrain of Black Richmond," 85.

16. Ibid., 101.

17. Cliff Weil Cigar Company Reference for James Jackson, June 14, 1914, Jackson Papers, box 1, folder 22.

18. Cooper Jackson, *This Is My Husband*, 12.

19. Esther Cooper Jackson, interview with author, November 17, 2008, Brooklyn, NY.

20. Cooper Jackson, *This Is My Husband*, 10.

21. Ibid., 11.

22. Ibid., 10. For information on resistance to restrictive covenant laws in the early twentieth century, including references to laws in Richmond, see Michael Jones-Correa, "The Origins and Diffusion of Racial Restrictive Covenants," *Political Science Quarterly* 115, no. 4 (Winter 2000–2001): 541–68; and *Shelley v. Kraemer,* 334 U.S. 1 (1948), Vinson, C.J., Opinion of the Court, Supreme Court of the United States, available at Legal Information Institute, Cornell University Law School, http://www.law.cornell.edu/supct/html/historics/USSC_CR_0334_0001_ZO.html.

23. Cooper Jackson, *This Is My Husband*, 12.

24. "The Niagara Movement," *Oxford W. E. B. Du Bois Reader*, ed. Eric J. Sundquist (New York: Oxford University Press, 1996), 373–76, 374. The Niagara movement was a group of black middle-class professionals who first organized in 1905 in Erie, Ontario, and resolved to fight for comprehensive citizenship rights for African Americans. When the NAACP was organized five years later, it absorbed most of the Niagara members.

25. Cooper Jackson, *This Is My Husband*, 10.

26. Booker T. Washington, "Atlanta Compromise," in *The Booker T. Washington Papers*, ed. Louis R. Harlan, 14 vols. (Urbana: University of Illinois Press, 1972–1989), 3:583–87.

27. Cooper Jackson, *This Is My Husband*, 10, 12.

28. For more on Washington, see McGerr, *A Fierce Discontent*, 195–200; Lewis R. Harlan, *Booker T. Washington: The Making of a Black Leader, 1856–1901* (New York: Oxford University Press, 1975), and *Booker T. Washington: The Wizard of Tuskegee, 1901–1915* (New York: Oxford University Press, 1983); Lewis, *W. E. B. Du Bois: Biography of a Race*; Michael Bieze, *Booker T. Washington and the Art of Self-Representation* (New York: Peter Lang, 2008); and Robert J. Norrell, *Up from History: The Life of Booker T. Washington* (Cambridge, MA: Belknap Press of Harvard University Press, 2009).

29. David Levering Lewis, *W. E. B. Du Bois: The Fight for Equality and the American Century, 1919–1963* (New York: Henry Holt, 2000), 523.

30. Cooper Jackson, *This Is My Husband*, 15.

31. Ibid., 16.

32. McGerr, *A Fierce Discontent*, 112. For more on manliness and masculinity in the early twentieth century, see Summers, *Manliness and Its Discontents;* and Ross, *Manning the Race.*

33. James E. Jackson to Esther Cooper, n.d., Jackson Papers, box 6, folder 27.

34. McGerr, *A Fierce Discontent*, 112.

35. McGerr, *A Fierce Discontent*, 111. See also Summers, *Manliness and Its Discontents.*

36. James E. Jackson to Esther Cooper, n.d., Jackson Papers, box 6, folder 27.

37. Cooper Jackson, *This Is My Husband*, 16; "Getting Blacks into Scouting Took Some Work," *Richmond Times Dispatch*, August 11, 1997, Jackson Papers, box 1, folder 3.

38. Cooper Jackson, *This Is My Husband*, 16.

39. Ibid.

40. Workers of the Writers' Program of the Works Progress Administration in the State of Virginia, *The Negro in Virginia* (1940; Winston-Salem, NC: John F. Blair, 1994), 294–304.

41. Cooper Jackson, *This Is My Husband,* 17.

42. Ira Katznelson, *When Affirmative Action Was White: An Untold History of Racial Inequality in Twentieth Century America* (New York: Norton, 2005), 13. For more on race during the Depression, see Sullivan, *Days of Hope;* Kelley, *Hammer and Hoe;* Naison, *Communists in Harlem;* and Korstad, *Civil Rights Unionism.*

43. Cooper Jackson, *This Is My Husband,* 17.

44. James E. Jackson to Esther Cooper, n.d., Jackson Papers, box 6, folder 27.

45. James E. Jackson Jr., "The Student and the World beyond the Campus," *Intercollegian,* October 1932, Jackson Papers, box 2, folder 5.

46. Amy Kaplan, *The Anarchy of Empire in the Making of U.S. Culture* (Cambridge, MA: Harvard University Press, 2002), 184.

47. Quoted in Robinson, *Black Marxism,* 276, 333–34n.

48. Lewis, *W. E. B. Du Bois: Biography of a Race,* 504–5.

49. Lewis, *W. E. B. Du Bois: The Fight for Equality,* 413.

50. Cooper Jackson, *This Is My Husband,* 17.

51. Nina Mjagkij, *A Light in the Darkness: African Americans and the YMCA, 1852–1946* (Lexington: University Press of Kentucky, 1994).

52. Cooper Jackson, *This Is My Husband,* 18.

53. James E. Jackson to Esther Cooper, n.d., Jackson Papers, box 6, folder 27.

54. Minkah Makalani, *In the Cause of Freedom: Radical Black Internationalism from Harlem to London, 1917–1939* (Chapel Hill: University of North Carolina Press, 2011); Horne, *Black Liberation/Red Scare;* Naison, *Communists in Harlem;* Kelley, *Hammer and Hoe.*

55. James Goodman, *Stories of Scottsboro* (New York: Vintage, 1994); Dan T. Carter, *Scottsboro: A Tragedy of the American South* (Baton Rouge: Louisiana State University Press, 1969); Herbert Aptheker, ed., *A Documentary History of the Negro People in the United States,* 7 vols. (New York: Citadel, 1951–1994), vol. 5.

56. Davis, *Communist Councilman from Harlem,* 53–81.

57. Cooper Jackson, *This Is My Husband,* 18.

58. Scales and Nickson, *Cause at Heart,* 62–63, 69.

59. Kelley, *Hammer and Hoe,* xii.

60. Hudson, *Black Worker in the Deep South,* 38.

61. James E. Jackson to Esther Cooper, n.d., Jackson Papers, box 6, folder 27.

62. Summers, *Manliness and Its Discontents,* 1.

63. Gaines, *Uplifting the Race,* 3–4, 5. The historian Darlene Clark Hine argues that African American cultural and social responses to the oppressive structure of racism in the United States, particularly in reaction to sexual violence

against black women, can be characterized as a "culture of dissemblance." Dissemblance, she writes, "involved [black women] creating the appearance of disclosure, or openness about themselves and their feelings, while actually remaining enigmatic." Darlene Clark Hine, *Hine Sight: Black Women and the Re-Construction of American History* (Indianapolis: Indiana University Press, 1997), 41. Gaines extends Hine's theory of dissemblance to apply to the politics of racial uplift. He writes: "Bitter, divisive memories of the violence and humiliations of slavery and segregation were and remain at the heart of uplift ideology's romance of the patriarchal family, expressed by black men and women's too-often-frustrated aspirations to protect and be protected." Gaines, *Uplifting the Race,* 5. Elite and middle-class black men, then, dissembled to guard themselves against the psychological harm racism caused and to create the appearance of a normative social and familial life to promote racial advancement.

64. Cooper Jackson, *This Is My Husband,* 20.

65. Gellman, *Death Blow to Jim Crow,* 64.

66. Scott J. Myers-Lipton, *Social Solutions to Poverty: America's Struggle to Build a Just Society* (Boulder, CO: Paradigm, 2006), 165–66.

67. James E. Jackson, "We Tell the Congressmen," *Student Review,* June 1935, 5–6.

68. Solomon, *The Cry Was Unity,* 304–5. See also Gellman, *Death Blow to Jim Crow.*

69. Johnetta Richards, "The Southern Negro Youth Congress: A History" (Ph.D. diss., University of Ohio, 1987), 19–20.

70. Gellman, *Death Blow to Jim Crow,* 4.

71. Record, *The Negro and the Communist Party,* 27.

72. Solomon, *The Cry Was Unity,* 170, 171.

73. Lewis, *W. E. B. Du Bois: The Fight for Equality,* 262–64.

74. Schrecker, *Many Are the Crimes,* 15. For more on the Popular Front movement, see Egerton, *Speak Now against the Day;* and Cohen, *When the Old Left Was Young.*

75. Augusta Jackson Strong, "Southern Youth's Proud Heritage," *Freedomways,* no. 1 (1964): 36.

76. Ibid., 38–39.

77. Ibid.

78. Kelley, *Hammer and Hoe,* 200.

79. Richards, "The Southern Negro Youth Congress," 201. See also "Memorandum: Second All-Southern Negro Youth Conference," Southern Negro Youth Congress Papers (hereafter SNYC Papers), Conferences, Moorland-Spingarn Research Center, Howard University, Washington, DC.

80. Richards, "The Southern Negro Youth Congress," 31.

81. Florence Castile to Johnnie A. Moore, Tuskegee Institute SNYC club president, October 10, 1947, SNYC Papers, Clubs and Councils.

82. Richards, "The Southern Negro Youth Congress," 32.

83. For more on the SNYC's first conference, see Gellman, *Death Blow to Jim Crow*, 63–108.

84. "Proclamation of Southern Negro Youth," ca. 1937, SNYC Papers, Publications. The "Proclamation of Southern Negro Youth" was printed in several formats throughout the SNYC's existence— in some instances in shortened form to read like a manifesto. The full text is approximately four pages long.

85. Ibid. For works that explore Marcus Garvey's influence, see Ula Taylor, *The Veiled Garvey: The Life and Times of Amy Jacques Garvey* (Chapel Hill: University of North Carolina Press, 2001); Judith Stein, *The World of Marcus Garvey: Race and Class in Modern Society* (Baton Rouge: Louisiana State University Press, 1991); Mary G. Rolinson, *Grassroots Garveyism: The Universal Negro Improvement Association in the Rural South, 1920–1927* (Chapel Hill: University of North Carolina Press, 2007); and Tony Martin, *Race First: The Ideological and Organizational Struggles of Marcus Garvey and the Universal Negro Improvement Association*, 2nd ed. (Dover, MA: Majority, 1986).

86. Kelley, *Hammer and Hoe*, 212.

87. "Proclamation of Southern Negro Youth," ca. 1937, SNYC Papers, Publications.

88. The SNYC's third conference program cover featured a photograph of Booker T. Washington in a specific attempt to appeal to black southerners who were put off by the organization's more radical reputation. Leaders made an effort to include multiple political aspirations in the conference proceedings.

89. Adult Advisory Board Members, n.d., SNYC Papers.

90. Dorothy Burnham, interview with author, January 23, 2003, Brooklyn, NY.

91. For further details on race and the YMCA/YWCA, see Nancy Robertson, *Christian Sisterhood, Race Relations, and the YWCA, 1901–1946* (Urbana: University of Illinois Press, 2007); Doug Rossinow, *The Politics of Authenticity: Liberalism, Christianity, and the New Left in America* (New York: Columbia University Press, 1998); and Mjagkij, *A Light in the Darkness.*

92. Manual of Organization, 1947, SNYC Papers, Administrative Files.

93. Strong, "Southern Youth's Proud Heritage," 41.

94. Richard Love, "In Defiance of Custom and Tradition: Black Tobacco Workers and Labor Unions in Richmond, Virginia, 1937–1941," *Labor History* 35, no. 1 (Winter 1994): 25–47, 26.

95. Gellman, *Death Blow to Jim Crow*, 67.

96. Workers of the Writers' Program, *The Negro in Virginia*, 339–40.

97. Gellman, *Death Blow to Jim Crow*, 66–67.

98. Korstad, *Civil Rights Unionism*, 38.

99. Ted Poston, "The Making of Mama Harris," *New Republic*, November 4, 1940, quoted in Love, "In Defiance of Custom and Tradition," 1.

100. James E. Jackson Jr., interview with author, December 12, 2002, Brooklyn, NY. See also Workers of the Writers' Program, *The Negro in Virginia,* 340. For a detailed history of the unionization of Richmond tobacco workers and this series of strikes, see Gellman, *Death Blow to Jim Crow,* 63–108; and Love, "In Defiance of Custom and Tradition." Love argues that the Richmond strikes constituted an assault on the "structure and status quo of racial segregation," led to the reification of racial lines within major labor unions, and challenged the exclusion of African American laborers from skilled ranks as mechanization isolated them at increasingly insufficient pay grades and poor labor conditions. Ibid., 26.

101. Love, "In Defiance of Custom and Tradition," 25, 29–30 (quote); Augusta V. Jackson, "A New Deal for Tobacco Workers," *The Crisis,* October 1938, 323; Gellman, *Death Blow to Jim Crow,* 78.

102. Jackson, "A New Deal for Tobacco Workers," 322–24, 330, 324.

103. Workers of the Writers' Program, *The Negro in Virginia,* 340.

104. See ibid.; Love, "In Defiance of Custom and Tradition"; and Gellman, *Death Blow to Jim Crow,* 67.

105. Love, "In Defiance of Custom and Tradition," 33 (quote), 35–36. See also Gellman, *Death Blow to Jim Crow,* 66–67.

106. Howard D. Samuel, "Troubled Passage: The Labor Movement and the Fair Labor Standards Act," *Monthly Labor Review* 123 (December 2000): 36.

107. Workers of the Writers' Program, *The Negro in Virginia,* 342.

108. Jackson, "A New Deal for Tobacco Workers," 323.

109. Workers of the Writers' Program, *The Negro in Virginia,* 341.

110. Ibid., 342.

111. Love, "In Defiance of Custom and Tradition," 38.

112. James E. Jackson Jr., interviews with author, December 12, September 25, 2002, Brooklyn, NY.

113. James E. Jackson Jr., interview with author, September 25, 2002, Brooklyn, NY.

114. Barbara Melosh, "Manly Work: Public Art and Masculinity in Depression America," in *Gender and American History since 1890,* ed. Barbara Melosh (New York: Routledge, 1993), 155–81, 178, 159.

115. James E. Jackson Jr., interview with author, September 25, 2002, Brooklyn, NY.

116. Korstad, *Civil Rights Unionism;* Michael Denning, *The Cultural Front* (London: Verso, 1997), 352.

117. Gellman, *Death Blow to Jim Crow,* 82–83.

118. Invitation to Second All-Southern Negro Youth Conference, 1938, SNYC Papers, Conferences.

119. See Laura McEnaney, "He-Men and Christian Mothers: The America First Movement and the Gendered Meanings of Patriotism and Isolationism,"

Diplomatic History 18 (Winter 1994): 47–57; Leonard Dinnerstein, *Antisemitism in America* (New York: Oxford University Press, 1994); and David M. Kennedy, *Freedom from Fear: The American People in Depression and War, 1929–1945* (New York: Oxford University Press, 2001).

120. C. L. R. James, George Breitman, Edgar Keemer, et al., *Fighting Racism in World War II: A Week-by-Week Account of the Struggle against Racism and Discrimination in the United States during 1939–1945*, ed. Fred Stanton (New York: Monad, 1980), 28–39, 31 (C. L. R. James, "Why Negroes Should Oppose the War").

121. Kennedy, *Freedom from Fear*; Von Eschen, *Race against Empire*; Plummer, *Rising Wind*; James H. Meriwether, *Proudly We Can Be Africans: Black Americans and Africa, 1935–1961* (Chapel Hill: University of North Carolina Press, 2002).

122. Kennedy, *Freedom from Fear*; James Yates, *Mississippi to Madrid: Memoir of a Black American in the Abraham Lincoln Brigade* (Greensboro, NC: Open Hand, 1989).

123. Kennedy, *Freedom from Fear*, 418–25.

124. Souvenir Journal for the Second All-Southern Negro Youth Conference, 1938, SNYC Papers, Conferences.

125. Walter A. Jackson, *Gunnar Myrdal and America's Conscience: Social Engineering and Racial Liberalism, 1938–1987* (Chapel Hill: University of North Carolina Press, 1990), 127. See also Gunnar Myrdal, *An American Dilemma: The Negro Problem and Modern Democracy* (New York: Pantheon, 1944).

126. "Mrs. Esther I. Cooper Dies, Dynamic in NAACP, Church," *Washington (DC) Afro-American*, February 17, 1970, Esther Irving Cooper Papers, Moorland-Spingarn Research Center.

127. Ibid.

128. Esther Cooper Jackson, interview with author, September 25, 2002, Brooklyn, NY.

129. Quoted in McDuffie, "Long Journeys," 289.

130. Temma Kaplan, *Taking Back the Streets: Women, Youth, and Direct Democracy* (Berkeley and Los Angeles: University of California Press, 2004); Yates, *Mississippi to Madrid*.

131. Esther Cooper Jackson, interviews with author, September 25, 2002, December 12, 2002, Brooklyn, NY.

132. McDuffie, "Long Journeys," 294.

133. Esther Cooper, "The Negro Woman Domestic Worker in Relation to Trade Unionism" (M.A. thesis, Fisk University, 1940), Jackson Papers, box 8, folder 31; McDuffie, "Long Journeys," 296–97.

134. Cooper, "The Negro Woman Domestic Worker."

135. Katznelson, *When Affirmative Action Was White*, 44.

136. James E. Jackson to Esther Cooper, n.d., Jackson Papers, box 6, folder

27. In this letter, Jack offers Esther a narrative of their relationship and quotes a letter of his to Ed Strong.

137. Cooper Jackson, *This Is My Husband;* Esther Cooper Jackson, interview with author, September 25, 2002, Brooklyn, NY.

138. Gellman, *Death Blow to Jim Crow,* 187.

139. Kelley, *Hammer and Hoe,* 205.

140. Esther and James Jackson: Memories of the Southern Negro Youth Congress, Esther Cooper Jackson and James E. Jackson Jr., interview with James Vernon Hatch, 1992, Brooklyn, NY.

141. Cooper Jackson, *This Is My Husband,* 26.

142. Kelley, *Hammer and Hoe,* 206. See also Esther Cooper Jackson, interview with author, September 25, 2002, Brooklyn, NY.

143. Esther Cooper Jackson, interview with author, December 12, 2002, Brooklyn, NY.

144. Esther Cooper Jackson, interview with author, September 25, 2002, Brooklyn, NY. See also Gerard Bekerman, *Marx and Engels: A Conceptual Concordance* (Totowa, NJ: Barnes & Noble, 1981), 190–91; and Weigand, *Red Feminism.*

145. Esther Cooper Jackson, interview with author, September 25, 2002, Brooklyn, NY. See also Friedrich Engels, *The Origin of the Family, Private Property, and the State, in Light of the Researches of Lewis H. Morgan* (New York: International, 1942).

146. For a discussion of couples who opted out of marriage, see Peggy Dennis, *The Autobiography of an American Communist: A Personal View of Political Life, 1925–1975* (Westport, CT: Lawrence Hill, 1977).

147. Coontz, *Marriage, a History,* 218–19.

148. Esther Cooper Jackson, interview with author, March 15, 2006; McDuffie, "Long Journeys," 313; Lewis, *W. E. B. Du Bois: The Fight for Equality.*

149. Esther Cooper Jackson, interview with author, September 25, 2002, Brooklyn, NY.

2. Radical Marriage on the Front Lines of the Double Victory Campaign

1. James Jackson to Esther Cooper, June 16, 1945, Jackson Papers, box 6, folder 41.

2. Esther Cooper to James Jackson, June 28, 1945, Jackson Papers, box 6, folder 24.

3. Cott, *Public Vows,* 182.

4. For discussions of the CPUSA in the World War II years, see Fried, ed., *Communism in America;* Klehr, Haynes, and Firsov, *The Secret World of American Communism;* Schrecker, *Many Are the Crimes;* and Isserman, *Which Side Were You On?*

5. Kennedy, *Freedom from Fear*, 468–69.

6. "Detour the Roosevelt Road to War!" *S.N.Y.C. News*, January 1941, SNYC Papers, Publications.

7. Ibid.

8. James E. Jackson Jr. to Sherman Williams, September 17, 1942, SNYC Papers, Correspondence.

9. "The Young Negro Woman Works for Peace," *S.N.Y.C. News*, November 1940, SNYC Papers, Publications.

10. Report of 1942 Conference in Tuskegee, 1942, SNYC Papers, Conferences.

11. "Address of Louis E. Burnham, Organizational Secretary, Southern Negro Youth Congress, Delivered on the 'Wings over Jordan' Radio Program," March 7, 1943, SNYC Papers, Publications. For a discussion of race and radio in World War II, see Barbara Dianne Savage, *Broadcasting Freedom: Radio, War, and the Politics of Race, 1938–1948* (Chapel Hill: University of North Carolina Press, 1999).

12. "We Recommend," *Monthly Bulletin* (SNYC, Birmingham, AL) 8, no. 4 (July 1944), SNYC Papers, Publications.

13. *The Negro Soldier*, produced by the US War Department/Special Service Division, Army Service Forces, directed by Frank Capra, 49 minutes (1944; Los Angeles: Spotlite Video, 1985), videocassette.

14. Herbert Garfinkel, *When Negroes March: The March on Washington Movement in the Organizational Politics for FEPC* (Glencoe, IL: Free Press, 1959), 7; David Lucander, *Winning the War for Democracy: The March on Washington Movement, 1941–1946* (Urbana: University of Illinois Press, 2014).

15. President's Committee on Fair Employment Practice, Negro Employment and Training Branch, Labor Division, War Production Board (WPB), and Minority Groups Branch, Labor Division, WPB, *Minorities in Defense* (Washington, DC: Social Security Building, 1942), 16–17.

16. John Morton Blum, *V Was for Victory: Politics and American Culture during World War II* (New York: Harcourt Brace Jovanovich, 1976), 196–97. For more on the FEPC, see Merl Elwyn Reed, *Seedtime for the Modern Civil Rights Movement: The President's Committee on Fair Employment Practice, 1941–1946* (Baton Rouge: Louisiana State University Press, 1991); and Andrew Kersten, *Race, Jobs, and the War: The FEPC in the Midwest, 1941–1946* (Urbana: University of Illinois Press, 2007).

17. Blum, *V Was for Victory*, 196.

18. Summary of Activities Conducted January 1–November 30, 1943, n.d., SNYC Papers, Administrative Files.

19. Ibid.

20. Richards, "The Southern Negro Youth Congress," 93–94.

21. Esther Cooper Jackson, interview with author, September 25, 2002,

Brooklyn, NY. For more on African American voting rights, see Steven F. Lawson, *Black Ballots: Voting Rights in the South, 1944–1969* (New York: Columbia University Press, 1976); and Ronald Walters, *Freedom Is Not Enough: Black Voters, Black Candidates, and American Presidential Politics* (Lanham, MD: Rowman & Littlefield, 2007).

22. Report of 1942 Conference in Tuskegee, 1942, SNYC Papers, Conferences.

23. "The Job Is Up to YOU," *Cavalcade: The March of the Southern Negro Youth,* May 1942, SNYC Papers, Publications.

24. Ibid.

25. Esther Cooper Jackson, interview with author, September 25, 2002, Brooklyn, NY.

26. Martin Duberman, *Paul Robeson: A Biography* (New York: New Press, 1988), 216 (quote), 254.

27. "Sings, Talks, Acts, Works, Lives in the Fight for Freedom," Invitation to Fifth SNYC Conference, 1942, SNYC Papers, Conferences.

28. *Cavalcade,* October 1941, SNYC Papers, Publications.

29. James Smethurst, *The Black Arts Movement: Literary Nationalism in the 1960s and 1970s* (Chapel Hill: University of North Carolina Press, 2005), 322; Lewis, Nash, and Leab, eds., *Red Activists and Black Freedom,* xv.

30. Esther Cooper and James Jackson World War II Correspondence, Jackson Papers, box 6; Esther Cooper Jackson and James Jackson, interviews with author, 2002–2006; Erik S. McDuffie, "Long Journeys"; Sarah Hart Brown, "Esther Cooper Jackson: A Life in the Whirlwind," in *"Lives Full of Struggle and Triumph": Southern Women, Their Institutions, and Their Communities,* ed. Bruce L. Clayton and John A. Salmond (Gainesville: University Press of Florida, 2003), 203–24; Kelley, *Hammer and Hoe.*

31. James Jackson to Esther Cooper, September 5, 1945, Jackson Papers, box 6, folder 44; James Jackson to Esther Cooper, April 25, 1945, Jackson Papers, box 6, folder 39; Esther Cooper to James Jackson, July 12, 1945, Jackson Papers, box 6, folder 25.

32. Esther Cooper to James Jackson, July 2, 1945, Jackson Papers, box 6, folder 25.

33. James Jackson to Esther Cooper, May 4, 1945, Jackson Papers, box 6, folder 40.

34. James Jackson to Esther Cooper, April 26, 1945, Jackson Papers, box 6, folder 39.

35. Historians such as Herbert Garfinkel, Richard M. Dalfiume, and Neil A. Wynn, writing in the 1950s, 1960s, and 1970s, had an interest in resurrecting black involvement in the seemingly forgotten war years from what appeared to be a historical abyss. Driven by the recent civil rights activism in the United States, they each sought an earlier manifestation of black revolt to explain that black

Americans had a long tradition of dissent and protest. The types of activism that they wrote about, then, naturally looked very similar to the sorts of activism that emerged in the 1950s and 1960s. Recently, historians have also taken interest in more radical forms of black activism. Ronald Takaki addresses race riots, David Levering Lewis has explored W. E. B. Du Bois's radical politics and thought in the war years, Patricia Sullivan and others have looked at the Popular Front and the Progressive Party, and Robin D. G. Kelley and George Lipsitz have examined patterns of everyday resistance. See Garfinkel, *When Negroes March;* Richard M. Dalfiume, "The Forgotten Years of the Negro Revolution," *Journal of American History* 55, no. 1 (June 1968): 90–106; Neil A. Wynn, *The Afro-American and the Second World War* (1975; New York: Holmes & Meier, 1993); Ronald Takaki, *Double Victory: A Multicultural History of America in World War II* (Boston: Little, Brown, 2000); Lewis, *W. E. B. Du Bois: The Fight for Equality;* Sullivan, *Days of Hope;* Robin D. G. Kelley, *Race Rebels: Culture, Politics, and the Black Working Class* (New York: Free Press, 1994); George Lipsitz, "Frantic to Join . . . the Japanese Army: Black Soldiers and Civilians Confront the Asia Pacific War," in *Perilous Memories: The Asia-Pacific War(s),* ed. T. Fujitani, Geoffrey M. White, and Lisa Yoneyama (Durham, NC: Duke University Press, 2001), 347–77; and Hall, "The Long Civil Rights Movement and the Political Uses of the Past."

36. Charles F. Romanus and Riley Sunderland, *United States Army in World War II, China-Burma-India Theater: Time Runs Out in CBI* (Washington, DC: Office of the Chief of Military History, Department of the Army, 1959), 291.

37. Ulysses Lee, *United States Army in World War II, Special Studies: The Employment of Negro Troops* (Washington, DC: Office of the Chief of Military History, United States Army, 1966), 457.

38. Esther Cooper Jackson, interview with author, April 6, 2006, Brooklyn, NY.

39. Romanus and Sunderland, *United States Army in World War II,* 294. *Uncle Sugar* became a replacement for both *United States* and *Uncle Sam.* In the 1944–1945 phonetic alphabet, the word *sugar* was used for the letter *s.*

40. Esther Cooper Jackson, interview with author, April 6, 2006, Brooklyn, NY.

41. James Jackson to Esther Cooper, February 5, 1945, Jackson Papers, box 6, folder 37.

42. James Jackson to Esther Cooper, October 2, 1945, Jackson Papers, box 6, folder 45.

43. Interviews with the Jacksons, 2002–present, SNYC Papers.

44. Esther Cooper to James Jackson, June 21, 1945, Jackson Papers, box 6, folder 24.

45. James Jackson to Esther Cooper, June 10, 1945, Jackson Papers, box 6, folder 41. According to Charles F. Romanus and Riley Sunderland, recreational facilities represented a main source of tension between black and white soldiers in

the CBI Theater. Early in the war, one base commander placed a recreation facility for black troops in an area of Calcutta deemed "out of bounds." In addition, black troops from the Stillwell Road area, the Ledo Road area, and other areas all crowded into the one small recreation center in Calcutta. This center was located near a brothel, which meant that "the venereal disease rate reached alarming proportions." By 1944, the situation was under investigation, and, by 1945, the base camp was moved to a better location. See Romanus and Sunderland, *United States Army in World War II*, 297–98.

46. James Jackson to Esther Cooper, n.d., Jackson Papers, box 6, folder 27. While this letter is undated, it was probably written around April 1944, when Jack was stationed in Tuskegee. This suggested dating is based on a nearby letter in the file; both letters mention plans for the SNYC's 1944 Atlanta conference.

47. James Jackson to Esther Cooper, April 15, 1944, Jackson Papers, box 6, folder 31.

48. Colonel Campbell C. Johnson, Address Delivered at the 6th Annual Conference of the Southern Negro Youth Congress, Atlanta, GA, December 2, 1944, SNYC Papers, Conferences.

49. Esther Cooper Jackson, interview with author, December 19, 2005, Brooklyn, NY.

50. Esther Cooper to James Jackson, July 11, 1945, Jackson Papers, box 6, folder 25.

51. Esther Cooper to James Jackson, July 12, 1945, Jackson Papers, box 6, folder 25. Recy Taylor was a black woman from Abbeville, Alabama, who was gang raped by a group of white men. The SNYC worked to attain justice on her behalf. See Danielle L. McGuire, *At the Dark End of the Street: Black Women, Rape, and Resistance—a New History of the Civil Rights Movement from Rosa Parks to the Rise of Black Power* (New York: Vintage, 2011).

52. James Jackson to Esther Cooper, July 22, 1945, Jackson Papers, box 6, folder 42.

53. Esther Cooper to James Jackson, July 22, 1945, Jackson Papers, box 6, folder 25.

54. James Jackson to Esther Cooper, August 13, 1945, Jackson Papers, box 6, folder 43.

55. Esther Cooper to James Jackson, July 21, 1945, Jackson Papers, box 6, folder 25.

56. James Jackson to Esther Cooper, n.d., Jackson Papers, box 6, folder 27.

57. Ibid.

58. Irene West, "Females Halfway to Hell," *Baltimore Afro-American*, June 23, 1945, and James Jackson to Editor, *Baltimore Afro-American*, July 6, 1945, both Jackson Papers, box 3, folder 21.

59. James Jackson to Editor, *Baltimore Afro-American*, July 6, 1945, box 3, folder 21.

60. Gwendolyn Midlo Hall, ed., *Love, War, and the 96th Engineers (Colored): The World War II New Guinea Diaries of Captain Hyman Samuelson* (Urbana: University of Illinois Press, 1995), xi. For a discussion of censorship during World War II, see George Roeder, *The Censored War: American Visual Experience during World War Two* (New Haven, CT: Yale University Press, 1993).

61. James Jackson to Esther Cooper, August 18, 1945, Jackson Papers, box 6, folder 43.

62. Esther Cooper to James Jackson, July 18, 1945, Jackson Papers, box 6, folder 25.

63. James Jackson to Esther Cooper, n.d., Jackson Papers, box 6, folder 27.

64. Nikhil Pal Singh, *Black Is a Country: Race and the Unfinished Struggle for Democracy* (Cambridge, MA: Harvard University Press, 2004), 118.

65. C. L. R. James and Walter White both emphasized the importance of colonial struggles to the fight against racism in the United States. When they offered their interpretations of the implications of World War II for black Americans, they drew from the immediacy of the situation. Their concerns were driven by a desire to produce and inspire immediate change. In recent years, historians concerned with black struggles during World War II have developed a much fuller understanding of the nuances and particularities of black radicalism and internationalism. Brenda Gayle Plummer, Barbara Dianne Savage, Penny M. Von Eschen, and Nikhil Pal Singh have offered new interpretations of black political struggle in the war years that draw both on White's and James's connections between domestic and international struggle and the more clear-cut civil rights organizing that Garfinkel, Dalfiume, and Wynn covered. See James et al., *Fighting Racism in World War II* (James, "Why Negroes Should Oppose the War"); Walter White, *A Rising Wind* (Garden City, NY: Doubleday, Doran, 1945); Plummer, *Rising Wind;* Savage, *Broadcasting Freedom;* Singh, *Black Is a Country;* and Von Eschen, *Race against Empire.*

66. James Jackson to Esther Cooper, September 7, 1944, Jackson Papers, box 6, folder 34.

67. Blum, *V Was for Victory,* 58–59.

68. Gary Gerstle, *American Crucible: Race and Nation in the Twentieth Century* (Princeton, NJ: Princeton University Press, 2001), 232.

69. Peery, *Black Fire,* 240–41.

70. James Jackson to Esther Cooper, January 15, 1945, Jackson Papers, box 6, folder 36. Jackson's observations contradict statements in the official military history of the CBI Theater. Romanus and Sunderland suggest that there were more issues between black soldiers and locals than between whites and locals. Their contention is problematic, however, because they did not engage in a substantial study of black soldiers' experiences in the CBI Theater. Despite their observation that over 60 percent of the engineering battalions were black, they address black soldiers in only four pages of their four-hundred-page book. Their

other claims, too, are rife with stereotypes about black soldiers: e.g., that they were poorly trained and had high morale but low efficiency. See Romanus and Sunderland, *The United States Army in World War II*, 297.

71. Cooper Jackson, *This Is My Husband*, 28.

72. Esther Cooper Jackson, interview with author, March 15, 2006, Brooklyn, NY.

73. Esther Cooper to James Jackson, July 13, 1945, Jackson Papers, box 6, folder 25.

74. Esther Cooper to Louis Burnham, series of correspondence, October 30–November 27, 1945, SNYC Papers, Correspondence.

75. Quoted by Jack in James Jackson to Esther Cooper, June 3, 1945, Jackson Papers, box 6, folder 41.

76. Ibid.

77. James Jackson to Esther Cooper, June 15, 1945, Jackson Papers, box 6, folder 41.

78. Esther Cooper to James Jackson, June 17, 1945, Jackson Papers, box 6, folder 24.

79. Esther Cooper to Louis Burnham, October 30, 1945, SNYC Papers, Correspondence.

80. Esther Cooper Jackson, interview with author, March 15, 2006, Brooklyn, NY. See also McDuffie, "Long Journeys," 392.

81. Esther Cooper Jackson, interview with author, March 15, 2006, Brooklyn, NY.

82. Gellman, *Death Blow to Jim Crow*, 185–91.

83. James Jackson to Esther Cooper, June 17, 1945, Jackson Papers, box 6, folder 41.

84. Esther Cooper to James Jackson, June 28, 1945, Jackson Papers, box 6, folder 24. Though both partners agreed on plans for the Rosenwald Fellowship, they never got around to applying. Applications were due on January 1, 1946, when both partners were overseas. Once they were resettled in the United States, Cooper and Jackson were immediately swept into organizing for the SNYC.

85. James Jackson to Esther Cooper, January 24, 1945, Jackson Papers, box 6, folder 36.

3. The Demise of the Black Popular Front in the Postwar Period

1. Esther Cooper Jackson, interview with author, March 15, 2006, Brooklyn, NY. See also McDuffie, "Long Journeys," 392.

2. James E. Jackson Jr., "Every Tenth American," quoted in Cooper Jackson, *This Is My Husband*, 29. In his 1941 State of the Union address, FDR outlined what he called the "four essential human freedoms": freedom of speech and expression, freedom of worship, freedom from want, and freedom from fear.

He promoted these Four Freedoms as universal values, and they became foundational to World War II rhetoric.

3. Steven F. Lawson, *Running for Freedom: Civil Rights and Black Politics in America since 1941* (Boston: McGraw-Hill, 1997); Douglas Massey and Nancy Denton, *American Apartheid: Segregation and the Making of the Underclass* (Cambridge, MA: Harvard University Press, 1998); Jennifer E. Brooks, *Defining the Peace: World War II Veterans, Race, and the Remaking of Southern Political Tradition* (Chapel Hill: University of North Carolina Press, 2004); Gail O'Brien, *The Color of Law: Race, Violence, and Justice in the Post–World War II South* (Chapel Hill: University of North Carolina Press, 1999); Steven F. Lawson, ed., *To Secure These Rights: The Report of President Harry S. Truman's Committee on Civil Rights* (Boston: Bedford St. Martin's, 2004). In 1948, after a landmark study called "To Secure These Rights," President Harry Truman issued Executive Order 9808, desegregated the armed forces, and established the President's Committee on Civil Rights. In *Smith v. Allwright* (1944), the Supreme Court determined that white primaries violated the Fourteenth Amendment. In *Shelley v. Kramer* (1948), it ruled that, under the Fourteenth Amendment, racially restrictive covenants were unenforceable.

4. Press Release, July 31, 1946, SNYC Papers, Press Releases.

5. "American Youth at the United Nations of Youth, World Youth Conference—1945: Youth Unite! Forward for Lasting Peace, Report of United States Delegation, World Youth Conference, London, November 1945," November 1945, SNYC Papers, Other Organizations.

6. Esther Cooper to Louis Burnham, November 13, 1945, SNYC Papers, Correspondence.

7. "American Youth at the United Nations of Youth, World Youth Conference—1945: Youth Unite! Forward for Lasting Peace, Report of United States Delegation, World Youth Conference, London, November 1945," November 1945, 12, SNYC Papers, Other Organizations.

8. Esther Cooper Jackson, interview with author, October 12, 2004, Brooklyn, NY.

9. Though officially documented lynching incidents were declining, the number of African Americans murdered by whites was still quite high. In 1951, William Patterson, the director of the Civil Rights Congress, issued a 225-page petition to the UN Secretariat in Paris titled "We Charge Genocide." The petition argued that African Americans were the victims of genocide because "systematized deprivation and insult and brutalization of a given population" fell under the UN definition of the term. Patterson detailed the incidences of murder and lynching in the United States and quoted a Southerner who argued that lynching was often overlooked because victims' "disappearance is shrouded in mystery, for they are dispatched quietly and without general knowledge." Patterson's report was ignored in the United States. Aptheker, ed., *A Documentary*

History of the Negro People in the United States, 5:30–52 (William Patterson, "We Charge Genocide").

10. Laura Wexler, *Fire in a Canebrake: The Last Mass Lynching in America* (New York: Scribner, 2003).

11. Ibid.

12. "Paris Confab Hears SNYC Leader Blast U.S. Fascism Accuses Byrnes of Harboring KKK-Fascism at Home and Preaching Democracy Abroad," press release, August 5, 1946, SNYC Papers, Publications. Burnham's reference to the Dorsey-Malcolm lynching suggests that, at this point, the details of the case were not clear. Despite the fact that the direct cause of the lynching was Roger Malcolm's altercation with his landlord, not an attempt to vote, the violence in the context of increased rights for African Americans in Georgia rendered the two inextricably connected.

13. Ibid.

14. Frances Damon to Louis Burnham, August 21, 1946, SNYC Papers, Other Organizations.

15. Dorothy Burnham, interview with author, November 1, 2004, Brooklyn, NY.

16. Von Eschen, *Race against Empire,* and *Satchmo Blows Up the World;* Dudziak, *Cold War Civil Rights;* Borstelmann, *The Cold War and the Color Line;* Plummer, *Rising Wind.*

17. Kelley, *Hammer and Hoe,* 206.

18. Florence Valentine, "Remarks on Jobs and Job Training for Negro Women," address delivered at the panel "Youth and Labor," Southern Youth Legislature, October 19, 1946, SNYC Papers, Conferences.

19. Aptheker, ed., *A Documentary History of the Negro People in the United States,* 5:483–84 (Vicki Garvin, "Negro Women Workers: Union Leader Challenges").

20. Kelley, *Hammer and Hoe,* 206.

21. Jack O'Dell, telephone interview with author, March 12, 2003.

22. SNYC Papers, Administrative Files. It is unlikely that the SNYC was able to hire any enthusiastic *Seventeen* readers, as its financial difficulties were mounting as anticommunism increased.

23. "The Southern Negro Youth Congress Presents Esther Cooper Jackson and James E. Jackson, Jr. in a Vital, Provocative Series of Lectures," March 17, 1946, SNYC Papers, Activities and Events.

24. Esther Cooper to Louis Burnham, November 13, 1945, SNYC Papers, Correspondence.

25. "The Southern Negro Youth Congress Presents Miss Esther V. Cooper in a Lecture on World Youth! and the Struggle for a Lasting Peace," ca. January 1946, SNYC Papers, Activities and Events.

26. "The Southern Negro Youth Congress Presents Esther Cooper Jackson

and James E. Jackson, Jr. in a Vital, Provocative Series of Lectures," March 17, 1946, SNYC Papers, Activities and Events.

27. Esther Cooper Jackson, interview with author, October 12, 2004, Brooklyn, NY.

28. Esther Cooper Jackson, interview with author, March 15, 2006, Brooklyn, NY.

29. Esther Cooper to James Jackson, July 2, 1945, Jackson Papers, box 6, folder 25.

30. Esther Cooper Jackson, interview with author, March 15, 2006, Brooklyn, NY.

31. Peter F. Lau, *Democracy Rising: South Carolina and the Fight for Black Equality since 1865* (Lexington: University Press of Kentucky, 2006), 146.

32. Winston Churchill, *Never Give In: The Best of Winston Churchill's Speeches* (New York: Hyperion, 2003).

33. Schrecker, *Many Are the Crimes*, 287.

34. Dudziak, *Cold War Civil Rights*, 19.

35. Plummer, *Rising Wind*, 35.

36. Lau, *Democracy Rising*, 184.

37. Ibid., 190.

38. Ibid., 182–90.

39. Meriwether, *Proudly We Can Be Africans*, 69.

40. Carol Anderson, *Eyes Off the Prize: The United Nations and the African American Struggle for Human Rights, 1944–1955* (Cambridge: Cambridge University Press, 2003), 2 (quote), 273.

41. Plummer, *Rising Wind*, 149.

42. Dudziak, *Cold War Civil Rights*, 45.

43. Hakim Adi, *West Africans in Britain, 1900–1960: Nationalism, Pan-Africanism, and Communism* (London: Lawrence & Wishart, 1998), 120.

44. Marika Sherwood, "There Is No New Deal for the Blackman in San Francisco," *International Journal of African Historical Studies* 29, no. 1 (1996): 71–94, 92.

45. "Call to the Southern Youth Legislature," 1946, SNYC Papers, Conferences.

46. Jack O'Dell, telephone interview with author, March 12, 2003.

47. "Call to the Southern Youth Legislature," 1946, SNYC Papers, Conferences.

48. Singh, *Black Is a Country*, 18–19.

49. Lewis, *W. E. B. Du Bois: The Fight for Equality*, 518–19, 523–24.

50. W. E. B. Du Bois, "Behold the Land," October 20, 1946, SNYC Papers, Conferences.

51. Singh, *Black Is a Country*, 214.

52. W. E. B. Du Bois, "Behold the Land," October 20, 1946, SNYC Papers, Conferences.

53. Dorothy Burnham, "International Youth Night at South Carolina U.S.A.: Negro Youth at the Southern Youth Legislature Celebrate World Youth Unity," October 19, 1946, SNYC Papers, Other Organizations.

54. Ibid.

55. Kelley, *Hammer and Hoe,* 207.

56. Dorothy Burnham, interview with author, January 23, 2003.

57. Dorothy Burnham, "International Youth Night at South Carolina U.S.A.: Negro Youth at the Southern Youth Legislature Celebrate World Youth Unity," October 19, 1946, SNYC Papers, Other Organizations.

58. Speech of A. Romeo Horton, October 19, 1946, and Speech of Theodore Baker, October 19, 1946, SNYC Papers, Conferences.

59. Schrecker, *Many Are the Crimes,* 131, 145.

60. Richard M. Fried, *Nightmare in Red: The McCarthy Era in Perspective* (New York: Oxford University Press, 1990).

61. Esther Cooper FBI Files, BH 100-1038, 6, in the possession of Esther Cooper Jackson, Brooklyn, NY.

62. "Add to Most Wanted: James E. Jackson, Well-Educated Red," unidentified newspaper clipping, July 18, 1951, Jackson Papers, box 2, folder 16.

63. "Red Leader in Jail, Fears to Be Freed," unidentified newspaper clipping, n.d., Jackson Papers, box 2, folder 16.

64. Esther Cooper FBI Files, NY 100-18618, 31.

65. Korstad, *Civil Rights Unionism,* 416.

66. "SNYC Statement on Atty. General's 'Subversive' List," *Young South Newsletter,* February 1948, SNYC Papers, Publications.

67. Diane McWhorter, *Carry Me Home: Birmingham, Alabama: The Climactic Struggle of the Civil Rights Revolution* (New York: Simon & Schuster, 2002); McDuffie, "Long Journeys"; Richards, "The Southern Negro Youth Congress"; Sullivan, *Days of Hope;* Gilmore, *Defying Dixie;* Kelley, *Hammer and Hoe.*

68. Louis E. Burnham, "A Birmingham Story," n.d., SNYC Papers, box 8, folder 5.

69. Foner, *Reconstruction,* 200–205. Connor had a reputation for conflict with other leftist organizations in the 1930s and had once attempted to shut down a Southern Conference for Human Welfare meeting in 1939. See Linda Reed, *Simple Decency and Common Sense: The Southern Conference Movement, 1938–1963* (Bloomington: Indiana University Press, 1994), 16.

70. Richards, "The Southern Negro Youth Congress."

71. Untitled story (first line: "Could this be America? Does freedom ring in Alabama too?"), n.d., SNYC Papers, box 8, folder 5.

72. Esther and James Jackson: Memories of the Southern Negro Youth Congress, Esther Cooper Jackson and James E. Jackson Jr., interview with James Vernon Hatch, 1992, Brooklyn, NY.

73. Sullivan, *Days of Hope,* 247. See also Gilmore, *Defying Dixie.*

74. Kelley, *Hammer and Hoe;* Sullivan, *Days of Hope.*

75. Richards, "The Southern Negro Youth Congress," 193.

76. Untitled story (first line: "Could this be America? Does freedom ring in Alabama too?"), n.d., SNYC Papers, box 8, folder 5.

77. "Judge Rules Senator Guilty for Attempt to Enter Front Door at SNYC Meet," press release, May 6, 1948, SNYC Papers, box 8, folder 34; "Taylor, under Bail in Alabama in Racial Case, Will Make Test," *New York Times,* May 3, 1948.

78. "Taylor, under Bail in Alabama in Racial Case, Will Make Test," *New York Times,* May 3, 1948, 1.

79. "Judge Rules Senator Guilty for Attempt to Enter Front Door at SNYC Meet," press release, May 6, 1948, SNYC Papers, box 8, folder 34.

80. Louis E. Burnham, "A Birmingham Story," n.d., SNYC Papers, box 8, folder 5.

81. Kelley, *Hammer and Hoe,* 226.

82. Dudziak, *Cold War Civil Rights;* Korstad, *Civil Rights Unionism;* Korstad and Lichtenstein, "Opportunities Found and Lost"; Kelley, *Hammer and Hoe;* Sullivan, *Days of Hope;* Anderson, *Eyes Off the Prize.*

83. Lau, *Democracy Rising,* 12.

84. Ibid., 191.

85. Louis E. Burnham, "A Birmingham Story," n.d., SNYC Papers, box 8, folder 5.

86. Schrecker, *Many Are the Crimes,* 91, 212.

87. Stein, "Why American Historians Embrace the 'Long Civil Rights Movement.'"

88. Gellman, *Death Blow to Jim Crow,* 259.

89. James E. Jackson, "Struggle against White Chauvinism," *Bulletin of the Michigan State Committee,* June 7, 1949, Jackson Papers, box 16, folder 24.

90. Isserman, *Which Side Were You On?,* 190 (Browder quote), 241.

91. Ibid., 246, 247.

92. Michigan Communist Party, "Truman Wants War but Not against KKK," ca. March–April 1948, Jackson Papers, box 2, folder 32.

93. Ibid.

94. James Jackson, "Statement on Behalf of Michigan CPUSA," July 11, 1949, Jackson Papers, box 2, folder 32.

95. Ibid. The reference is to Judge Harry Medina, whose behavior in the trial was biased and influenced by anti-Communist sentiment.

96. Esther Cooper FBI Files, DE 100-16825, 3–4. The names of the informant and his or her collaborator, along with the individual who suggested the setup, are obscured in the files.

97. McDuffie, "Long Journeys."

98. Esther Cooper FBI Files, NY 100-18618, 22.

99. Anderson, *Eyes Off the Prize,* 119 (quote), 121.
100. Esther Cooper FBI Files, DE 100-16825, 3.
101. Gerald Horne, *Communist Front? The Civil Rights Congress, 1946–1956* (Rutherford, NJ: Fairleigh Dickinson University Press, 1988), 29–30.
102. Hutchinson, *Blacks and Reds,* 198–200, 201.
103. Horne, *Communist Front?*
104. McDuffie, "Long Journeys"; Esther Cooper FBI Files, DE 100-16825, 10.
105. Rosa Lee Ingram was a black Georgia woman who, along with her two teenaged sons, was sentenced to execution on January 26, 1948, for the death of her white neighbor, John Stratford. Stratford, angry because Ingram's mules and pigs had wandered to his farm, brutally beat Ingram when she came to drive her animals back. Three of Ingram's sons witnessed the beating, and the oldest intervened, grabbing Stratford's gun and striking him on the head with it in a fatal blow. Ingram and her sons were tried by an all-white jury, and, after outrage among African Americans across the nation, the death sentences were converted to life in prison.

On January 27, 1948, in Trenton, New Jersey, a white husband and wife were attacked in their store. William Horner, the husband, died. His wife described the three assailants as "white or light-skinned Blacks." Police subsequently picked up six black men, only one of whom, James Thorpe, was light skinned. Thorpe had one arm and would have been easily identified by that characteristic. The trial of the six men lasted fifty-five days, and all were sentenced to die. Most of the men were eventually released after new trials and international outrage, but not before police officers brutalized Trenton's black neighborhoods.

In each of these cases, the CRC played a role in the defense. On Ingram, see Aptheker, ed., *A Documentary History of the Negro People in the United States,* 5:400–406. On the Trenton Six, see Horne, *Communist Front?,* 131–54.
106. Esther Cooper FBI Files, DE 100-16825, 10.

4. Family and the Black Freedom Movement in the Early Cold War Years

1. Albert E. Kahn, *The Game of Death: Effects of the Cold War on Our Children* (New York: Cameron & Kahn, 1953), 159.
2. Alfred Kahn, *The Vengeance on the Young: The Story of the Smith Act Children* (New York: Hour, June 1952), 9.
3. Ibid., 10.
4. Schrecker, *Many Are the Crimes,* 98.
5. See also *Dennis v. United States,* 341 U.S. 494 (1951).
6. "BIRMINGHAM'S FASCIST ORDINANCE, OUTLAWING THE COMMUNIST PARTY," n.d., Jackson Papers, box 11, folder 17.

7. Ibid. The fact sheet was published anonymously, likely because the organization responsible was attempting to shield itself from persecution in the face of the law it criticized.

8. Kelley, *Hammer and Hoe*, 224–31; Sullivan, *Days of Hope;* Michael K. Honey, *Southern Labor and Black Civil Rights* (Urbana: University of Illinois Press, 1993); Korstad and Lichtenstein, "Opportunities Found and Lost."

9. Reed, *Simple Decency and Common Sense.*

10. Mona Smith, *Becoming Something: The Story of Canada Lee: The Untold Tragedy of the Great Black Actor, Activist, and Athlete* (New York: Faber & Faber, 2004); Schrecker, *Many Are the Crimes;* Gerald Horne, *The Final Victim of the Hollywood Blacklist: John Howard Lawson, Dean of the Hollywood Ten* (Berkeley and Los Angeles: University of California Press, 2006); David Robinson, *Chaplin: His Life and Art* (New York: McGraw-Hill, 1985); Duberman, *Paul Robeson;* Lewis, *W. E. B. Du Bois: The Fight for Equality;* John D'Emilio, *Sexual Politics, Sexual Communities: The Making of a Homosexual Minority in the United States, 1940–1970* (Chicago: University of Chicago Press, 1983); Catherine Fosl, *Subversive Southerner: Anne Braden and the Struggle for Racial Justice in the Cold War South* (New York: Palgrave Macmillan, 2002); Sally Belfrage, *Un-American Activities: A Memoir of the Fifties* (New York: Harper Collins, 1994).

11. J. Edgar Hoover, *Masters of Deceit: The Story of Communism in America and How to Fight It* (New York: Henry Holt, 1958), 82–83.

12. Belfrage, *Un-American Activities,* 115–17. The *Guardian*'s conflict with the CPUSA was long-standing and derived from the paper's refusal to consistently support Party ideology, even though it supported the Party's right to political liberty. Sally Belfrage writes: "The CP's fury peaked in 1949–1950 when the *Guardian* defended Anna Louise Strong, an American radical journalist, after the Russians accused her of spying; and until Stalin's death in 1953 there was party animosity over the paper's siding with Tito against the Soviet Union." Ibid., 116.

13. Washington, *The Other Blacklist,* 11–13.

14. Smith, *Becoming Something,* 350.

15. Friedman, "The Strange Career of Annie Lee Moss," 452. For more on HUAC hearing strategies, see Jeff Woods, *Black Struggle, Red Scare: Segregation and Anti-Communism in the South, 1948–1968* (Baton Rouge: Louisiana State University Press, 2004).

16. Hoover, *Masters of Deceit,* 82.

17. Thomas Patterson, *On Every Front: The Making of the Cold War* (New York: Norton, 1979).

18. Gil Green, *Cold War Fugitive: A Personal Story of the McCarthy Years* (New York: International, 1984), 33 (quotes), 35.

19. Ibid., 35; Deborah A. Gerson, "Is Family Devotion Now Subversive? Familialism against McCarthyism," in Meyerowitz, ed., *Not June Cleaver,* 151–76, 154.

20. Green, *Cold War Fugitive*, 68–69.
21. Ibid., 69 (first two quotes), 59 (third quote).
22. Ibid., 71.
23. Kathryn A. Jackson, "Trauma Survivors: Adult Children of McCarthyism and the Smith Act" (Ph.D. diss., Temple University, 1991).
24. May, *Homeward Bound;* Thomas J. Sugrue, *The Origins of the Urban Crisis: Race and Inequality in Postwar Detroit* (Princeton, NJ: Princeton University Press, 1996); Arnold Hirsch, *Making the Second Ghetto: Race and Housing in Chicago, 1940–1960* (Chicago: University of Chicago Press, 1998); Massey and Denton, *American Apartheid;* Katznelson, *When Affirmative Action Was White;* Stephanie Coontz, *The Way We Never Were: American Families and the Nostalgia Trap* (New York: Basic, 1993), and *Marriage, a History.*
25. May, *Homeward Bound*, 121, 12.
26. Kahn, *The Game of Death*, 154. See also Green, *Cold War Fugitive.*
27. Green, *Cold War Fugitive*, 80.
28. Kahn, *The Game of Death*, 156.
29. Kahn, *Vengeance on the Young*, 11.
30. Gerson, "Is Family Devotion Now Subversive?" 151, 153–54. The Families Committee was an effective avenue for many activists who had built families as they engaged in social justice movements. For some Communists, having children conflicted with activism. William Z. Foster, one of the indicted leaders, had no children of his own with his wife, Esther (who did have two children from a prior relationship), because he "had been influenced by the French syndicalist notion that children inhibited the actions of militants and furnished the capitalist with a 'new supply of slaves.'" Barrett, *William Z. Foster and the Tragedy of American Radicalism*, 62. Devoted Communists often had personal conflicts about how to incorporate children into their activist lives, but many, like Cooper Jackson and the others involved in the Families Committee, prioritized a "normal" life for their children, as much as possible. See ibid.; and Dennis, *Autobiography of an American Communist.*
31. Weigand, *Red Feminism*, 70. More on radical and Communist women can be found in Gore, *Radicalism at the Crossroads;* Jacqueline Castledine, *Cold War Progressives: Women's Interracial Organizing for Peace and Freedom* (Urbana: University of Illinois Press, 2012); and Barbara Ransby, *Eslanda: The Large and Unconventional Life of Mrs. Paul Robeson* (New Haven, CT: Yale University Press, 2014).
32. Feldstein, *Motherhood in Black and White*, 85 (quote), 92–94. Feldstein discusses the way in which Mamie Till Bradley, the mother of fourteen-year-old Mississippi murder victim Emmett Till, represented an ideal of good black motherhood. Bradley, a World War II widow, feared "that [her son's] murder would be used by the Communists for anti-American propaganda." Ibid., 93. Her activism in the wake of her son's murder energized the civil rights struggle and gar-

nered sympathy among liberal whites and northerners. See also May, *Homeward Bound;* and Cuordileone, *Manhood and American Political Culture in the Cold War.*

33. See Goodman, *Stories of Scottsboro;* Plummer, *Rising Wind;* Horne, *Communist Front?;* Hutchinson, *Blacks and Reds;* and Aptheker, ed., *A Documentary History of the Negro People in the United States,* vol. 5.

34. Manfred Berg, "Black Civil Rights and Liberal Anticommunism: The NAACP in the Early Cold War," *Journal of American History* 94 (June 2007), 75–96, 78–79.

35. Ibid. See also Anderson, *Eyes Off the Prize;* and Plummer, *Rising Wind.*

36. Ben Green, *Before His Time: The Untold Story of Harry T. Moore, America's First Civil Rights Martyr* (New York: Free Press, 1999).

37. Ibid., 12, 88 (quote), 96. See also Steven F. Lawson, *Civil Rights Crossroads: Nation, Community, and the Black Freedom Struggle* (Lexington: University Press of Kentucky, 2003), 177–95.

38. Lawson, *Civil Rights Crossroads,* 186–87.

39. Green, *Before His Time,* 12–13.

40. Ibid., 10.

41. Ibid., 174–75.

42. Kahn, *The Game of Death,* 158n.

43. Green, *Before His Time,* 61.

44. Kelley, *Hammer and Hoe.*

45. Green, *Before His Time,* 178.

46. Ibid., 193–97.

47. "To the Editor of the Readers' Column," from Peggy Dennis and Sophie Gerson, n.d., Jackson Papers, box 11, folder 9.

48. Kahn, *The Game of Death,* 157.

49. Esther Cooper Jackson to the Editor, *The Union,* January 31, 1952, Jackson Papers, box 11, folder 3.

50. Kahn, *The Game of Death,* 158.

51. Ibid., 157.

52. Green, *Cold War Fugitive,* 175.

53. See Gerson, "Is Family Devotion Now Subversive?"

54. "To the Editor of the Readers' Column," from Peggy Dennis and Sophie Gerson, n.d., Jackson Papers, box 11, folder 9.

55. Ibid.

56. Kahn, *The Game of Death,* 160.

57. Works that address the decline of the Popular Front include Sullivan, *Days of Hope;* Reed, *Simple Decency and Common Sense;* Kelley, *Hammer and Hoe;* Korstad, *Civil Rights Unionism;* and Gilmore, *Defying Dixie.*

58. Smethurst, *The Black Arts Movement,* 123–24.

59. Washington, *The Other Blacklist,* 6.

60. Ibid.; Arnesen, "Civil Rights and the Cold War at Home"; Gore, "'The Danger of Being an Active Anti-Communist.'"

61. Manning Marable, *Malcolm X: A Life of Reinvention* (New York: Viking, 2011), iBooks edition, chap. 3.

62. Timothy Tyson, *Radio Free Dixie: Robert F. Williams and the Roots of Black Power* (Chapel Hill: University of North Carolina Press, 1999), 69–70.

63. For works that address the changes in the black freedom movement during the Cold War, see Kelley, *Hammer and Hoe;* Duberman, *Paul Robeson;* Lewis, *W. E. B. Du Bois: The Fight for Equality;* Fosl, *Subversive Southerner;* Dudziak, *Cold War Civil Rights;* Von Eschen, *Race against Empire,* and *Satchmo Blows Up the World;* Singh, *Black Is a Country;* Plummer, *Rising Wind;* Anderson, *Eyes Off the Prize;* and Borstelmann, *The Cold War and the Color Line.*

64. Hutchinson, *Blacks and Reds,* 196–97, 200 (quote).

65. The Reverend Edward D. McGowan, Pastor, "In Defense of Negro Leadership," 1953, Edward Strong Papers, box 6, folder 12, Moorland-Spingarn Research Center.

66. Horne, *Black Liberation/Red Scare,* 105.

67. The Reverend Edward D. McGowan, Pastor, "In Defense of Negro Leadership," 1953, Strong Papers, box 6, folder 12.

68. Horne, *Black Liberation/Red Scare,* 105.

69. The Reverend Edward D. McGowan, Pastor, "In Defense of Negro Leadership," 1953, Strong Papers, box 6, folder 12.

70. Cooper Jackson, *This Is My Husband,* 5.

71. Ibid., 7.

72. Ibid., 6, 33 (see generally 7–17).

73. Ibid., 28.

74. Ibid.

75. Ibid., 34–35.

76. Ibid., 35, 32.

77. Ibid., 36.

5. The Communist Party USA and Black Freedom in the 1950s

1. James Jackson's Notes on CPUSA Meeting, ca. fall 1957, Jackson Papers, box 2, folder 22.

2. Ibid.

3. Fried, ed., *Communism in America,* 340, 390–93.

4. Ibid., 397–403.

5. Martha Biondi, *To Stand and Fight: The Struggle for Civil Rights in Postwar New York City* (Cambridge, MA: Harvard University Press, 2003); Schrecker, *Many Are the Crimes.*

6. Lawson, *Civil Rights Crossroads,* 79.

7. Taylor Branch, *Parting the Waters: America in the King Years, 1954–1963* (New York: Simon & Schuster, 1988); David Garrow, *Bearing the Cross: Martin Luther King, Jr. and the Southern Christian Leadership Conference* (New York: Vintage, 1986), and *The FBI and Martin Luther King, Jr.: From "Solo" to Memphis* (New York: Norton, 1981); McWhorter, *Carry Me Home*.

8. Scales and Nickson, *Cause at Heart*, 224.

9. Ethel Devine, interview with author, July 1, 2007, Brooklyn, NY; Esther Cooper Jackson, interview with author, March 15, 2006, Brooklyn, NY.

10. Green, *Cold War Fugitive*, 105.

11. Esther Cooper Jackson, telephone interview with author, January 8, 2015; James and Esther Cooper Jackson, interview with Mary Helen Washington, 2001, Jackson Papers, box 1, folder 23; Green, *Cold War Fugitive*.

12. Hoover, *Master of Deceit*, 76.

13. Green, *Cold War Fugitive*, back cover.

14. Eugene Dennis, *Letters from Prison* (New York: International, 1956), 9.

15. Korstad, *Civil Rights Unionism*, 417. For more on the decline of the Popular Front, see Egerton, *Speak Now against the Day*; Sullivan, *Days of Hope*; Kelley, *Hammer and Hoe*; Biondi, *To Stand and Fight*; Von Eschen, *Race against Empire*, and *Satchmo Blows Up the World*; Dudziak, *Cold War Civil Rights*; Lewis, *W. E. B. Du Bois: The Fight for Equality*; Anderson, *Eyes Off the Prize*; Lau, *Democracy Rising*; and Ellen Schrecker, *Cold War Triumphalism: The Misuse of History After the Fall of Communism* (New York: New Press, 2004).

16. See Lau, *Democracy Rising*.

17. Dennis, *Letters from Prison*, 5.

18. CPUSA Report, p. 41, n.d., Jackson Papers, box 3, folder 14.

19. Esther Cooper Jackson, interview with author, March 15, 2006, Brooklyn, NY. Esther's mother started a fund for Harriet, "just in case" the United States was not a Communist nation by the early 1960s.

20. Scales and Nickson, *Cause at Heart*, 227.

21. Green, *Cold War Fugitive*, 118.

22. Naison, *Communists in Harlem*; Kelley, *Hammer and Hoe*.

23. Branch, *Parting the Waters*; Fried, ed., *Communism in America*; Horne, *Black Liberation/Red Scare*; Isserman, *If I Had a Hammer*.

24. Scales and Nickson, *Cause at Heart*, 249, 225.

25. Green, *Cold War Fugitive*.

26. "Universal Suffrage . . . the Gauge of the Maturity of the Working Class," by Charles P. Mann, August 1952, Strong Papers, box 4, folder 14; James E. Jackson Jr., *Revolutionary Tracings* (New York: International, 1974).

27. For additional information on anti–poll tax movements, see Lawson, *Black Ballots*; Sullivan, *Days of Hope*; and Gilmore, *Defying Dixie*.

28. Jackson, "Universal Suffrage," 1.

29. Ibid., 3.

30. George Lewis, *The White South and the Red Menace: Segregationists, Anti-Communism, and Massive Resistance, 1945–1965* (Gainesville: University Press of Florida, 2004), 49, 92; Woods, *Black Struggle, Red Scare.*

31. Jackson, "Universal Suffrage," 2. On US diplomacy and the start of apartheid in South Africa, see Borstelmann, *The Cold War and the Color Line.*

32. Jackson, "Universal Suffrage," 4.

33. Ibid., 5. Maceo Snipes, a World War II veteran, was the first black person to vote in Taylor County, Georgia, in 1946. A day after he exercised his right to the franchise, he was shot in the back by four white men. He died two days later, and to this day the murder remains unsolved. Elliot Minor, "Answers Sought in 1946 Ga. Killing," *Washington Post,* February 13, 2007.

34. Jackson, "Universal Suffrage," 10.

35. Ibid.

36. Dudziak, *Cold War Civil Rights,* 13–14.

37. Branch, *Parting the Waters;* Douglas Brinkley, *Rosa Parks* (New York: Penguin, 2000).

38. Isserman, *If I Had a Hammer,* 109.

39. Charles P. Mann and Frederick C. Hastings, "For a Mass Policy in Negro Freedom's Cause," *Political Affairs* 34 (March 1955): 7–29, 8, 11, Jackson Papers, box 16, folder 30.

40. See *Brown v. Board of Education of Topeka,* 347 U.S. 483 (1954).

41. Mann and Hasting, "For a Mass Policy," 11.

42. Ibid., 29.

43. Ibid., 11, 17, 20–22.

44. Ibid., 17–18.

45. Charles Payne, *I've Got the Light of Freedom: The Organizing Tradition and the Mississippi Freedom Struggle* (Berkeley and Los Angeles: University of California Press, 1995), 36–37, 39–40. Till's murderers were acquitted and shortly thereafter confessed to the killing in a magazine interview.

46. Mann and Hastings, "For a Mass Policy," 19.

47. Ibid., 21.

48. "Red Aide Missing since '51 Gives Up," *New York Times,* December 3, 1955.

49. "Red Party Hails Yielding of Two," *New York Times,* December 5, 1955, Jackson Papers, box 11, folder 3.

50. Statement Released by James E. Jackson Jr. at the Federal Courthouse Building, New York City, Friday, December 2, 1955, Jackson Papers, box 11, folder 3.

51. "Smith Act Trial of 7 Starts Here Monday," unidentified clipping, April 6, 1956, Jackson Papers, box 11, folder 3.

52. Testimony by James E. Jackson Sr. and W. E. B. Du Bois, June 26, 29, 1956, Jackson Papers, box 11, folder 8.

53. "United States Court of Appeals for the Second Circuit to Be Argued by Morton S. Robson," unidentified clipping, September 17, 1956, Jackson Papers, box 11, folder 1.

54. "Six Second-String Reds Guilty," *Daily News,* August 1, 1956, Jackson Papers, box 11, folder 3.

55. James E. Jackson Jr., Statement Before Sentencing, September 17, 1956, Jackson Papers, box 11, folder 11.

56. Ibid.

57. David Caute, *The Great Fear: The Anticommunist Purge under Truman and Eisenhower* (New York: Simon & Schuster, 1978), 208. See also *Yates v. United States,* 354 U.S. 298 (1957).

58. James Jackson to Kathy Jackson, December 9, 1955, in possession of Esther Cooper Jackson.

59. Esther Cooper Jackson, interview with author, January 8, 2015, Brooklyn, NY.

60. Ibid.

61. Ibid.

62. James Jackson to Roy Wilkins, February 24, 1956, Jackson Papers, box 5, folder 46.

63. Statement of the CPUSA on the Events in Little Rock, September 9, 1957, Jackson Papers, box 2, folder 34.

64. Aptheker, ed., *A Documentary History of the Negro People in the United States,* 6:394–96 (Roy Wilkins, "Little Rock, Arkansas [1957]"). Other works that address the Little Rock crisis include Daisy Bates, *The Long Shadow of Little Rock: A Memoir* (New York: David McKay, 1962); Melba Patillo Beals, *Warriors Don't Cry: A Searing Memoir of the Battle to Integrate Little Rock's Central High School* (New York: Washington Square, 1994); Grif Stockley, *Daisy Bates: Civil Rights Crusader from Arkansas* (Oxford: University Press of Mississippi, 2005); and John Kirk, *Beyond Little Rock: The Origins and Legacies of the Central High Crisis* (Fayetteville: University Press of Arkansas, 2007), and *Redefining the Color Line: Black Activism in Little Rock, Arkansas, 1920–1970* (Gainesville: University Press of Florida, 2002).

65. Statement of the CPUSA on the Events in Little Rock, September 9, 1957, Jackson Papers, box 2, folder 34.

66. Ibid.

67. Aptheker, ed., *A Documentary History of the Negro People in the United States,* 6:396 (Roy Wilkins, "Little Rock, Arkansas [1957]").

68. "The Communist Party Appeal for Continued Action," September 23, 1957, Jackson Papers, box 2, folder 34.

69. Ibid. It is likely that, even if the *State Press* had received ads from unions, it would not have printed them. The *State Press* was forced out of business in the second year of the Little Rock crisis, and, in the run-up to its demise, Daisy and

Lucius Christopher avoided printing much that would have given the white citizen councils cause to harass them further. See Kirk, *Redefining the Color Line,* and *Beyond Little Rock;* and Stockley, *Daisy Bates.*

70. James E. Jackson, *The Bold, Bad '60s: Pushing the Point for Equality Down South and Out Yonder* (New York: International, 1992), 10.

71. Ibid., 17.

72. James Jackson, "A Correct Marxist Approach to a Theoretical Presentation to the Negro Question in the US," n.d., Jackson Papers, box 2, folder 24.

73. Ibid. The Civil Rights Act of 1960 fixed some of the flaws in the 1957 Civil Rights Act, which specifically targeted voting rights. The 1957 act granted the federal government jurisdiction in situations where qualified black voters were disenfranchised. However, it did little to rectify the disenfranchisement of blacks who could not get through the inscrutable voter registration process in many southern locales. The 1960 act was largely ineffective, leaving 70 percent of black voters disenfranchised. See Steven F. Lawson and Charles Payne, *Debating the Civil Rights Movement, 1945–1968* (Lanham, MD: Rowman & Littlefield, 1998), 16.

74. James Jackson, "A Correct Marxist Approach to a Theoretical Presentation to the Negro Question in the US," n.d., Jackson Papers, box 2, folder 24.

75. "Working Material for a C.P. Discussion Resolution on Theoretical Aspects of the Negro Question," n.d., Jackson Papers, box 2, folder 24. See also Horne, *Black Liberation/Red Scare.*

76. Notes on a Discussion of the Structure of the National Committee, n.d., Jackson Papers, box 2, folder 22.

6. Radical Journalism in the Civil Rights Years

1. James E. Jackson and Esther Cooper Jackson to Mr. Abramowitz, n.d., Jackson Papers, box 5, folder 17.

2. James E. Jackson to John and Margrit Pittman, March 8, 1960, Jackson Papers, box 5, folder 41. See also generally John Pittman Papers, Tamiment Library.

3. Esther Cooper Jackson, interview with Erik McDuffie, n.d., Jackson Papers, box 1, folder 25.

4. Robeson was prevented from performing overseas after his passport was revoked in 1950. As his popularity as a performer waned in the United States when anti-Communist sentiment increased, he was no longer able to make a living by performing. These challenges scarred him, and he fought to stand by his principles, finding a new medium for doing so by publishing *Freedom.* See Duberman, *Paul Robeson;* and Lindsey R. Swindall, *Paul Robeson: A Life of Activism and Art* (Lanham, MD: Rowman & Littlefield, 2013), and *The Path to a Greater, Freer, Truer World: Southern Civil Rights and Anticolonialism, 1937–1955* (Gainesville: University Press of Florida, 2014).

5. Esther Cooper Jackson and Constance Pohl, eds., *Freedomways Reader: Prophets in Their Own Country* (Boulder, CO: Westview, 2000), xxi.

6. Jack H. O'Dell to Diane Nash Bevels, February 8, 1967, Jackson Papers, box 7, folder 2.

7. Michael Schwerner to Esther Cooper Jackson, March 18, 1964, Jackson Papers, box 7, folder 44. COFO was founded in 1961 by the Mississippi activist Aaron Henry and was revitalized by Bob Moses of the SNCC, Tom Gaither of CORE, and Medgar Evers of the NAACP in 1962 to unite all the groups working in Mississippi. See John Dittmer, *Local People: The Struggle for Civil Rights in Mississippi* (Urbana: University of Illinois Press, 1995), 118–19. Michael Schwerner was a white CORE activist and the director of CORE projects in six counties in Mississippi. Just three months after he wrote to *Freedomways* to request copies for the community center library, he became a part of one of the nation's worst civil rights tragedies. He, along with James Chaney and Andrew Goodman, was driving from Oxford to Meridian in June, and the three were arrested outside Philadelphia, Mississippi. They were released and rearrested shortly thereafter and were subsequently handed off to a mob. Schwerner, Chaney, and Goodman disappeared and were lynched in Neshoba County around June 21, 1964. The FBI was slow to respond but along with other COFO volunteers eventually began searching for the missing activists. On August 4, the FBI recovered the bodies. See Dittmer, *Local People*, 246–83; and Payne, *I've Got the Light of Freedom*.

8. Michael Nash and D. J. Leab, "Freedomways," *American Communist History* 7, no. 2 (December 2008): 227–37, 236.

9. Cooper Jackson and Pohl, eds., *Freedomways Reader*, xix.

10. Ibid.

11. James Baldwin to Potential Subscribers, 1964, Jackson Papers, box 6, folder 48.

12. Cooper Jackson and Pohl, eds., *Freedomways Reader*, xx.

13. Nash and Leab, "Freedomways," 228.

14. Von Eschen, *Race against Empire*, and *Satchmo Blows Up the World*; Dudziak, *Cold War Civil Rights*; Borstelmann, *The Cold War and the Color Line*; Plummer, *Rising Wind*; Biondi, *To Stand and Fight*.

15. Clayborne Carson, *In Struggle: SNCC and the Black Awakening of the 1960s* (Cambridge, MA: Harvard University Press, 1981), 1; Barbara Ransby, *Ella Baker and the Black Freedom Movement: A Radical Democratic Vision* (Chapel Hill: University of North Carolina Press, 2003); Lawson and Payne, *Debating the Civil Rights Movement*; Payne, *I've Got the Light of Freedom*.

16. Branch, *Parting the Waters*, 292.

17. Carson, *In Struggle*, 2 (quotes), 105–7.

18. Smethurst, *The Black Arts Movement*, 126.

19. Nash and Leab, "Freedomways," 232.

20. Ian Rocksborough-Smith, "Filling the Gap: Intergenerational Black Radicalism and the Popular Front Ideals of *Freedomways* Magazine, 1961–1965," *Afro-Americans in New York Life and History* 31, no. 3 (2007): 7–42, 29–31 (quote 31). See also Ian Rocksborough-Smith, "Bearing the Seeds of Struggle: *Freedomways* Magazine, Black Leftists, and Continuities in the Black Freedom Movement" (M.A. thesis, Simon Fraser University, 2005).

21. David Howard-Pitney, *Martin Luther King, Jr., Malcolm X, and the Civil Rights Struggle of the 1950s and 1960s* (Boston: Bedford St. Martin's, 2004), 120.

22. Robert F. Williams, *Negroes with Guns* (Detroit: Wayne State University Press, 1998), 26.

23. Howard-Pitney, *Martin Luther King, Jr.,* 98.

24. Rocksborough-Smith, "Filling the Gap."

25. Bruce J. Schulman, *Lyndon B. Johnson and American Liberalism: A Brief History with Documents* (Boston: Bedford St. Martin's, 1995).

26. Massey and Denton, *American Apartheid;* Peniel E. Joseph, *Waiting 'til the Midnight Hour: A Narrative History of Black Power in America* (New York: Henry Holt, 2006); Thomas J. Sugrue, *Sweet Land of Liberty: The Forgotten Civil Rights Struggle in the North* (New York: Random House, 2008), and *The Origins of the Urban Crisis.*

27. "Jesse Gray, 64, Leader of Harlem Rent Strikes," *New York Times,* April 5, 1988.

28. Joseph, *Waiting 'til the Midnight Hour,* 110. For more details on the Harlem and Bedford-Stuyvesant riots, see Janet L. Abu-Lughotd, *Race, Space, and Riots in Chicago, New York City, and Los Angeles* (New York: Oxford University Press, 2007).

29. Brooklyn was home to a radical chapter of CORE that engaged in mass demonstrations and theatrical protests against all the borough's racist institutions. Housing and neighborhood conditions in Bedford-Stuyvesant were particularly poor, triggering rent strikes, protests for better sanitation in the neighborhood, an end to employment discrimination, and safer traffic patterns. Blacks were isolated in a few Brooklyn neighborhoods, and CORE documented a widespread pattern of blatant housing discrimination across the city. See Arnie Goldwag Brooklyn Congress of Racial Equality Collection, Brooklyn Historical Society, Brooklyn, NY; and Brian Purnell, *Fighting Jim Crow in the County of Kings: The Congress of Racial Equality in Brooklyn* (Lexington: University Press of Kentucky, 2013).

30. Gene Roberts and Hank Klibanoff, *The Race Beat: The Press, the Civil Rights Struggle, and the Awakening of a Nation* (New York: Vintage, 2006), 400.

31. Joseph, *Waiting 'til the Midnight Hour,* 132–42.

32. Ibid., 146, 197.

33. William Van Deberg, *New Day in Babylon: The Black Power Movement in American Culture, 1965–1975* (Chicago: University of Chicago Press, 1992), 10.

34. Rocksborough-Smith, "Bearing the Seeds of Struggle," 53.

35. Roberts and Klibanoff, *The Race Beat*, 368–71. For more on the FBI's efforts to subvert civil rights efforts, see Garrow, *The FBI and Martin Luther King*.

36. See Branch, *Parting the Waters*.

37. See Conferences Files, SNYC Papers; Gerald Horne, "The Southern Negro Youth Congress," in *Organizing Black America: An Encyclopedia of African American Associations*, ed. Nina Mjagkij (New York: Garland, 2001), 551–52.

38. Jonathan Scott Holloway, *Confronting the Veil: Abram Harris Jr., E. Franklin Frazier, and Ralph Bunche, 1919–1941* (Chapel Hill: University of North Carolina Press, 2002), 183.

39. Korstad, *Civil Rights Unionism*, 416–17. See also Korstad and Lichtenstein, "Opportunities Found and Lost"; and Honey, *Southern Labor and Black Civil Rights*.

40. James Jackson to Gus Hall, n.d., Jackson Papers, box 5, folder 32.

41. Honey, *Southern Labor and Black Civil Rights*, 276, 277.

42. Michael K. Honey, introduction to Martin Luther King Jr., *All Labor Has Dignity*, ed. Michael K. Honey (Boston: Beacon, 2011), xvi–xvii. See also William P. Jones, *The March on Washington: Jobs, Freedom, and the Forgotten History of Civil Rights* (New York: Norton, 2013).

43. David Sentner, "Reds Plan to Sneak in D.C. March," *Baltimore News Post*, August 27, 1963, Jackson Papers, box 2, folder 4.

44. Jack O'Dell, a former member of the SNYC Miami chapter, met with Martin Luther King Jr. in 1959 and became an executive assistant to him in 1962 after the attorney Stanley Levison recommended him for the job. Levison, a white socialist, had long supported progressive and humanitarian causes, including the defense of the Smith Act defendants in 1949 and the Rosenbergs from 1950 to 1953. He was active as a civil rights attorney and formed an organization with Bayard Rustin in 1956 called In Friendship, through which he met King. His relationship with King raised eyebrows, but, as the historian Taylor Branch notes, King "found nothing objectionable about Levison, least of all his radical connections." King was no Communist, but he "never wavered in support of the victims of McCarthyism or in his sympathy with Communist advocacy for the oppressed." The FBI and the Kennedys believed King's association with Levison was problematic, and, when O'Dell entered the mix, FBI surveillance of the SCLC increased. The bureau was well aware of O'Dell's history and believed that he was elected to the CPUSA's national committee in 1959 using the name "Cornelius James." When it learned of O'Dell's new role in the SCLC, one agent wrote: "In view of the continued activity of Levison and O'Dell and the fact they exert influence on King, it is deemed advisable to again ask for a review of the appropriate field office files to determine if any [Communist Party] direction and infiltration of the SCLC

has developed." O'Dell remained in the SCLC fold quietly until 1963, when, in the midst of the organization's massive, decisive campaign in Birmingham, the *Birmingham News* reported that he continued to receive a paycheck from the organization. When the news broke that O'Dell had not actually resigned from the SCLC, King and others met with him and formally removed him from the organization's roster. See McWhorter, *Carry Me Home*; Garrow, *The FBI and Martin Luther King*, 50–51; Branch, *Parting the Waters*, 209.

45. *The Negro Family in the United States* argued that social circumstances shaped the structure of black families in the United States. Frazier's argument that race was not a sole determinant of behavior shaped scholarly and political ideas about black families for decades to come. Most notably, his work provided a scholarly foundation for Daniel Patrick Moynihan's *The Negro Family: A Case for National Action*. Moynihan's work characterized African American family structures as "a tangle of pathology" and cited maternalism and weakened manhood as key sources of problems in black communities. See E. Franklin Frazier, *The Negro Family in the United States* (Chicago: University of Chicago Press, 1966); and Daniel Patrick Moynihan and Office of Policy and Planning, Department of Labor, *The Negro Family: The Case for National Action* (Washington, DC: US Government Printing Office, 1965).

46. Whitney M. Young Jr., "What Price Prejudice? On the Economics of Discrimination," *Freedomways*, no. 3 (1962): 237–42, 239.

47. Ibid., 241.

48. Clayborne Carson et al., eds., *The Eyes on the Prize Civil Rights Reader* (New York: Penguin, 1991). See also *Boynton v. Virginia*, 364 U.S. 454 (1960).

49. Jimmy McDonald, "A Freedom Rider Speaks His Mind," *Freedomways*, no. 2 (1961): 158–63, 161, 159.

50. Lester Davis, "NAACP—a Leadership Dilemma," *Freedomways*, no. 3 (1961): 275–81, 280.

51. Robert F. Williams used his position in the Monroe NAACP to advocate self-defense against rampant racial violence. He believed that blacks should not succumb to racial violence but should instead show a willingness to fight back as a form of defense. In a few instances he succeeded by showing that whites were unlikely to attack armed blacks. He was expelled from the NAACP and forced to leave the country. He lived in Cuba and China before returning to the United States in the late 1960s. See Timothy Tyson, "Robert F. Williams, 'Black Power,' and the Roots of the African American Freedom Struggle," in Williams, *Negroes with Guns*, xv–xxxiv, and *Radio Free Dixie*.

52. Davis, "NAACP—a Leadership Dilemma," 277.

53. Ibid., 281.

54. Ibid.

55. Ralph Ellison to John Henrik Clarke, March 13, 1964, Jackson Papers, box 7, folder 14.

56. Rocksborough-Smith, "Bearing the Seeds of Struggle"; Nash and Leab, "Freedomways"; Smethurst, *The Black Arts Movement;* Gerald Horne, *Race Woman: The Lives of Shirley Graham Du Bois* (New York: New York University Press, 2000).

57. Smethurst, *The Black Arts Movement,* 125.

58. Patricia Sullivan, ed., *Freedom Writer: The Letters of Virginia Foster Durr* (New York: Routledge, 2006), 351. For a biographical sketch of Durr, see Sullivan, *Days of Hope,* 110–14.

59. Virginia Durr to Esther Cooper Jackson, December 5, 1966, Jackson Papers, box 7, folder 13.

60. Virginia Durr to Esther Cooper Jackson, March 1, 1967, Jackson Papers, box 7, folder 13.

61. Horne, *Race Woman,* 223.

62. Rocksborough-Smith, "Bearing the Seeds of Struggle," 53, 66, 82. The Black Panther Party was established in 1966 by Black Power advocates in Oakland, California. The Panthers based their philosophy on Mao Tse-tung's *Little Red Book* and mobilized Maoist Marxism to advocate for "revolutionary nationalism." They sold copies of the book and used the profits to finance the purchase of guns to protect local communities from the police. The organization created a "ten-point program" that outlined the needs of Oakland-area blacks, including an end to police brutality, adequate access to necessities like food, housing, clothing, and education, and an end to exploitation. See Joseph, *Waiting 'til the Midnight Hour.*

63. Rocksborough-Smith, "Filling the Gap," 31.

64. Smethurst, *The Black Arts Movement,* 7.

65. Ruby Dee, "The Culture and Cause of Black Freedom," in Cooper Jackson and Pohl, eds., *Freedomways Reader,* 290.

66. Smethurst, *The Black Arts Movement,* 142–43.

67. Smethurst, *The Black Arts Movement,* 127, 141.

68. Cooper Jackson and Pohl, eds., *Freedomways Reader,* 322.

69. Rocksborough-Smith, "Bearing the Seeds of Struggle," 98. For more on the political spectrum that *Freedomways* sought to represent, see Rocksborough-Smith, "Filling the Gap."

70. For more on the links between earlier artistic expression and *Freedomways,* see Rocksborough-Smith, "Filling the Gap," 30.

71. Cooper Jackson and Pohl, eds., *Freedomways Reader,* 293.

72. Alice Childress, "The Negro Woman in American Literature," *Freedomways,* no. 1 (1966): 8–25, 15, 19. For more on popular stereotypes of Black women, see "On Jezebel and Mammy," in Deborah Gray White, *Ar'n't I a Woman? Female Slaves in the Plantation South* (New York: Norton, 1999), 27–61.

73. Max Roach, "Jazz," *Freedomways,* no. 2 (1962): 173–77, 173–74.

74. Abbey Lincoln, "Black Women Singers-Artists," *Freedomways,* no. 1 (1966): 8–25, 13.

75. Milton Galamison, "Bedford-Stuyvesant—Land of Superlatives," in Clarke, ed., *Harlem*, 187–97, 191, 195 (quote). For more on Galamison, see Clarence Taylor, *Knocking at Our Own Door: Milton A. Galamison and the Struggle to Integrate New York City Schools* (New York: Columbia University Press, 1997).

76. Galamison, "Bedford-Stuyvesant," 196.

77. E. U. Essien-Udom, "The Nationalist Movements of Harlem," in Clarke, ed., *Harlem*, 97–104, 98, 104.

78. Smethurst, *The Black Arts Movement*, 367.

79. Jackson, *The Bold, Bad '60s*, 86–89.

80. Ibid., 90–91.

81. James E. Jackson, "Justice, No Frameup, Is Harlem's Demand," *The Worker*, July 26, 1964.

82. James Jackson, Notebook 2, n.d., Jackson Papers, box 9, folder 40.

83. James Jackson to "Daughter," August 3, 1967, Jackson Papers, box 1, folder 21.

84. "Negro Unity and Negro-White Unity Are Needed for Freedom Power," September 4, 1966, Jackson Papers, box 2, folder 13.

85. James E. Jackson Jr., *The Meaning of Black Power* (1966), 9–10, Jackson Papers, box 16, folder 41.

86. Stokely Carmichael, "What We Want" (1966), in *The Radical Reader*, ed. Timothy Patrick McCarthy and John McMillan (New York: New Press, 2003), 390–96, 395.

87. Stokely Carmichael and Charles V. Hamilton, *Black Power: The Politics of Liberation* (New York: Vintage, 1992), 23.

88. James E. Jackson Jr., *The Meaning of Black Power* (1966), 13, Jackson Papers, box 16, folder 41.

89. Ibid., 13–14.

90. Ibid., 15.

91. Joseph, *Waiting 'til the Midnight Hour*, 153–54.

92. Caute, *The Great Fear*, 564n. In 1965, the Supreme Court overturned the McCarran Act, agreeing that it did violate the Fifth Amendment.

93. Schrecker, *Many Are the Crimes*, 141.

94. James E. Jackson Jr., *The View from Here: Commentaries on Peace and Freedom* (New York: New Press, 1963), 10–12.

95. James E. Jackson Jr., "Our Democratic Heritage," *The Worker*, February 11, 1962.

96. Lawson and Payne, *Debating the Civil Rights Movement*, 22–24.

97. Jackson, *The View from Here*, 87–88.

98. James Jackson to Harriet Jackson, August 4, 1962, Jackson Papers, box 1, folder 21.

99. Schrecker, *Many Are the Crimes*, 393–94.

100. George Murphy to Carl, February 5, 1962, Jackson Papers, box 6, folder 11.

101. Lowery was a New Yorker from a wealthy family. When the freedom riders arrived in Monroe, they met the former NAACP leader and self-defense advocate Robert F. Williams. Both Williams and the freedom riders hoped to prove the other's philosophy to be ineffective. The freedom riders encountered substantial violence in Monroe, and a number of them were arrested. See Tyson, *Radio Free Dixie*, 264–79.

102. John C. Lowery to James E. Jackson, May 18, 1962, Jackson Papers, box 5, folder 37.

103. Jackson, *The View from Here*, 98.

104. During his presidential campaign, Kennedy made a phone call to Coretta Scott King while her husband was in jail, securing African American votes. See Carson et al., eds., *The Eyes on the Prize Civil Rights Reader*.

105. For information on Meredith, see Carson et al., eds., *The Eyes on the Prize Civil Rights Reader*, 63. Barnett had extensive conversations with Kennedy about the turmoil in his state surrounding James Meredith's enrollment at the University of Mississippi and attempted to use interposition to prevent the government from interfering in Mississippi's rights. Two people were killed in Oxford, Mississippi, before the Kennedy administration took action.

106. Lee C. White to James Jackson, August 13, 1962, Jackson Papers, box 3, folder 36.

107. Jackson, *The View from Here*, 97.

108. John F. Kennedy, "Civil Rights Message," June 11, 1963, in *Ripples of Hope: Great American Civil Rights Speeches*, ed. Josh Gottheimer (New York: Basic, 2003), 227–32, 231; James E. Jackson Jr., "Kennedy and the Segregation Crisis: An Editorial," June 11, 1963, Jackson Papers, box 2, folder 10.

109. James E. Jackson Jr., "DEFEND AMERICA! Punish the Assassins, Unite for Democracy!," November 23, 1963, Jackson Papers, box 2, folder 10. For discussions of right-wing politics in the 1960s, see Rebecca Klatch, *A Generation Divided: The New Left, the New Right, and the 1960s* (Berkeley and Los Angeles: University of California Press, 1999); and Donald Critchlow, *Phyllis Schlafly and Grassroots Conservatism: A Woman's Crusade* (Princeton, NJ: Princeton University Press, 2005).

110. James E. Jackson Jr., "With Bloody Hands, They Try to Smear Others," *The Worker*, December 16, 1963, Jackson Papers, box 2, folder 10. Oswald emigrated to the Soviet Union, living there from 1959 to 1962, but associated with Russian anti-Communists on his return. His murky political affiliations contribute to the air of mystery around the Kennedy assassination. See Gerald Posner, *Case Closed: Lee Harvey Oswald and the Assassination of JFK* (New York: Anchor Books, 1993).

111. Jackson, "With Bloody Hands."

112. "The People Will Fight Back," CPUSA Statement on Kennedy Assassination, 1963, Jackson Papers, box 2, folder 10. William Moore was a white postal worker from Baltimore, Maryland, who planned to walk from Chattanooga, Tennessee, to Mississippi to protest segregation. He was gunned down in Alabama. See Branch, *Parting the Waters,* 748–49; and Payne, *I've Got the Light of Freedom.*
113. "Another Disgraceful Chapter," *Freedomways,* no. 1 (1964): 5–6, 6. The six children slain in Birmingham were the four young girls who were killed when the Sixteenth Street Baptist Church was bombed on September 15, 1963. In the aftermath, two Eagle Scouts shot two black boys on a bicycle, one of whom was killed. Another black Birmingham man was killed fleeing a confrontation with whites. For more on racial violence in Birmingham, see Branch, *Parting the Waters.*
114. "Another Disgraceful Chapter," 6.

7. *Freedomways,* the Communist Party USA, and Black Freedom in the Post–Civil Rights Years

1. Jackson Speech at 60th Birthday Celebration, 1974, Jackson Papers, box 1, folder 1.
2. Van Gosse, *Rethinking the New Left: An Interpretive History* (New York: Palgrave Macmillan, 2005); Cohen, *When the Old Left Was Young.*
3. Jackson Speech at 60th Birthday Celebration, 1974, Jackson Papers, box 1, folder 1.
4. Jack's lectures and writings in this period covered a wide range of theoretical and political questions and fill multiple boxes. A small sampling of titles includes "Capitalism's Ornery Nature: An Economics Teaching from Marxism-Leninism," "Dialectical Materialism," "Falsifiers of Marxism," "Historical Materialism," "Contemporary World Politics," "Left-Wing Communism," "Philosophy," "Revolutionary Processes," "Strategy and Tactics," "Philosophical Falsifiers," "The State and the Nature and Character of Fascism," and "The Socialist Countries and the Class Struggle in the Capitalist Countries." These are located in ser. VII, XI, XIII, and XIV of the Jackson Papers, boxes 8, 9, 12, 13, 16–21. For more historical context, see Hutchinson, *Blacks and Reds.*
5. Weigand, *Red Feminism,* 156. See also ibid., 139–58; McDuffie, *Sojourning for Freedom;* and Gore, *Radicalism at the Crossroads.*
6. James Jackson, Lecture on the Woman Question, transcribed, 1977, Jackson Papers, box 10, folder 65.
7. Ibid.
8. Ibid.
9. Esther Cooper Jackson, interview with author, June 24, 2014, Brooklyn, NY.
10. Vietnam Trip Notes, May 1968, Jackson Papers, box 19, folder 32.

11. Gosse, *Rethinking the New Left*, 90.

12. Adam Fairclough, *To Redeem the Soul of America: The Southern Christian Leadership Conference and Martin Luther King, Jr.* (Athens: University of Georgia Press, 1987).

13. Martin Luther King Jr., "Time to Break Silence," *Freedomways*, no. 2 (1967): 103–17, 105, 115.

14. Martin Luther King Jr., "Honoring Dr. Du Bois," *Freedomways*, no. 2 (1968): 104–11, 109.

15. After the passage of the 1965 Voting Rights Act, King and the Southern Christian Leadership Conference confronted urban riots and rebellions in the North and increasingly turned their attention to the economic inequality that both stemmed from and spurred racial strife. King's efforts to promote the Poor People's Campaign drew criticism from his more moderate colleagues in the National Association for the Advancement of Colored People and the National Urban League because it highlighted socialistic aspects of his perspective. His incorporation of democratic socialism into his agenda simultaneously gave fodder to his critics and highlighted the tensions McCarthyism had brought just a decade earlier. Overall, it was detrimental to his reputation. See Fairclough, *To Redeem the Soul of America*, 357–84.

16. Editors, "Farewell to 'A Drum Major for Justice and Peace,'" *Freedomways*, no. 2 (1968): 101–2.

17. Clayborne Carson and Kris Shepard, eds., *A Call to Conscience: The Landmark Speeches of Dr. Martin Luther King, Jr.* (New York: Hachette, 2001), 223.

18. Vietnam Trip Notes, May 1968, Jackson Papers, box 19, folder 32.

19. Ibid.

20. Ibid. See also Nguyen Thi Dinh, *No Other Road to Take: Memoir of Mrs. Nguyen Thi Dinh*, trans. Mai V. Elliot (Ithaca, NY: Cornell Southeast Asia Program Publications, 1976).

21. Out of a commitment to participatory democracy, New Left organizations were often wary of Communists, who focused on a rigid organizational and hierarchical structure. The New Left did not, however, condemn Communism outright, and many groups were openly critical of a broad anti-Communist agenda in the United States. See Gosse, *Rethinking the New Left*.

22. Diane Nash, "Journey to North Vietnam," *Freedomways*, no. 2 (1967): 118–28.

23. In the wake of widespread black criticism of Nixon's position on civil rights, Daniel Patrick Moynihan and Nixon agreed that a policy of "benign neglect" would benefit racial progress in the United States, that is, that earlier policies had alleviated the most pressing racial injustices and that "a period in which Negro progress continues and racial rhetoric fades" would eliminate any lingering racial strife. Not surprisingly, black leaders did not respond well to a recommendation that the president ignore their grievances, limit spending on

civil rights objectives, and withdraw from public discussion of racial problems. See Dean J. Kotlowski, *Nixon's Civil Rights: Politics, Principle, and Policy* (Cambridge, MA: Harvard University Press, 2009), 172–75.

24. Editors, "The Pentagon's 'Secret Papers,'" *Freedomways*, no. 3 (1971): 233–36, 233, 235.

25. Ibid., 235. See also "Ethiopians Seeking New Arms from U.S.," *New York Times*, March 17, 1971, 16; "Eritrean Liberation Group Pursuing Its Struggle at the U.N.," *New York Times*, December 15, 1971, 12; and "Brooklyn G.I. Slain in Ethiopia Region of Guerilla Activity," *New York Times*, January 22, 1971, 4.

26. Editors, "The Pentagon's 'Secret Papers,'" 236.

27. Bettina Aptheker, *The Morning Breaks: The Trial of Angela Davis* (Ithaca, NY: Cornell University Press, 1997); Hutchinson, *Blacks and Reds;* Angela Davis, *Angela Davis: An Autobiography* (New York: Random House, 1974).

28. Aptheker, *The Morning Breaks;* Hutchinson, *Blacks and Reds;* Davis, *Angela Davis.*

29. Hutchinson, *Blacks and Reds,* 289–90.

30. Jackson, *Revolutionary Tracings,* 53–56 ("Three Philosophers: Frederick Engels, Herbert Marcuse and Angela Davis"). When Jack says that Davis is "in transition from Marcuse to Marx and Lenin," he means that she has bridged the intellectual distances between ideological trends.

31. James E. Jackson Jr., Statement Before Sentencing, September 17, 1956, Jackson Papers, box 11, folder 11. See also Jackson, *Revolutionary Tracings,* 57–59 ("The Triumph of Angela Davis").

32. Lieutenant William Calley was the only American soldier convicted of crimes in the March 16, 1968, My Lai massacre. In April 1971, President Nixon converted Calley's life sentence to house arrest at Fort Benning, pending an appeal. Within a few years, the government ceased pursuit of punishment for Calley. See James S. Olson and Randy Roberts, *My Lai: A Brief History with Documents* (Boston: Bedford St. Martin's Press, 1998).

33. Editorial, "Free Angela Davis!" *Freedomways*, no. 2 (1971): 139.

34. Jackson, *Revolutionary Tracings,* 58, 59 ("The Triumph of Angela Davis").

35. Hutchinson, *Blacks and Reds,* 296.

36. "Communist Party, USA," in *Encyclopedia of the American Left* (2nd ed.), ed. Mari Jo Buhle, Paul Buhle, and Dan Georgakas (Oxford: Oxford University Press, 1998), 146–56; Membership Records and CPUSA Applications for Membership, Communist Party USA Papers, box 266, folders 8–9, and box 275, folder 39.

37. Ernest Kaiser, "Review: *U.S. Negroes in Battle: Little Rock to Watts*," *Freedomways*, no. 4 (1967): 367–70, and "Review: *Revolutionary Tracings in World Politics and Black Liberation*," *Freedomways*, no. 2 (1975): 119–22.

38. James E. Jackson, "*Freedomways* Media Issue: A Valued Contribution to Struggle vs. Racism," n.d., Jackson Papers, box 7, folder 32.

39. Ibid.

40. Maryemma Graham, "The Color Purple," *Freedomways*, no. 4 (1983): 278–81.

41. James Jackson, "The Destructive Design of *The Color Purple*," *Political Affairs* 51 (March 1986): 26–30, Jackson Papers, box 17, folder 17. Jack is quoting Loyle Hairston, "Alice in the Mainstream," *Freedomways*, no. 3 (1984): 182–91.

42. Jackson, "The Destructive Design of *The Color Purple*."

43. Alice Walker to Esther Cooper Jackson, April 30, 1984, Jackson Papers, box 8, folder 22.

44. Alice Walker to Esther Cooper Jackson, May 28, 1985, Jackson Papers, box 8, folder 22.

45. Esther Cooper Jackson, interview with author, June 24, 2014, Brooklyn, NY.

46. Ibid.

47. Jack O'Dell, telephone interview with author, March 12, 2003.

48. Bettye Collier-Thomas and V. P. Franklin, *Sisters in Struggle: African American Women in the Civil Rights–Black Power Movement* (New York: New York University Press, 2001); McGuire, *At the Dark End of the Street;* Christina Greene, *Our Separate Ways: Women and the Black Freedom Movement in Durham, North Carolina* (Chapel Hill: University of North Carolina Press, 2005); Ransby, *Ella Baker and the Black Freedom Movement;* Chana Kai Lee, *For Freedom's Sake: The Life of Fannie Lou Hamer* (Urbana: University of Illinois Press, 2000).

49. For more on this, see McDuffie, *Sojourning for Freedom;* and Gore, *Radicalism at the Crossroads.*

50. Esther Cooper Jackson, interview with author, June 24, 2014, Brooklyn, NY.

51. These included Jean Carey Bond, "The Media Image of Black Women," *Freedomways*, no. 1 (1975): 34–36, and "Keeping the Faith: Writings by Contemporary Black American Women," *Freedomways*, no. 2 (1975): 125–26; Akosua Barthwell and Patricia A. Roberts, "Two Young Black Women Speak of African Liberation," *Freedomways*, no. 3 (1975): 212–14; Elizabeth V. Murrell, "World Congress for the International Women's Year: Many Women—One Goal," *Freedomways*, no. 4 (1975): 249–57; Elizabeth S. Landis, "Apartheid and the Disabilities of African Women in South Africa," *Freedomways*, no. 4 (1975): 272–75; and Magdalena Nahambo Shamena, "Letter from a Namibian Woman," *Freedomways*, no. 4 (1975): 276–79.

52. Editors, "Black Women: Internationalizing the Struggle," *Freedomways*, no. 1 (1975): 5–7, 5.

53. Augusta Strong, "Negro Women in Freedom's Battles," *Freedomways*, no. 4 (1967): 302–15, 303, 314. See also McGuire, *At the Dark End of the Street;*

Greene, *Our Separate Ways;* Ransby, *Ella Baker and the Black Freedom Movement;* and Lee, *For Freedom's Sake.*

54. Peter Novick, *That Noble Dream: The "Objectivity Question" and the American Historical Profession* (Cambridge: Cambridge University Press, 1988), 475–77. Starobin later committed suicide.

55. Martha Biondi, *The Black Revolution on Campus* (Berkeley and Los Angeles: University of California Press, 2012), 175–76.

56. Smethurst, *The Black Arts Movement,* 2. See also Biondi, *The Black Revolution on Campus,* 13–42.

57. Cooper Jackson and Pohl, eds., *Freedomways Reader,* xxix.

58. See John Henrik Clarke, ed., *William Styron's Nat Turner: Ten Black Writers Respond* (Boston: Beacon, 1968).

59. Esther Cooper Jackson to Martin Duberman, October 3, 1983, Jackson Papers, box 8, folder 10.

60. See Herbert Aptheker, *American Negro Slave Revolts* (New York: Columbia University Press, 1943).

61. Vincent Harding, "You've Taken My Nat and Gone," in Clarke, ed., *William Styron's Nat Turner,* 23–44, 24, 30.

62. John A. Williams, "The Manipulation of History and Fact: An Ex-Southerner's Apologist Tract for Slavery and the Life of Nat Turner; or, William Styron's Faked Confessions," in ibid., 45–49, 45–46.

63. Eugene D. Genovese, "The Nat Turner Case," *New York Review of Books,* September 12, 1968, http://www.nybooks.com/articles/archives/1968/sep/12/the-nat-turner-case.

64. Anna Mary Wells, Mike Thelwell, and Eugene D. Genovese, "An Exchange on Nat Turner," *New York Review of Books,* November 7, 1968, http://www.nybooks.com/articles/archives/1968/nov/07/an-exchange-on-nat-turner.

65. Eugene D. Genovese, *Roll, Jordan, Roll: The World the Slaves Made* (New York: Vintage, 1974).

66. Earl Smith, "Roll, Apology, Roll!" *Freedomways,* no. 1 (1975): 46–50, 46.

67. Esther Cooper Jackson to Martin Duberman, October 3, 1983, Jackson Papers, box 8, folder 10.

68. Martin Duberman, "Historical Fictions," *New York Times,* August 11, 1968.

69. Sterling Stuckey, "The Cultural Philosophy of Paul Robeson," *Freedomways,* no. 1 (1971): 78–90, 79, 90.

70. Ibid., 80.

71. Jack O'Dell, "A Rock in a Weary Lan'," *Freedomways,* no. 1 (1971): 34–49, 37.

72. Ibid., 34, 49.

73. Gellman, *Death Blow to Jim Crow,* 259.

74. Virginia Durr to Esther Cooper Jackson, May 6, 1971, Jackson Papers, box 8, folder 13.

75. See Virginia Durr to Esther Cooper Jackson, March 21, 1979, Jackson Papers, box 8, folder 13.

76. George Murphy to Esther Cooper Jackson, June 23, 1971, and George Murphy to Virginia Durr, June 23, 1971, Jackson Papers, box 8, folder 13.

77. Virginia Durr to Esther Cooper Jackson, March 21, 1979, Jackson Papers, box 8, folder 13.

78. Esther Cooper Jackson to Virginia Durr, March 30, 1979, Jackson Papers, box 8, folder 13.

79. Paul Robeson Jr., "Paul Robeson: Black Warrior," in *Paul Robeson: The Great Forerunner*, by Freedomways Associates (New York: Dodd, Mead, 1978), 3–16.

80. Philip S. Foner, ed., *Paul Robeson Speaks: Writings, Speeches, and Interviews, a Centennial Celebration* (New York: Citadel, 1978); Paul Robeson Jr. to Mr. H. L. Mazel, cc Esther Jackson, November 22, 1978, Jackson Papers, box 7, folder 17.

81. "Lloyd L. Brown, 89, Journalist and Paul Robeson Biographer," obituary, *New York Times*, April 14, 2003.

82. Lloyd L. Brown Memorandum on Paul Robeson Biography, March 16, 1982, Jackson Papers, box 7, folder 6.

83. Ibid.

84. Ibid.

85. Martin Duberman to Esther Cooper Jackson, September 9, 1983, Jackson Papers, box 8, folder 10.

86. Esther Cooper Jackson to Martin Duberman, October 3, 1983, Jackson Papers, box 8, folder 10.

87. Novick, *That Noble Dream*, 469–91.

88. In his memoir, the historian Mark Naison recounts his experience as the only white faculty member in Fordham University's Institute for Afro-American Studies, beginning in 1970. He recalled that he developed a strong rapport with many of his students and colleagues, black and white, but that some students remained reluctant to acknowledge him in the program. Other white historians offered significant interventions in the field of African American history, including Kenneth Stampp, August Meier, Elliot Rudwick, Eric Foner, Leon Litwack, William Chafe, Steven Lawson, and John Dittmer, to name a few. See Mark Naison, *White Boy: A Memoir* (Philadelphia: Temple University Press, 2002), 146–71.

89. Sterling Stuckey, "The Twilight of Our Past: Reflections on the Origins of Black History," in *Amistad 2*, ed. John A. Williams and Charles F. Harris (New York: Vintage, 1971), 261–95, 291.

90. Nash and Leab, "Freedomways," 236; Esther Cooper Jackson, interview with author, June 24, 2014, Brooklyn, NY.

91. Jack O'Dell, "Tracing the Freedom Way," *Freedomways*, no. 3 (1985): 131–34.

92. Editorial, *Freedomways*, no. 4 (1983): 211; Editorial, *Freedomways*, no. 4 (1984): 227.

93. James E. Jackson to Gus Hall, Judith LeBlanc, and National Board, CPUSA, January 21, 1992, Jackson Papers, box 5, folder 44.

Conclusion

1. Robin D. G. Kelley to Esther Cooper Jackson, May 18, 1989, Jackson Papers, box 8, folder 1.

2. Grant Application: Written History of the Southern Negro Youth Congress, titled "Like the Dew They Covered Dixie," 1990, Jackson Papers, box 8, folder 27.

3. See, e.g., McWhorter, *Carry Me Home;* Kelley, *Hammer and Hoe;* Solomon, *The Cry Was Unity;* Egerton, *Speak Now against the Day;* Sullivan, *Days of Hope;* McDuffie, *Sojourning for Freedom;* and Gellman, *Death Blow to Jim Crow.*

4. Patricia Sullivan to James and Esther Jackson, August 11, 1995, Jackson Papers, box 8, folder 1.

5. Roger L. Green to James and Esther Jackson, April 15, 1996, Jackson Papers, box 7, folder 44.

6. Esther Jackson to Friend of the Du Bois Foundation, January 23, 1996, Jackson Papers, box 8, folder 24.

7. Sara Sue Koritz to Esther Jackson, February 26, 1998, Jackson Papers, box 7, folder 45.

8. Tim Wheeler, "James Jackson: Fighter for Equality, Democracy, Peace and Socialism," *People's Weekly World Newspaper,* December 6, 2001.

9. Angela Davis, "James and Esther Jackson: Connecting the Past to the Present," *American Communist History* 7, no. 2 (December 2008): 271–76, 273.

10. James Jackson to Esther Cooper, June 21, 1945, World War II Correspondence, Jackson Papers, box 6, folder 41.

Selected Bibliography

Primary Sources

Interviews

Burnham, Dorothy, January 23, 2003, November 11, 2004, Brooklyn, NY.
Cooper Jackson, Esther, September 25, 2002, December 12, 2002, October 12, 2004, March 15, 2006, June 24, 2014, January 8, 2015, Brooklyn, NY.
Devine, Ethel, July 1, 2007, Brooklyn, NY.
Jackson, James E., Jr., September 25, December 12, 2002, Brooklyn, NY.
O'Dell, Jack, March 12, 2003, by telephone.

Manuscript Collections

Communist Party USA Papers, Tamiment Library, New York University, New York, NY.
Esther Irving Cooper Papers, Moorland-Spingarn Research Center, Howard University.
James and Esther Cooper Jackson Papers, Tamiment Library, New York University, New York, NY.
Arnie Goldwag Brooklyn Congress of Racial Equality Collection, Brooklyn Historical Society, Brooklyn, NY.
Esther Cooper Jackson FBI Files, in possession of Esther Cooper Jackson, Brooklyn, NY.
Southern Negro Youth Congress Papers, Moorland-Spingarn Research Center, Howard University.
Edward Strong Papers, Moorland-Spingarn Research Center, Howard University.

Secondary Sources

Adi, Hakim. *West Africans in Britain, 1900–1960: Nationalism, Pan-Africanism, and Communism.* London: Lawrence & Wishart, 1998.
Alexander, Eleanor. *Lyrics of Sunshine and Shadow: The Tragic Courtship and Marriage of Paul Laurence Dunbar and Alice Ruth Moore: A History of Love and Violence among the African American Elite.* New York: New York University Press, 2001.
Anderson, Carol. *Eyes Off the Prize: The United Nations and the African*

American Struggle for Human Rights, 1944–1955. Cambridge: Cambridge University Press, 2003.

———. "'The Brother in Black Is Always Told to Wait': The Communist Party, African American Anticommunism, and the Prioritization of Black Equality—a Reply to Eric Arnesen." *Labor* 3, no. 4 (2006): 65–68.

Aptheker, Bettina. *The Morning Breaks: The Trial of Angela Davis.* Ithaca, NY: Cornell University Press, 1997.

Aptheker, Herbert, ed. *A Documentary History of the Negro People in the United States.* 7 vols. New York: Citadel, 1951–1994.

Arnesen, Eric. "No 'Graver Danger': Black Anticommunism, the Communist Party, and the Race Question." *Labor* 3, no. 4 (2006): 13–52.

———. "The Red and the Black: Reflections on the Responses to 'No "Graver Danger."'" *Labor* 3, no. 4 (2006): 75–79.

———. "Civil Rights and the Cold War at Home: Postwar Activism, Anticommunism, and the Decline of the Left." *American Communist History* 11, no. 1 (April 2012): 5–44.

———. "The Final Conflict? On the Scholarship of Civil Rights, the Left, and the Cold War." *American Communist History* 11, no. 1 (2012): 63–80.

Barrett, James R. *William Z. Foster and the Tragedy of American Radicalism.* Urbana: University of Illinois Press, 1999.

Belfrage, Sally. *Un-American Activities: A Memoir of the Fifties.* New York: Harper Collins, 1994.

Berg, Manfred. "Black Civil Rights and Liberal Anticommunism: The NAACP in the Early Cold War." *Journal of American History* 94 (June 2007): 75–96.

Biondi, Martha. *To Stand and Fight: The Struggle for Civil Rights in Postwar New York City.* Cambridge, MA: Harvard University Press, 2003.

———. "Response to Eric Arnesen." *Labor* 3, no. 4 (2006): 59–63.

———. *The Black Revolution on Campus.* Berkeley and Los Angeles: University of California Press, 2012.

Blum, John Morton. *V Was for Victory: Politics and American Culture during World War II.* New York: Harcourt Brace Jovanovich, 1976.

Borstelmann, Thomas. *The Cold War and the Color Line: American Race Relations in the Global Age.* Cambridge, MA: Harvard University Press, 2001.

Branch, Taylor. *Parting the Waters: America in the King Years, 1954–1963.* New York: Simon & Schuster, 1988.

———. *Pillar of Fire: America in the King Years, 1963–1965.* New York: Simon & Schuster, 1998.

———. *At Canaan's Edge: America in the King Years, 1965–1968.* New York: Simon & Schuster, 2006.

Brinkley, Douglas. *Rosa Parks*. New York: Penguin, 2000.

Brown, Elsa Barkley. "Womanist Consciousness: Maggie Lena Walker and the Independent Order of Saint Luke." *Signs: Journal of Women in Culture and Society* 14, no. 3 (Spring 1989): 610–33.

Brown, Elsa Barkley, and Gregg D. Kimball. "Mapping the Terrain of Black Richmond." In *The New African American Urban History*, ed. Kenneth W. Goings and Raymond A. Mohl, 66–115. Thousand Oaks, CA: Sage, 1996.

Carmichael, Stokely, and Charles V. Hamilton. *Black Power: The Politics of Liberation*. New York: Vintage, 1992.

Carson, Clayborne. *In Struggle: SNCC and the Black Awakening of the 1960s*. Cambridge, MA: Harvard University Press, 1981.

Castledine, Jacqueline. *Cold War Progressives: Women's Interracial Organizing for Peace and Freedom*. Urbana: University of Illinois Press, 2012.

Caute, David. *The Great Fear: The Anticommunist Purge under Truman and Eisenhower*. New York: Simon & Schuster, 1978.

Chafe, William H. *Civilities and Civil Rights: Greensboro, North Carolina, and the Black Struggle for Freedom*. Oxford: Oxford University Press, 1980.

Clarke, John Henrik, ed. *Harlem: A Community in Transition*. New York: Citadel, 1964.

———, ed. *William Styron's Nat Turner: Ten Black Writers Respond*. Boston: Beacon, 1968.

Clayton, Bruce L., and John A. Salmond, eds. *"Lives Full of Struggle and Triumph": Southern Women, Their Institutions, and Their Communities*. Gainesville: University of Florida Press, 2003.

Cohen, Robert. *When the Old Left Was Young: Student Radicals and America's First Mass Student Movement, 1929–1941*. New York: Oxford University Press, 1993.

Collier-Thomas, Bettye, and V. P. Franklin. *Sisters in Struggle: African American Women in the Civil Rights–Black Power Movement*. New York: New York University Press, 2001.

Coontz, Stephanie. *The Way We Never Were: American Families and the Nostalgia Trap*. New York: Basic, 1993.

———. *Marriage, a History: How Love Conquered Marriage*. New York: Penguin, 2006.

Cooper Jackson, Esther. *This Is My Husband: Fighter for His People, Political Refugee*. New York: National Committee to Defend Negro Leadership, 1953.

Cooper Jackson, Esther, and Constance Pohl, eds. *Freedomways Reader: Prophets in Their Own Country*. Boulder, CO: Westview, 2000.

Cott, Nancy. *Public Vows: A History of Marriage and the Nation.* Cambridge, MA: Harvard University Press, 2000.

Cruse, Harold. *The Crisis of the Negro Intellectual.* New York: New York Review of Books, 1967.

Cuordileone, K. A. *Manhood and American Political Culture in the Cold War.* London: Routledge, 2005.

Curwood, Anastasia. "Three African American Marriages in the World of E. Franklin Frazier, 1932–1967." Ph.D. diss., Princeton University, 2003.

Davis, Angela. *Angela Davis: An Autobiography.* New York: Random House, 1974.

Davis, Benjamin J. *Communist Councilman from Harlem: Autobiographical Notes Written in a Federal Penitentiary.* 2nd ed. New York: International, 1991.

Dennis, Eugene. *Letters from Prison.* New York: International, 1956.

Dennis, Peggy. *The Autobiography of an American Communist: A Personal View of Political Life, 1925–1975.* Westport, CT: Lawrence Hill, 1977.

Dittmer, John. *Local People: The Struggle for Civil Rights in Mississippi.* Urbana: University of Illinois Press, 1995.

Draper, Theodore. *The Roots of American Communism.* New York: Viking, 1957.

Duberman, Martin. *Paul Robeson: A Biography.* New York: New Press, 1988.

Du Bois, W. E. B. *The Souls of Black Folk.* 1903. New York: Modern Library, 2003.

———. *Black Reconstruction in America, 1860–1880.* 1935. New York: Free Press, 1998.

———. *Color and Democracy: Colonies and Peace, a Ringing Challenge to Postwar Peace Plans from the Point of View of the Colored Races.* New York: Harcourt, Brace, 1945.

———. *The World and Africa: An Inquiry into the Part Which Africa Has Played in World History.* 1946. New York: International, 1990.

Dudziak, Mary. *Cold War Civil Rights: Race and the Image of American Democracy.* Princeton, NJ: Princeton University Press, 2000.

Egerton, John. *Speak Now against the Day: The Generation Before the Civil Rights Movement in the South.* New York: Knopf, 1994.

Ellison, Ralph. *Invisible Man.* New York: Random House, 1952.

Fairclough, Adam. *To Redeem the Soul of America: The Southern Christian Leadership Conference and Martin Luther King, Jr.* Athens: University of Georgia Press, 1987.

Feldstein, Ruth. *Motherhood in Black and White: Race and Sex in American Liberalism, 1930–1965.* Ithaca, NY: Cornell University Press, 2000.

Foner, Eric. *Reconstruction: America's Unfinished Revolution, 1863–1877.* New York: Harper & Row, 1988.

Foner, Philip S., ed. *Paul Robeson Speaks: Writings, Speeches, and Interviews, a Centennial Celebration.* New York: Citadel, 1978.

Fosl, Catherine. *Subversive Southerner: Anne Braden and the Struggle for Racial Justice in the Cold War South.* New York: Palgrave Macmillan, 2002.

Freedomways Associates. *Paul Robeson: The Great Forerunner.* New York: Dodd, Mead, 1978.

Fried, Albert, ed. *Communism in America: A History in Documents.* New York: Columbia University Press, 1997.

Fried, Richard M. *Nightmare in Red: The McCarthy Era in Perspective.* New York: Oxford University Press, 1990.

Friedman, Andrea. "The Strange Career of Annie Lee Moss: Rethinking Race, Gender, and McCarthyism." *Journal of American History* 94, no. 2 (September 2007): 445–68.

Gaines, Kevin K. *Uplifting the Race: Black Leadership, Politics, and Culture in the Twentieth Century.* Chapel Hill: University of North Carolina Press, 1995.

Galamison, Milton. "Bedford-Stuyvesant—Land of Superlatives." In *Harlem: A Community in Transition,* ed. John Henrik Clarke, 187–97. New York: Lyle Stewart, 1969.

Garfinkel, Herbert. *When Negroes March: The March on Washington Movement in the Organizational Politics for the FEPC.* Glencoe, IL: Free Press, 1959.

Garrow, David. *The FBI and Martin Luther King, Jr.: From "Solo" to Memphis.* New York: Norton, 1981.

———. *Bearing the Cross: Martin Luther King, Jr. and the Southern Christian Leadership Conference.* New York: Vintage, 1986.

Gellman, Erik. *Death Blow to Jim Crow: The National Negro Congress and the Rise of Militant Civil Rights.* Chapel Hill: University of North Carolina Press, 2012.

Gellman, Erik, and Jarod Roll. *The Gospel of the Working Class: Labor's Southern Prophets in New Deal America.* Urbana: University of Illinois Press, 2011.

Gerstle, Gary. *American Crucible: Race and Nation in the Twentieth Century.* Princeton, NJ: Princeton University Press, 2001.

Gilmore, Glenda. *Defying Dixie: The Radical Roots of Civil Rights, 1919–1950.* New York: Norton, 2008.

Goodman, James. *Stories of Scottsboro.* New York: Vintage, 1984.

Gore, Dayo. *Radicalism at the Crossroads: African American Women Activists in the Cold War.* New York: New York University Press, 2010.

———. "'The Danger of Being an Active Anti-Communist': Expansive Black Left Politics and the Long Civil Rights Movement." *American Communist History* 11, no. 1 (2012): 45–48.

Gosse, Van. *Rethinking the New Left: An Interpretive History.* New York: Palgrave MacMillan, 2005.

Gramsci, Antonio. *Selections from the Prison Notebooks of Antonio Gramsci.* New York: International, 1971.

Green, Ben. *Before His Time: The Untold Story of Harry T. Moore, America's First Civil Rights Martyr.* New York: Free Press, 1999.

Green, Gil. *Cold War Fugitive: A Personal Story of the McCarthy Years.* New York: International, 1984.

Greene, Christina. *Our Separate Ways: Women and the Black Freedom Movement in Durham, North Carolina.* Chapel Hill: University of North Carolina Press, 2005.

Hall, Gwendolyn Midlo, ed. *Love, War, and the 96th Engineers (Colored): The World War II New Guinea Diaries of Captain Hyman Samuelson.* Urbana: University of Illinois Press, 1995.

Hall, Jacquelyn Dowd. "The Long Civil Rights Movement and the Political Uses of the Past." *Journal of American History* 91, no. 4 (March 2005): 1233–63.

Harlan, Lewis R. *Booker T. Washington: The Wizard of Tuskegee, 1901–1915.* New York: Oxford University Press, 1983.

Haynes, John Earl. "Reconsidering Two Questions: On Arnesen's 'No "Graver Danger"': Black Anticommunism, the Communist Party, and the Race Question.'" *Labor* 3, no. 4 (2006): 53–57.

Haywood, Harry. *A Black Communist in the Freedom Struggle: The Life of Harry Haywood.* Edited by Gwendolyn Midlo Hall. Minneapolis: University of Minnesota Press, 2011.

Hobbs, Richard. *The Cayton Legacy: An African American Family.* Pullman: Washington State University Press, 2002.

Holloway, Jonathan Scott. *Confronting the Veil: Abram Harris Jr., E. Franklin Frazier, and Ralph Bunche, 1919–1941.* Chapel Hill: University of North Carolina Press, 2002.

Honey, Michael K. *Southern Labor and Black Civil Rights: Organizing Memphis Workers.* Urbana: University of Illinois Press, 1993.

Hoover, J. Edgar. *Masters of Deceit: The Story of Communism in America and How to Fight It.* New York: Henry Holt, 1958.

Horne, Gerald. *Black and Red: W. E. B. Du Bois and the Afro-American*

Response to the Cold War, 1944–1963. Albany: State University of New York Press, 1986.

———. *Communist Front? The Civil Rights Congress, 1946–1956*. Rutherford, NJ: Fairleigh Dickinson University Press, 1988.

———. *Black Liberation/Red Scare: Ben Davis and the Communist Party*. Newark: University of Delaware Press, 1994.

———. *Race Woman: The Lives of Shirley Graham Du Bois*. New York: New York University Press, 2000.

———. *The Final Victim of the Blacklist: John Howard Lawson, Dean of the Hollywood Ten*. Berkeley and Los Angeles: University of California Press, 2006.

Horowitz, Daniel. *Betty Friedan and the Making of the Feminine Mystique: The American Left, the Cold War, and Modern Feminism*. Amherst: University of Massachusetts Press, 1998.

Howard-Pitney, David. *Martin Luther King, Jr., Malcolm X, and the Civil Rights Struggle of the 1950s and 1960s*. Boston: Bedford St. Martins, 2004.

———. *African American Jeremiad: Appeals for Justice in America*. Philadelphia: Temple University Press, 2005.

Howe, Irving. *The American Communist Party: A Critical History, 1919–1957*. Boston: Beacon, 1957.

Hudson, Hosea. *Black Worker in the Deep South: A Personal Record*. New York: International, 1972.

Hughes, C. Alvin. "We Demand Our Rights: The Southern Negro Youth Congress, 1937–1949." *Phylon Quarterly* 48, no. 1 (1st Quarter 1987): 38–50.

Hutchinson, Earl Ofari. *Blacks and Reds: Race and Class in Conflict, 1919–1990*. Lansing: Michigan State University Press, 1995.

Isserman, Maurice. *Which Side Were You On? The American Communist Party during the Second World War*. Middletown, CT: Wesleyan University Press, 1982.

———. *If I Had a Hammer . . . : The Death of the Old Left and the Birth of the New Left*. New York: Basic, 1987.

Jackson, James E., Jr. *The View from Here: Commentaries on Peace and Freedom*. New York: New Press, 1963.

———. *U.S. Negroes in Battle: Little Rock to Watts*. Moscow: Progress, 1967.

———. *Revolutionary Tracings in World Politics and Black Liberation*. New York: International, 1974.

———. *The Bold, Bad '60s: Pushing the Point for Equality Down South and Out Yonder*. New York: International, 1992.

Jackson, Kathryn A. "Trauma Survivors: Adult Children of McCarthyism and the Smith Act." Ph.D. diss., Temple University, 1991.

Jackson, Walter A. *Gunnar Myrdal and America's Conscience: Social Engineering and Racial Liberalism, 1938–1987.* Chapel Hill: University of North Carolina Press, 1990.

James, C. L. R., George Breitman, Edgar Keemer, et al. *Fighting Racism in World War II.* Edited by Fred Stanton. New York: Monad, 1980.

James, Joy. *Transcending the Talented Tenth: Black Leaders and American Intellectuals.* New York: Routledge, 1997.

Janken, Kenneth R. "Anticommunism or Anti–Communist Party? A Response to Eric Arnesen." *Labor* 3, no. 4 (2006): 69–74.

Jones, William P. *The March on Washington: Jobs, Freedom, and the Forgotten History of Civil Rights.* New York: Norton, 2013.

Joseph, Peniel E. *Waiting 'til the Midnight Hour: A Narrative History of Black Power in America.* New York: Henry Holt, 2006.

Kahn, Albert E. *The Game of Death: Effects of the Cold War on Our Children.* New York: Cameron and Kahn, 1953.

Kahn, Alfred. *The Vengeance on the Young: The Story of the Smith Act Children.* New York: Hour, June 1952.

Kaiser, Ernest, ed. *Freedomways Reader: Afro-America in the Seventies.* New York: International, 1977.

Katznelson, Ira. *When Affirmative Action Was White: An Untold History of Racial Inequality in Twentieth Century America.* New York: Norton, 2005.

Kelley, Robin D. G. *Hammer and Hoe: Alabama Communists during the Great Depression.* Chapel Hill: University of North Carolina Press, 1990.

———. "'But a Local Phase of a World Problem': Black History's Global Vision, 1883–1950." In "The Nation and Beyond: Transnational Perspectives on United States History," special issue, *Journal of American History* 86, no. 3 (December 1999): 1045–77.

Kennedy, David M. *Freedom from Fear: The American People in Depression and War, 1929–1945.* New York: Oxford University Press, 2001.

Kersten, Andrew. *Race, Jobs, and the War: The FEPC in the Midwest, 1941–1946.* Urbana: University of Illinois Press, 2007.

King, Martin Luther, Jr. *"All Labor Has Dignity."* Edited by Michael K. Honey. Boston: Beacon, 2011.

Kirk, John. *Redefining the Color Line: Black Activism in Little Rock, Arkansas, 1920–1970.* Gainesville: University Press of Florida, 2002.

———. *Beyond Little Rock: The Origins and Legacies of the Central High Crisis.* Fayetteville: University Press of Arkansas, 2007.

Klatch, Rebecca. *A Generation Divided: The New Left, the New Right, and the 1960s.* Berkeley and Los Angeles: University of California Press, 1999.

Klehr, Harvey. *The Heyday of American Communism: The Depression Decade.* New York: Basic, 1984.

Klehr, Harvey, John Earl Haynes, and Fridrikh Igorevich Firsov. *The Secret World of American Communism.* New Haven, CT: Yale University Press, 1995.

Korstad, Robert Rodgers. *Civil Rights Unionism: Tobacco Workers and the Struggle for Democracy in the Mid-Twentieth-Century South.* Chapel Hill: University of North Carolina Press, 2003.

Korstad, Robert, and Nelson Lichtenstein. "Opportunities Found and Lost: Labor, Radicals and the Early Civil Rights Movement." *Journal of American History* 75, no. 3 (December 1988): 786–81.

Kotlowski, Dean J. *Nixon's Civil Rights: Politics, Principle, and Policy.* Cambridge, MA: Harvard University Press, 2009.

Lau, Peter F. *Democracy Rising: South Carolina and the Fight for Black Equality since 1865.* Lexington: University Press of Kentucky, 2006.

Lawson, Steven F. *Black Ballots: Voting Rights in the South, 1944–1969.* New York: Columbia University Press, 1976.

———. "Freedom Then, Freedom Now: The Historiography of the Civil Rights Movement." *American Historical Review* 96, no. 2 (April 1991): 456–71.

———. *Running for Freedom: Civil Rights and Black Politics in America since 1941.* Boston: McGraw-Hill, 1997.

———. *Civil Rights Crossroads: Nation, Community, and the Black Freedom Struggle.* Lexington: University Press of Kentucky, 2003.

———, ed. *To Secure These Rights: The Report of President Harry S. Truman's Committee on Civil Rights.* Boston: Bedford St. Martin's Press, 2004.

Lawson, Steven F., and Charles Payne. *Debating the Civil Rights Movement, 1945–1968.* Lanham, MD: Rowman & Littlefield, 1998.

Lee, Chana Kai. *For Freedom's Sake: The Life of Fannie Lou Hamer.* Urbana: University of Illinois Press, 1999.

Lewis, David Levering. *W. E. B. Du Bois: Biography of a Race, 1868–1919.* New York: Henry Holt, 1993.

———. *W. E. B. Du Bois: The Fight for Equality and the American Century, 1919–1963.* New York: Henry Holt, 2000.

Lewis, David Levering, Michael H. Nash, and Daniel J. Leab, eds. *Red Activists and Black Freedom: James and Esther Jackson and the Long Civil Rights Revolution.* London: Routledge, 2010.

Lewis, George. *The White South and the Red Menace: Segregationists, Anti-Communism, and Massive Resistance, 1945–1965.* Gainesville: University Press of Florida, 2004.

Lichtenstein, Alex. "Consensus? What Consensus?" *American Communist History* 11, no. 1 (2012): 49–53.

Lichtenstein, Nelson. *The Most Dangerous Man in Detroit: Walter Reuther and the Fate of American Labor.* New York: Basic, 1995.

Lipsitz, George. *A Life in the Struggle: Ivory Perry and the Culture of Opposition.* Philadelphia: Temple University Press, 1988.

Love, Richard. "In Defiance of Custom and Tradition: Black Tobacco Workers and Labor Unions in Richmond, Virginia, 1937–1941." *Labor History* 35 (1994): 25–47.

Lucander, David. *Winning the War for Democracy: The March on Washington Movement, 1941–1946.* Urbana: University of Illinois Press, 2014.

Marable, Manning. *Malcolm X: A Life of Reinvention.* New York: Viking, 2011. iBooks edition.

Massey, Douglas, and Nancy Denton. *American Apartheid: Segregation and the Making of the Underclass.* Cambridge, MA: Harvard University Press, 1998.

May, Elaine Tyler. *Great Expectations: Marriage and Divorce in Post-Victorian America.* Chicago: University of Chicago Press, 1980.

———. *Homeward Bound: American Families in the Cold War Era.* New York: Basic, 1999.

McDuffie, Erik S. "Long Journeys: Four Black Women and the Communist Party, U.S.A., 1930–1956." Ph.D. diss., New York University, 2003.

———. *Sojourning for Freedom: Black Women, American Communism, and the Making of Black Left Feminism.* Durham, NC: Duke University Press, 2011.

McGerr, Michael. *A Fierce Discontent: The Rise and Fall of the Progressive Movement in America, 1870–1920.* Oxford: Oxford University Press, 2003.

McGuire, Danielle. *At The Dark End of the Street: Black Women, Rape, and Resistance—a New History of the Civil Rights Movement from Rosa Parks to the Rise of Black Power.* New York: Vintage, 2011.

McGuire, Danielle, and John Dittmer, eds. *Freedom Rights: New Perspectives on the Civil Rights Movement.* Lexington: University Press of Kentucky, 2011.

McWhorter, Diane. *Carry Me Home: Birmingham, Alabama: The Climactic Struggle of the Civil Rights Revolution.* New York: Simon & Schuster, 2002.

Melosh, Barbara, ed. *Gender and American History since 1890.* New York: Routledge, 1993.

Meriwether, James H. *Proudly We Can Be Africans: Black Americans and*

Africa, 1935–1961. Chapel Hill: University of North Carolina Press, 2002.

Meyerowitz, Joanne, ed. *Not June Cleaver: Women and Gender in Postwar America, 1945–1960*. Philadelphia: Temple University Press, 1994.

Mitchell, Michele. *Righteous Propagation: African Americans and the Politics of Racial Destiny after Reconstruction*. Chapel Hill: University of North Carolina Press, 2004.

Mjagkij, Nina. *A Light in the Darkness: African Americans and the YMCA, 1852–1946*. Lexington: University Press of Kentucky, 1994.

Myrdal, Gunnar. *An American Dilemma: The Negro Problem and Modern Democracy*. New York: Pantheon, 1944.

Naison, Mark. *Communists in Harlem during the Depression*. New York: Grove, 1984.

———. *White Boy: A Memoir*. Philadelphia: Temple University Press, 2002.

Norrell, Robert J. *Up from History: The Life of Booker T. Washington*. Cambridge, MA: Belknap Press of Harvard University Press, 2009.

Novick, Peter. *That Noble Dream: The "Objectivity Question" and the American Historical Profession*. Cambridge: Cambridge University Press, 1988.

Painter, Nell Irvin. *The Narrative of Hosea Hudson: His Life as a Negro Communist in the South*. Cambridge, MA: Harvard University Press, 1979.

Payne, Charles. *I've Got the Light of Freedom: The Organizing Tradition and the Mississippi Freedom Struggle*. Berkeley and Los Angeles: University of California Press, 1995.

Peery, Nelson. *Black Fire: The Making of an American Revolutionary*. New York: New Press, 1994.

Plummer, Brenda Gayle. *Rising Wind: Black Americans and U.S. Foreign Affairs, 1935–1960*. Chapel Hill: University of North Carolina Press, 1996.

Purnell, Brian. *Fighting Jim Crow in the County of Kings: The Congress of Racial Equality in Brooklyn*. Lexington: University Press of Kentucky, 2013.

Ransby, Barbara. *Ella Baker and the Black Freedom Movement: A Radical Democratic Vision*. Chapel Hill: University of North Carolina Press, 2003.

———. *Eslanda: The Large and Unconventional Life of Mrs. Paul Robeson*. New Haven, CT: Yale University Press, 2014.

Record, Wilson. *The Negro and the Communist Party*. Chapel Hill: University of North Carolina Press, 1951.

Reed, Linda. *Simple Decency and Common Sense: The Southern Conference Movement, 1938–1963*. Bloomington: Indiana University Press, 1994.

Reed, Merl Elwyn. *Seedtime for the Modern Civil Rights Movement: The Presi-

dent's Committee on Fair Employment Practice, 1941–1946. Baton Rouge: Louisiana State University Press, 1991.

Richards, Johnetta. "The Southern Negro Youth Congress: A History." Ph.D. diss., University of Ohio, 1987.

Roberts, Gene, and Hank Klibanoff. *The Race Beat: The Press, the Civil Rights Struggle, and the Awakening of a Nation.* New York: Vintage, 2006.

Roberts, Sam. *The Brother: The Untold Story of the Rosenberg Case.* New York: Random House, 2003.

Robinson, Cedric J. *Black Marxism: The Making of the Black Radical Tradition.* London: Zed, 1983.

Rocksborough-Smith, Ian. "Bearing the Seeds of Struggle: *Freedomways* Magazine, Black Leftists, and Continuities in the Black Freedom Movement." M.A. thesis, Simon Fraser University, 2005.

———. "Filling the Gap: Intergenerational Radicalism and the Popular Front Ideals of *Freedomways Magazine,* 1961–1965." *Afro-Americans in New York Life and History* 31, no. 3 (January 2007): 7–42.

Romanus, Charles F., and Riley Sunderland. *United States Army in World War II, China-Burma-India Theater: Time Runs Out in CBI.* Washington, DC: Office of the Chief of Military History, Department of the Army, 1959.

Ross, Marlon. *Manning the Race: Reforming Black Men in the Jim Crow Era.* New York: New York University Press, 2004.

Savage, Barbara Dianne. *Broadcasting Freedom: Radio, War, and the Politics of Race, 1938–1948.* Chapel Hill: University of North Carolina Press, 1999.

Scales, Junius Irving, and Richard Nickson. *Cause at Heart: A Former Communist Remembers.* Athens: University of Georgia Press, 1987.

Schrecker, Ellen. *Many Are the Crimes: McCarthyism in America.* Boston: Little, Brown, 1998.

Sherwood, Marika. "There Is No New Deal for the Blackman in San Francisco." *International Journal of African Historical Studies* 29, no. 1 (1996): 71–94.

Sherwood, Marika, and Hakim Adi. *The 1945 Manchester Pan African Congress Revisited.* London: New Beacon, 1995.

Singh, Nikhil Pal. *Black Is a Country: Race and the Unfinished Struggle for Democracy.* Cambridge, MA: Harvard University Press, 2004.

Smethurst, James Edward. *The Black Arts Movement: Literary Nationalism in the 1960s and 1970s.* Chapel Hill: University of North Carolina Press, 2005.

Smith, Mona Z. *Becoming Something: The Story of Canada Lee: The Untold*

Tragedy of the Great Black Actor, Activist, and Athlete. New York: Faber & Faber, 2004.

Solomon, Marc. *The Cry Was Unity: Communists and African Americans, 1917–1936*. Jackson: University Press of Mississippi, 1998.

Stein, Judith. *The World of Marcus Garvey: Race and Class in Modern Society*. Baton Rouge: Louisiana State University Press, 1991.

———. "Why American Historians Embrace the 'Long Civil Rights Movement.'" *American Communist History* 11, no. 1 (2012): 55–58.

Stockley, Grif. *Daisy Bates: Civil Rights Crusader from Arkansas*. Jackson: University Press of Mississippi, 2005.

Styron, William. *The Confessions of Nat Turner*. New York: Random House, 1967.

Sugrue, Thomas J. *The Origins of the Urban Crisis: Race and Inequality in Postwar Detroit*. Princeton, NJ: Princeton University Press, 1996.

———. *Sweet Land of Liberty: The Forgotten Civil Rights Struggle in the North*. New York: Random House, 2008.

Sullivan, Patricia. *Days of Hope: Race and Democracy in the New Deal Era*. Chapel Hill: University of North Carolina Press, 1996.

———, ed. *Freedom Writer: Virginia Foster Durr, Letters from the Civil Rights Years*. New York: Routledge, 2003.

———. *Lift Every Voice: The NAACP and the Making of the Civil Rights Movement*. New York: New Press, 2009.

Summers, Martin. *Manliness and Its Discontents: The Black Middle Class and the Transformation of Masculinity, 1900–1930*. Chapel Hill: University of North Carolina Press, 2004.

Swindall, Lindsay R. *Paul Robeson: A Life of Activism and Art*. Lanham, MD: Rowman & Littlefield, 2013.

———. *The Path to the Greater, Freer, Truer World: Southern Civil Rights and Anticolonialism, 1937–1955*. Gainesville: University Press of Florida, 2014.

Tyson, Timothy B. *Radio Free Dixie: Robert F. Williams and the Roots of Black Power*. Chapel Hill: University of North Carolina Press, 2000.

Van Deberg, William. *New Day in Babylon: The Black Power Movement in American Culture, 1965–1975*. Chicago: University of Chicago Press, 1992.

Von Eschen, Penny M. *Race against Empire: Black Americans and Anticolonialism, 1937–1957*. Ithaca, NY: Cornell University Press, 1997.

———. *Satchmo Blows Up the World: Jazz Ambassadors Play the Cold War*. Cambridge, MA: Harvard University Press, 2004.

Washington, Mary Helen. *The Other Blacklist: The African American Liter-

ary and Cultural Left of the 1950s. New York: Columbia University Press, 2014.

Weigand, Kate. *Red Feminism: American Communism and the Making of Women's Liberation*. Baltimore: Johns Hopkins University Press, 2001.

Wexler, Laura. *Fire in a Canebrake: The Last Mass Lynching in America*. New York: Scribner, 2003.

White, Deborah Gray. *Too Heavy a Load: Black Women in Defense of Themselves, 1894–1994*. New York: Norton, 1998.

White, Walter. *A Rising Wind*. Garden City, NY: Doubleday, Doran, 1945.

———. *How Far the Promised Land?* New York: Viking, 1955.

Williams, John A., and Charles F. Harris, eds. *Amistad 2*. New York: Vintage, 1971.

Williams, Robert F. *Negroes with Guns*. Detroit: Wayne State University Press, 1998.

Woods, Jeff. *Black Struggle, Red Scare: Segregation and Anti-Communism in the South, 1948–1968*. Baton Rouge: Louisiana State University Press, 2004.

Workers of the Writers' Program of the Works Progress Administration in the State of Virginia. *The Negro in Virginia*. 1940. Winston-Salem, NC: John F. Blair, 1994.

Wright, Richard. *Black Boy (American Hunger)*. New York: Harper & Bros., 1945.

Zieger, Robert H. "Déjà Vu All over Again." *American Communist History* 11, no. 1 (2012): 59–62.

Index

Progressive Party, 110, 114, 119–20,
121, 263–64, 299n35
Progressive Voter's League (PVL),
139–40
progressivism (Progressive era),
15–18, 39, 50, 53, 289n13
Proletarian Students Party, 33
Provisional Committee for the
Defense of Ethiopia, 47

racism, 11, 12, 18–20, 23, 25, 27, 28,
30–32, 47, 49, 52, 62, 65, 69–70,
72, 74–76, 83, 87, 90, 93–94, 100,
103–4, 112–14, 125–26, 142, 145,
148, 166, 168, 174, 180–82, 184,
188, 190, 197–99, 201, 202, 204,
209–10, 213, 217–19, 221, 224–
26, 234, 248, 250, 257, 259–60,
263, 264–65, 269, 277, 292n63,
302n65, 319n29
Randolph, A. Philip, 63, 201, 203
Rankin, John, 166
rape, 9, 29, 75, 81, 136, 138, 301n51
Reagan, Ronald, 246–47
Reconstruction Congressmen, 103
Recy Taylor Committee, 74
Red Squad, Detroit, 114
Reeves, Frank, 174
rent strikes, 197, 319n29
"Resolution on Theoretical Aspects
of the Negro Question" (Jackson,
James), 183–84
respectability, 9, 10, 15, 19, 22, 25,
28, 32, 40, 46, 50
restrictive covenants, 20, 90, 290n22,
304n3
Reuther, Walter, 203
Richards, Johnetta, 273
Richardson, Benjamin, 146
Richmond Times-Dispatch, 26
Richmond, VA, 148–50; race in,
18–22, 25–26, 31–32, 290n14,

290n22; SNYC founding, 38–39;
tobacco strikes, 40–46, 295n100
Right to Vote campaign (SNYC), 65
Roach, Max, 213
Roberson, Willie, 29
Robeson, Eslanda Goode, 9, 267
Robeson, Paul, 9, 145, 195, 247,
257, 267–70, 274; and *Freedom,*
144, 191; and *Freedomways,*
191, 261–67; and McCarthyism,
317n4; and SNYC, 66–67, 106
Robeson, Paul, Jr., 266–68
Roosevelt, Eleanor, 101, 139
Roosevelt, Franklin Delano, 33, 36, 47,
52, 59, 60, 63, 65, 77, 102, 110
Roosevelt, Theodore, 21
Roosevelt University, 37
Rosenberg, Ethel, 129, 320n44
Rosenberg, Julius, 129, 320n44
Rosenwald Fellowship, 57, 86, 303
Royce, Edward, 261
Rustin, Bayard, 156, 320n44

Scales, Junius, 30–31, 158, 164
Schwellenbach, Lewis, 145
Schwerner, Michael, 191, 318n7
Scottsboro boys, 29, 33, 35, 120,
136, 138, 245, 254
Seale, Bobby, 247
second cadre, 130–34, 158–60, 161,
164, 173, 185, 187
second stringers, 130
See It Now, 128
Seeger, Pete, 65, 67, 229
segregation, 1, 5, 7–8, 20–21, 23,
27–28, 30–31, 33, 38, 51, 58,
61, 66, 74, 81–82, 85, 87, 89,
91, 92, 94–95, 104–5, 136, 145,
168, 169, 176, 194, 196, 206–8,
219, 224–26, 237–38, 246, 275,
293n64, 295n100, 325n112; and
anticommunism, 100, 109–13,

CIVIL RIGHTS AND THE STRUGGLE FOR BLACK EQUALITY
IN THE TWENTIETH CENTURY

SERIES EDITORS
Steven F. Lawson, Rutgers University
Cynthia Griggs Fleming, University of Tennessee

Freedom's Main Line: The Journey of Reconciliation and the Freedom Rides
Derek Charles Catsam

Subversive Southerner: Anne Braden and the Struggle for Racial Justice in the Cold War South
Catherine Fosl

Constructing Affirmative Action: The Struggle for Equal Employment Opportunity
David Hamilton Golland

River of Hope: Black Politics and the Memphis Freedom Movement, 1865–1954
Elizabeth Gritter

James and Esther Cooper Jackson: Love and Courage in the Black Freedom Movement
Sara Rzeszutek Haviland

Sidelined: How American Sports Challenged the Black Freedom Struggle
Simon Henderson

Becoming King: Martin Luther King Jr. and the Making of a National Leader
Troy Jackson

Civil Rights in the Gateway to the South: Louisville, Kentucky, 1945–1980
Tracy E. K'Meyer

In Peace and Freedom: My Journey in Selma
Bernard LaFayette Jr. and Kathryn Lee Johnson

Democracy Rising: South Carolina and the Fight for Black Equality since 1865
Peter F. Lau

Civil Rights Crossroads: Nation, Community, and the Black Freedom Struggle
Steven F. Lawson

Selma to Saigon: The Civil Rights Movement and the Vietnam War
Daniel S. Lucks

In Remembrance of Emmett Till: Regional Stories and Media Responses to the Black Freedom Struggle
Darryl Mace

Freedom Rights: New Perspectives on the Civil Rights Movement
edited by Danielle L. McGuire and John Dittmer

This Little Light of Mine: The Life of Fannie Lou Hamer
Kay Mills

After the Dream: Black and White Southerners since 1965
Timothy J. Minchin and John A. Salmond

Fighting Jim Crow in the County of Kings: The Congress of Racial Equality in Brooklyn
Brian Purnell

Roy Wilkins: The Quiet Revolutionary and the NAACP
Yvonne Ryan

Thunder of Freedom: Black Leadership and the Transformation of 1960s Mississippi
Sue [Lorenzi] Sojourner with Cheryl Reitan

For a Voice and the Vote: My Journey with the Mississippi Freedom Democratic Party
Lisa Anderson Todd

Art for Equality: The NAACP's Cultural Campaign for Civil Rights
Jenny Woodley

For Jobs and Freedom: Race and Labor in America since 1865
Robert H. Zieger

CPSIA information can be obtained at www.ICGtesting.com
Printed in the USA
BVOW08*0540180915

418504BV00001B/1/P